Faith, Honor, Integrity and Tradition

A History of Catholic Central Football

Volume I

1908-1963

BY

Steve Grinczel
with
David R. Wood

GRCL Publications
Grand Rapids, MI

Printed in the United States of America

First Printing, 2012

ISBN 978-0-9839196-1-2

GRCL Publications
800 Burke NE
Grand Rapids, MI 49503

www.GRCLPublications.com

Cover Photo: Catholic Central/West Catholic Archives - 1945

Dedication

This book is dedicated to the Catholic Central High School boosters, alumni and friends whose many contributions have built and maintained the Cougar football tradition.

Table of Contents

About the Authors

Steve Grinczel is the online columnist for Michigan State University's athletic website, MSUspartans.com. He is an award-winning journalist who covered MSU athletics for Booth Newspapers of Michigan, an eight-paper chain including The Grand Rapids Press, from 1986-2009. He was the Big Ten correspondent for Sports Illustrated for 20 years and has contributed to various other publications such as Athlon and Sporting News preseason football and basketball guides, and he wrote centerpiece features for the NCAA Basketball Tournament Final Four game programs in 2009 and 2004. He provided extensive coverage of the Detroit Tigers and the Detroit Pistons, including their 2004 NBA championship. He was Booth Newspapers' point man at Olympics in: Calgary (1988), Barcelona (1992), Atlanta (1996) and Sydney (2000), and the Pan American Games in Havana, Cuba (1991). He covered 14 NCAA Basketball Tournament Final Fours, 14 college football bowl games, two Super Bowls, two Major League Baseball All-Star games, the 1994 soccer World Cup from kickoff in Chicago to its conclusion in Pasadena, Calif., the 1994 U.S. Figure Skating Championships and two Boston Marathons. He is the author of three other books: "Michigan State Football, They Are Spartans" (Arcadia, 2003); "Gregory Kelser's Tales of Michigan State Basketball" (Sports Publishing 2006); "A History of Grand Rapids City League Track and Field" with David Wood (GRLC Publications, 2011).

Dave Wood is in his 17th season as the Head Track and Field Coach at Aquinas College. Competing as an athlete and a coach in the Grand Rapids area since 1970, Wood parlayed his interest in history and his passion for the Grand Rapids City League into a publishing company, GRCL Publications, that has produced two books covering high school sports in Grand Rapids. The first, "A History of Grand Rapids City League Track and Field" (GRCL Publications) hit the shelves in the fall of 2011.

Foreword

Football. In many communities, certainly ours, no other activity generates so much excitement, emotion and school spirit. Yet, about the time Catholic Central football began, President Teddy "Roughrider" Roosevelt was petitioned to ban the sport on the grounds it was too rough and dangerous for young men. He did not concur.

I believe this excerpt from his 1910 speech reflected his position: *"It is not the critic who counts;... the credit belongs to the man who is actually in the arena, whose face is marred by dust and sweat and blood; who strives valiantly; who errs,... but who does actually strive to do the deeds; ... who spends himself in a worthy cause; who at the best knows in the end the triumph of high achievement, and who at the worst, if he fails, at least fails while daring greatly, so that his place shall never be with those cold and timid souls who neither know victory nor defeat."*

Reading the President's words takes me back to the dustbowl "arena" that was Buckley Field, the Cougars' football practice site for hundreds of Catholic Central students in the first half of the 20th Century. It was there, an unkempt dirt field five blocks southwest of the school, that the coaches leading the CC football program molded boys into young men. Physical and mental skills were pushed beyond their comfort zone in the pursuit of Cougar excellence. In the heat of August two-a-day practices you could not help but be "marred by dust and sweat and blood." I believe that to a man, those experiences in the dirt and stones at Buckley Field instilled strength of character that generated the energetic leadership so many Cougar football alumni came to exhibit as faith-based citizens in our community, our state and our country.

In this two-volume "History of Catholic Central Football," Steve Grinczel and Dave Wood provide detailed insight to the overwhelming success of a scholastic program that has excited a community for over 100 years. Volume 1, covering 1910-1963, describes a different world than we know today. Back then off-season workouts consisted of playing multiple sports at local public parks, perhaps a few jogs around Garfield or Richmond parks, or maybe lakeshore dunes. Weight rooms did not exist. Energy drinks were salt tablets in tepid water. Ed Mead filmed every game on grainy 16mm black-and-white film. Yet the lessons learned under the tutelage of men such as Ted Sowle and Joe Godleski were then, and are today, the same lessons we hope each Catholic Central football player takes into his adult life.

Leaving the Sheldon Avenue campus in the early '60s, I took with me a mental notebook of Cougar football experiences. I recalled those situations many times in my four years at West Point and the Army career that followed. Absorbing the challenging skills and overcoming the exhaustion of Ranger School seemed possible because I had endured CC's football regimen. A few years later, in a foreign land where blood and sweat took a different meaning, it was Ranger skills and attention to detail—traits first learned in Cougar pre-game tasks—that guided our actions. Connect the dots.

Thirty-two years after leaving Catholic Central's classrooms, it was my honor to return to campus as Athletic Director. On my first Friday night back in Grand Rapids, I witnessed the football team's exciting overtime win with a performance that let me know Cougar football was still representing our school with great energy, discipline and teamwork.

For more than a century Catholic Central families have sacrificed to keep the school and co-curricular programs available for new generations. As you will learn in this enjoyable collection of Cougar lore, the faces change, many family names are repeated through the years, and technology and modern training techniques create bigger, faster, stronger athletes. However, the contribution of Catholic Central football to the school's mission always was, and remains, an essential pillar in the foundation of our Christ-centered institution. Regardless of the career paths our football graduates choose, I remain convinced more than ever that:

"On these fields of friendly strife are sown the seeds that, on other days and other fields, will bear the fruits of victory."

— Douglas MacArthur

It's a Great Day to be a Cougar!
Mike Neuman, CC '63
Colonel, US Army (Ret.)
Athletic Director 1995-2008

Acknowledgements

Researching, compiling and producing "Faith, Honor, Integrity and Tradition" would not have been possible without the help and support of a variety of people.

The staff of the History and Special Collections Department of the Grand Rapids Public Library was again truly amazing. Their technical advice, countless retrieval of high school yearbooks and overall encouragement made the hours and hours of research enjoyable and productive. Thank you again Benjamin Boss, Chris Byron, Heather Edwards, Karolee Gillman, Jennifer Morrison, Julie Tabberer and Department Head Tim Gleisner.

The Catholic Central/West Catholic archives collection supervised by Deb Moore and Pat Nugent provided an invaluable resource for the book and Maureen Korte's assistance in working with the archive was greatly appreciated.

A great deal of thanks goes out to editor Paul Keep and The Grand Rapids Press for granting their permission for the use of a many of photos in the book. Their generous gesture enabled the story to be told.

And a special thanks to Steve Grinczel for his attention to detail and his ability to weave a great story through each year of games and Deb Moore for her proof work insuring the book properly reflects the quality of the writing.

David R. Wood
November 1, 2012

Introduction

After Catholic Central High School fielded its first official, faculty-sanctioned football team with its first paid adult head coach, compensated by donations from boosters and nearby businesses, in 1912, it was also known by its street address upon second reference in news accounts. For example, a sportswriter at The Grand Rapids Herald or The Grand Rapids Press might wax poetic about how the players from the Sheldon Avenue establishment or institution withstood a scoring threat mounted by their cross-town rivals, "the Unions." Catholic Central's first players were a scruffy bunch, with student-athletes playing in full or partial uniforms they purchased themselves, or in street clothes.

Starting the following season, sportswriters avoided monotonous repetition by dubbing CC "the Catholics" in game stories and in 1914, the boosters provided the money needed to buy full uniforms for every player and the team also had a new unofficial nickname, "Holloway's men" or "Holloway eleven" in honor of coach Phil Holloway. In 1916, much was made about the new dark blue jerseys purchased for the team by the Catholic Central alumni association.

A new way to identify the CC "aggregate" dawned with the hiring former Notre Dame captain George Fitzpatrick in 1921 as the program's first full-time head coach. Catholic Central's affinity with the iconic college program located a couple of hours away in South Bend, IN started when Fitzpatrick patterned his program after the way he did things at ND as a player. The bond grew even stronger when legendary Fighting Irish coach Knute Rockne served as the keynote speaker at Catholic Central's postseason football banquet. Starting with the 1922 season, CC's moniker of "the Catholics" was inexplicably replaced with "the Parochials," though "the Irishmen," in deference to Fitzpatrick's ancestry and alma mater, also caught on. The team also was commonly referred to as the "Blue and White," just as Union was known as the "Red and White" and South High the "Red and Blue."

The bond between Catholic Central and Notre Dame grew even stronger when former ND letter winner George Haller replaced Fitzpatrick as head coach in the fall of '27 and the team was routinely called "the Irish" in game accounts throughout the season. Although Haller resigned amid controversy four games into the '28 season, he returned in 1929.

In 1930, Tony McCracken, a devotee of University of Illinois coach Bob Zuppke, took over as head coach, and Catholic Central was referred to as "the Cougars" for the first time in the local newspapers and that's how they've been know since.

Faith, Honor, Integrity and Tradition

A History of Catholic Central Football

Volume I

1908-1963

Chapter 1
The Birth of Catholic Central Football
1908-1920

A high Mass in St. Andrew's Cathedral on Wednesday, September 5, 1906 celebrated the creation of the first Catholic high school in the city of Grand Rapids. In fact, it was a celebration of two new high schools with the boys to be located in St. Andrew's School and the girls housed in Sacred Heart Academy on Fountain Street. The Sisters of Charity took the teaching assignment at St. Andrew's while the Sisters of St. Dominic were to oversee the instruction of the girls at Sacred Heart.

By February of that first school year *The Grand Rapids Press* was already reporting on a basketball team from Catholic Central High School playing various club and organizational teams around the city. Track and field showed up as a team sport at CC in the spring of 1908 and indications are that some sort of football activity took place during the fall of 1908.

During the fall of 1909 *The Grand Rapids Press* reported Catholic Central played Union High School (at that point Union only went through the eleventh grade) in a practice football game on October 2. The game ended in a 5-5 tie. A week later Catholic played Belding High School, falling by the score of 11-5.

Failing to get the support of Father Schmitt, the school's principal, for a Catholic Central football team during the fall of 1910, a collection of students secured sponsorship from local tavern owner Ernie Reed. Known as the Ernie Reeds, the Catholic Central students played a schedule of local club teams and engaged in a football game with Union High School, winning the game of 6-5.

CC/WC Archives

The 1910 Ernie Reeds Football Team

By the fall of 1911 athletics at Catholic Central gained more momentum and the football team embarked on its most ambitious schedule to date. With the Catholic Central faculty demonstrating a distinct lack of interest in fielding a high school football team, the responsibility of assembling a squad for CC's 1911 season fell completely to the student-athletes, who understandably got off to a late start. Nevertheless, under the direction of player-coach and team captain Robert Murray, "the Catholics" as they were called by the local newspapers, were deemed ready to take the field against cross-town rival Union High School.

Catholic Central		Union High
Rooney	LE	Gilleo
Kirchgessner	LT	Kingsley
Noonen	LG	Kramer
Francis O'Donnell	C	Hansen
O'Brien	RG	Snellink
Minardo	RT	Gill
McKenna	RE	Adrian
T. Colleton	QB	Loucks
Holland	LH	Beck
Hugh O'Donnell	RH	Goosman
Murray	FB	Johnson

Catholic	0	0	0	0	0
Union	0	5	0	5	10

Touchdowns – Goosman 1, Johnson 1.
Referee– Crell, Umpire– Bullick, Head Linesman–Rachl.

Union 10
Catholic Central 0
Saturday, October 14 at John Ball Park

The "Unions" had already lost their season opener against Sparta. Lester Stiles, Murray and Alfred Holland comprised the Catholic Central backfield, which was described as heavy, fast and experienced. Unfortunately, the rest of the team was regarded as "exceptionally light" and under prepared. It didn't help matters that the game was played in miserable weather. The Catholics were penalized repeatedly for going offside and Stiles also had a "punt hit" blocked in the first quarter.

Although Stiles, CC's so-called "heavy man", shredded Union with a few nice gains in the first half, Catholic Central failed to sustain much of an attack. After Union got the ball back on downs in the second quarter, John Bek, its right half, ran for successive 20-yard gains to set up a touchdown by left half A. Johnson, and the West Siders led, 5-0. For unexplained reasons, the officials put the ball back into the field of play before Union could dropkick the extra point, known as a "goal from touchdown." Bek's 25-yard rush in the fourth quarter set up Gooseman's rushing touchdown from the left halfback position, but the officials didn't allow Union a try-at-goal after that score, either.

Right half Hugh O'Donnell stood out for Catholic Central on defense by stopping every Union ball-carrier who ran in his direction. The fair-sized crowd assembled at John Ball Park was criticized by *The Grand Rapids Herald* for "a lack of concerted yelling."

Sparta 22
Catholic Central 6
Saturday, October 28 at Garfield Park

O'Donnell delivered the first significant building block in the foundation underlying Catholic Central's storied football tradition, appropriately enough, in sensational fashion.

The shifty ball-carrier received the opening kickoff from Sparta and then brilliantly evaded tacklers until he crossed the goal line for the initial touchdown in school history. Holland kicked the goal-from-touchdown to give the Catholics a 6-0 lead, but it was short-lived.

Catholic Central entered the game shorthanded because Murray was out with an injury sustained two weeks earlier against Union. O'Donnell replaced Murray at fullback, the playmaker position in the single-wing formation, but Sparta

Catholic Central		Sparta
Frair	LE	F. Wolcott
Noonan	LT	E. Johnson
Egan	LG	Crawford
Francis O'Donnell	C	Light
Carmondy	RG	Carrey
Rooney	RT	Stebbins
T. Colleton	RE	Burnett
McKenna	QB	Moore
Kirchgessner	LH	A. Johnson
Holland	RH	Burgett
Hugh O'Donnell	FB	Frank Wolcott

Catholic	6	0	0	0	6
Sparta	6	0	0	10	22

Touchdowns – H. O'Donnell, Burgett 2, Moore
PAT – Holland, Burgett.
Filed Goals - Burgett
Referee– Crell, Umpire– Bullick, Head Linesman–Rachl.

John "Hugh" O'Donnell
Catholic Central
1912

Hugh O'Donnell attended St. Andrew's School and graduated from Catholic Central in 1912. A football star on the 1911 Catholic Central team, O'Donnell entered Notre Dame in the fall of 1912.

A two-year letter-winner in Football at Notre Dame, O'Donnell was elected the first president of Notre Dame's Monogram Club.

After graduating from Notre Dame in 1916, O'Donnell entered the Novitiate at Notre Dame and eventually was ordained to the Priesthood at Sacred Heart Academy in Grand Rapids on December 28, 1921.

Rev. O'Donnell was named President of the University of Notre Dame in 1940 after previously serving the university in various positions. Responsible for establishing the Navy ROTC program at the South Bend campus, O'Donnell cemented the relationship with Navy's football team that exists to this present day.

Rev. O'Donnell passed away on June 13, 1947 after suffering from cancer.

GR Herald Photo

(l-r) Notre Dame President Rev. Hugh O'Donnell, Monsignor Michael J. Ready, Joseph Kennedy and Monsignor Sheen at Notre Dame's 1940 commencement.

proved to be too fast and experienced at nearly every position. Spartans right half Burgett scored two touchdowns on end sweeps off buck laterals in addition to a field goal. Moore, the Sparta quarterback, added a touchdown reception.

Although the Catholics were overmatched physically, they were given credit for holding a superior opponent to just 22 points.

Union 5
Catholic Central 0
Saturday, November 4 at Garfield Park

Union coach Mazurkiewicz went into the rematch with Catholic Central expecting a decisive, if not lopsided, victory, but the Catholics almost made him pay for his lack of respect.

The 9:30 a.m. game between the Unions, from Grand Rapids' near west side, and the Catholics, who hailed from east of the Grand River, generated area-wide interest because it featured the city's two smallest high schools. The West Siders missed Bek, their star left halfback, and Catholic Central seized the early momentum with a 15-yard pass and rushes of 20 and 10 yards on the opening possession. The drive stalled, however, and CC punted.

Union took over at its own 40 and "line bucks" into the middle of the CC defense by Loucks, the quarterback, left half Campbell and fullback Kingsley, netted 40 yards to the Catholic Central 25 as the first quarter expired. On the first play of the second quarter, Johnson, who was listed in Union's starting lineup as the right tackle, galloped around end for 10 yards and on the next play Kingsley went off tackle for 5 more to set up Johnson's 5-yard plunge for the game's only score. Gilleo missed the goal, and Catholic was only a touchdown and an extra point away from victory.

Catholic Central		Union High
Mead	LE	Gilleo
Egan	LT	Kramer
O'Brien	LG	Gill
Francis O'Donnell	C	Hansen
Carmondy	RG	Snellink
Noonan	RT	Johnson
Rooney	RE	Adrian
McKenna	QB	Loucks
Kirchgessner	LH	Campbell
Stiles	RH	Rich
Hugh O'Donnell	FB	Kingsley

Catholic	0	0	0	0	0
Union	0	5	0	0	5

Touchdowns – Johnson 1.
Referee– Monroe, Umpire– Frair, Head Linesman– Ray Murray.

Catholic Central tried to move the ball through the air in the third quarter, but most of the passes were dropped. With time running out in the fourth quarter, a series of three 5-yard runs by O'Donnell and Stiles moved the ball deep into Union territory. Catholic appeared to have moved even closer to the goal line when quarterback James McKenna lofted a perfect pass to Dan Mead, the left end. However, Mead lost control of the ball and Union recovered the fumble at its 5-yard line. Johnson gave Union some breathing room with a 15-yard pass to Gilleo, and the game ended with Union in possession of the ball near midfield.

Despite playing Union to a draw for more than three quarters, Catholic Central would have to wait for its first victory until the following season.

1911 Schedule/Results
Head Coach – Robert Murray

Date	Opponent	Result		Location
Oct. 14	Union	Lost	0-10	John Ball Park
Oct. 28	Sparta	Lost	6-22	Garfield Park
Nov. 4	Union	Lost	0-5	Garfield Park

	Record	Pts. Scored	Pts. Allowed
Overall	0-3	6	37

-1912-

In 1911, Catholic Central had a football team. A year later, it had a program.

For the first time, according to *The Grand Rapids Herald*, the CC faculty officially sanctioned interscholastic athletics at the "Sheldon Avenue establishment." That support, in turn, motivated area businesses to contribute financial aid, which allowed the school to hire its first coach. In early October, the biggest "mass meeting" in school history was held by the CC Alumni Association in the school hall "for the purpose of inspiring" Catholic Central's teams "with a little more enthusiasm." Students, alumni and anyone else interested in CC athletics were invited. The Alumni Association realized, *The Herald* reported, that for the student-athletes to succeed, they "must get the proper encouragement, something which they have never fallen heir to before."

The most significant rule change going into the season increased from three to four the number of downs the offense had to move the ball 10 yards for a first down. It was believed this modification would encourage more trick plays. It also promised to divide teams into two styles: heavy teams that went the slow and strenuous route by "bucking the line," and speedy teams attempting to move the ball by "circling the ends" off buck laterals. Because of its team speed, Catholic Central was suited for the wide-open latter style of play. The value of a touchdown was also increased from five points to six. A week before Catholic Central opened the season against St. Joseph's Seminary, Muskegon High School set an interscholastic world scoring record with a 216-0 victory over Hastings.

Catholic Central 19
St. Joseph's Seminary 12
Saturday, October 5

Catholic Central defeated the Seminarians, 19-12, in a hard-fought battle to notch the first victory in program history. Afterward, Coach Tierney said he was happy with the players' performance. Team captain Robert Murray, who served as player-coach during CC's inaugural season, and Lester Stiles were the leading ground-gainers while William Kirchgessner led the defensive charge.

Catholic Central 19		Sparta High 33
Doran	LE	Fred Walcott
Francis O'Donnell	LT	Elkin
John Carey	LG	Bolender
Whalen	C	Nelson
Stiles	RG	John Johnson
Madigan	RT	J. McIver
Murray	RE	R. Covell
Kirchgessner	QB	Moore
Holland	LH	E. Johnson
Mead	RH	O. Johnson
Colleton	FB	Frank Wolcott

Touchdowns – E. Johnson 2, Moore 2, Frank Wolcott, Kirchgessner (CC) 2, Colleton (CC).
Referee– Monroe, Umpire– smith, Head Linesman– Ducey.

Sparta 33
Catholic Central 19
Saturday, October 12 at Garfield Park

Catholic Central girded for its first big test of the season but was no match for Sparta quarterback Moore, who by all accounts was a one-man wrecking crew. When Moore wasn't powering his way through the CC line, he was bedazzling the Catholics with end sweeps. Moore scored two touchdowns and ran the Spartans offense with great precision.

Kirchgessner scored two of Catholic Central's touchdowns and Thomas Colleton ran for the other, but Murray and Dan Mead were the team's most productive rushers.

1912 Schedule/Results
Head Coach – Tierney

Date	Opponent	Result	Location
Oct. 5	St. Joe Seminary	Won 19-12	Garfield Park
Oct. 12	Sparta	Lost 19-33	Garfield Park

	Record	Pts. Scored	Pts. Allowed
Overall	1-1	38	45

-1913-

Catholic Central entered the season with high hopes after scoring a pair of touchdowns in the second of two preseason scrimmages against Union High School. First-year coach John Bek was encouraged by the rushing of quarterback Brian Ducey and the end play of Edward Leonard. With student enthusiasm for football on the upswing, record crowds were predicted and the best season in Grand Rapids city football history was anticipated.

Then, the season started.

Plainwell 77
Catholic Central 0
Saturday, September 27 at Plainwell

A team of 15 regulars made the road trip south, where CC's speedy mighty-mites were no match for the "beefy aggregation" from Plainwell. Outweighed by "10 pounds per man," the Catholics were overwhelmed and apparently stricken with "stage fright," according to the account in *The Grand Rapids Herald*. Walter Ducey was the lone bright spot for Catholic Central in the 77-0 drubbing.

Hope College 81
Catholic Central 0
Saturday, October 4 at Holland

Things went from bad to worse for CC the week after being trounced by Plainwell. Bek resigned suddenly as the Catholics' head coach, citing the inability to devote the necessary time to the team. Phil Holloway, a former local star, was chosen to fill the vacancy and his first assignment, thank you very much, was to guide CC into battle on the road against a college team.

A "mass meeting," or pep rally, was held at the school to boost team morale for its game the following day against Hope College in Holland, but to no avail. Not surprisingly, Catholic Central was at an even greater weight disadvantage against the collegians than it was at Plainwell. *The Grand Rapids Press* called it "a case of the giants against the midgets, and of course, the giants won" by the score of 81-0. Considering the fact that soon after sizing up their opponent the Catholics thought they might give up 200 points, they left Holland with a hard-earned moral victory.

Despite the margin of defeat, CC battled from start to finish and won the crowd over with its courage. If the Catholics only had enough time to learn some trick plays, they would have been able to counter some of Hope's size advantage, noted one newspaper account.

Catholic Central 30
Nashville 0
Saturday, October 11 at Nashville

If Catholic Central was demoralized by getting outscored 158-0 in its previous two games including one against a college team it didn't show at Nashville High School. In fact, the Catholics vented their frustrations by drubbing their hosts to the south, 30-0.

Catholic Central moved the ball with such dizzying flair, the Nashville defenders were often left grasping at air. John Holland scored first for the Catholics from his halfback position three minutes into the game and Ducey, the quarterback, added a touchdown three minutes later.

William Kirchgessner scored two second-quarter touchdowns and one in the fourth to close out the second win in school history.

Catholic Central		Union High
Kirchgessner	LE	Adrian
Murray	LT	Blandford
Sunseri	LG	Baker
Carmondy	C	Anderson
Eagen	RG	Hammond
Murphy	RT	Gilson
Joe Holland	RE	Drunbrook
Ducey	QB	Powers
Middleton	LH	Hanish
John Holland	RH	Dake
Carey	FB	Knowlton

Catholic	0	6	6	0	12
Union	0	13	6	0	19

Touchdowns – Ducey, Kirchgessener, Hanish 2, Brown.
Referee– Bennett, Umpire– Butler, Head Linesman– Coffey.

Union 19
Catholic Central 12
Saturday, October 18 at Ramona Park

For the first time in its short existence, the Catholic Central football team was going into a game with realistic expectations of coming out of it with a victory. The Catholics were coming off an overwhelming shutout victory at Nashville and had already matched up well against its next opponent, Union, in two preseason scrimmages.

The West Siders won, 19-12, before a crowd of 200 at the Ramona Park field in East Grand Rapids, but CC more than satisfied its fans, who would have been happy to see their team merely score a touchdown against the well-established rival.

On the game-opening possession, Union drove deep into Catholic Central territory, but Ducey ended the threat by intercepting a pass and returning it to his own 15-yard line. Early in the second quarter, the Catholics took over on downs in good field position. Good gains by fullback John Cary, Ducey and Kirchgessner set up Ducey's 12-yard touchdown run. To the amazement of just about everyone, CC led, 6-0.

After the ensuing kickoff, Union replaced Powers with Brown who marched the team down the field and scored the equalizer on a 3-yard run. However, Brown missed the kick for goal and the score remained tied. The Catholics fumbled the ball on the second play of their next series to give Union a short field. Joe Hanish ran in for the touchdown and Dake kicked the extra point to give the West Siders a 13-6 lead going into halftime.

Ray "Stub" Murray returned Union's second-half kickoff to the 50-yard line, and Kirchgessner and Ducey moved the ball into scoring position with back-to-back 15-yard gains. Catholic Central's drive ended, however, on an interception by Dunbrook, and Union trampled the CC defense en route to Hanish's touchdown for a 19-6 lead.

Catholic Central countered quickly on Kirchgessner's 75-yard touchdown reception late in the third quarter but Cary missed the extra point. Union had a chance to put the game out of reach in the fourth quarter, but CC's stout goal-line stand stopped the West Siders for no gain on four consecutive plunges into the line. The Catholics moved the ball out of the shadow of their own goalpost, but time ran out on them 75 yards away from the end zone. Catholic Central left the field knowing it could play with an established team, and the West Siders went home fully aware that they earned a hard-fought victory.

Rockford 15
Catholic Central 0
Saturday, October 25 at John Ball Park

Catholic Central had enough speed and quickness to move the ball against Rockford High School, but lacked the size required on defense to stop its husky opponents from the north. And yet, the Catholics might have had a chance, if they hadn't lost several fumbles after getting within range of Rockford's goal line.

Rockford overcame numerous offside penalties by repeatedly steamrolling Catholic's defensive wall en route to a 15-0 victory. Rockford took an early 2-0 lead on a safety scored by Thompson, who starred along with Baker. Kirchgessner, John Holland, Cary and Ducey stood out for CC.

Rockford 19
Catholic Central 0
Saturday, November 8 at Rockford

Holloway was confident his team could avenge the 15-0 spanking it suffered at the hands of Rockford High School two weeks earlier on home turf if it just kept mistakes to a minimum in the rematch on the road.

Holloway had to juggle his lineup because standout right half John Holland was suffering from a severe cold. Ray Murray moved from right tackle to the backfield and Casper Droste, a new addition to the team, took his place in the line. With Holland out, all the passing would be done by Ducey, the diminutive, but fiery, quarterback. CC was further depleted when star left guard James Egan left the game with an injury.

CC/WC Archives

1913 Catholic Central Football Team

Back Row (l-r) - Ray Murray, Butler, John Cary, John Holland, Coach Holloway, Frank Murphy, James Holland, Madigan
Middle Row - Finney, Joseph Riley, William Kirchgessner, James Sunseri, James Carmondy
Front Row - Art Middleton, Edward Leonard, Bill Ducey

The Catholics gave Rockford its best game to date, according to *The Grand Rapids Herald*, but couldn't overcome 19 unanswered points by their hosts in the third quarter.

Catholic Central 38
Sparta 0
Saturday, November 15 at Sparta

Catholic Central ended a two-game losing streak against Sparta with a resounding 38-0 road victory. It was a milestone win for the Catholics because it avenged the 33-19 defeat they suffered at the hands of the Spartans at the end of the 1912 season and provided evidence they could compete with the area's better teams.

Catholic Central 52
Nashville 0
Saturday, November 22 at John Ball Park

Seven different players accounted for eight touchdowns in the Catholic Central football team's best showing in its short history. The Catholics kept Nashville off-balance with a variety of trick plays and fumbled infrequently despite the waterlogged condition of the John Ball Park field.

After a long series of line bucks and buck laterals around end, right halfback John Holland scored CC's first touchdown in the first quarter, and Ducey scored the first of his two touchdowns a few minutes later. Catholic, which dominated every phase throughout the game, scored three touchdowns in the second quarter. Left end Jimmy Holland and left half Art Middleton stood out for their 20- and 30-yard receptions, respectively.

Catholic Central 14
CC Alumni 0
Thursday, November 27 at Houseman Field

Catholic Central		CC Alumni
James Holland	LE	Rooney
Murphy	LT	Jannausch
Kelly	LG	Jullian
Carmondy	C	Morrissey
Droste	RG	Welch
Murray	RT	Schmidt
Kirchgessner	RE	Eble
Ducey	QB	T. Colleton
John Holland	LH	McNearny
Middleton	RH	Stiles
Carey	FB	Murray

Catholic	0	2	6	6	14
Union	0	0	0	0	0

Touchdowns – Middleton, Jimmy Howward
Referee– Hugh O'Donnell, Umpire– Murray, Head Linesman– Walter Pipp.

The progress being made by the Catholic Central football program wasn't reflected in the way the Varsity defeated the Alumni Team, 14-0, before a large crowd in lousy weather. It was the way the youngsters looked doing it.

Just two years earlier, Catholic Central's founding players were considered too light to compete against bulkier opposition. Even though they now outweighed their successors by 10 pounds per man, the current squad of CC players proved that speed and quickness could beat size and strength.

After the Varsity took a 2-0 second-quarter lead when Kirchgessner trapped the Alumni punter, McNearney, in his own endzone for a safety, the rest of the half turned into a punter's duel. Ducey threw a touchdown pass to Middleton in the third quarter and after the attempt at goal field, the Varsity led 8-0. Jimmy Holland scored the Varsity's final touchdown off an Alumni punt.

1913 Schedule/Results
Head Coach – John Bek/Phil Holloway

Date	Opponent	Result		Location
Sep. 27	Plainwell	Lost	0-77	Plainwell
Oct. 4	Hope College	Lost	0-81	Hope College
Oct. 11	Nashville	Won	30-0	Nashville
Oct. 18	Union	Lost	12-19	Ramona Park
Oct. 25	Rockford	Lost	0-15	John Ball Park
Nov. 8	Rockford	Lost	0-19	Rockford
Nov. 15	Sparta	Won	38-0	Sparta
Nov. 22	Nashville	Won	52-0	John Ball Park
Nov. 27	Alumni	Won	14-0*	Houseman Field

	Record	Pts. Scored	Pts. Allowed
Overall	3-5	132	210

* Not included in team record

-1914-

The Catholic Central football program continued to build momentum off and on the field heading into preseason training. Boosters rallied to provide financial backing, which allowed all the players to be fully equipped for the first time. The return of coach Phil Holloway for a second season had the student body excited and some 30 players, the most ever, went out for the team while nearly every member of CC's successful 1913 campaign was back. Consequently, the allotment of season tickets was nearly sold out before the first game and it was likely more would have to be printed to meet demand.

Catholic Central 20
Allegan 6
Saturday, October 3 at John Ball Park

The optimistic Catholics expected to be tested right out of the gate by the Allegan High eleven, which had the advantage of playing two games before CC lined up for its first. Allegan lost to Holland High, 3-0, and scored a touchdown on the road at Lansing High, which was considered one of the strongest teams in the state. The challenge appeared even more difficult because fullback and newly selected captain John Cary was sidelined by a broken wrist.

Allegan was bigger, but Catholic continued to use the speed it demonstrated the previous season to its advantage to take an early lead and finish with a 20-6 victory. Quarterback Bill Ducey and the Holland twins, Jimmy and John, at the halfback positions and fullback Ray "Stub" Murray dominated play.

On the first possession of the game, Ducey capped a 75-yard drive by running 5 yards for a touchdown and CC had a 7-0 lead. Allegan cut into Catholic's lead in the second quarter when Brady ran 19 yards for a touchdown. He missed the goal from touchdown, however, and Allegan trailed 7-6.

It was all Catholic Central the rest of the way. Jimmy Holland's 20-yard gain set up Ducey's 12-yard broken-field run for a touchdown in the third quarter. A few minutes later, John Kelly's interception and John Holland's 20-yard sweep around end led to Murray's 3-yard plunge into the end zone.

A financial windfall from an exceptionally strong gate provided CC with a second victory.

Plainwell 20
Catholic Central 7
Saturday, October 17 at Plainwell

Cary returned to Catholic Central's starting lineup, but it wasn't enough to prevent a 20-7 loss to Plainwell on the road. Holloway played Cary, who missed the opener against Allegan because of a mending broken wrist, at left end instead of his customary fullback position to limit contact.

A case of the nerves was blamed for Catholic's ineffective play on defense in the first quarter, and Plainwell scored first but missed the goal from touchdown. After settling down, Cary's second-quarter touchdown, followed by a successful goal-after, gave the Catholics a one-point advantage over the team it lost to by a score of 77-0 the previous season.

However, with Plainwell playing aggressively and trying to dictate the tempo in the third quarter, Catholic Central appeared to be content to sit on the lead and milk the clock. At one point, CC took over on downs at the Plainwell 2-yard line but failed to muster enough effort to score. Catholic Central made a fatal error by thinking it had the game in hand because Plainwell scored 14 unanswered points in the fourth quarter to seal the victory.

Catholic Central 72
Sparta 9
Saturday, October 24 at John Ball Park

Banged up physically and hurting mentally from an inexcusable loss the previous week at Plainwell, Catholic Central appeared to be in trouble heading into its game against Sparta. The Spartans had beaten CC in two of the three previous meetings, and after a slow start to the season, were expected to give the Catholics all they could handle.

So much for predictions. Catholic more than made up for its lack of offensive assertiveness at Plainwell by burying Sparta, 72-9, on the strength of the Holland twins' nine touchdowns. The points were the most scored in school history.

The backfield of Ducey, Murray and John and Jimmy Holland repeatedly hammered the Spartan line for 30- and 40-yard gains. John Holland led the way with five scores and Jimmy had four. Cary played end despite his sore arm, and hauled in a 35-yard pass. He did his best work on the other side of the ball, however. The Cary-led defense attacked with such savagery, it literally tore three jerseys off Elkins, the Sparta end.

Catholic Central (72)		Sparta (9)
Cary	LE	Elkins
Roonan	LT	Taylor
B. Ducey	LG	Anderson
Butler	C	Miller
Drostie	RG	Snowden
Rasch	RT	Laubeck
Friar	RE	Jacobs
Bill Ducey	QB	Wilcox
Jim Holland	LH	J. Johnson
John Holland	RH	H. Johnson
Murray	FB	Holt

Touchdowns – John Holland (5), Jim Holland (4), Ducey, Friar, Eikins
Field Goal: Holt
Referee– Friar, Umpire– Moore,

Catholic Central 6
Rockford 6
Saturday, October 31 at Rockford

A controversial 6-6 tie ended Rockford's series dominance, but Catholic Central returned home less than satisfied with the result.

Baker provided Rockford with a 6-0 lead in the first quarter, but CC dominated the rest of the game. Ducey's touchdown evened the score, and in the third quarter Catholic believed it had forced a safety when a Rockford player downed the ball in his own end zone. However, instead of awarding CC with what would have been the decisive two points, the officials ruled the ball was downed for a touchback and spotted the ball at the 20-yard line.

The Catholics had only themselves to blame for not coming away with a victory, however. They subsequently had the ball within easy reach of the Rockford goal line on three occasions, but came up empty each time, twice fumbling the ball away at the 1-yard line.

Cary split time between left end and his familiar fullback position, and his power runs into the line were considered the highlight of the game, but such recognition provided little consolation.

Catholic Central 27
Belding 6
Saturday, November 7 at Belding

Holloway's desire to have Catholic Central's football program regarded on par with the best in the state suffered a setback when its formal application to play a game against Muskegon High School was rejected by the West Michigan powerhouse. Even cross-town rival Union turned down CC's challenge for a game because of a scheduling conflict. Union had moved its game with Grand Haven to Nov. 17, a Tuesday, and a critical game with Grand Rapids Central followed on Saturday. The only open date Union had was before Thanksgiving, but coach Elmer Mitchell didn't want to subject his players to three games in nine days or extend the season beyond the holiday.

Consequently, Catholic Central was extra-determined during that week's practice to put on a show against Belding in order to get noticed by the big boys. Ducey, the small-in-stature but elusive quarterback, set the tone by running for a 75-yard touchdown on the first play from scrimmage, and CC went on to crush the Silk-Millers

John Cary
Catholic Central
1915

John Cary attended St. Andrew's School and graduated from Catholic Central in 1915.

A three-year varsity player at CC, Cary entered the University of Michigan in the fall of 1915 and played on the football team from 1915 through 1919 with a year off in 1918 while he attended naval flight school.

Cary earned his varsity letter in 1919, becoming the first Catholic Central alumni to wear the block "M".

Earning his law degree from U of M in 1922, Cary returned to Grand Rapids to practice law.

John Cary passed away in Grand Rapids on June 1, 1977

27-6 on their own field. Catholic Central overpowered Belding with superior speed, and, for a change, size.

Catholic's edge dropped to 7-6 five minutes later when Belding's Jersey scooped up a CC fumble and returned it 15 yards for a touchdown. Nevertheless, the Millers couldn't move the ball against Cary and the Catholic defense, considered the best ever to play in Belding.

In the second quarter, Catholic Central confused Belding with a double-shift and John Holland swept the end for a touchdown. Kelly ran for a touchdown to open up a 21-6 lead in the third quarter and Jimmy Holland capped the scoring with a fourth-quarter touchdown. John Holland converted three of four goal-from-touchdown drop-kick attempts.

Whether CC impressed the state's power teams is debatable; Belding considered itself successful for not being beaten by a bigger margin.

Dowagiac 20
Catholic Central 14
Saturday, November 14 at Dowagiac

Catholic Central went into Dowagiac anticipating its toughest challenge of the season. The Catholics got it, and then some, thanks to a costly mistake made by the referee. The Indians' strength was gauged by the fact they lost at South Bend (Ind.) High only by the score of 24-0 one week earlier. Meantime, CC star halfback Jimmy Holland was sidelined by a sprained ankle sustained in practice.

Despite operating with the relatively inexperienced John Kelly at halfback, the Catholics opened up a 14-0 lead on a pair of John Holland touchdowns and two goal-from-touchdown drop-kicks. Dowagiac made it a 14-6 game just before halftime, and cut the deficit to one point in the third quarter when Gwilt, an Indians defender, recovered a CC fumble and ran it back for a touchdown.

The Catholics appeared to secure the victory late in the fourth quarter when they threw the Dowagiac ball-carrier for a loss on fourth-and-5 to go at the CC 12-yard line. However, the referee declared it was only third down and the Indians picked up first-down yardage on the extra play. Dowagiac fullback Warren Allen's second touchdown proved to be the game-winner.

CC Alumni 24
Catholic Central 19
Thursday, November 26 at Reeds Lake, Ramona Park

The Catholics closed out their best season ever against the CC Alumni on Thanksgiving Day. The game was scheduled for the morning so the players would be able to watch Central High's pivotal game at Muskegon later that day. A crowd of 900 watched the Alumni All-Stars defeat the Varsity, 24-19.

Catholic Central (19)		Alumni (24)
Cary	LE	Rooney
Kelley	LT	Allen
Droste	LG	D. O'Brien
Butler	C	Carmondy
Rasch	RG	Sutherland
Murphy	RT	Miller
Schenkelberg	RE	R. O'Brien
Bill Ducey	QB	Kirchgessner
Jim Holland	LH	T. Holland
John Holland	RH	Stiles
Ray Murray	FB	Bob Murray

Touchdowns – T. Holland, Kirchgessner (2), Stiles, Ducey, John Holland, Murphy

Trailing entering the fourth quarter, the Varsity put on an offensive show with nifty laterals and a completed forward pass from Ducey to halfback John Holland to score a touchdown and close within five points. After stopping the Alumni following the ensuing kick-off, the Varsity advanced the ball to the Alumni's 4-yard line. But the Varsity couldn't punch the ball over the goal line against the Alumni, who enjoyed a 30-pound-per-man weight advantage, and the referee called the game in time for the players to head west.

1914 Schedule/Results
Head Coach – Phil Holloway

Date	Opponent	Result		Location
Oct. 3	Allegan	Won	20-6	John Ball Park
Oct. 17	Plainwell	Lost	7-20	Plainwell
Oct. 24	Sparta	Won	72-9	John Ball Park
Oct. 31	Rockford	Tie	6-6	Rockford
Nov. 7	Belding	Won	27-6	Belding
Nov. 14	Dowagiac	Lost	14-20	Dowagiac
Nov. 27	Alumni	Lost	19-24*	Ramona Park

	Record	Pts. Scored	Pts. Allowed
Overall	3-2-1	132	210

* Not included in team record

-1915-

With all four members of his 1914 backfield lost to graduation, third-year Catholic Central coach Phil Holloway acknowledged he was probably in for a rebuilding year. The high-scoring Holland twins, Jimmy and John, had to be replaced at the halfback positions, as did quarterback Bill Ducey and fullback Ray "Stub" Murray. The line was also decimated.

Bryant Ducey was among the inexperienced players competing for the quarterback job, but Holloway had no idea what kind of team he'd have despite *The Grand Rapids Herald* headline declaring that "Catholic Central's Team Looks Formidable."

Otsego 56
Catholic Central 6
Saturday, October 9 at Otsego

Holloway found out swhat he had soon enough in the 56-6 season-opening loss at Otsego, which plowed CC's undersized defensive line into the turf. With Otsego leading 19-0 in the second quarter, Catholic Central end Eddie Gallagher got open on a crisscross pattern and caught a 15-yard touchdown pass. However, Otsego outscored CC 25-0 in the third quarter and 12-0 in the fourth to complete the rout.

The score didn't look quite as bad in retrospect considering the Otsego fullback identified by *The Herald* as "Kelly" had previous playing experience at the University of Detroit and St. Louis University. A week later, the Catholics were still scratching their heads over how Kelly and two other grown men could have possibly been eligible to play for Otsego.

Catholic Central		Union H. S.
Gallagher	LE	Everts
Butler	LT	Bock
Bolger	LG	Kellogg
Norton	C	Swigerl
Friar	RG	Swanson
Sullivan	RT	Townsend
Stace	RE	Seymour
Brown	QB	Griffin
Rasch	LH	Scharmack
Droste	RH	Cornwell
O'Brien	FB	Thorndyk

Catholic	0	0	0	0	0
Union	11	13	19	26	72

Touchdowns – Cornwell (3), Griffin, Scharmack, Seymour (2), Thorndyk (3), Knowlton
PAT: Cornwell (6)
Referee– Fled, Umpire– Shaw, Head Linesman– Grimes.

Union 72
Catholic Central 0
Saturday, October 16 at Ramona Park, Reeds Lake

In the wake of CC's 50-point season-opening loss at Otsego, Holloway had no choice but to rearrange his lineup for Union, which was considered one of the state's strongest and biggest teams. To beef up his offensive line, Holloway moved Ducey from quarterback to guard and Bob Brown, who had virtually no experience but plenty of natural ability, took over at quarterback. Holloway put Jimmy Bolger, another first-year player, at the other guard spot.

What Catholic Central lacked in size - it was reportedly the lightest squad in program history - it tried to make up for with courage. Unfortunately, the Catholics didn't have nearly enough to compete with Union, which beat CC, 72-0.

Catholic Central put up a stubborn fight in the first half, and with the help of numerous offside, unnecessary roughness and holding penalties level against the Unions for 96 yards, trailed only 27-0 going into the third quarter. Union used its overwhelming brawn to wear down CC, which ended the game with just one first down the rest of the way.

In spite of the way CC was beaten, Brown emerged from the wreckage as a budding star because of his play at quarterback.

GR Herald Photo

Catholic Central's O'Brien punting during the game against South.

Catholic Central		South H. S.
Gallagher	LE	Bolden
Butler	LT	Fisher
Bolger	LG	Shives
G. Butler	C	Fish
Friar	RG	Pixley
Droste	RT	Freeland
Stace	RE	Nicholl
Brown	QB	Mohr
Schenkelberg	LH	Walbridge
Rasch	RH	Perkins
O'Brien	FB	Molesta

Catholic	0	0	0	0	0
South	0	0	0	3	3

Field Goal - Wallbridge
Referee– O. F. Field, Umpire– Stanley Joseph, Head Linesman–Mike Monroe.

South 3
Catholic Central 0
Friday, October 29 at Ramona Park

Being outscored by a combined 128-6 in its first two games didn't stop Catholic Central from being favored to defeat South High Schools first-year varsity squad, referred to as "the infants" and the "little eleven" by several touchdowns. The Catholics held their own defensively in what quickly evolved into a fierce battle for every inch of territory, but exhibited little offensive firepower in the 3-0 loss.

GR Herald Photo
(t-b)Eddie Gallagher, Clancey O'Brien and Bob Brown

For the most part, Catholic Central bent but didn't break against the suddenly efficient South eleven, who solved the fumbling problems that plagued them in previous games. South moved the ball into scoring position several times, but CC denied it access to the end zone each time.

In the second quarter, South drop-kicker Wallbridge missed a 22-yard field-goal attempt. Unfortunately, Catholic Central couldn't move the ball on offense and played most of the game in its own territory. Wallbridge drop-kicked the game-winning field goal from the 9-yard line with about four minutes remaining.

Catholic Central's most effective weapon during the game was its punter.

Grand Haven 33
Catholic Central 0
Saturday, November 6 at Grand Haven

The Grand Rapids Press reported Catholic Central fought gamely and succeeded in holding the heavier Grand Haven squad to only 33 points.

Wayland 13
Catholic Central 0
Saturday, November 13 at Wayland

Wayland scored once in the third quarter and once in the fourth quarter to hold off the scrappy visitors from Grand Rapids and keep the Catholic school winless for the 1915 season.

GR Herald Photo

1915 Catholic Central Football Team

Catholic Central 0
CC Alumni 0
Thursday, November 25 at Island Park

Catholic Central's speed gave it a chance to beat the much bigger CC Alumni, but the annual game against the old-timers ended in a scoreless tie. Its speed also prevented another loss.

In the third quarter, Alumni defensive end Al Zeits intercepted a pass at the 50-yard line and had the goal line in sight. However, a Varsity defender ran him down from behind and tackled him 12 yards short of the end zone. The Varsity could at least boast that it stalemated a team loaded with former CC stars, such as Bob and "Stub" Murray and Bill Ducey.

1915 Schedule/Results

Head Coach – Phil Holloway

Date	Opponent	Result		Location
Oct. 9	Otsego	Lost	6-56	Otsego
Oct. 16	Union	Lost	0-72	Ramona Park
Oct. 29	South	Lost	0-3	Ramona Park
Nov. 6	Grand Haven	Lost	0-33	Grand Haven
Nov. 13	Wayland	Lost	0-13	Wayland
Nov. 27	Alumni	Tie	0-0*	Island Park

	Record	Pts. Scored	Pts. Allowed
Overall	0-5	6	171

* Not included in team record

-1916-

While fourth-year Catholic Central coach Phil Holloway was off on his honeymoon, former CC players Robert Murray and John Cary volunteered to put the squad of 35 players through its paces during preseason drills at John Ball Park. Although the Catholics returned an experienced backfield, developing a physical line, which was constantly overrun the previous season, was the No. 1 priority.

Holloway came back in time to take over the team a couple of days before the season opener at Grand Haven High. The CC Alumni Association also announced that new dark-blue jerseys - sporting a series of thin white stripes on the sleeves - had been purchased for the players.

However, Catholic Central's outlook for a successful season dimmed significantly when the parents of Pete Pipp indicated they weren't going to let their son join the team. Pipp was Holloway's best all-around prospect and the younger brother of New York Yankees first baseman Wally Pipp, who in 1925 would be famously replaced in the lineup by a rookie named Lou Gehrig. In an ironic precursor to Wally Pipp becoming a folk legend for giving way to the beloved Yankee, who became known as "The Iron Horse" while playing in a record 2,130 consecutive games, *The Grand Rapids Herald* headline announcing CC's expected loss read: "PIPP MAY NOT PLAY FOR CATHOLIC HIGH."

Grand Haven 18
Catholic Central 6
Saturday, September 30 at Grand Haven

With Pipp out of the lineup, undersized CC lost to their much bigger foes at Grand Haven, 18-6. Catholic's touchdown came on a 70-yard run by Don Stace, the quarterback.

Cadillac 32
Catholic Central 13
Saturday, October 14 at Island Park

Pipp's parents apparently relented and let their son play for CC after all, and the Catholics donned their new blue and white jerseys for the first time when they took to the Island Park field to host Cadillac High School. The Catholics scored the game's first 13 points and appeared in good shape for a win. However, they were eventually overpowered by their much bigger opponent and suffered a 32-13 loss before a crowd of 300.

Stace bettered the 70-yard touchdown run he had in the opener against Grand Haven with an 80-yarder against Cadillac. However, Cadillac right half Mace stole the show with a 96-yard jaunt to the end zone. Catholic Central found it all but impossible to penetrate the middle of Cadillac's line, and its best running plays were sweeps by Pipp and Rudy Schmidt from their right and left end positions. Catholic's offense was also hampered by its inability to complete a forward pass against Cadillac.

Catholic Central		South H. S.
Schmidt	LE	Moore
O'Brien	LT	Osborne
Gallagher	LG	McManamy
Norton	C	Worth
Riordan	RG	DeRuiter
F. Peet	RT	Swanson
Pipp	RE	Brough
Stace	QB	Molesta
Rasch	LH	Shives
N. Peet	RH	Perkins
Bolger	FB	Freeland

Catholic	0	6	3	6	15
South	0	0	3	6	9

Touchdowns – Pipp, Bolger, Swanson
Field Goals – Pipp, Swanson
Referee – Monroe, Umpire – Daane, Head Linesman - Wikstrom

Catholic Central 15
South 9
Tuesday, October 24 at Island Park

A steady downpour that turned the Island Park field into a sea of mud caused Catholic Central's game against South High to be postponed twice from Thursday, Oct. 19 to the following Tuesday. Both teams were reportedly "on edge" after taking time off, enduring chalk-talks by their respective coaches Holloway at CC and South's "Pop" Churm and participating in light walk-throughs.

The time off was reflected in the sloppy, turnover-plagued play of both teams, which were locked in a 9-9 tie until Catholic Central fullback Jimmy Bolger intercepted a pass and returned it 60-plus yards as time expired.

South outgained CC by a wide margin, but Pipp dominated with his kicking, running and defense and the Catholic Central defense forced several turnovers to stop promising South drives short of the goal line. Pipp intercepted a South pass to stop one of those threats at the end of the first quarter.

In the second quarter, a 20-yard holding penalty called against South and Pipp's second interception set up Catholic Central's first score, which came off the game's initial trick play. After running a fake cross-buck that drew the South defense to the right side of the line, Pipp reversed from his right end position behind the line of scrimmage, took the ball and ran 40 yards for a touchdown.

South drove to the CC 30-yard line on its first possession of the second half, but the Catholic defense stopped the south enders on fourth down. Catholic's offense failed to advance the ball, but after another punt by Pipp, South lost 20 more yards on a holding penalty, fumbled the ball on the next play and recovered at its own 1-yard line. After a weak South punt from the end zone, Catholic Central got the ball back just 10 yards from the goal line, but netted just 1 yard on three plays and settled for a short field goal from Pipp, who had a drop-kick blocked in the first quarter.

South's Swanson drop-kicked a 30-plus-yard field goal to cut Catholic's lead to 9-3 in the third quarter and then tied the score after a bizarre sequence in the fourth quarter. South drove 79 yards to the CC 1-yard line but failed to score on fourth down. Catholic Central lost a fumble at its 6-yard line and two plays later Swanson plunged into the end zone from the 1-foot mark. Osborn missed the go-ahead extra-point try. After South lost another fumble and Pipp had two more drop-kicks blocked, Catholic Central fumbled a punt and South recovered.

But Bolger forced the last turnover of the day and Catholic Central ended a seven-game losing streak spanning three seasons.

Catholic Central 19
Hastings 0
Saturday, October 28 at Hastings

Brimming with confidence and suddenly clicking on offense, Catholic Central used its speed and athleticism to counteract Hastings' bulk in a 19-0 road victory.

Stace, the CC quarterback, scored touchdowns in the first and second quarters, but Schmidt provided the biggest highlight of the game. Schmidt, who switched from his usual end position to halfback in place of the injured Herbert Rasch, brought the crowd to its feet with a school-record, 95-yard, broken-field touchdown run.

Pipp continued to kick the Catholics out of trouble with long, high punts, but he had a long drop-kick for a field goal nullified by a technicality. Pipp converted one of three point-after attempts.

Catholic Central		Union H. S.
Schmidt	LE	Kreumheur
Gallagher	LT	Guguski
Ehrhardt	LG	Nelson
Norton	C	Bowbeer
Riordan	RG	Quigley
F. Peet	RT	Clemens
Pipp	RE	Van Wingen
Stace	QB	Cornwell
Rasch	LH	Rivard
N. Peet	RH	Boch
Bolger	FB	Throndyk

Catholic	0	0	0	0	0
Union	0	7	6	0	13

Touchdowns – Thorndyk (2)
PAT – Cornwell
Referee – Monroe, Umpire – Herrick

Otsego 46
Catholic Central 0
Saturday, November 11 at Otsego

Pipp's sure tackling and strong punting was about all that kept Catholic Central from losing to the monstrous Otsego football team by more than seven touchdowns. After a scoreless first quarter, Otsego scored 19 points in the second to break the game open. Otsego scored a pair of touchdowns in each of the final two stanzas and Catholic Central's modest win streak was snapped at two games.

Union 13
Catholic Central 0
Friday, November 17 at Island Park

Pipp won the punting duel, a closely watched aspect of football during this era, but Union High School was better in every other phase of the game while defeating Catholic Central 13-0 on an Island Park field frozen by unseasonably cold weather.

Pep rallies, known then as "mass meetings," were held at each school before the game, which handicappers picked to have a similar result as Union's 72-0 victory a year earlier.

Everyone in attendance was surprised, therefore, to see the first quarter end in a 0-0 tie, thanks in large part to Pipp's magnificent punting. Union battered the CC defense with a series of line bucks, and on the third play of the second quarter, Thorndyke, the West Sider's fullback, plowed into the end zone from the 8-yard line and Clyde Cornwell drop-kicked the extra point for a 7-0 lead.

The Catholics picked up their initial first down of the game on the ensuing possession, and Pipp's 12-yard run to the Union 30 resulted in their best shot at scoring in the game. The offense stalled, however, and Pipp's 30-yard drop-kick for a field goal sailed wide. Thorndyke put the game out of reach with his second touchdown.

Catholic Central 9
CC Alumni 0
Thursday, November 30 at Island Park

Age, attrition and a dearth of fitness finally started to catch up with the Catholic Central Alumni, who were thrashed by the Varsity, 9-0, on Thanksgiving morning. The Alumni had barely enough players to field an eleven, and once the referee blew his whistle for the opening kickoff, "the motley array of the older boys… found that little short of a fatality would excuse them during the course of the game," read *The Grand Rapids Herald* account of the contest.

On the Varsity's first offensive play, Pipp, from his right end position, threw a 20-yard touchdown pass to Schmidt, his bookend on the left side of the line. Pipp also kicked the goal from touchdown and CC added a safety in the second quarter to complete the scoring.

Catholic Central		CC Alumni
Schmidt	LE	Hessman
Gallagher	LT	Williams
Ehrhardt	LG	Kelly
Norton	C	Friar
Riordan	RG	Droste
F. Peet	RT	Middleton
Pipp	RE	Brown
Stace	QB	Ducey
Rasch	LH	Murray
N. Peet	RH	Schenkleberg
Bolger	FB	Host

Catholic	7	2	0	0	9
CC Alumni	0	0	0	0	0

Touchdowns – Schmidt
PAT – Pipp
Referee – Monroe, Umpire – Hollaway, Head Linesman - Brown

Meanwhile, the Associated Press reported that 14 athletes, including 14-year-old Francis B. Moriarty of Detroit, died playing football nationwide in 1916. That was two fewer than the previous year, but one more than in '14.

"In most cases," the AP story said, "those who lost their lives were members of high school, semi-professional and prairie elevens. Only one of the victims was a college player. Two of the players suffered broken necks, but a majority died from internal injuries."

1916 Schedule/Results

Head Coach – Phil Holloway

Date	Opponent	Result		Location
Sep. 30	Grand Haven	Lost	6-18	Grand Haven
Oct. 14	Cadillac	Lost	13-32	Island Park
Oct. 24	South	Won	15-9	Island Park
Oct. 28	Hastings	Won	19-0	Hastings
Nov. 11	Otsego	Lost	0-46	Otsego
Nov. 17	Union	Lost	0-13	Island Park
Nov. 30	Alumni	Won	9-0*	Island Park

	Record	Pts. Scored	Pts. Allowed
Overall	2-4	53	118

* Not included in team record

-1917-

CC/WC Archives

CC's Bill Cary

Uncertainty at key positions weighed heavily on CC coach Phil Holloway's mind 10 days before the Sheldon Avenuers' season opener at Wayland High School. Catholic Central's chief needs were at quarterback and both guard positions. Shanahan showed good leadership while handling the quarterback duties for a few practices, but Holloway thought him too light to handle the rigors of the position. After considering every player on the team, Holloway decided to move Bill Cary into the QB spot. Meanwhile, Mehan was in danger of losing his job at end because, according to The *Grand Rapids Herald*, he "took the day off to celebrate with his rural playmates at the fair."

A week later, Cary was lined up as a starting guard, the pint-sized Frank Doran had won the quarterback competition and Mehan was off the team.

Catholic Central 26
Wayland 0
Saturday, September 29 at Wayland

Doran acquitted himself quite well in the 26-0 victory against Wayland. He received credit for running the team efficiently, scooting for good gains around the end and ducking under the defensive line while scoring his two touchdowns. Fullback Jimmy Bolger and Don Stace, a halfback, also scored touchdowns.

Although Catholic Central's defense looked impressive while stopping Wayland several times on fourth down, it was considered a misleading development because the line was considered too light to handle the more powerful offenses it would face later in the season.

Catholic Central		Union H. S.
P. Carey	LE	Miller
O'Brien	LT	Bowbeer
Teal	LG	Blickley
Riordan	C	Walker
W. Carey	RG	Rubinkowitz
Patt	RT	Clemens
Friar	RE	Mervenne
Doran	QB	Cornwell
F. Peet	LH	Small
Stace	RH	Krumheur
Bolger	FB	Coleman

Catholic	0	0	0	0	0
Union	0	12	12	18	42

Touchdowns – Coleman (2), Cornwell (2), Small (3), Krumheur

Referee – Mike Monroe, Umpire – Cash, Head Linesman – W. A Monroe

Union 42
Catholic Central 0
Saturday, October 6 at Island Park

When the Catholics played their next game, against archrival Union High, on paper, they liked their chances. They only lost to the West Siders by 13 points a year earlier, and they improved while Union appeared to be no better after beating Newaygo and Belding.

Catholic Central's theory appeared to have merit during the scoreless first quarter. And when Union right tackle Clemens was ejected for rough play and the attendant penalty moved the ball from the West Siders' 40-yard line to the 20, the Catholics thought they were onto something. Unfortunately, CC was too light to power the ball through the Unions' defense, and its best chance of the day ended on downs at the 12.

Catholic Central did get one last chance to score when on the next play, it fell inches short of trapping Union fullback Coleman in the end zone for a safety near the end of the first quarter. The momentum shifted to Union after Coleman punted out of the end zone and on CC's next play, Union's Mervenne recovered a fumble at his own 40. Union spent the next several minutes pulverizing the Catholic Central defense with runs up the middle and off tackle, and Coleman dragged defenders into the end zone for the first score.

Union converted CC end Pat Cary's fumble at his own 15-yard line into another touchdown by quarterback Clyde Cornwell, and the West Siders led, 12-0, at halftime. Doc Meyers thrilled Union's fans when he returned the second-half kickoff to the Catholic Central 18 and Small scored the first of his three touchdowns to put the game out of reach.

GR Herald Photo
(l-r) Frank Doran, Bill Cary and Bryant Ducey.

Shelby 20
Catholic Central 0
Saturday, October 13 at Shelby

Catholic Central came out of its game against Union battered and bruised and Holloway didn't even make the westward trip to Shelby with the 14-man squad which included Mehan, who was back on the roster. Doran, the CC quarterback, left tackle and team captain Clancey O'Brien and backup guard Goetz stayed back because of injuries.

The Catholics put up a good fight, but overcoming Holloway's unexplained absence and Shelby's daunting size was too much to ask of CC's patchwork eleven. After a scoreless first quarter, Shelby scored 13 points in the second quarter and seven in the fourth to upend Catholic Central, 20-0.

Stace, who moved from halfback to quarterback in place of Doran, drove the Catholics to the Shelby 10-yard line on two occasions, but CC failed to move the ball with any consistency.

Cadillac 80
Catholic Central 0
Saturday, October 20 at Cadillac

With seven of 11 starters unable to practice, the situation looked bleak for Catholic Central going into the game at Cadillac. Stace, who played quarterback in place of the injured Doran during the loss at Shelby was back at halfback, and Cary, who lined up at halfback against Shelby, was back at quarterback, the position he played during preseason drills.

Only six regulars from the beginning of the season made the trip north, and CC's team made up primarily of reserves was destroyed by Cadillac, 80-0. Carey picked up a couple of first downs on end sweeps, but the Catholics were never in position to score.

Hastings 7
Catholic Central 0
Saturday, October 27 at Hastings

Catholic Central looked to Hastings, which was playing its first game of the season, for relief from its injury-woes. Even in its depleted state, CC matched up well with Hastings, as was evident by the 0-0 deadlock through three-plus quarters.

The Catholics suffered yet another setback a few minutes into the rain-soaked game when left halfback Freddie Peet left with an injury. With Stevens in at halfback and the game plan Holloway designed with Peet in mind out the window, Catholic Central penetrated deep into enemy territory only once. That threat was extinguished when Randall, the Hastings captain, intercepted a CC pass.

Hastings wore Catholic down in the fourth quarter and Randall plowed into the endzone for the game's only touchdown with five minutes remaining, much to the delight of the local fans who witnessed a long home losing streak come to an end.

Catholic Central		South H. S.
P. Carey	LE	Howell
O'Brien	LT	Hodges
Doherty	LG	McManamy
Reilly	C	Worth
Dierdorf	RG	Otten
Patt	RT	Swanson
W. Carey	RE	Wikop
Doran	QB	LeBaron
F. Peet	LH	Osborne
Stace	RH	Bolden
Teal	FB	DeRuiter

Catholic	0	0	0	0	0
South	20	7	21	27	75

Touchdowns – DeRuiter (3), Bolden (2), LaBaron (2), Witkop (2), Swanson, Siemons
PAT – DeRuiter 9 of 11
Referee – Daane, Umpire – Winslow, Head Linesman – Bennett

South 75
Catholic Central 0
Tuesday, November 6 at Island Park

Holloway welcomed some of Catholic Central's walking wounded back for a snowy week of practice for the game against South High, but doctors declared Bolger out for the season. Catholic Central even held one practice indoors at the Knights of Columbus gymnasium because of the poor weather, which caused the game to be postponed by four days.

Not that any of it mattered. South took no pity on the beleaguered Catholics and avenged its disappointing 15-9 loss to CC in 1916 with a 75-0 rout. South set a new scoring record one week after defeating Belding, 74-0.

South's desire to run up the score became evident early on when Worth, the team captain, insisted on playing full 15-minute quarters. Catholic Central trailed only by 27 points at halftime, but was overmatched at every position and in every phase of the game. The Catholics stopped the South scoring machine twice on downs in the fourth quarter, but still gave up 27 points, including a touchdown off a blocked punt, in the final period. The game took so long it ended just before total darkness set in.

Catholic Central 18
Grand Haven 7
Saturday, November 17 at Island Park

As Catholic Central's humiliating season neared its end, an analysis of the situation by *The Grand Rapids Herald* concluded that the school's sorry showing in sports was a result of inadequate, or non-existent, athletic training in the parochial elementary schools.

The Herald pointed out that public school boys begin training early on by playing soccer in a well-developed, citywide program. Once in high school, public school boys also had access to gymnasiums in the winter and the opportunity to try out for basketball, which CC didn't offer. Spring sports were also made available by the development of a municipal recreation department. *The Herald* asserted that it was Catholic Central's patriotic duty to make sure its young students had every opportunity to develop athletically at an early age by developing grammar school programs.

On the field, the Catholics hoped to save face by announcing their intention to beat Grand Haven "worse than South did." They fell short by a touchdown, but the Pat Cary-led 18-7 victory was a welcome respite from the misery they had endured, nonetheless.

Grand Haven throttled Catholic Central in the first quarter and it looked like more of the same for CC, although neither team scored. A 15-yard run by Freddie Peet, the left half, and a 40-yard reception by Patt, the right end, set up quarterback Doran's 6-yard touchdown run that put CC ahead 6-0 in the second quarter. The Catholics lost the lead a few minutes later when Slingerian returned an interception 50 yards for a touchdown and then drop-kicked the extra point.

However, Catholic's 12-point third quarter got started when Doran ran the second-half kickoff to the Grand Haven 35. On the first play from scrimmage, Doran connected with Pat Cary for a 65-yard touchdown pass to regain the lead. Grand Haven fumbled the ensuing kickoff back to CC, and Pat Cary put the game out of reach five plays later with a 15-yard touchdown run.

CC Alumni 7
Catholic Central 0
Thursday, November 29 at Island Park

The season thankfully came to an end for Catholic Central with a 7-0 loss to the CC Alumni on Thanksgiving morning. The ground was too slippery and the Varsity was too light to give the burly Alumni much competition. John Cary's 5-yard rushing touchdown in the third quarter was all the Alumni needed.

At least none of the Catholics were among the 12 youths killed nationwide while playing football.

Catholic Central		CC Alumni
P. Cary	LE	Pettit
O'Brien	LT	J. Cary
Goetz	LG	Mead
Reilly	C	Norton
Dierdorf	RG	Riordan
Teal	RT	Carmondy
Patt	RE	McGough
Doran	QB	Murray
F. Peet	LH	Schmidt
Stace	RH	Stiles
Schenckelberg	FB	Peet

Catholic	0	0	0	0	0
CC Alumni	0	0	0	0	7

Touchdowns – J. Carey
PAT – Stiles
Referee – Madigan, Umpire – Murray, Head Linesman – Milton Peet

1917 Schedule/Results
Head Coach – Phil Holloway

Date	Opponent	Result		Location
Sep. 29	Wayland	Won	26-0	Wayland
Oct. 6	Union	Lost	0-42	Island Park
Oct. 13	Shelby	Lost	0-20	Shelby
Oct. 20	Cadillac	Lost	0-80	Cadillac
Oct. 27	Hastings	Lost	0-7	Hastings
Nov. 6	South	Lost	0-70	Island Park
Nov. 17	Grand Haven	Won	18-7	Island Park
Nov. 29	Alumni	Lost	0-7*	Island Park

	Record	Pts. Scored	Pts. Allowed
Overall	2-5	44	226

* Not included in team record

-1918-

After Phil Holloway resigned during preseason drills, former player John Cary took over as the new Catholic Central head coach. But size, or the lack thereof, was the same old problem for CC going into the season opener. South High, whose fledgling program just a few years earlier was called the "infants" and the "little eleven," had already caught and passed CC. In a tale-of-the-tape chart printed by *The Grand Rapids Herald*, South's starting lineup averaged 147 pounds per man to 143 for the Catholics.

South 35
Catholic Central 0
Friday, September 27 at Island Park

Whatever edge CC thought it had in the speed department didn't pan out during the 35-0 loss. It was South's third victory in four games against Catholic.

Fullback Freddie Peet became a fan-favorite with his spirited play, but CC had little else to be happy about. South took a 7-0 lead two minutes into the game on South fullback DeRuiter's 30-yard run around end. On its ensuing possession, Catholic Central drove to the South 10-yard line and appeared to be on the verge of tying the score, but DeRuiter intercepted a pass at the 3. DeRuiter all but put the game out of reach with a 50-yard touchdown run in the second quarter, and South finished off CC with 21 second-half points.

Catholic Central		South H. S.
Pat Carey	LE	Howell
McKenna	LT	Hodges
Kelly	LG	DeHoog
Reilly	C	Jacques
Dougherty	RG	Fleckner
Murray	RT	Otten
Friar	RE	Siemons
O"Brien	QB	LeBaron
Meyers	LH	Osborne
Peet	RH	Bolden
Teele	FB	DeRuiter

Catholic	0	0	0	0	0
South	7	7	7	14	35

Touchdowns – DeRuiter (2), Bolden, Hodges, LeBaron, Osborne
PAT – DeRuiter 5 of 5
Referee – Roe, Umpire – Bouwman, Head Linesman – Trusedale

Union 21
Catholic Central 10
Saturday, October 12 at Island Park

Catholic Central		Union H. S.
P. Carey	LE	VanWingen
Stevens	LT	Blickley
Dougherty	LG	DeYoung
Reilly	C	Walker
Kelly	RG	Boller
Murray	RT	Clemens
Friar	RE	Cherry
O'Brien	QB	Cornwell
Vinnie Meyers	LH	Meyers
Peet	RH	Mindell
Teele	FB	Tufts

Catholic	3	0	7	0	10
Union	7	14	0	0	21

Touchdowns – Tufts, Meyers, Mindell, Vinnie Meyers
PAT – Cornwell 3 of 3, Friar 1 of 1
FG - Friar

Union went into its annual grudge match with Catholic Central sporting an even bigger weight advantage than South did, 11 pounds per man, and outweighed CC at 10 of 11 positions. Back then, size was the biggest single indicator of success, and this game ran true to form when the West Siders defeated Catholic, 21-10, before a small crowd at Island Park.

The game featured a showdown between the Meyers brothers: "Doc" of Union and Vinnie for Catholic. It also marked the end of Cary's short tenure as the CC head coach. Cary finally got word that his application for naval flight service had been accepted and was headed to military duty shortly after the game.

Tufts capped Union's first drive with a rushing touchdown that resulted in a 7-0 lead, but CC wasn't daunted. The Catholics moved into scoring position at the Union 25-yard line with Bernie Friar's 20-yard reception on a crisscross pattern. After Union sniffed out a fake drop-kick and dropped CC for a 10-yard loss, Bernie Friar booted a 35-yard field goal to cut the deficit to 7-3.

Union pulled away in the second quarter with a 20-yard touchdown reception by right half Mindell, and a dive into the end zone by Doc Meyers. Catholic scored the game's final points in the third quarter when Union's Clyde Cornwell fielded a punt at his 10-yard line and fumbled after a 5-yard return. Vinnie Meyers picked up the loose ball and ran 15 yards for a touchdown. Union had the best chance to score in the final quarter, but Catholic Central repelled the West Siders on both occasions.

Muskegon 13
Catholic Central 0
Wednesday, November 13 at Hackley Field

GR Herald Photo

(l-r) Vinnie Meyers, Bob O'Brien, Elgin Teale and Freddie Peet.

With Catholic Central's next game at Dowagiac canceled due to an outbreak of the Spanish flu at the host school, the Sheldon Avenuers were without a game and coach. The school tried to solve the latter problem by trying to lure Holloway back, but he declined, citing a work conflict. Ray Murray, a CC halfback from 1913-14, accepted the job but would have to wait nearly a month to make his debut.

When the flu epidemic reached Grand Rapids, local health officer Dr. C.C. Siemons ordered all games on Oct. 24 and 25 be cancelled. Central coach Heinie Lightner and South coach Pop

Churm protested the ban on the grounds that since the games were being played outdoors and in fresh air, fans would be able to spread out and wouldn't be of danger of contracting the virus from each other. Union coach John Truesdale lamented that the cancellations came just as his team was rounding into mid-season form and gunning for a state championship.

Catholic Central was just happy to get out of the weekend without another loss. On Oct. 21, Gov. Albert E. Sleeper issued a ban on games throughout the state until further notice.

While the Catholics were idle on Nov. 9, Central High School junior quarterback Gordon Scott, 17, broke his neck while being tackled during the second quarter of the game against Union. It was believed Scott was injured when he was pounced on by Union players while trying to recover his own fumble. Before he died at Blodgett Memorial Hospital three days later, according to *The Grand Rapids Herald*, Scott regained consciousness long enough to issue a statement exonerating the Union players of any wrongdoing. Nevertheless, the West Side school called off the rest of its games.

It was under a pall, therefore, that Catholic Central lined up for its final game, at Muskegon on the Tuesday Scott died. Five days after CC's 13-0 loss to the Muskies, the 1918 season was declared "a complete failure" by *The Herald* in a story under the byline of Werner C. Groening.

Reasons for the breakdown ranged from the loss of coaches who joined the military to serve during World War I to the statewide ban on games due to a flu epidemic to Scott's death. *The Herald* even declined to name an All-City Team, and there were calls for the abandonment of high school football in Michigan.

1918 Schedule/Results

Head Coach – John Cary/Holland/Ray Murray

Date	Opponent	Result		Location
Sep. 27	South	Lost	0-35	Island Park
Oct. 12	Union	Lost	10-21	Island Park
Nov. 13	Muskegon	Lost	0-13	Hackley Field

	Record	Pts. Scored	Pts. Allowed
Overall	0-3	10	69

-1919-

Grand Haven 19
Catholic Central 0
Saturday, September 27 at Grand Haven

Faced with an opportunity to try out for the University of Michigan's football team coached by Fielding Yost, John Cary's agreement to coach his alma mater ended two weeks after classes started at Catholic Central. The school replaced Cary with Heinie Lightner, who guided Central High's team in 1918 and was at Union earlier in the decade. Lightner's debut was inauspicious, thanks to a 19-0 season-opening beating by Grand Haven.

Catholic Central		Union H. S.
Fulgoni	LE	Maas
Quinn	LT	Major
Brown	LG	Eckert
Reilly	C	Walker
Bolger	RG	Hultman
Kelly	RT	Bowbeer
Grant	RE	Schuiling
O'Brien	QB	C. Cornwell
Weiden	LH	R. Cornwell
Curran	RH	Tufts
Friar	FB	Coleman

Catholic	0	0	0	0	0
Union	21	7	9	21	58

Touchdowns – Coleman (3), R. Cornwell (2), Mindell (2), Guthan
PAT – C. Cornwell 8 of 8
Safety - Friar

Union 58
Catholic Central 0
Saturday, October 4 at Island Park

Lightner's first game as the CC coach against his old team, Union, couldn't have gone worse. Not only did the Catholics get wiped out by a score of 58-0, star fullback Bernie Friar was believed to be lost for the season with a knee injury.

Furthermore, Catholic Central looked uncompetitive and uninspired against the clearly superior West Siders. The Catholics were behind 21-0 before the end of the first quarter. They put up their best fight in the second quarter when Union scored just one touchdown, but Friar's injury in the third quarter appeared to demoralize CC. Catholic Central went to the air to try to catch up, but Union intercepted three passes which it promptly converted into long runs for touchdowns.

Muskegon 27
Catholic Central 0
Saturday, October 11 at Island Park

Lightner inexplicably didn't even show up for Catholic Central's next game. And because of so many injuries to first-string players, the Catholics had to rely heavily on reserves. Nevertheless, CC put up a spirited fight and was given credit for limiting Muskegon to only a 27-0 win. Muskegon scored a touchdown in each quarter but CC never sniffed the goal line.

Catholic Central 7
Big Rapids 0
Saturday, November 8 at Big Rapids

Playing a wide-open style based on passing the football and running it around end, Catholic Central snapped a six-game losing streak dating back to the 1918 season opener with a 7-0 victory over Big Rapids High.

Bob O'Brien, CC's tiny quarterback, was the star of the show. He provided the margin of victory by scoring a touchdown in the fourth quarter and drop-kicking the extra point. Catholic

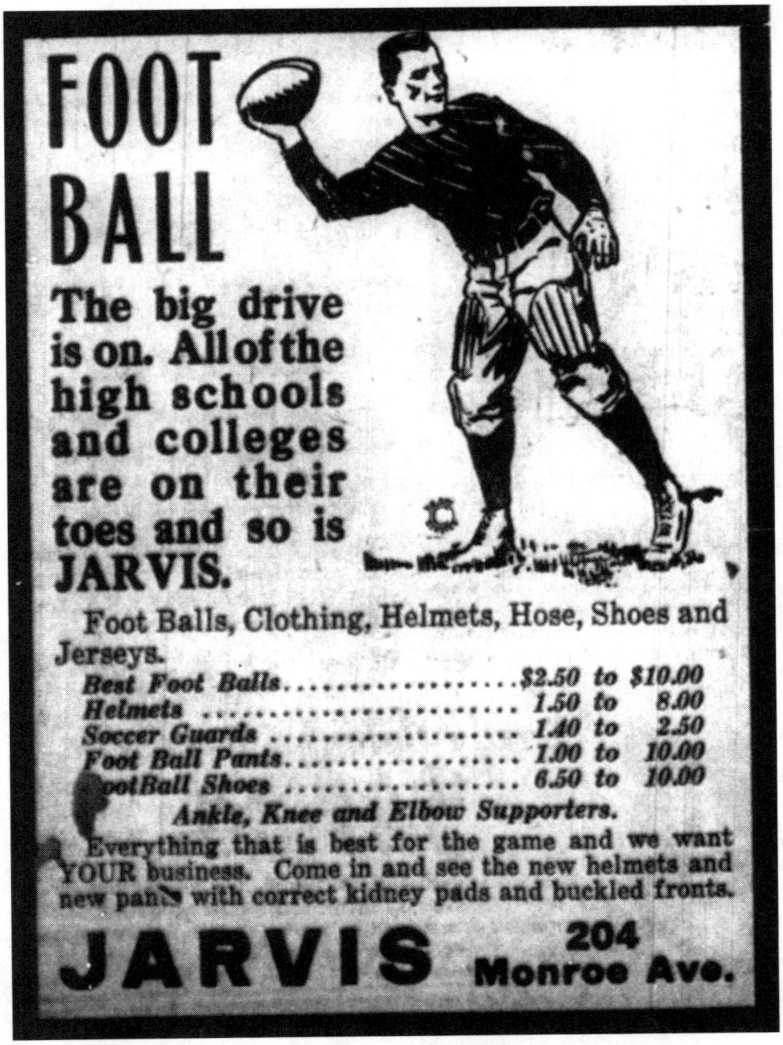

GR Herald Photo

Advertisement from The Grand Rapids Herald.

Central may have been even more successful through the air if a fierce wind hadn't been blowing throughout the game.

Allegan 74
Catholic Central 0
Saturday, November 15 at Allegan

Before playing Allegan on a muddy field, Catholic Central captain Fred Curran's request to have the quarters shortened from 15 minutes to 12 was granted. Curran thought that by shortening the game, CC would have a chance to keep the score close. All it really accomplished, however, was to prevent Allegan from scoring 100 points.

At the beginning of the season, Allegan expected the game with Catholic Central to be one of the toughest on the schedule. That quickly became the overestimation of the year after Allegan put 21 points on CC in the first quarter and went on to win, 74-0. Catholic Central clearly didn't want to be there, and hastened its departure by picking up just two first downs. Injury was added to insult when Curran left the game with a broken ankle.

Catholic Central		CC Alumni
Fulgoni	LE	R. B. O'Brien
Quinn	LT	B. Cary
Johnson	LG	Braun
Reilly	C	Riordan
F. Bolger	RG	Geotz
Murray	RT	C. O'Brien
Al Ducey	RE	F. Peet
Bob O'Brien	QB	B. Murray
Weiden	LH	V. Meyers
Murray	RH	R. Murray
Teal	FB	J. Bolger

Catholic	0	7	0	0	7
CC Alumni	0	0	0	0	0

Touchdowns – Teal
PAT – Bob O'Brien

Catholic Central 7
CC Alumni 0
Thursday, November 27 at Island Park

Catholic Central suffered through another disappointing season, but at least it ended on a light note. The game between the CC Varsity and the CC Alumi featured three brother acts: the Murrays (one on the Varsity, two on the Alumni), the O'Briens (one on the Varsity and two on the Alumni) and the Bolgers (one each).

The sibling rivalries provided much entertainment for the crowd of 100. The old-timers hoped to score a lot of points in the first quarter and hang on for dear life as their fitness levels dwindled, but they never got a chance to score. Elgin Teale's 5-yard touchdown in the second quarter proved to be the game-winner.

1919 Schedule/Results
Head Coach – Heine Lightner

Date	Opponent	Result		Location
Sep. 27	Grand Haven	Lost	0-19	Grand Haven
Oct. 4	Union	Lost	0-58	Island Park
Oct. 11	Muskegon	Lost	0-27	Island Park
Nov. 8	Big Rapids	Lost	0-7	Big Rapids
Nov. 15	Allegan	Lost	0-74	Allegan
Nov. 27	Alumni	Won	7-0*	Island Park

	Record	Pts. Scored	Pts. Allowed
Overall	0-4-1	0	200

* Not included in team record

-1920-

Catholic Central 13
Rockford 13
Saturday, October 2 at Island Park

For the first time since 1917, Catholic Central didn't open the season with a loss. And for a team as inexperienced as CC's, a 13-13 tie with Rockford was almost as good as a win, and if not for missed opportunities it would have been one.

Catholic's first possession of the season ended with a fumble at the Rockford 5-yard line. Unfazed, the Catholics marched right back down the field on their next drive, and fullback Larry Minogue posted a 6-0 lead with his 5-yard rushing touchdown. Bill Grant missed the drop-kick for the goal-from-touchdown to prevent CC from earning a full complement of points.

Catholic Central momentarily led 13-0 in the second quarter after right end Larry Ducey lofted a perfect 40-yard touchdown pass to Minogue and this time, Grant converted. The Catholics stuck to the air on their next possession, but the strategy backfired when Rockford's Graves intercepted a pass and returned it 30 yards to the CC 5-yard line. Ron Finch, the Rockford fullback, rammed the ball into the end zone from there and also kicked the extra point.

Finch scored another touchdown on an end sweep in the fourth quarter, but missed what would have been the game-winning extra point and the teams played to a stalemate the rest of the way.

Lansing St. Mary's 19
Catholic Central 0
Friday, October 8 at Lansing

Lansing St. Mary's Academy sounded like school with a background similar to Catholic Central's, but things aren't always as they appear.

St. Mary's threw its five-pound weight advantage around while scoring a touchdown in every period but the second. Robert Crowley, Minogue and Ducey played well defensively, but Catholic Central struggled offensively. The Catholics reached St. Mary's 1-yard line in the fourth quarter, but couldn't get the ball over the goal line.

As luck would have it, Catholic Central's best chance for a victory dissipated when St. Mary's of Jackson called to cancel its game against CC scheduled for Oct. 16 at Island Park. Jackson St. Mary's had so many players out with injuries that it didn't have enough healthy players to field a competitive team.

Catholic Central 12
CC Alumni 0
Saturday, October 23 at Island Park

No report of the 1920 alumni game could be found in either *The Grand Rapids Herald* or *The Grand Rapids Press*.

Union 67
Catholic Central 0
Friday, October 29 at Island Park

Catholic Central's undersized and undermanned team was almost out of the game before it started. Union left end

Hice intercepted CC's first pass of the game early in the first quarter and returned it 30 yards for a touchdown to start the scoring binge. A few minutes later, Union blocked a punt to set up its next touchdown and another score made it 19-0 before the first quarter came to an end.

Union played big and fast, and the Catholics were ill-equipped to slow the West Siders down.

Plainwell 27
Catholic Central 0
Saturday, November 13 at Plainwell

Too light in the saddle to hold its ground against a heavy team on a wet, slippery field, Catholic Central left Plainwell High School with a 27-0 defeat. It was the Catholic's third straight game without scoring a point. Although CC failed to pick up much yardage on the ground, it had some success through the air. Ruse scored all of Plainwell's points on four touchdowns, including two in the third quarter, and three extra points.

Catholic Central's inability to catch a break extended to the next weekend when it traveled to Grand Haven for its next game, presumably against Grand Haven High School. However, the GHHS team failed to show up and local officials had lined up a squad of independents, called the Army and Navy Athletic Club, to face the Catholics from Grand Rapids. Catholic Central refused to play the game and returned home.

Albion 74
Catholic Central 0
Thursday, November 25 at Albion

Catholic Central's relative strength at the end of the decade was illustrated by the fact only one of its players received all-star accolades. Left tackle Bert Scannell was named second-team All-City by *The Grand Rapids Herald*.

The Catholics had to be wishing they had 10 more like him after losing the season finale at Albion High School, 74-0. Wet weather grounded the aerial attacks of both teams, and Albion ran the ball through the CC defense without much resistance.

1920 Schedule/Results
Head Coach – Bill Cary

Date	Opponent	Result		Location
Oct. 2	Rockford	Tie	13-13	Island Park
Oct. 8	Lansing St. Marys	Lost	0-19	Lansing
Oct. 23	Alumni	Won	12-0*	Island Park
Oct. 29	Union	Lost	0-67	Island Park
Nov. 13	Plainwell	Lost	0-27	Plainwell
Nov. 25	Albion	Lost	0-74	Albion

	Record	Pts. Scored	Pts. Allowed
Overall	0-5	0	185

* Not included in team record

CHAPTER 2

Catholic Central Gets Serious About Football
1921-1926

-1921-

After eight years of a lukewarm commitment to football, Catholic Central made a bold statement by hiring George Fitzpatrick as its first fulltime football coach. Boosters made the move possible with financial support. It was just what CC needed to attract the type of players who avoided the school in previous years because they wanted to play for a winner. A former Alpena (Mich.) high school star who played three seasons for the Fighting Irish of Notre Dame University, Fitzpatrick brought strong credentials to the position.

He captained the Irish freshman team in 1915 and earned a starting position on the varsity the following season. Fitzpatrick's college career was interrupted by World War I, and after two years in the Army he returned to Notre Dame for the 1919 campaign. Fitzpatrick roomed with George Gipp, a native of Calumet in Michigan's Upper Peninsula, and backed up the legendary halfback the entire season. Fitzpatrick transferred to the University of Detroit before his senior season and finished his collegiate career as an end for the U of D team.

Three years after Grand Rapids city league football was declared a disaster, 75 students, 30-35 more than normal, turned out for Union's first practice at Ninth Street Field. Based on numbers alone, coach John Truesdale expected the size of the team to jump by 10 pounds per player to 145 pounds. Notoriously small Catholic Central benefitted from no such infusion of size, but tryout numbers also were up at the Sheldon Avenue school, and the Catholics made up for their physical deficiencies in other ways. In the wake of numerous football-related deaths in previous seasons, new rules favoring size-challenged teams like CC were implemented. Fitzpatrick placed a major emphasis on fundamentals and installed techniques, plays, strategies and formations he learned at Notre Dame and Detroit.

Catholic Central 13
Lansing St. Mary's 0
Friday, September 23 at Island Park

With white stripes ringing their navy blue jersey sleeves, the Catholics played like hungry cougars in their opener against Lansing St. Mary's Academy, a team they lost to by 19 points a year earlier. The game was greeted by unseasonably hot temperatures and Catholic got on the board in the first minute of the second quarter when Robert Crowley, the left half, crossed the goal line on a running play. Bill Grant dropkicked the extra point to make the score 7-0.

CC/WC Archives
CC's Robert Crowley

Two plays after fielding a deep kickoff, St. Mary's fumbled and Thomas Murphy recovered for CC on the 15-yard line. The Catholics pounded St. Mary's line relentlessly, and Louis Norman bulled his way into the end zone from the 1. The extra-point kick failed.

Catholic Central's defense thwarted St. Mary's threats in an evenly played second half and most of the action took place in the middle of the field. Catholic held on for the 13-0 win, and based on its disciplined play and work ethic was given a good chance to enjoy success as its level of experience rose.

GR Herald Photo

Catholic Central's Coach George Fitzpatrick

Catholic Central 19
Muskegon Heights 0
Saturday, October 1 at Muskegon Heights

Catholic Central traveled to Muskegon Heights High School for its second game. Although CC weighed in at just 135 pounds per man, it used scrappy play and flawless precision to prevent its physically superior opponent from picking up a first down. The Catholics blocked and tackled so well, even the Muskegon Heights fans applauded their effort en route to a 19-0 victory.

Frank Slattery, the CC quarterback, struck paydirt in the first quarter and Grant kicked the extra point for a 7-0 lead. Slattery's 40-yard punt return and a 10-yard pass from Crowley to Murphy, the left end, set up Bert Scannell's second-quarter touchdown and the Catholics led 13-0 at halftime.

The Catholic Central offense stopped itself with penalties in the third quarter, but with the game firmly in hand, Fitzpatrick substituted liberally in the fourth period. Bill Powers made the reserves proud with a scamper around the end to score six and the Catholics left the Sawdust City with their first 2-0 start in school history.

Catholic Central 82
Muskegon St. Mary's 0
Friday, October 7 at Island Park

Muskegon Heights fans might have been impressed by Catholic Central's technique, but Coach Fitzpatrick wasn't. He ran his players through tough blocking and tackling practice all week to clean up what he thought were glaring weaknesses. The extra work translated into a school-record 82-0 victory over Muskegon St. Mary's.

Long runs of 10 to 50 yards around end and powerful rushes off tackle were the staple of the CC offense. Fitzpatrick intentionally ran a no-frills attack because he didn't want to reveal any tactics to the South High School scouts who were watching from the sideline. Carroll Powers started the barrage five minutes into the game with the first of CC's three first-quarter touchdowns.

South 7
Catholic Central 0
Friday, October 14 at Island Park

Catholic Central		South
Murphy	LE	Waterman
Grant	LT	Bailey
Wolfe	LG	Hodson
Norman	C	Hondorp
Blaszczyk	RG	Lilly
VanGorp	RT	McMillian
L. Ducey	RE	Ederle
Slattery	QB	P. Robinson
Crowley	LH	Finch
C. Powers	RH	Gruver
Scannell	FB	Snyder

Catholic	0	0	0	0	0
South	0	0	0	0	7

Touchdowns – Snyder 1.
PAT – Robinson 1/1
Referee– Daane, Umpire – Edwards, Head Linesman - Churm

Coach Fitzpatrick held a "demon practice" earlier in the week to set the tone for the biggest game Catholic Central would play since it began playing football in 1911. Either the "Parochials," as CC was now informally known, or South High School would be virtually eliminated from city championship contention in the Friday-afternoon showdown.

The pivotal game was decided early in the first quarter when Crowley set up to pass and was quickly met by a heavy rush. A South defender who broke through the line hit Crowley and knocked the ball out of his hand just before he could release it. Many in attendance thought it was an incomplete pass, but the officials ruled it a fumble. South's Snyder gathered in the loose ball and returned it 50 yards for the game's only touchdown, and Robertson converted.

Catholic Central was content to wage a defensive battle until the beginning of the fourth quarter when it started to launch the ball downfield. The Parochials finally got their one chance to score after forcing a South punt late in the period. Starting from the CC 40-yard line, quarterback Slattery picked up big chunks of yardage with 30- and 15-yard passes to right end Larry Ducey. Slattery then made a decision that would be questioned and criticized after the game. Starting at the 15, he called for running plays into the center of the line on the next two downs. Slattery's third-and-10 pass fell incomplete, and CC fell short on fourth down. South took over and although the Parochials forced another punt, Crowley fumbled and South recovered. Catholic Central had one more possession, but couldn't reach the end zone.

The Parochials threw South ball-carriers for several big losses and were complimented for their superior technical performance, but South, which had several regulars sidelined by injuries, played with admirable determination.

Catholic Central 68
Plainwell 7
Saturday, October 22 at Island Park

Catholic Central took out the frustration left over from its 7-0 loss to South by beating Plainwell for the first time with the help of Billy Manns, a backup left halfback who set up several touchdowns and scored two, and Norman's outstanding kicking. The 68-7 thumping made a dent in the series' lopsided scoring discrepancy. Plainwell came into the game with a combined 124-7 edge in three previous meetings.

After a 40-yard gain by Manns, Slattery, the CC quarterback, scored the first of his four touchdowns on the first possession of the game. In the second quarter, Manns put Catholic Central in position for its third touchdown with a 25-yard punt return. Manns' interception led to a Slattery touchdown that made the score 27-0, and Manns' 15-yard reception and 5-yard run led to his 12-yard touchdown run just before halftime. Manns added a 27-yard touchdown run in the fourth quarter.

Norman put on a show with his strong leg. He wowed the crowd with several kickoffs that reached the end zone and one of his punts flew 60 yards.

Catholic Central		Union H. S.
Murphy	LE	Waterman
Grant	LT	Bailey
Wolfe	LG	Hodson
Norman	C	Hondorp
Blaszczyk	RG	Lilly
VanGorp	RT	McMillian
L. Ducey	RE	Ederle
Slattery	QB	P. Robinson
Crowley	LH	Finch
C. Powers	RH	Gruver
Scannell	FB	Snyder

Catholic	0	0	0	0	0
Union	0	0	7	7	14

Touchdowns – Fulgoni 2.
PAT – Cherry 2/2.
Referee– Churm, Umpire – Tapping, Head Linesman - Swanson

Union 14
Catholic Central 0
Friday, October 28 at Island Park

Union coach John Truesdale made a prophetic statement heading into the annual grudge match against Catholic Central.

"A considerable number of fans believe that Union will have an easy time in subduing the Parochials," Truesdale said. "The fact is, we will have a hard time to defeat them. According to comparative scores, Fitzpatrick's boys are 14 points better than we are. That's not to say we're ready to be licked, but every man on my team will have to play his best in order to win."

Fitzpatrick concurred by saying, "I believe my men have an even chance of taking the measure of Union tomorrow. The boys have shown a great improvement and their aerial attack cannot be beat."

The game more than lived up to the hype as the Parochials and the "Unionites" battled to a scoreless tie after nearly three quarters. The Catholic Central defense, which had so brilliantly repelled dangerous Union forays 5 and 10 yards from the goal line in the first half, finally buckled when on fourth-and-3, Union left half George Fulgoni (who played for CC during the 1919 season) ran 8 yards for the game's first touchdown with one minute remaining in the third quarter.

The West Siders mounted a methodical drive for their second touchdown, also scored by Fulgoni, early in the fourth quarter to secure the 14-0 victory. If CC played as well on offense as it did on defense, it might have gotten the measure of Union, but Crowley was Catholic's only productive offensive player.

Catholic Central 7
Fremont 0
Saturday, November 5 at Fremont

Catholic Central went into its game against Fremont all but certain it wouldn't be able to win by trying to power the ball up the middle. So, CC threw the ball over the top of its thick foe to win 7-0.

The Catholics completed 5 of 7 passes for good yardage, and set up their only touchdown on a long Carroll Powers-to-Les Lennon completion early in the fourth quarter. Holland burrowed through the Fremont defense for the final 5 yards, but it was the most life the running attack showed all game.

In addition to a passing game that confused Fremont, CC's superior conditioning also played a role in the win.

Catholic Central 14
Greenville 9
Friday, November 11 at Greenville

Catholic Central defeated a previously unbeaten Greenville, 14-9, on Armistice Day to become the frontrunner in the race for the Class B state championship. The Grand Rapids school dazzled the crowd with an array of criss-cross plays and a spectacular passing game usually diplayed by collegiate teams.

Greenville took a 9-7 lead going in to the fourth quarter but three passes from Slattery to Murphy and two from

Powers to Lennon took the ball down to the three-yard line. Four plays later Scannell bullied his way across the goal to give Catholic Central claim to the West Michigan class B crown.

Despite losing a hard-fought game Greenville displayed admirable sportsmanship by hosting a post-game banquet and dance for the visiting team.

CC/WC Archives
All-City Guard Louis Norman

Catholic Central 6
Saginaw St. Peter and Paul's 0
Saturday, November 19 at Saginaw

After 10 formative years that ended mostly in futility, Catholic Central prepared for the last game of the season with something other than pride on the line. If CC could defeat defending Saginaw Valley Catholic Schools Conference champion St. Peter and Paul's on its own field, it would be declared the state parochial school champion and winners of the mythical Class B high school title.

The Catholics pulled off the impressive "double" by defeating St. Peter and Paul's 6-0 in a most unlikely way. With the host geared to stop CC's vaunted passing attack, the Catholics stuck to the ground on a field that had been reduced to a mud bath as snow fell steadily throughout the game.

Catholic Central's decisive drive came in the fourth quarter and covered 55 yards on a series of line plunges. Carroll Powers powered the ball over the goal line for the touchdown that secured a sparkling 7-2 record and CC's first of many championships.

Catholic Central 17
CC Alumni 0
Thursday, November 24 at Island Park

The season ended on a symphony of high notes for the Catholic Central football team. Louis Norman, the outstanding center, was the first CC player to be selected to *The Grand Rapids Herald's* All-City Eleven first team and Thomas Murphy was named second-team quarterback.

Catholic Central		CC Alumni
Murphy	LE	Hessman
VanGorp	LT	Geitzen
Wolfe	LG	M. Peet
Norman	C	Reilly
Blaszczyk	RG	Slovinski
Scannell	RT	Quinn
Lennen	RE	Carey
Slattery	QB	N. Peet
Crowley	LH	Schenkleberg
C. Powers	RH	Frair
Holland	FB	Middleton

Catholic	0	0	7	10	17
Alumni	0	0	0	0	0

Touchdowns – C. Powers, Murphy.
PAT – Slattery 2/2, Field Goals - Slattery
Referee– Murray, Umpire – Goodrich, Head Linesman - Madigan

The Catholics won state parochial and Class B championships, and the Varsity downed the Alumni, 17-0, in the annual Thanksgiving Day affair. The Alumni threatened first when Art Middleton rambled 58 yards before slipping to the ground 5 yards from the end zone. The Varsity stood fast, however, and pulled away with a 20-yard touchdown run by Powers in the third quarter and Murphy's 30-yarder in the fourth. Slattery drop-kicked a 35-yard field goal to finish off the old-timers.

Finally, the team was addressed by legendary Notre Dame coach Knute Rockne and Fighting Irish captain Eddie Anderson at the team banquet held in downtown Grand Rapids at the luxurious Pantlind Hotel.

"Football was not a game for those muscle-bound around the neck or those lacking intestinal strength," Rockne told the gathering of 200, "but a game that would bring out the best in a fellow."

Rockne was speaking in generalities, but he might as well have been talking about Catholic Central in particular.

1921 Schedule/Results
Head Coach – George Fitzpatrick

Date	Opponent	Result		Location
Fri., Sep. 23	Lansing St. Mary's	Won	13-0	Island Park
Sat., Oct. 1	Muskegon Hts.	Won	19-0	Muskegon
Fri., Oct. 7	Muskegon St. Mary's	Won	82-0	Island Park
Fri., Oct. 14	South	Lost	0-7	Island Park
Sat., Oct. 22	Plainwell	Won	68-7	Island Park
Fri., Oct. 28	Union	Lost	0-14	Island Park
Sat., Nov. 5	Fremont	Won	7-0	Fremont
Fri., Nov. 11	Greenville	Won	14-9	Greenville
Sat., Nov. 19	St. Peter & Paul	Won	6-0	Saginaw
Thu., Nov. 24	Alumni	Won	17-0*	Island Park

	Record	Pts. Scored	Pts. Allowed
Overall	7-2	209	37

* Not included in team record

-1922-

Catholic Central 26
Sparta 0
Saturday, September 16 at Island Park

Speed had always been Catholic Central's forte, but there was something different about the team going into the season opener against Sparta. Fitzpatrick deemed the 1922 CC squad the strongest, from a purely physical standpoint, in school history. The Parochials used that combination of speed and strength to easily hammer the Spartans, 26-0.

GR Herald Photo

Catholic Central cheerleader Ronald Chinnick.

Although CC lacked the precision it demonstrated the previous season, it overpowered its opponent after a 0-0 stalemate in the first quarter. Ernie Couture, the pint-sized transplant from Alpena, starred for the Parochials. An evasive scatback who dipped and darted for long gains throughout the game,

GR Herald Photo

Billy Manns scores Catholic's second touchdown against Sparta with a quarterback sneak.

Couture put CC ahead 6-0 in the second quarter on a plunge through the line, and Billy Manns plowed into the end zone for the first score of the second half.

Catholic Central moved ahead 19-0 later in the third when Thomas Murphy blocked a punt and Couture ran it back 10 yards for a touchdown. In the fourth quarter, Couture set up his third touchdown of the game by throwing a 30-yard pass to Murphy. Couture's final tally came on an end sweep. Meantime, the CC defense stopped Sparta like "a stone wall," according to *The Grand Rapids Herald.*

Catholic Central 39
Lansing St. Mary's 0
Friday, September 29 at Lansing

The offensive front seven led CC to an easy 39-0 victory over Lansing St. Mary's by dominating the line of scrimmage. Fitzgerald's blockers paved the way for three touchdowns in the first half and three in the second. Parochial's left halfback Carroll Powers faced virtually no resistance while running for three touchdowns, and Couture scampered for a pair.

It's no surprise that Chick Landry also was considered among CC's standouts for his long, high kickoffs. He had plenty of practice.

Catholic Central 25
Allegan 0
Saturday, October 7 at Ramona Park

For the third game in a row, a lethargic first quarter left Catholic Central faithful wondering what to expect from their team. Those doubts were answered in short order by a fierce demonstration of aggression and a knack for navigating a muddy field during the 35-0 rout of Allegan.

GR Herald Photo

Ernie "Cootch" Couture

The CC line pummeled Allegan's front seven in the second quarter until Powers blasted through for his first touchdown of the game. Powers completed a similar drive early in the third quarter, and a subsequent long march, capped by Powers' third score of the day, took the wind completely out of Allegan's sails. Les Lennon, the Parochials' right end, finished Allegan off in the fourth quarter by blocking a punt, gathering in the loose ball and running it back 10 yards for a touchdown.

Catholic Central 44
Muskegon Heights 0
Saturday, October 14 at Ramona Park

A state power was rapidly emerging on Grand Rapids' East Side. And this time, Catholic Central wasted no time scoring for a change. After charging out to a 12-0 lead in the first quarter and a 31-0 bulge by halftime, the Parochials went on to whip Muskegon Heights, 44-0.

Landry, the CC fullback, started the landside by sweeping around end for his first of three touchdowns against the Heights. Robert Crowley then completed a scoring pass to Couture, who also reached the end zone three times, once while going the distance with an interception.

Parochial's quarterback Manns stood out for guiding the team with the efficiency of a tested veteran and by averaging 25 yards per punt return. Catholic Central's otherwise stellar play was marred in the fourth quarter by constant bickering among teammates, which in turn led to poor play.

Catholic Central 39
East Lansing 0
Saturday, October 21 at Ramona Park

The points kept coming in bunches for Catholic Central, while the scoring drought continued for CC opponents.

"Displaying a varied attack and a stonewall defense, Catholic Central had no difficulty in defeating East Lansing 39 to 0 yesterday afternoon at Ramona Athletic Park, Reeds Lake," wrote Everett C. Swanson of *The Grand Rapids Herald*, who declared that the Parochials had shown so much improvement, "they are 100 percent stronger than last season."

Catholic Central gained the upper hand early by battering East Lansing quarterback Olin so badly in the first quarter, he left the game and didn't return until the second half. With its field general sidelined, East Lansing played into CC's hands by running repeatedly into the center of the line without success.

Manns, meantime, orchestrated a devastating array of line plunges, end sweeps and long passes to move the ball effortlessly down the field. Couture and Landry scored two touchdowns each while Powers and Manns added one each.

With its low tackling and blocking being compared favorably to that of collegiate teams, Catholic Central was undefeated, untied and unscored upon after five games. Meanwhile, the Parochials had outscored their opponents, 173-0.

Catholic Central 57
Sturgis 13
Saturday, October 28 at Ramona Park

Adversity visited Catholic Central for the first time all season when Richards, the star right guard, suffered his second appendicitis attack of the season early in the week and was ruled out for the remainder of the season. Fitzpatrick also feared that with Ed Dierda, another guard, set to miss his second straight game because of injury, Catholic could be vulnerable against a Sturgis High School team that evoked rave reviews from the CC scouts. The situation became gloomier later in the week when Couture apparently sprained his ankle while participating in a tough scrimmage during practice and was considered doubtful for the game. The chances of Catholic Central beating Sturgis were said to be "slim."

CC/WC Archives
Harold "Chick" Landry

Fitzpatrick needn't have worried, however.

Yes, Sturgis was the first team to score when it returned a Catholic fumble on the opening kickoff for a touchdown. But its 6-0 lead didn't last long. The Parochials came out of the first period with a 20-6 advantage and led 32-6 at halftime before winning, 57-13.

The infuriated CC defense blew up Sturgis' plays before they got started while the offense ripped off gains of 10-45 yards with regularity. Couture, who earlier in the week looked doubtful, stood out with a pair of sweeps of 40 and 45 yards, and two touchdowns. Landry had three CC tallies, as did Shook. Powers, Manns and Crowley also reached the end zone.

South Bend (Ind.) 27
Catholic Central 0
Saturday, November 4 at the University of Notre Dame

The stage couldn't have been bigger or the task more difficult for the Catholic Central eleven's seventh game of the season.

The Parochials were scheduled to travel across the state line to play South Bend High School at Notre Dame's Cartier Field in an 11:30 a.m. preliminary to the Fighting Irish's homecoming showdown against Indiana University.

It was bad enough that standout linemen Dierda and Richards were out and Couture was hobbling on a bad ankle. Lennon was carried off the field earlier in the week after getting clobbered in a dummy practice, Murphy injured his knee and was doubtful and Landry would play South Bend with an injured hand protected by a splint.

Furthermore, South Bend outweighed CC by 10 pounds per man, was considered the best high school team in the state of Indiana and had already defeated Kalamazoo High School and Flint, a contender for the state championship. "Not so sweet," is how Coach Fitzpatrick characterized the situation after one practice.

The game followed suit for Catholic, which fell, 27-0, with about 200 fans from Grand Rapids watching from the stands.

The Parochials put up a brave fight from the outset and might have gone into halftime tied 7-7, but an apparent

3-yard touchdown pass from Powers to Couture was nullified because the receiver was judged to be out of the end zone when he caught the ball. South Bend exploited weak spots in the CC defensive line to score a pair of touchdowns in the third quarter and another in the fourth.

Lennon stood out for his role in Catholic's aerial attack, which completed 6 of 7 passes. Incidentally, Notre Dame defeated Indiana, also by a score of 27-0.

Catholic Central 0
Pontiac 0
Saturday, November 11 at Pontiac

Catholic Central traveled from one corner of the region to another in the span of a week, and while the outcome was better in Pontiac than it was in South Bend, the 0-0 tie against Pontiac High School left much to be desired.

The Parochials moved the ball all over the field via the ground and the air, but couldn't break through for a score. Catholic's best opportunity came at the end of the first half when Powers broke free for a 40-yard gain to the Pontiac 10-yard line, but time expired before it could run another play. Pontiac's most effective weapon was the leg of Heitch, who kept CC at bay with punts averaging 45 yards, including a 50-yarder.

Grand Haven 10
Catholic Central 6
Saturday, November 18 at Grand Haven

Sporting its healthiest lineup in weeks, Catholic Central journeyed to Michigan's West Coast for a game against Grand Haven, which Coach Fitzpatrick's scouts reported was one of the "sweetest teams in the state."

Grand Haven's 3-0 lead on a field goal stood until the fourth quarter when Bert Scannell blocked a punt that CC recovered at the 1-yard line. Crowley's second crack at the Grand Haven line was successful, and Catholic Central led, 6-3. However, the Parochials' next possession ended with a fumble that the Havenites recovered at the CC 20-yard line. Den Herder covered the distance on the very next play with a pass to Duffield for Grand Haven's winning touchdown with two minutes remaining.

Catholic Central outgained Grand Haven by 61 yards, 183-122, but gave back 37 on penalties. Catholic Central's Louis Norman also lost the punting duel to Van Toll by an average of 20 yards.

The game ended on a controversial note when the jubilant Grand Haven players ran off the field after scoring their final touchdown and couldn't be rounded up for several minutes. Fitzpatrick appealed to University of Michigan coach Fielding Yost for a ruling on whether Grand Haven was guilty of an infraction, but the score was upheld.

Catholic Central		Belding
Blaszczyk	LE	J. Hudnutt
Mooney	LT	Johnson
Landry	LG	Noddins
Pozniak	C	Rahell
Dierda	RG	Conn
Norman	RT	McGuire
Lennon	RE	Fitzjohn
Manns	QB	K. Hudnutt
Boggiano	LH	Lamberton
McPhilmy	RH	McKidie
Scannell	FB	Hawley

Catholic	0	12	0	13	25
Belding	0	6	0	0	6

Touchdowns – Hawley (Belding), McPhilmy 2, Lennon, Scannell.
PAT – Norman 1/4, Belding 0/1
Referee– Buss, Umpire – Daane, Head Linesman - Brown

Catholic Central 25
Belding 6
Friday, November 24 at Ramona Park

With Powers nursing a broken hand and Crowley laid up with a fractured elbow, Catholic Central was again battling the injury bug. Plus, Couture had left the team to be with his gravely ill father in Detroit.

Thanks to the improvement of key reserves, CC overcame the absences while beating Belding, 25-6, in a swirling snowstorm.

Belding broke out to a 6-0 lead in the second quarter when Hawley returned an interception 70 yards for a touchdown. Catholic countered with two touchdowns before halftime on a 1-yard dive by backup halfback Ed McPhilamy, a 15-year-old freshman, and Lennon's 40-yard reception.

After a scoreless third quarter, Catholic Central intercepted a pass in the bitter cold to set up McPhilamy's touchdown plunge off right tackle and Scannell added an insurance score in the final minutes. Despite wearing a cast on his arm, Crowley entered the game as a substitute.

Catholic Central 6
Fort Wayne (Ind.) Catholic Central 6
Thursday, November 30 at Ramona Park

Catholic Central thought it played Indiana's best high school team at the beginning of the month. Then, Fort Wayne Catholic Central came to town with an eleven averaging 170 pounds per man.

When FWCC took a 6-0 lead in the first quarter, it looked like it was going to be a long day for Grand Rapids' Parochials. But that only served to get CC's anger up. Later in the quarter, when Manns returned a FWCC punt 25 yards and CC's next offensive play netted 35 to the FWCC 4-yard line, the overconfident visitors were suddenly back on their heels. A first-down run advanced the ball to the 2, but CC lost 3 yards on second down, gained 3 on third and failed to score on fourth. Nevertheless, FWCC knew it was in for a fight.

Catholic Central stymied FWCC time after time with critical stops behind the line of scrimmage and several touchdown-saving tackles, including a one-handed takedown by Lennon early in the third quarter. Later in the third, Landry's 40-yard run put CC in business at the FWCC 1-yard line, but the Parochials were once again turned back by a goal-line stand. Undaunted by failing to score twice from short yardage, Crowley finally broke through for the game-tying touchdown, but Couture's dropkick for the extra point missed the mark. Neither team threatened in the final 10 minutes, which were played in darkness.

Given Coach Fitzpatrick's heritage and the way his players battled for the tie, every member of CC's team was duly christened "a fighting Irishman."

Union 12
Catholic Central 0
Saturday, December 2 at Island Park

The fluid nature of high school football in the Roaring Twenties was on full display after a showdown between Union, a serious contender for the state championship until it suffered its only loss to Kalamazoo, and Catholic Central was hastily arranged. Although Union had dispatched Grand Rapids rivals Central and South, it couldn't legitimately claim the city championship, contended Catholic Central, because the city schools refused to play the Sheldon Avenue team. After CC backers openly insinuated that the public schools "were afraid" to play their parochial counterpart, Union

Catholic Central		Union H. S
Blaszczyk	LE	Malewitz
Mooney	LT	Wolven
Lau	LG	Ginmich
Pozniak	C	Cornwell
Dierda	RG	Williams
Norman	RT	Douglass
Lennon	RE	Harrigan
Manns	QB	VanLet
Boggiano	LH	Ferguson
McPhilmy	RH	Quinten
Scannell	FB	Fulgoni

Catholic	0	0	6	6	12
Union	0	0	0	0	0

Touchdowns – Harrigan, Fulgoni
Referee– Buss, Umpire – Churm, Head Linesman - Daane

GR Herald Photo

Catholic Central's "Chick" Landry goes around left end to score in the Union game.

picked up the gauntlet. It was believed that the Exchange Club, which had donated the city championship trophy, would be forced to give it to Catholic Central in the event it beat Union, because the Parochials would have defeated the team that put down Central and South.

The potentially awkward situation never arose, much to the relief of organizers. The Unionites defeated CC, 12-0, at about the same time Jim Thorpe's Oorang Indians, of Cleveland, were getting crushed 29-0 by the Durant Stars, the undisputed professional football champions of Michigan, 70 miles away in Lansing.

Fans of both schools and interested independents began showing up at the Island Park field more than an hour before the 2:20 p.m. kickoff. The overflow crowd spilled out of the bleachers and covered every square yard of sideline space.

The scoreless first half was a battle of alternating possessions. When Union wasn't giving the ball to CC with a pair of fumbles, it was punting, and the Parochials would kick it right back after failing to pick up first downs. The trend appeared destined to continue in the third quarter when Catholic Central's first possession ended on Landry's 47-yard punt. However, Union methodically marched the ball downfield and took a 6-0 lead on Venlet's 12-yard touchdown pass to Harrigan.

The see-saw battle resumed, with each team giving the ball back either on downs or with punts. Union finally took control of the game after CC was stopped for no gain on fourth-and-2 at the Union 37. From there, the West Siders made to the Catholic Central 20 before running out of downs. The Parochials couldn't move the ball, and after a 40-yard Landry punt and minus-12 yard return by Ferguson, Union engineered a bone-crunching 15-play drive, which included gains of 16 and 10 yards, and resulted in first-and-goal-to go at the CC 1. George Fulgoni plowed in from there on the next play to sew up the win and the city title.

Catholic Central harbored no shame in ending what was considered its greatest season of all time in such a way while finishing with a 7-3-2 record.

Off-field Maneuvers

The Catholic Central administration then took a leadership role in the statewide fight to have parochial schools recognized by the Michigan Interscholastic Athletic Association, the forerunner of today's Michigan High School Athletic Assocation. Public school opposition revolved around eligibility concerns, although Father Emmet Fitzpatrick of Catholic Central tried to allay such fears at the MIAA's annual meeting in Lansing.

"As far as Catholic Central is concerned, I can say we will live up to the rules of the MIAA," Rev. Fitzpatrick, the brother of the CC head coach, told the gathering. "Our books and class records are open to anybody who wishes to verify our statements relative to the standing of any player.

"We desire only one thing and that is to be placed on even terms in regards to athletics with other schools, and are willing to do everything in our power to bring this about. We hope to be admitted to the MIAA and if we are, and then fail to live up to the rules, we are willing to be summarily expelled. We seek no special favors."

An amendment to the MIAA constitution had the strong support of public schools in Grand Rapids, Saginaw and Detroit, and appeared destined for approval. However, an 11th-hour change of heart by the smaller-community schools, apparently fearful of a power shift to private schools, resulted in a 28-24 vote against the amendment. Without the MIAA endorsement, Catholic Central and other parochial schools had difficulty scheduling public-school rivals, who had little to gain and much to lose by playing them.

While speaking at CC's annual postseason banquet for the second consecutive year, Notre Dame coach Knute Rockne heaped high praise on the Parochials.

"The Catholic Central eleven of this year was a miniature edition of Notre Dame," he said. "Its spirit has been wonderful and I believe the day is coming when Catholic Central will have one of the greatest teams in the country. Football is necessary. It is one of the greatest aids in developing squareness and honor in the younger generation."

1922 Schedule/Results
Head Coach – George Fitzpatrick

Date	Opponent	Result		Location
Sep. 16	Sparta	Won	26-0	Island Park
Sep. 29	Lansing St. Mary's	Won	39-0	Lansing
Oct. 7	Allegan	Won	35-0	Ramona Park
Oct. 14	Muskegon Hts.	Won	44-0	Ramona Park
Oct. 21	East Lansing	Won	39-0	Ramona Park
Oct. 28	Sturgis	Won	57-13	Ramona Park
Nov. 4	South Bend	Lost	0-27	Notre Dame
Nov. 11	Pontiac	Tie	0-0	Pontiac
Nov 18	Grand Haven	Lost	6-10	Grand Haven
Nov. 24	Belding	Won	25-6	Ramona Park
Nov. 30	Ft. Wayne CC	Tie	6-6	Ramona Park
Dec. 2	Union	Lost	0-12	Island Park

	Record	Pts. Scored	Pts. Allowed
Overall	7-3-2	277	74

-1923-

Two new monikers came to be used to identify Catholic Central on the dawning of the 1923 season. With "Red" Fitzpatrick, who reportedly was a candidate to join Knute Rockne's staff at Notre Dame, back as head coach for a third season, CC was becoming known as the "Irishmen" given their coach's nationality and its affinity with the revered South Bend institution. A successful season was being predicted for the "Blue and White" due to the high number of returning veterans and the help of former Notre Dame star lineman Hugh O'Donnell as a volunteer assistant coach in preseason camp.

Catholic Central 26
Muskegon St. Mary's 0
Saturday, September 15 at Island Park

Catholic Central, now in possession of above-average size to go with exceptional speed and its trademark fighting nature, had no trouble defeating Muskegon St. Mary's Academy, 26-0, in the first game of a season-opening doubleheader that featured Union and Rockford in the second contest. After just one game, CC was in the state championship conversation, and given Union's 40-0 victory, anticipation was already growing for the season finale between the Irishmen and the West Siders.

Louis Norman showed all-state form at the center position and Ray Cudahy, a newcomer to the starting backfield, stood out with two touchdowns. Carroll Powers also scored and Billy Manns, the Blue and White quarterback, brought the crowd to its feet with a 55-yard touchdown run during which he appeared to avoid each of the 11 St. Mary's tacklers at least once.

Catholic Central incurred several offside and backfield-in-motion penalties, but Fitzpatrick wasn't upset with his charges. "I was not angry with my men losing so many yards through penalties," he said. "(The infractions) to me showed an eagerness and willingness to play football for all they're worth."

Catholic Central 68
Sparta 0
Saturday, September 22 at Ramona Park

The Catholic Central-Sparta game figured to be the marquee matchup of a doubleheader that featured Union against Lansing Vocational in the prelim. The game failed to live up to its billing, except to fans of wipeouts. The Irishmen scored at will in a 68-0 thrashing of the Spartans. Had Fitzpatrick kept his regulars in the game beyond halftime, the Blue and White could have easily won by double the score.

CC/WC Archives

Ernie "Cootch" Couture perfects his tackling skills at Island Park.

Catholic Central's reserves started getting considerable playing time soon after Fitzpatrick saw his team jump out to a 13-0 lead with ease in the first quarter. Sparta was guilty of numerous fumbles and picked up only two first downs while all but giving up in the second half. After leading 19-0 at halftime, CC tagged on 19 points in the third quarter and 24 in the fourth. The Irishmen put on quite a show for Saginaw Eastern coach Beatty and several of his star players, who were scouting from the Ramona Athletic Park grandstand.

Saginaw Eastern 14
Catholic Central 0
Saturday, October 6 at Saginaw

The Blue and White found out how they measured up on a statewide basis in a 14-0 defeat suffered at the hands of

Saginaw Eastern in hostile territory. In one respect, CC discovered that its hosts were as good as they were big. On the other hand, Catholic Central discovered it was so well-respected, it suspected Eastern needed a diet of home cooking provided by an allegedly crooked officiating crew to survive.

Certainly, the Irishmen contributed mightily to their own demise against their yellow-and-black adversaries. In the first quarter, Fredericks, the Eastern center, blocked a CC punt and teammate Jerome pounced on the ball just 10 yards from the goal line. Catholic threw Eastern for a 5-yard loss on first down, but was penalized for offside on second down, and the officials placed the ball on the original spot. Eastern's path "to the 1-yard line was strewn with lilies," wrote *The Grand Rapids Herald's* Francis McCarthy. Those 9 yards were provided by back-to-back "unaccounted for penalties which the referee and the head linesmen took turns calling." CC held firm on Eastern's first plunge into the line, but Bothwell bored into the end zone on the second try and the Blue and White trailed, 7-0.

Catholic Central fumbled the second-half-opening kickoff and Eastern recovered at the CC 20. Despite big defensive stops by Manns and Norman, Eastern advanced the ball to the 2-yard line with the help of another offside penalty and Bothwell plowed in for the score. The Irishmen had a sizeable advantage in yards gained, especially in the open field, but lost 80 yards on penalties in the first half alone. Norman greatly outplayed Fredericks, the 1922 all-state center, and Harold "Chick" Landry, Manns and Ernie "Cootch" Couture also performed well.

The Herald subsequently reported that the officials were allegedly being investigated for betting heavily on the game. "One of the officials," according to the story, "who had most to do with the heavy penalties, is said to have been barred from officiating in the MIAA back in 1919."

Catholic Central 19
Allegan 0
Saturday, October 13 at Allegan

A sloppy field, an incessant drizzle and the fast Allegan High defense couldn't conspire to stop Catholic Central's air attack. Actually, the Blue and White simply did a better job of adjusting to the deteriorating conditions while storming to a 19-0 victory.

In the first quarter, Catholic Central executed a 99-yard drive mostly by throwing the ball and took a 6-0 lead on Couture's 30-yard touchdown pass to Cudahy. Powers' long reception and a 20-yard sweep around end put CC in position for its second score. And after Landry carried four Allegan tacklers with him to the 2-yard line, Powers smashed through the line for a 13-0 lead. Couture added a touchdown in the third quarter and the Irishmen were content to slog it out the rest of the way.

Catholic Central 92
Lansing Vocational 0
Saturday, October 20 at Ramona Athletic Park

Only the final whistle stopped the Catholic scoring machine, which tallied a school-record number of points in a 92-0 massacre of Lansing Vocational. Seconds after Vocational fumbled the ball to CC on the first play from scrimmage, Blue and White fullback Powers swept around left end for a 30-yard touchdown. The score was 14-0 only a few minutes later when Manns made up for the touchdown which was called back because of a roughing penalty, by throwing a scoring pass to Fred Erhardt.

Things escalated from there. The Irishmen scored 20 points in the second quarter, 27 in the third and 20 in the fourth. Cudahy accounted for four touchdowns, Powers, Manns and Couture had three each and Erhardt and Fred Blaszczyk had one each.

GR Herald Photo

Ray Cudahy

Catholic Central 52
Detroit Southwestern 0
Saturday, October 27 at Ramona Park

"The Fitzies" were expected to beat Detroit Southwestern High School handily, maybe even by four touchdowns. But no one saw CC's 52-0 romp coming, especially DSHS players who had a difficult time seeing much of anything the dazzling Irishmen were doing with blinding quickness.

Couture, the miniature halfback, could often be seen smiling at would-be tacklers as he swept around end like the wind. He scored two touchdowns before leaving the game with a displaced kneecap. The Blue and White led 32-0 at halftime. Cudahy also accounted for two touchdowns and Manns, Powers, Lennon and Fred Boggiano had one apiece. Couture was taken to St. Mary's Hospital where he was listed in "favorable" condition.

So resounding was the win that fans were left to wonder where CC would be situated in the state title race if not for the controversial loss at Saginaw Eastern.

Catholic Central 29
Grand Haven 0
Saturday, November 3 at Ramona Park

It was a sign of the times that betting on high school football games was so commonplace newspapers openly served as unofficial oddsmakers before games. Grand Haven fans were reportedly so confident about the Havenites' chances against Catholic Central, that "they are willing to wager even money that (their) team will win and are coming to Grand Rapids Saturday prepared to cover anything that the Catholic adherents may offer."

At Catholic Central's biggest pep rally of the season, new cheers were practiced and the new school song, which was written by former students Robert Murray and Charles Norton and entitled "Victory," was sung publicly for the first time. The St. James and St. Andrew's grade school teams of the parochial league, serving as a feeder system for CC football, were scheduled to play in the preliminary game.

Catholic Central sent Grand Haven fans home with lighter wallets after handing the lakeshore team its worst defeat of the season, 29-0. The resounding victory established CC's newly dubbed "Blue Devils" as the team to beat in the city, despite cries to the contrary by South High School.

The 3,500 CC fans were spellbound by their team's near-flawless execution of majestic sweeps, confounding trick plays and pinpoint passing. With Couture out with a knee injury, Cudahy continued to establish himself as the most complete back in the area, if not West Michigan.

Catholic Central asserted itself on the scoreboard just two minutes and nine seconds after the opening whistle on Powers' 25-yard run, which was set up by Manns' 25-yard rush. Catholic's next possession got going on a 15-yard pass from Cudahy to Landry, followed by Cudahy's 12-yard run and Landry's 3-yard plunge into the end zone for a 13-0 first quarter lead. A 20-yard reception by Ray Blaszczyk gave CC a first down on the Grand Haven 5-yard line and two plays later Manns squirmed across the goal line for a 19-0 lead that stood until the third quarter. The Irishmen fumbled away an opportunity at the Grand Haven 2-yard line, but still got points out of the situation when GHHS punter Den Herder couldn't handle a high snap while standing in his own end zone and was trapped for a safety. Catholic Central closed out the game with a 50-yard drive that ended on Bogganio's 1-yard plunge across the goal line.

Catholic Central 16
Pontiac 0
Saturday, November 10 at Ramona Park

Anticipation for Catholic Central's home game against Pontiac was off the charts. The weekend started with a pep rally in the community room at St. Andrew's Cathedral and demand for tickets greatly exceeded supply. Not only was former Union High School multi-sport star Eddie Powers returning to his hometown for the first time as the Pontiac head coach, Pontiac was coming off a convincing victory over Saginaw Eastern, which handed CC its only loss so far. That 14-0 decision, which was marred by a suspected gambling scandal allegedly involving the officials, presumably cost Catholic a shot at the state championship.

However, the Irishmen would get an opportunity to restate their case if they could saddle Pontiac with a convincing defeat, which they did, 16-0.

The 3,000 fans jammed into Ramona Athletic Park knew going into the game that CC boasted a star-studded backfield. However, it was the standout end tandem of Les Lennon and Ray Blaszczyk that led the way for Catholic Central. On offense, both made a number of amazing catches, including several off their shoetops. On defense, each was a disruptive force against Pontiac's sweeps.

CC/WC Archives
Les Lennon

Couture provided all the scoring the Blue and White would need when he dropkicked a 25-yard field goal in the first quarter. Lennon all but broke the game open in the second quarter when he caught a pass from Cudahy while seated on the ground. Stunned by the circus catch, the Pontiac defenders watched as Lennon got up and completed the 80-scoring play. Catholic Central's Power ended a promising Pontiac drive with an interception at his own 8-yard line, and time ran out on the first half.

Manns finished Pontiac off with a 2-yard touchdown plunge that came at the end of what amounted to a tedious 11-play, 63-yard drive that was delayed for five minutes while the trainer treated a Pontiac player's split lip, which was bleeding profusely.

More than 1,000 CC fans continued the postgame celebration into the night with a parade led by the Grand Rapids Elks Band through town. The Irishmen felt they had vindicated their loss to Saginaw Eastern and could rightly be counted among the very best teams the state had to offer. They had just shut out their fifth straight opponent while winning those games by a combined score of 208-0 for an average tally of 42-0 during that span.

In a portent of things to come, Catholic Central's junior varsity team won its first game, 7-0, against South in the prelim.

CC/WC Archives
Bert Scannell

Catholic Central 24
South 6
Friday, November 16 at Island Park

The game between Catholic Central and South for city football supremacy was the talk of the town. More than 6,000 fans descended upon Island Park for the game, and although South was supremely confident coming off its 13-12 victory over Central, the Irishmen were favored.

In what was considered the seminal victory in CC's relatively short football history, the resounding 24-6 decision in the cold rain not only put the Sheldon Avenue school in the driver's seat for the city championship, it established the Blue and White as a bona fide power among the local teams. No longer would Catholic Central be seen as the most-welcomed homecoming opponent or chance for an easy win between tough games.

What's more, Catholic Central cleaned South's clock without relying on fancy forward passes or timely trick plays: it repeatedly drove the ball down the field playing tough-nosed, hard-charging, straight-ahead football. The Blue and White attempted just one pass against South.

"In straight football playing, they have no equal," Dick Remington, one of the state's foremost experts on prep high school football, said after refereeing the game.

Catholic Central dominated on offense, defense and special teams. The Irishmen scored five minutes into the game after Landry blocked Helms' punt. Catholic Central took over at the 1-yard line and Manns needed just one play to reach the end zone.

South rose to meet the challenge on the ensuing possession. Formama, the South fullback, opened the 77-yard drive with a 15-yard pass to Smith, the right half, and an 18-yarder to his left end, Holden. Gesitert, the South quarterback, called his own number on the final play and his 7-yard bullet pass to Smith in the back the end zone knotted the score at 6-6.

However, CC took control in the second quarter. Lennon scored off a criss-crossing triple lateral that allowed him to score around left end from 10 yards out. Later in the quarter, Landry broke through to block his second punt of the game, gathered in the ball and returned it 45 yards for a touchdown that put the Irishmen ahead 18-6. After Catholic and South traded possessions on an interception and downs in the third quarter, CC took a commanding lead on Powers' dash around end. The fourth quarter was largely uneventful, and after Cudahy intercepted South's last pass, Catholic ran out the clock with six straight running plays.

Catholic Central won because it outgained South by 221 yards. The Blue and White complete the only pass it attempted, and all but 2 of its 445 yards came on the ground.

Catholic Central		South H. S
Ray Blaszczyk	LE	Holden
Scannell	LT	Hicks
Mooney	LG	Rittenger
Norman	C	Clatworthy
Hurnowitz	RG	Joslin
Landry	RT	Helms
Lennon	RE	Hall
Manns	QB	Geistert
Cudahy	LH	Yonkman
Couture	RH	Smith
Carroll Powers	FB	Formama

Catholic	6	12	6	0	24
Belding	6	0	0	0	6

Touchdowns – Lennon, Couture, Manns, Landry, Smith
Referee– Remmington, Umpire – Buss, Head Linesman – Hoeker, Field Judge - Cary

Catholic Central 43
Port Huron 6
Saturday, November 24 at Island Park

Although considerably below full strength, Catholic had no trouble dispatching Port Huron, 43-6. Norman, CC's standout center, was sidelined by a cracked rib, while utility backup lineman Chuck Pozniak was battling pneumonia and Blaszczyk was on crutches with his leg in a cast. Landry, Cudahy and Couture played despite coming out of the South game with a variety of bumps and bruises. Fitzpatrick was left to rely on a ninth-grader named Frank McGavin, who earned his stripes in the first half of the win over South.

Cudahy stopped hobbling long enough early in the first quarter to break through the line for a 60-yard touchdown, and the rout was on. Manns ran 45 yards to set up Cudahy's second touchdown of the period, and Port Huron quickly lost any interest in putting up a fight. Catholic only put up six points in the second quarter, but outscored the Huronites 19-0 in the third. Cudahy ended up with four touchdowns to strengthen his bid for a spot on the all-state team.

Catholic Central 18
Union 0
Saturday, December 1 at Island Park

Mathematically speaking, the Blue and White was still in danger of losing the city title. Catholic would be outright champs if it beat Union, but a loss would create a four-way tie among CC, Union, Central and South.

Catholic Central settled the discussion by winning the so-called "battle for blood," 18-0.

Union was underpowered coming into the game but put up a valiant fight. George Fulgoni, one of the best running backs Grand Rapids football fans had ever seen, was declared ineligible earlier in the season because of irregularities involving his transfer from Catholic Central in 1919. And Gimmick, one of the state's top tackles, was held out of the game for academic reasons.

Meanwhile, CC's star center, Norman, was back in the lineup. The Irishmen took a 2-0 lead on a first-quarter safety and never trailed, but it was on the strength of its "little Frenchman," Couture, that the Blue and White won its first city championship. Couture accounted for nearly every CC yard in the first three quarters. Catholic claimed 15 white sweaters and a silver schooner as its prizes for winning the title, and took the "little brown jug" rivalry trophy away from Union, but its shot at a state championship was denied when powerhouse Muskegon High, with nothing more to gain, turned down its challenge for a one-game playoff.

Catholic Central dominated *The Grand Rapids Herald* All-City Eleven with an unprecedented five first-team berths filled by Couture, Lennon, Manns, Landry and guard Frank Hurnowitz. Norman, the standout center, who missed significant playing time because of a rib injury, Ray Blaszczyk, Scannell, Cudahy and Bill Mooney were named to the second team and Powers was an honorable mention.

CC/WC Archives

Billy Manns

Analysis of Union-Catholic Game

	CATHOLIC 1st. Per.	2nd. Per.	3rd. Per.	4th. Per.	To.	UNION 1st. Per.	2nd. Per.	3rd. Per.	4th. Per.	To.
Ground gained on rushes	89	123	80	90	282	22	9	17	9	67
First downs..........	4	6	5	4	19	1	0	1	3	5
First down on penalties	0	0	1	0	1	0	0	0	0	0
Punts	4	1	0	2	7	4	2	3	1	10
Av. distance on punts..	28	25	0	15½	29½	31	35½	24	20	28½
Distance punts run back	3	0	0	0	3	0	0	0	3	3
Forward passes attem'd	0	3	4	3	10	3	1	3	8	15
Forward passes comp..	0	1	3	1	5	0	0	1	4	5
Gain on forward passes	0	15	49	0	64	0	0	13	51	64
Forward passes interc'd	0	1	0	1	2	0	1	0	1	2
Penalties............	1	3	1	1	6	2	0	1	1	4
Ground lost on penalties	15	25	15	5	60	20	0	3	5	28
Fumbles...............	0	1	1	0	2	0	0	1	0	1
Own fumbles recovered.	0	1	0	0	1	0	0	0	0	0
Op. fumbles recovered.	0	0	1	0	1	0	0	1	0	1
Field goals attempted..	0	0	0	1	1	0	0	0	2	2
Field goals made.....	0	0	0	0	0	0	0	0	0	0

At CC's postseason awards banquet, with Notre Dame coach Knute Rockne attending as the featured guest for the third straight year, former Cornell University football captain and Olympic hurdling champ R.O. Weldgon said, "A real team is one that can come back after a defeat and go out and win games, and that's what Catholic Central did."

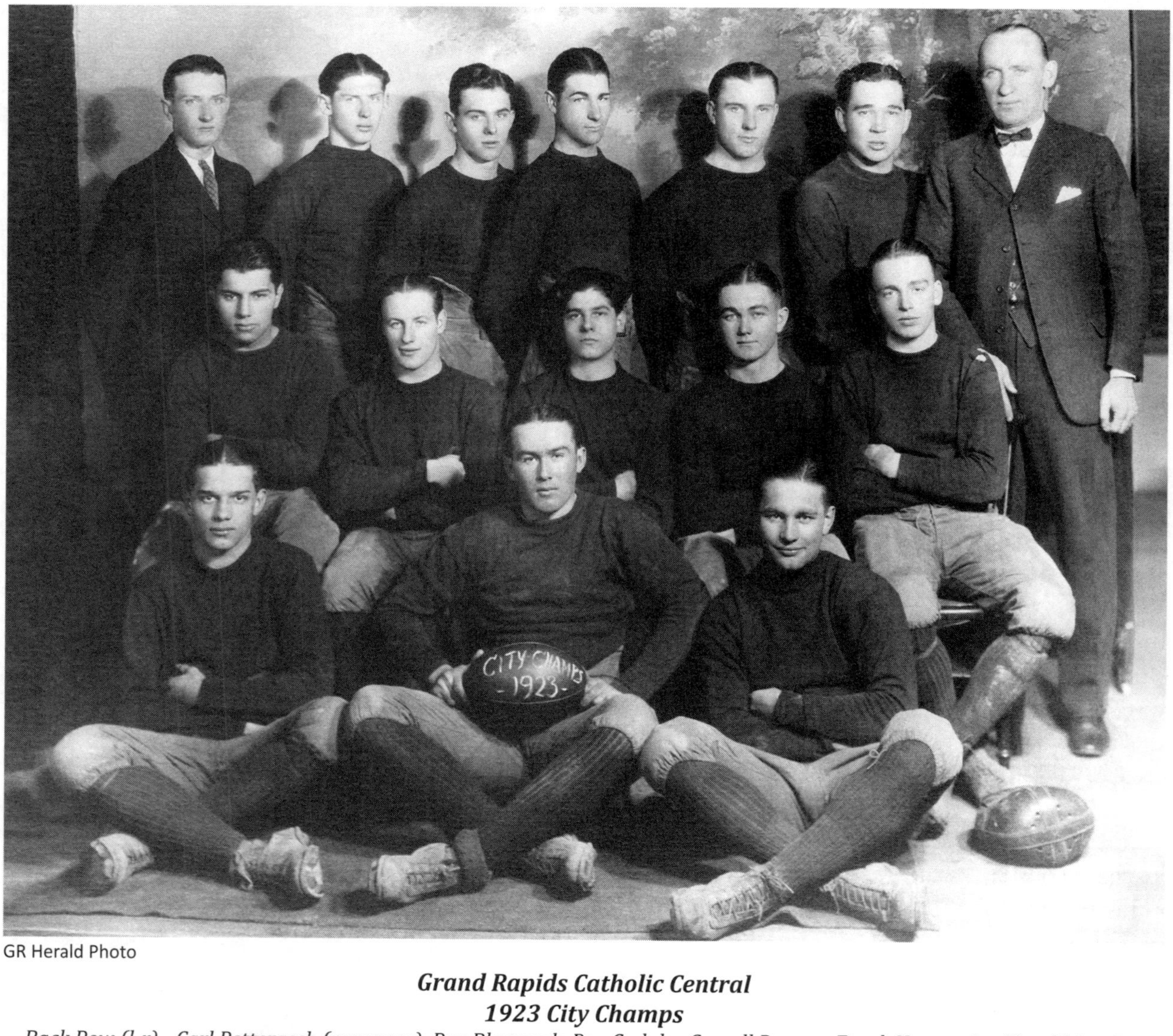

GR Herald Photo

Grand Rapids Catholic Central
1923 City Champs

Back Row (l-r) - Carl Petterasch (manager), Ray Blaszczyk, Ray Cudahy, Carroll Powers, Frank Hurnowitz, Harold Landry, George Fitzpatrick

Middle Row - Fred Boggiano, Ernie Couture, Fred Blaszczyk, Thomas Bowen, Bill Manns

Front Row - Fred Erhardt, Bert Scannell, Edward Dierda

Missing - Les Lennon, Charles Pozniak, Bill Mooney, Louis Norman

1923 Schedule/Results
Head Coach – George Fitzpatrick

Date	Opponent	Result		Location
Sep. 15	Muskegon St. Mary's	Won	26-0	Island Park
Sep. 22	Sparta	Won	68-0	Ramona Park
Oct. 6	Saginaw Eastern	Lost	0-14	Saginaw
Oct. 13	Allegan	Won	19-0	Allegan
Oct. 20	Lansing Vocational	Won	92-0	Ramona Park
Oct. 27	Detroit Southwestern	Won	52-0	Ramona Park
Nov. 3	Grand Haven	Won	29-0	Ramona Park
Nov. 10	Pontiac	Won	16-0	Ramona Park
Nov. 16	South	Won	24-6	Island Park
Nov. 24	Port Huron	Won	43-6	Island Park
Dec. 1	Union	Won	18-0	Island Park

	Record	Pts. Scored	Pts. Allowed
Overall	10-1	387	26

-1924-

Catholic Central entered a season knowing that for the first time each of its city rivals, Union, South and Central, were on the schedule. Before playing any of them, however, coach George Fitzpatrick had to rebuild his starting eleven.

Catholic Central 68
Sparta 0
Saturday, September 13 at Ramona Park

Despite returning no veterans from the previous season's 10-1 city championship team in the lineup, the Blue and White picked up where it left off with a 59-0 season opening slaughter of Sparta.

Bill Mooney and Carroll Powers were back, but ailing and not in uniform. The other familiar names on the field belonged to former reserves Frank McGavin and Fred Erhardt, the team captain who was nursing a shoulder injury.

GR Herald Photo

Larry (left) and Jack Montroy

The Montroy brothers, Jack and Larry, filled the halfback spots formerly manned by standouts Couture and Cudahy.

GR Herald Photo

CC cheerleaders Shane Bolen (left) and Bernard DeVries.

Jack Montroy made a good accounting of himself by scoring six touchdowns and having a hand in 48 points.

Catholic Central 10
Ovid 0
Saturday, September 20 at Ramona Park

On a water-logged afternoon, Catholic Central and Ovid might have been drier had they played in Reeds Lake than on the nearby field at Ramona Athletic Park. The Blue and White did a better job of negotiating the mud-covered field to win 10-0.

Erhardt provided all the scoring CC would need with a remarkable, given the conditions, 35-yard dropkick for a second-quarter field goal. The 3-0 advantage stood until the fourth quarter when Ovid turned the ball over at its own 15-yard line on an interception. The Montroy brothers took over from there.

Larry splashed through the Ovid defense for 5 yards like a land shark and Jack went forward for 4 more. On third-and-one at the 6, Jack swam in for the touchdown and kicked the extra point with his right flipper, as well.

Catholic Central 20
Lowell 12
Saturday, September 27 at Ramona Park

The Irishmen passed their first major test of the season when they came from behind to upend Lowell, billed as a Class-A-level power disguised as a Class-B competitor, 20-12. Catholic Central was outweighed and outplayed, but won thanks to a skillfully executed trick play down the stretch.

Catholic broke out on top after blocking a Lowell punt and taking over on the 50-yard line. After two runs moved the ball to the Lowell 30, CC quarterback Martin "Shorty" Stapleton called for a pass. Larry Montroy, the left half, set up to throw, and delivered the ball to his brother, Jack, the right half who was waiting for it at the 15. From there, Jack broke two tackles and zig-zagged his way into the end zone for a 6-0 lead. However, after exploiting CC's undersized defensive line with a series of hard-charging plunges, Lowell tied the score on Fineis' 5-yard dive.

The Lowellites punished CC's defense on the first possession of the second half, and Fineis ran the ball in from 1 yard to put Catholic behind on the scoreboard for the first time since the third game of the '23 season against Saginaw Eastern. Trailing 12-6 at the end of the third quarter, CC got a break when it recovered a Wingeier fumble.

Fitzpatrick finally put Erhardt, who missed a week of practice and appeared to be in street clothes at the beginning of the game, on the field and Catholic Central seemed to find its rhythm. Five minutes into the fourth quarter, after back-to-back passes moved the ball to the Lowell 25, Fitzpatrick called for his favorite trick play. The confusing, quickly executed criss-crosses in the backfield had the Lowellites grasping at every Irishman but Jack Montroy, who tucked the ball and scampered 25 yards for the score. Erhardt dropkicked the go-ahead extra point for a 13-12 lead, although Jack Montroy added an insurance marker with a 13-yard touchdown around end later in the quarter.

Otsego 6
Catholic Central 0
Saturday, October 4 at Ramona Park

The scuttlebutt preceding Catholic's game against Otsego was that CC would have a difficulty winning with Jack Montroy and Erhardt in the lineup. Without them, well, it would be easy pickins for the team that previously held Central's powerful team scoreless. As it turned out, Montroy, who was responsible for 95 percent of Catholic Central's touchdowns, didn't suit up because he was being investigated on eligibility grounds, and Erhardt's injured shoulder kept him on the sideline. But, the Blue and White wasn't an easy "out" for Otsego, which was fortunate to get out of town with a 6-0 victory.

Trailing by six points since the second quarter when Otsego's McNutt returned Larry Montroy's fumble 5 yards for a touchdown, and in danger of falling behind further, Catholic Central got the break it desperately needed. A furious rush caused Otsego to fumble and McGavin recovered at the CC 5-yard line with five minutes remaining. Stapleton smartly got the ball out of trouble when his pass from behind the goal line was caught by Red Everhart, who fought off three Otsego defenders to make the catch. Stapleton connected with Everhart on the next two plays, as well.

Stapleton's fourth pass of the series to Everhart gave Catholic a first down at the Otsego 8 with two minutes remaining. Two line plunges and a sweep moved the ball to the 3. However, with Larry Montroy playing the role of his older brother on the criss-cross play that beat Lowell a week earlier, CC was stopped a foot short of the goal line on fourth down.

Central 36
Catholic Central 7
Friday, October 17 at Houseman Field

The restoration of Jack Montroy's eligibility was the good news Catholic Central was waiting to hear, but his return to the lineup made little difference in the 36-7 loss to Central before a record crowd of more than 5,000 at Houseman Field. With Montroy back in the stable, CC was favored to win, but the Hilltoppers weren't fazed by the game that was played incessently in the newspaper.

Catholic Central		Central H. S
Sokolski	LE	Bonstrom
Mooney	LT	Peck
Kampfschulte	LG	Leavenworth
McGavin	C	Steckman
Roach	RG	Fitzgerald
Erhardt	RT	Monten
Everhart	RE	Green
Stapleton	QB	Hodgson
L.Montroy	LH	Ray
J. Montroy	RH	Hall
Ducey	FB	VerMerris

Catholic	0	0	7	0	7
Central	0	6	7	23	36

Touchdowns – Ray (3), Hodgson, Steckman, J. Montroy
PAT – Erhardt 1 of 1, Grabill 1 of 1, Bowstrom 2 of 2
FG – Hodgson
Referee– Page, Umpire – Remington, Head Linesman – Churm, Field Judge - Beard

After the teams played to a scoreless draw in the first quarter, Central won ideal field position when left halfback Jimmy Ray fielded Catholic's punt from the back of the end zone at the CC 23-yard line. Although Central failed to convert a field-goal attempt, Catholic Central couldn't move the ball and the Hilltoppers regained possession on a CC punt at the 34. Eight plays later, Ray scored a 1-yard touchdown for the first lead of the game. Catholic Central moved ahead on the scoreboard after getting the ball back on a Ray fumble, and Larry Montroy connected with brother Jack for a 65-yard touchdown pass. Erhardt kicked the extra point, but CC's 7-6 advantage was short-lived and far too small.

A 35-yard pass from standout quarterback Jack Hodgson to Grabill gave the Hilltoppers a first down at the Blue and White 12-yard line, and after CC was penalized 5 yards, Ray ran 7 yards off tackle for the go-ahead touchdown. Central then shocked the Irishmen in the fourth quarter with 23 unanswered points, the last of which came on Steckman's 20-yard interception return for a touchdown.

Pontiac 19
Catholic Central 6
Saturday, October 25 at Ramona Park

Catholic Central		South H. S
Lynch	LE	Hall
Mooney	LT	Joslin
Kampfschulte	LG	Hicks
McGavin	C	Bremer
Gilbert	RG	Snyder
Erhardt	RT	Van Hoven
Everhart	RE	Linder
Stapleton	QB	Geistert
L.Montroy	LH	Smith
J. Montroy	RH	Witzel
Papa	FB	Zoerner

Catholic	0	0	0	0	0
South	19	13	7	14	47

Touchdowns – Smith, Bremer, Giestert (3), Witzel, Fox
PAT – Giestert 4 of 7
Referee– Lawton, Umpire – Duncan, Head Linesman – Buchanan

Trailing Pontiac High School 12-6 with five minutes remaining, Catholic Central was in position to take the lead with a touchdown and an extra point. However, after CC picked up good yardage with a pass, it dipped to the aerial well one time too many. A Pontiac defender came out of nowhere to pluck the ball out of the air before it could reach Everhart, and returned the interception 20 yards before being tackled. Pontiac went on to score a touchdown as time ran out to secure a 19-6 victory over the Irishmen.

Catholic Central appeared to be much improved over the way it played against Central thanks to the Montroy brothers and a lift provided by Peter Papa, a backup fullback playing in place of Ducey. And when Pontiac took a 6-0 lead in the first quarter, the Blue and White didn't flinch. Jack Montroy scored early in the second half, and the game was tied until Boardman regained the lead for Pontiac in the fourth quarter and then added to it at the very end.

Catholic Central 47
Grand Rapids Vocational 0
Friday, November 7 at Ramona Park

Jack Montroy ran for five touchdowns to lead Catholic Central to a 47-0 victory over Grand Rapids Vocational, the forerunner of Davis Tech, and remain in contention for the city scoring title. Montroy scored Catholic's first four touchdowns against the first-year program on runs of 15, 5, 31 and 1 yards. Papa, the fullback, broke Montroy's streak by ending a long drive with a touchdown, but Montroy capped a similar possession to finish his day. Earhardt scored CC's final touchdown when he recovered a bad Vocational snap in the end zone.

GR Herald Photo
CC's All-City Left Tackle Bill Mooney

South 47
Catholic Central 0
Saturday, November 22 at Ramona Park

South exacted its revenge on Catholic Central and enhanced its status as the frontrunner for the state championship with a 47-0 victory. A week earlier, South moved to the front of the pack with a 7-6 victory over powerful Jackson High before 10,000 fans at Island Park. A year earlier, its chances for a city championship were all but dashed by a 24-6 loss to CC.

With city and state championships on the line, South showed no mercy while running up the score against the Catholics. South scored a touchdown in the game's first 30 seconds and never let up. Catholic Central was no match for the Red and Blue backfield of quarterback Mike Geistert, "Rabbit" Smith, Witzel and Zoerner, whose names resonated like those of Layden, Crowley, Miller and Stuhldrehrer, Notre Dame's fabled Four Horsemen, in local circles.

The Catholic Central defense was given credit for stopping South drives on just a couple of occasions, while giving up 19 points in the first quarter, 13 in the second and 14 in the third before Coach Guckert called off the dogs. Geistert left the game with three touchdowns to retake the city scoring lead from CC's Jack Montroy.

GR Herald Photo

(l-r) - Jack Montroy, Larry Montroy and Red Everhart show the strain of the game with Union.

Catholic Central 38
Muskegon St. Mary's 0
Thursday, November 27 at Ramona Park

The four inches of snow covering the Ramona Athletic Park field proved to be no obstacle for Catholic Central and neither did Muskegon St. Mary's defense. The Irishmen won what amounted to a glorified scrimmage, 38-0, but Jack Montroy's five touchdowns counted in the city scoring race, nonetheless. Catholic's other touchdown was scored by Jack's younger brother, Larry.

Jack Montroy scored on back-to-back punt returns of 30 and 40 yards in the second quarter. A couple of days later, he was named to *The Grand Rapids Herald* All-City First Eleven team, as was CC's Bill Mooney at left tackle. Erhardt was a second-team selection at tackle.

Catholic Central 13
Union 13
Saturday, December 6 at Ramona Park

Catholic Central and Union saved their best games of the season for last, which made the 13-13 draw in the mud at Ramona Athletic Park all the more fitting. Few who witnessed the battle left disappointed.

Catholic Central		Union H. S
Lynch	LE	Schaubel
Mooney	LT	Zegunis
Kampfschulte	LG	Gimmick
McGavin	C	Griffin
Gilbert	RG	Weidenfeller
Erhardt	RT	Seborg
Everhart	RE	Strockis
Ducey	QB	Parsaca
L.Montroy	LH	Lamphear
J. Montroy	RH	Plachecki
Papa	FB	Hart

Catholic	7	0	6	0	13
Union	0	6	0	7	13

Touchdowns – Schaubel, Parsaca, J. Montroy, Papa
PAT – Strockis, Erhardt
Referee– Remmington, Umpire – Hoeker, Head Linesman – Beard

Fitzpatrick was relegated to bed rest by a foot infection, but he was kept apprised of the developments by a CC agent manning a telephone in the park. Father Emmett Fitzgerald handled the coaching duties for his brother.

Jack Montroy, who was making his last appearance in a Catholic Central uniform, scored the game's first points on a 1-yard run four minutes into the first quarter. Erhardt dropkicked the extra point for a 7-0 CC advantage. Catholic Central astonished the crowd in the second quarter when it stopped Union short of the goal line on four straight tries from the 1-yard line. However, after the Blue and White gave the ball back with a punt, quarterback Rocky Parsaca got Union on the board with a 15-yard touchdown pass to left end Schaubel. Catholic Central broke through the line to block the extra point, and led 7-6 at halftime.

In the third quarter, Jack and Larry Montroy took turns completing passes to each other to set up CC's second touchdown. On third down, Larry Montroy threw a 20-yard touchdown pass to Papa, the fullback, and Catholic led 13-6. However, Parsaca countered with a 10-yard touchdown run and then lined up with his knee on the ground to hold for Alex Strokis' all-important place-kick for the extra point. The snap and hold were good, and so was the kick to tie the score.

The "Trusies," so-nicknamed in honor of coach John Truesdale, had one more chance to score, and actually got the ball to the Catholic Central 10-yard with 50 seconds remaining. For some inexplicable reason, Union continued to try for a touchdown instead of a field goal. Parsaca ran the ball to the 6 and Bunny Placheki drove to the 3, but CC stopped Parsaca at the 2 as time expired on the most exiting finish of the season. Catholic's last stand allowed it to finish with a 5-4-1 record.

1924 Schedule/Results

Head Coach – George Fitzpatrick

Date	Opponent	Result		Location
Sep. 13	Sparta	Won	59-0	Ramona Park
Sep. 20	Ovid	Won	10-0	Ramona Park
Sep. 27	Lowell	Won	20-12	Ramona Park
Oct. 4	Otsego	Lost	0-6	Ramona Park
Oct. 17	Central	Lost	7-36	Houseman Field
Oct. 25	Pontiac	Lost	6-19	Ramona Park
Nov. 7	Davis Tech	Won	47-0	Ramona Park
Nov. 16	South	Lost	0-47	Ramona Park
Nov. 27	Muskegon St. Mary's	Won	38-0	Ramona Park
Dec. 6	Union	Tie	13-13	Ramona Park

	Record	Pts. Scored	Pts. Allowed
Overall	5-4-1	200	133

-1925-

Unlike the previous season when he had to rebuild his entire team after it was ravaged by graduation, Catholic Central coach George Fitzpatrick returned a veteran lineup in 1925 with one exception. And, what a big exception it was. Jack Montroy, who scored 23 touchdowns the previous season, was gone and not even his younger brother Larry could be expected to match his production, though he was named team captain.

Catholic Central 26
Ovid 0
Saturday, September 12 at Ramona Park

Ovid didn't pose much of an opening-game challenge for the Blue and White, which won handily 26-0. Ovid had been practicing in street clothes because a fire that broke out at the school the previous winter destroyed the building and everything inside of it, including the team's football equipment. The Ovid players donned football gear, which was graciously donated by South High School, for the very first time minutes before playing CC.

With many of its players weighing in the vicinity of 100 pounds, Ovid punted often on first down and had no hope of beating Catholic, which took a 13-0 lead in the first quarter and never looked back. Fitzpatrick actually used two lineups in the game to sort out his best players.

Catholic Central 34
Rockford 0
Saturday, September 19 at Ramona Park

Fitzpatrick had every reason to expect a sterner test from Rockford High School, which returned an experienced lineup which included talented halfback Roy Whittall, "the Red Grange of the county schools." It was not to be as Catholic Central humbled Rockford's grossly overconfident squad, 34-0.

Fitzpatrick liked his backfield combination of Chapman at quarterback, Andy Papa playing fullback and Larry Montroy and Martin "Shorty" Stapleton as halfbacks. With the line providing exceptional blocking, CC counted several gains of 10, 20 and 30 yards. Whittall was repeatedly stopped in his tracks by Catholic defensive stars Red Everhart and Ted Kroon. In the first quarter, Kroon's holding penalty moved CC from the Rockford 4-yard line to the 19, but Montroy made up that yardage and then some by scoring on the next play. He also kicked the extra point to put Catholic ahead, 7-0. Montroy threw a 15-yard touchdown pass to Chapman in the second quarter and the Blue and White broke the game open with two scores in the third.

GR Herald Photo
1925 Captain Larry Montroy

Catholic Central 75
Muskegon St. Mary's 0
Saturday, September 26 at Ramona Park

The most significant developments pertaining to Catholic Central's game against Muskegon St. Mary's Academy was the installation of 800 new bleacher seats at Ramona Athletic Park, not that many fans were still sitting in them at the end of the 75-0 drubbing.

"Peewee" Duemier scored CC's first touchdown on a 1-yard plunge and Stapleton scored the second on a 70-yard jaunt. It was the first of five touchdowns scored by Stapleton, who ended the game with 32 points. When the first quarter ended with Catholic holding a 24-0 lead, Fitzpatrick started to clear his bench, but St. Mary's couldn't stop the reserves, either.

The game also marked the debut of Catholic Central's first paid assistant coach. George Haller, a former Notre Dame player and Columbia College coach, was hired to help manage CC's bourgeoning program. Fitzpatrick put Haller in charge of the third and fourth squads.

Catholic Central 18
Fort Wayne Catholic Central 13
Saturday, October 3 at Ramona Park

The competition level promised to move up a few notches with Fort Wayne Catholic Central, the defending Indiana Catholic school champs, coming to town. Displeased with his team's lackluster fighting spirit in the first three games, Fitzpatrick finally got the Parochials to play with passion en route to a hard-fought 18-13 victory.

The game pitted two teams running Notre Dame-style attacks, and except for Catholic Central's 6-0 advantage in the third quarter, the game was a stalemate.

GR Herald Photo

CC's Backfield (l-r) - Chapman, Stapleton, Papa, Montroy

The first quarter ended in a 0-0 deadlock, which Everhart worked hard to break in the second quarter. While running downfield, Everhart had to twist and turn to locate the ball thrown high into the air by Montroy. After making the catch, Everhart completed the 25-yard play by diving over the goal line with a FWCC defender in tow. FWCC promptly tied the score on a 25-yard pass play of its own.

Montroy masterfully followed Everhart's blocking to record the only score in the third quarter, and Stapleton's touchdown gave CC a 18-6 lead in the fourth quarter. FWCC answered with a 50-yard scoring pass, but it had little else to say about the outcome. Both teams were lauded for playing one of the cleanest games in recent memory.

Catholic Central 34
Lowell 0
Saturday, October 10 at Ramona Park

When Catholic Central wasn't running over Lowell's undersized defense, it was running around it and the result was a 34-0 victory. Stapleton's sprint around left end broke a 0-0 tie in the second quarter, and Montroy's 15-yarder around right end increased the lead to 13-0. Chapman's 10-yard off-tackle touchdown run put CC ahead 20-0 going into halftime. Stapleton and Chapman each scored again in the third quarter and Lowell never threatened.

Central 6
Catholic Central 0
Saturday, October 17 at Ramona Park

Catholic Central		Central H. S
Kroon	LE	German
Roach	LT	Bartholic
Kampfschulte	LG	Brockmier
McGavin	C	Lyons
Starr	RG	Pearsall
Jackaboice	RT	Montes
Everhart	RE	Green
Champman	QB	Roseberry
L.Montroy	LH	Jones
Stapleton	RH	Sutfin
Papa	FB	Geiser

Catholic	0	0	0	0	0
Central	0	0	0	6	6

Touchdowns – Geiser
Referee– Olds, Umpire – Dunn, Head Linesman – Lightner

Catholic Central was motivated to avenge the humiliating 36-7 loss it suffered against Central a year earlier. Both teams needed to win to stay in contention for the city championship. More than 5,000 fans turned out on a golden October afternoon to witness the CC-Central battle, which lived up to its billing as a competition between two evenly matched teams.

On its final play from the final yard in the final minute, Hilltopper bronking bull fullback Ed Geiser scored the touchdown that would send the Blue and White off the mushy field with a heartbreaking 6-0 defeat that snapped a five-game win streak. Catholic Central took little consolation being told it had just been involved in what would stand up forever as great a defensive struggle as had ever been witnessed in Grand Rapids. Tears flowed into a mixture of blood, sweat and mud.

Defensively, CC rose to the occasion all but one time. The Irishmen struggled offensively because they were usually operating on a long field. Central punter Green had a major effect on field position with spellbinding kicks traveling up to 60 yards.

Early in the third quarter, Central penetrated deep into CC territory with Montez, "the Spanish Duke," banging forward for 6 yards to the 16-yard line. However, the next play resulted in a 5-yard loss and Fitzpatrick's "Fitzies" held on downs.

CC/WC Archives
All-City Center Frank McGavin

The Catholic Central offense finally came to life early in the fourth quarter when consecutive passes from Montroy to Stapleton netted 30 yards. Papa moved the line 6 yards to the Hilltopper 15, and CC fans desperately pleaded for a touchdown. Montroy twice tried to batter Central's middle, but was repelled for no gain and a third-down pass fell incomplete. However, with the way the game was going, CC knew it could win with just a field goal and Montroy lined set up for a 22-yard placekick, which was coming into vogue after years of dropkicking. The snap from McGavin was perfect and Stapleton's hold was flawless, but Montroy's kick was low and the ball sailed under the crossbar.

It was from there that Central began its decisive drive, with quarterback George "Rosie" Roseberry and the helmetless Geiser, who stood head and shoulders over everybody else on the field, took turns marching the ball down the field. All game long, when tacklers didn't bounce or slip off Geiser, he dragged them with him.

On fourth down at the CC 12 with two minutes to play, Roseberry darted 6 yards for the first down. Sutfin carried for 2 yards and Roseberry picked up one more to the 3. On third down, Catholic Central's defense stuffed Geiser 1 yard short of the goal line. But with one minute to play, he

GR Herald Photo

CC's Guards Martin Starr (left) and Elmer Kampfschulte

followed the block of his center, Lyons, and dove into the end zone.
Catholic got the ball back on the ensuing kickoff with less than a minute to play, but wasn't about to surrender. On the first play of the last possession, Montroy completed a 30-yard pass to Chapman. Stapleton threw a 10-yard pass to Montroy, but the only Gold and White defender between him and the goal line threw him out of bounds at the Central 15. The Parochials had one last shot at the end zone, but their pass fell to the ground as time expired.

Catholic Central had been all but mathematically eliminated from the city and state championship hunts.

Traverse City 7
Catholic Central 6
Saturday, October 24 at Traverse City

For the first time in seven games, Catholic Central ventured away from Ramona Athletic Park. The longest road trip in school history landed the Blue and White in the North Country where it knocked heads with Traverse City High School. The physically imposing host scored a touchdown in the first quarter, and the extra point held up as the difference in a 7-6 CC defeat.

Catholic Central won the coin toss and elected to kick off to Traverse City, which quickly found out it could move the ball by blocking down on CC's ends. A 20-yard run around left end set up TC quarterback Curtis' 5-yard touchdown run around right end, and McGuire kicked what would be the decisive extra point.

Catholic responded in the second quarter with a series of Notre Dame-shift plays that confused the Traverse City defenders. By running its backs around end off double and triple laterals, CC efficiently drove the ball to the TC 30. From there, Montroy launched a pass that was tipped by Traverse City fullback Glauch into the hands of Catholic halfback Stapleton, who dashed into the end zone. Montroy, who missed a field goal a week earlier in the 6-0 loss to Central, was off-target again, and his botched extra point loomed large the rest of the way.

The Parochials averted disaster in the third quarter after TC recovered Montroy's fumble at the CC 10-yard line. Catholic held its ground to force a field goal, but McGuire's short kick flew wide of the goal post. A few minutes later, Catholic Central recovered a fumble deep in Traverse City territory just before time expired in the third quarter.

After failing to pick up first-down yardage on three tries from the TC 12-yard line, Fitzpatrick had to make a crucial fourth-down decision: call on Montroy to try a field goal or go for it. Fitzpatrick chose the latter and Stapleton was stopped short while trying to sweep around the end.

Both teams picked up nine first downs. Catholic Central completed 8 of 12 passes for 45 yards, one touchdown and one interception, while TC completed 1 of 6 for 10 yards. Catholic Central received credit for playing an exceptionally clean game, but it was reeling from a two-game losing streak, and things were about to get worse.

Union 21
Catholic Central 0
Saturday, October 31 at Island Park

Catholic Central		Union H. S
Kroon	LE	Schaubel
Roach	LT	Seborg
Kampfschulte	LG	McKay
McGavin	C	Griffin
Starr	RG	Hultman
Jackaboice	RT	Zegunis
Everhart	RE	Cornwell
Duemler	QB	Parsaca
L.Montroy	LH	Betterridge
Stapleton	RH	Lamphear
Papa	FB	Hart

Catholic	0	0	0	0	0
Union	0	7	14	0	21

Touchdowns – Schaubel, Lamphear, Hart
PAT – Parsaca 3 of 3
Referee– Remmington, Umpire – Lawton, Head Linesman – Hoeker

Although Catholic Central had lost two in a row, it was still mathematically in contention for the city championship going into what was being touted as the biggest sporting day in Grand Rapids history. The race would be sorted out by a doubleheader at Island Park with the Navy Blue of Catholic Central and the Red of Union kicking off at 1:15 p.m., and Central and South doing battle at 2:45.

Coach Fitzpatrick shook up his lineup in the wake of losses to Central and Traverse City, but to no avail, as Union spanked CC 21-0 before a record crowd of more than 10,000.

The Blue and White entered the game knowing it had to win to retain a slim chance at the title. Catholic had a 1-4-1 all-time record against its archrival, but it also won and tied the last two meetings. Union quarterback Rocky Parsaca was also motivated by recent history, and he ran the West Siders' offense with surgical precision.

Catholic Central's opportunity to score came when Union fumbled the ball away on its first possession. On first down, however, CC quarterback Jimmy Duemler became woozy when he was accidentally kicked in the head and remained that way until the third quarter. Union forced Catholic to punt and the Red and White defense remained just as stingy the rest of the game.

After meticulously driving Union into scoring position, Parsaca threw a 20-yard touchdown pass to Schaubel for a 7-0 lead. Early in the third quarter, Parsaca's 50-yard pass to Schaubel, who was run down from behind by the hustling Stapleton, set up Hart's 1-yard touchdown run on the next play. Later in the quarter, Parsaca intercepted a Montroy pass to end what was shaping up as a dangerous CC threat, and completed a 35-yard pass to Red Lamphear, who was tackled at the Catholic 10-yard line. Lamphear ran it in from there for Union's final score.

Although several CC players left the field with injuries, they were quoted by *The Grand Rapids Herald* as saying, "Union tackles hard and clean. Their players are the cleanest bunch of players we've faced this season. They shut their mouths and play hard, clean football."

Flint Central 28
Catholic Central 2
Saturday, November 7 at Flint

When Coach Fitzpatrick sealed a two-year deal earlier in the season to play defending co-state champion Flint Central, it seemed like a good idea at the time. Playing such a high-profile opponent would enhance CC's statewide status, Fitzpatrick reasoned. "It's opposition my boys want," Fitzpatrick said at the time, "and we expect to get plenty of it next month in the Flint game."

After giving up 28 unanswered points before losing 28-2, Fitzpatrick may have thought his players should have been more careful about what they wished for. Instead of CC using Flint Central to its advantage, the home team exploited the Blue and White to bolster its state-title credentials.

Catholic Central left the Vehicle City with accolades for putting up a strong fight in rain-soaked and mud-covered conditions described as the worst imaginable. But Flint Central was clearly the stronger team. It opened the game with a 60-yard touchdown drive, and although CC fought hard to hold the score to 7-0 at halftime, it ran out of gas in the second half. Flint Central came out of the game with a 20-2 advantage in first downs.

South 20
Catholic Central 0
Saturday, November 14 at Island Park

The Blue and White went into the final game of the season with a sense of "deadly earnestness," according to one writer, but that wasn't enough to avoid a fifth straight defeat. The 20-0 loss to South left CC with a 5-5 record and a 0-4 mark against city rivals.

The Catholic Central defense had no answer for the running of South's Witzel, who rushed for more than 100 yards, and Keister, who broke loose for several long-gainers. Witzel ran off tackle for a 17-yard touchdown that put CC behind 6-0 in the first quarter. South went up 13-0 in the second quarter when from 8 yards out, Witzel fumbled before reaching the goal line and Lowing recovered for South in the end zone. After a scoreless third quarter, Keister's 41-yard end sweep for touchdown put the game out of reach. Catholic stopped South from scoring one last time with a goal-line stand that ended when time expired before the Red and Blue could run a play on fourth down.

With Parsaca drop-kicking field goals of 42, 40 and 25 yards, Union defeated previously unbeaten South 9-0 to wrap up the city championship and earn a share of the state title. Montroy, McGavin and Elmer Kampfschulte, the right guard, represented Catholic Central on *The Grand Rapids Herald's* first-team All-City Team and Everhart earned second-team recognition.

CC/WC Archives

1925 Catholic Central Varsity Team

Standing (l-r) - Coach Fitzpatrick, Erhardt, Montroy, Everhardt, Starr. Gilbert, McGavin, Kampfschulte, Roach, Papa, McKinney, George Jackoboice

Kneeling - Cummings, Riley, Kishkorn, Alexander, Chapman, Duemler, Stapleton, Murphy, Jeroze, O'Brien, Meade, McKenna

1925 Schedule/Results
Head Coach – George Fitzpatrick

Date	Opponent	Result		Location
Sep. 12	Ovid	Won	26-0	Ramona Park
Sep. 19	Rockford	Won	34-0	Ramona Park
Sep. 26	Muskegon St. Mary's	Won	75-0	Ramona Park
Oct. 3	Ft. Wayne Catholic	Won	18-13	Ramona Park
Oct. 10	Lowell	Won	34-0	Ramona Park
Oct. 17	Central	Lost	0-6	Ramona Park
Oct. 24	Traverse City	Lost	6-7	Traverse City
Oct. 31	Union	Lost	0-21	Island Park
Nov. 7	Flint Central	Lost	2-28	Flint
Nov. 14	South	Lost	0-20	Island Park

	Record	Pts. Scored	Pts. Allowed
Overall	5-5	195	95

-1926-

Catholic Central 71
Ovid 0
Saturday, September 11 at Ramona Park

Preseason prognostications of Catholic Central dominating the city league in 1926 appeared more credible after the Parochials swamped Ovid, 71-0, in the season opener. The criticism of being too light to compete, which dogged CC for years, was a distant memory. Coach Fitzpatrick's line averaged 175 pounds from end-to-end with center Ted Feldpausch tipping the scales at 195 and veteran tackle Tom Roach going 192. Mature fullback Ted Cummings and halfback Norm O'Brien weighed in at 170 and 175, respectively. What Catholic lacked, according to scouting reports, was a heady quarterback and a breakaway threat at halfback.

Despite its huge size advantage over Ovid, CC was downgraded for being weak in the blocking department, though the shortcoming was attributed to a lack of practice time. Eight different Blue and White players scored touchdowns, but a candidate for the featured halfback job didn't emerge.

Catholic Central 32
Kalamazoo Catholic Central 0
Saturday, September 18 at Ramona Park

Catholic Central scored a touchdown in each of the first three quarters and two in the fourth to subdue Kalamazoo Catholic Central, 32-0. Judging by the score CC was a far superior team, and it was, for the most part. However, it was still flawed in several areas.

None of the three quarterbacks Fitzpatrick used in the game looked sharp, the linemen came out of their stances too high, CC appeared to be slow on the flanks and special teams were mistake-prone. What Catholic did exceptionally well was defend. None of the Kazooks' plays went for more than 5 yards and they failed to pick up a first down.

GR Herald Photo

Catholic Central quarterback Bill Murphy plunges through the Ovid line.

O'Brien, a triple-threat with a pair of touchdowns against KCCHS, ran 6 yards for CC's first touchdown, and set up the second with a 15-yard pass to Dave Mead, the right half. Harold Riley, Catholic's most productive quarterback in the game, made it 12-0 on a 2-yard plunge. Fitzpatrick relied on reserves for the remainder of the first half and the entire second half.

Catholic Central 6
Benton Harbor 0
Saturday, September 25 at Houseman Field

Benton Harbor High School's eleven didn't even flinch upon laying eyes on Catholic Central's impressive size. The Harborites took the fight to CC, which wouldn't face a harder-blocking or fiercer-tackling team the rest of the season. To their credit, the Parochials stood up to the challenge and left Houseman Field with a well-deserved 6-0 victory.

Catholic adroitly manipulated field position in the first quarter to manufacture the decisive touchdown. When CC's first possession failed to penetrate beyond Benton Harbor's 20-yard line, O'Brien punted the ball out of bounds at the 5. When two runs into the line yielded zero yards, BHHS's Walker set up to punt from his own end zone on third down. A heavy CC rush caused Walker to hurry the kick, which traveled only 25 yards. Cummings returned the ball 13 yards, and three plays later scored the game-winner on a 4-yard off-tackle rush.

Later in the game, Fitzpatrick replaced O'Brien with CC fan-favorite Tony Mitchell, who launched a 70-yard punt.

Catholic Central 26
Cadillac 0
Saturday, October 2 at Cadillac

GR Herald Photo
Fullback Ted Cummings

Just when it looked like Catholic Central's rushing attack was getting untracked, it stalled in the second and third quarters against Cadillac High School, only to fire back up in the fourth. The result was an odd, but satisfying, 26-0 victory.

The Parochials wasted no time in marching the ball downfield in the first quarter, and Cummings sparked the scoring frenzy with a 6-yard rush into the end zone. Mead added a touchdown at the end of the first quarter to give CC a 13-0 advantage. Things got interesting, if not mind-boggling, from that point. Catholic Central's line seemed to lose interest in firing off the line and finishing blocks, and the running backs had difficulty finding much room to maneuver.

The Blue and White perked up in the fourth quarter after Cadillac's Smith fumbled a punt just outside his own goal line and Bill Murphy recovered for CC. Mitchell burrowed into the end zone on the next play, and ran for a 30-yard touchdown a few minutes later.

Catholic Central 37
Alma 3
Saturday, October 9 at Ramona Park

A fast start, a lull, a strong finish: the trend continued for Catholic Central, which overwhelmed Alma, 37-0, for its fifth consecutive victory.

The Parochials quickly moved the ball into scoring position on their game-opening drive, and Mead's 10-yard run provided a 6-0 lead barely five minutes into the game. The CC offense then went quiet for the rest of the first half while Alma scored a field goal on Ward's 27-yard place-kick.

The Blue and White came back to life in the third quarter after Mitchell hit end Jack McKinney with a 59-yard touchdown pass. Cummings upped the score to 19-3 by taking a cross-buck off tackle and racing 28 yards to the end zone. Catholic scored three fourth-quarter touchdowns, including a 30-yarder by Cummings, one on another Mitchell-to-McKinney pitch-and-run and a 50-yard run by Mead.

It wasn't a bad way to go, as long as it produced wins.

Central 13
Catholic Central 6
Saturday, October 16 at Houseman Field

The key matchup in Catholic Central's city league opener against Central pitted CC All-City guard Elmer Kampfschulte against the Hilltoppers' backfield, led by quarterback George Roseberry. Whichever captain's unit got the better of the other's was almost certain to be on the winning side.

True to its season-long form, CC scored first. This time, however, the offense failed to spring back to life, and Central put up two second-half touchdowns to hand the Blue and White its first defeat of the season, 13-6, and its third series loss in as many seasons.

Cummings, said to have played the greatest game of his career, almost singlehandedly carried Catholic Central to scoring position in the first quarter. His 28-yard gain set up his 6-yard touchdown, which stood as the lone marker until halftime.

Catholic Central outrushed Central, 116-86, but 102 of those yards were gained in the first quarter. For whatever reasons, Cummings, who accounted for 75 percent of CC's first-half rushing yards, barely handled the ball in the second half. Meantime, Roseberry's boys ran for 56 of its yards in the second half against Kampfschulte's line, which paved the way for just 5 rushing yards after halftime. The Hilltoppers also completed 2 of 12 passes for 23 yards and one interception while CC connected on just 1 of 11 passes for 1 yard and four interceptions.

Catholic Central		Central H. S
McKinney	LE	Gorman
Roach	LT	Mee
Kampfschulte	LG	Jachang
Feldpausch	C	Russell
Starr	RG	Brockmier
Kishkorn	RT	Montez
Paganelli	RE	Graves
Murphy	QB	Hicks
Mitchell	LH	Jones
O'Brien	RH	Peck
Cummings	FB	Koets

Catholic	6	0	0	0	6
Central	0	0	13	0	13

Touchdowns – Cummings, Roseberry, Russell
PAT - Koets
Referee– Olds, Umpire – Dunn, Head Linesman – Lightner

Catholic Central 33
Traverse City 6
Saturday, October 23 at Ramona Park

When it played up to its potential, CC's offensive line was state-championship caliber. Although not especially explosive, it was big, smart and fairly athletic. Any team in Michigan would have loved to have the guard tandem of Kampfschulte and Martin Starr. At 195 pounds, Feldpausch was a stout anchor at center and Roach and Bill Kishkorn were a running-back's dream on off-tackle plays. In McKinney and Santi Paganelli, Fitzpatrick had a pair of ends who were effective blockers and capable receivers.

What the Blue and White desperately continued to search out, five wins and one loss into the season, was a capable field general at quarterback and a reliable halfback to complement Cummings, the do-it-all fullback. Fitzpatrick called his backs a collection of "motionless wonders." Although any of the four backs in the single wing could be called upon to throw a pass, the quarterback was responsible for calling the plays. What Murphy brought to the field in terms of spirit and energy was all-but negated by his lack of feel for the game. CC threw four interceptions in the loss to Central while Cummings touched the ball very few times in the second half.

As a result, Fitzpatrick shook up his lineup for Traverse City. O'Brien, a splendid athlete who had a penchant for avoiding gaping holes like the plague, was relegated to the second team and Murphy was doomed to a similar fate if he didn't start making better decisions.

The Parochials responded with a resounding 33-6 pounding of Traverse City, but Cummings still carried most of the load. Cummings broke through the middle for a 30-yard gain to set up his first of two touchdowns, and he passed Catholic into position for two more scores later in the game. Not surprisingly, Cummings, Kampfschulte, Starr and Roach were named the stars of the game.

Union 10
Catholic Central 7
Saturday, October 30 at Ramona Park

On the schedule, it read "Catholic Central vs. Union." In reality, it was Ted Cummings vs. Rocky Parsaca. The West Side quarterback's virtuoso performance was three points better than that of the CC fullback, who try as he might, couldn't prevent the Blue and White from suffering a 10-7 city league loss.

Union broke out on top in the first quarter on Mol's 35-yard touchdown run and Parsaca dropkicked the extra point. Later in the period, a Red and White drive ground to a halt at the CC 30-yard line, but Parsaca coolly dropkicked the field goal that would hold up as the game-winner for the next three quarters.

GR Herald Photo

Catholic Central's Tony Mitchell prepares to pass in the Union Game.

However, in a game Catholic had to win to stay in the city league title race given its previous loss to Central, the Blue and White was far from beaten. Cummings repeatedly gashed the Union defense for gains of 10, 12 and 15 yards to get CC into scoring position. But except for Murphy's quarterback sneak followed by Cummings' extra point in the third quarter, Union stopped Catholic Central on downs every time it reached the shadow of the West Siders' goalpost.

The game was decided, for all intents and purposes, in a dramatic fourth-quarter duel involving Parsaca and Cummings. After Catholic Central blocked Parsaca's second field-goal attempt, Cummings gathered in the loose ball and fought off three Union tacklers while trying to break free for the go-ahead score. With the entire Union team in rabid pursuit, Cummings traveled 43 yards before being hunted down from behind.

Catholic Central		Union H. S
McKinney	LE	McCellen
Roach	LT	Kirwin
Kampfschulte	LG	Bolter
Erhardt	C	Irwin
Kishkorn	RG	Mekrigan
Feldpausch	RT	Hultman
Paganelli	RE	Jaroski
Murphy	QB	Parsaca
Mitchell	LH	Steponski
Mead	RH	Decker
Cummings	FB	Mol

Catholic	0	0	7	0	7
Union	10	0	0	0	10

Touchdowns – Mol, Cummings
PAT – Cummings, Parsaca
FR - Parsaca
Referee– Bassett, Umpire – Hoeker, Field Judge – Houston, Head Linesman – Wilson

Catholic Central 8
Flint Central 3
Saturday, November 6 at Ramona Park

The Blue and White suffered another major setback following the Union loss when Cummings was automatically declared ineligible upon reaching is 20th birthday. Fitzpatrick could only try to fill the massive void with Stephen Ollis.

Cummings' absence made it difficult for CC to move the ball against Flint Central High School's brick-wall defense, so the Blue and White passed its way to an 8-3 victory over the perennial powerhouse.

In an attempt to create breaks in good field position, FCHS often punted on first down and attempted just six rushes and eight passes in the first half. Catholic Central scored all the points it needed early in the opening stanza when Mitchell lofted the ball 20 yards downfield to Mead, who wisely followed his blockers for the final 50 yards of a 70-yard touchdown play. Cummings wasn't on hand to dropkick the extra point, so Ollis attempted a pass for the point after touchdown (PAT) but it fell incomplete.

Catholic Central added two more points to its ledger near the end of the first quarter when Roach and McKinney tackled Vehics punter Glidden in his own end zone for a safety.

Catholic Central		South H. S
McKinney	LE	Maxey
Roach	LT	McGrath
Kampfschulte	LG	Hall
Erhardt	C	Kutsche
Kishkorn	RG	Holland
Feldpausch	RT	Joslin
Paganelli	RE	Hoogesteger
Murphy	QB	Boelens
Mitchell	LH	Driscal
Mead	RH	Turnwall
Gillis	FB	Russo

Catholic	0	0	0	0	0
South	3	0	0	6	9

Touchdowns – Driscal
FG – Driscal
Referee– Jack Dunn, Umpire – Genebach, Head Linesman – Hoeker

After Glidden dropkicked a 28-yard field goal in the third quarter, re-energized Flint Central opened up its attack. However, Murphy, the beleaguered CC quarterback, put on a show in the defensive secondary by batting down several dangerous passes.

South 9
Catholic Central 0
Friday, November 12 at Island Park

"Like a ship without a rudder, a foundering Catholic Central eleven wallowed through a veritable sea of mud yesterday…." And so began *The Grand Rapids Herald's* tale of how the Irishmen lost their last shot at city league respectability. The 9-0 defeat against South on the snow-softened Island Park field dropped CC's record against the locals to 0-3. Driscal, the triple-threat quarterback, accounted for all of the Southenders' points with a 14-yard field goal in the first quarter and a touchdown in the fourth.

Catholic Central never missed Cummings more than when it had first and goal to go at the South 1-foot line in the second quarter. The Blue and White's massive offensive line couldn't budge South's light defenders in the ankle-deep mud on three plunges. The Parochials' only legitimate scoring opportunity of the game ended when Murphy called for a sweep around end, and the Southenders dropped Mead for a 4-yard loss.

Paganelli and McKinney played their best games of the season, but CC was done-in by three consecutive second-half interceptions, each of which was secured by South's Jay Boelens, and a fumble by backup fullback Martin "Cowboy" Schnur, which led to Driscal's 1-yard touchdown.

From beginning to end, wrote *The Herald's* Heinie Martin, South was just "smarter and cleverer" while making a bid for a share of the city championship.

Catholic Central 13
Highland Park 0
Saturday, November 20 at Ramona Park

It was fitting that a player known as "Cowboy" helped Catholic Central ride off into the sunset with a 13-0 victory in the home finale on the snow-covered plain at Reeds Lake.

Martin Schnur, the lanky fullback from Arizona, did his best Ted Cummings imitation by bludgeoning the Highland Park High School defense with such ferocity, three of its players had to be carried off the field.

At the end of the first quarter, Bernard Erhardt blasted through the Highland Park line to block a punt, and recovered the ball on the 7-yard line. On the second play of the second quarter, Ollis' 3-yard plunge gave CC a 6-0 lead. Schnur, who replaced Ollis at fullback in the second half, then took it upon himself to finish what the Irishmen started.

Schnur churned up big hunks of yardage, while leaving HPHS tacklers in his muddy wake in the third quarter. Then, in the fourth, he gave CC fans something to talk about during the impending offseason, when he knocked a couple of Highlander defenders off their feet and hauled in a pass from Murphy. On the next play, Schnur was on the throwing end of a long completion to Murphy. Schnur then completed the scoring drive by knocking three or four would-be tacklers out his way with a vicious stiff-arm throughout his 35-yard run to paydirt. On defense, Schnur hit HPHS' McCracken so hard, the star receiver left the game with a broken nose.

The victory raised CC's record to 8-3, and even better days appeared to be right around the corner because the Blue and White junior varsity team defeated South, 16-14, in the preliminary to capture the city reserve championship.

Bay City 18
Catholic Central 0
Thursday, November 25 at Bay City

If local observers saw Catholic Central as a "light" team, one can only imagine how big the Bay City High eleven appeared to CC in the final game of the season. The Wolves used two blocked punts and a pair of interceptions to vanquish the Irishmen, 18-0.

The first block came early in the first quarter and Bay City took over at Catholic Central's 1-foot line. The Wolves found it tough to move the ball 12 inches, and needed three smashes into the line by Wheeler to score. Catholic's next possession ended on an interception, but the defense didn't yield and the Wolves had to punt. Unfortunately for CC, the ball was downed at its own 1-yard line, and that's where BCHS eventually recovered the second blocked punt. This time Wheeler needed only two attempts to score. Wheeler then ended Catholic's next possession by picking off a pass and running the ball back 30 yards to the CC 17-yard line. He scored from there on the next play.

Kampfschulte and Roach represented 8-4 Catholic Central on *The Herald* All-City Team but Cummings, unquestionably the best fullback in Grand Rapids through the first eight games, was left off the so called mythical all-star squad because he became immediately ineligible upon turning 20 on Oct. 31, the day after he seriously outplayed Union's Mol, the eventual all-city pick, in the three-point loss.

"In selecting All-State or All-American teams, writers do not consider players who fail to play out the entire season," rationalized *Herald* sports reporter Heinie Martin, who selected the All-City Team.

Some birthday present.

CC/WC Archives

1926 Catholic Central Varsity Team

1926 Schedule/Results
Head Coach – George Fitzpatrick

Date	Opponent	Result		Location
Sep.11	Ovid	Won	71-0	Ramona Park
Sep. 18	Kalamazoo CC	Won	32-0	Ramona Park
Sep. 25	Benton Harbor	Won	6-0	Houseman Field
Oct. 2	Cadillac	Won	26-0	Cadillac
Oct. 9	Alma	Won	37-3	Ramona Park
Oct. 16	Central	Lost	6-13	Houseman Field
Oct. 23	Traverse City	Won	33-6	Ramona Park
Oct. 30	Union	Lost	7-10	Ramona Park
Nov. 6	Flint Central	Won	8-3	Ramona Park
Nov.12	South	Lost	0-9	Island Park
Nov.20	Highland Park	Won	13-0	Ramona Park
Nov. 25	Bay City	Lost	0-18	Bay City

	Record	Pts. Scored	Pts. Allowed
Overall	8-4	239	62

CHAPTER 3
The Haller and McCracken Era
1927-1933

After George Fitzpatrick left Grand Rapids to join the staff of legendary University of Dayton head man Harry C. Baujan, Catholic Central High School once again tapped into the pipeline between it and the University of Notre Dame for a football coach. George Haller, who led the CC reserves to a city championship in 1926, was promoted to the top job. Haller never played for the Fighting Irish, but he was classmates with Fitzpatrick at ND and was a member of one of the school's renowned "interhall teams" which play intramural tackle football in full gear. Before returning from the West Coast to rejoin Fitzpatrick, Haller worked as an assistant coach in Washington and California. Described in *The Grand Rapids Herald* as having "a quiet, modest and extremely retiring nature..., he is well-liked by the boys and his methods of coaching have brought fine results with the reserve teams."

Haller welcomed back what was considered the city's strongest line, led by all-state tackle and team captain Tom Roach who tipped the scales at 200 pounds, but would go into the season without a bona fide featured back. Archival Union also entered the season with a new head coach due to the resignation of John Truesdale, who moved on to Grinnell College. John Hess, who according to the *Herald* "is of a quiet, modest, yet forceful nature," inherited a team of West Siders with a line as good as Catholic Central's, but with a backfield to match. October 29, the date of what shaped up as the city league's biggest game of the season, was circled on Blue and White and Red and White calendars on both sides of the Grand River.

Despite starting out with so much hope and promise, Haller's tenure at Catholic Central would prove to be short and tumultuous.

-1927-

Catholic Central 26
Shelby 0
Saturday, September 17 at Ramona Athletic Park

The sultry weather was better suited for a swimming in nearby Reeds Lake than battling it out in football equipment covered with thick moleskin jerseys. Nevertheless, Catholic Central's stable of unproven ball-carriers thrived in the heat while leading the Blue and White to a 26-0 victory over Shelby.

GR Herald Photo
Coach George Haller

Martin "Cowboy" Schnur, who made a name for himself with his aggressive fullback play at the tail end of the '26 season, quarterback Henry Milan and halfback Ray Jennings ran roughshod over Shelby. Halfback Tony Mitchell, who bulked up 180 pounds by working with a pick and shovel all summer, snapped off a long-gainer before scoring CC's first touchdown of the season on a nifty run around end, and Milan sneaked in for the touchdown that upped the lead to 13-0.

After Jennings left the game with a broken leg late in the first half, a mighty mite named Alex Liberacki wasted no time in setting up his first touchdown with a wild romp around end and Robert Lynch hauled in a 35-yard pass from Johnny Farrell for the game's final touchdown in the waning moments. It was only the second pass CC attempted in the game.

Catholic Central 13
Benton Harbor 6
Saturday, September 24 at Benton Harbor

The breaks went all Catholic Central's way in a 13-6 victory against Benton Harbor High School.

The Parochials scored all the points they'd need early in the second quarter when center Bernard Erhardt blocked a BHHS punt and Charles Weiks grabbed the loose ball and returned it 20 yards for a touchdown. Martin Starr booted the decisive extra point for a 7-0 lead.

Benton Harbor pulled to within one point in the third quarter when a series of completed passes advanced the ball deep into CC territory. Catholic Central's stellar defensive line broke down for the only time of the game when BHHS smashed into the end zone with a line buck, but the extra point failed.

Catholic Central sealed the victory late in the fourth quarter after Benton Harbor sent Bernard, its center, into the game as a substitute for a second time in the same quarter. The whopping 35-yard penalty assessed for illegal substitution gave CC the ball at the Benton Harbor 35, and the Parochials pounded the ball in from there with 90 seconds remaining.

Catholic Central 26
Ottawa Hills 7
Saturday, October 1 at Ramona Athletic Park

The first-ever meeting between Catholic Central and Ottawa Hills High School, which wasn't considered part of the city league because it played in a lower class, was a contrast in experience. The Parochials' superior organization and outstanding line development showed in a 28-7 victory, but the Indians picked up a moral victory with their first touchdown of the season even if it did come at the expense of CC's second string.

Captain Tom Roach led a fearsome defensive rush that repeatedly dropped OHHS running backs for negative yardage. On offense, CC ran the Notre Dame-influenced criss-cross action in the backfield to perfection. A combination of plunges and tricky cross-bucks led to Mitchell's touchdown before the game was five minutes old.

Liberacki and Schnur stayed with that theme while contributing second-quarter touchdowns, and Catholic led 19-0 at halftime. Ottawa Hills outplayed the CC reserves in the third quarter and set up its only touchdown with a 40-yard run around end and a 10-yard penalty tacked on for a late hit out of bounds. Despite throwing an incomplete pass on the extra-point try, the Indians were awarded the extra point anyway after the officials penalized the Parochials for pass interference. Milan countered that score with one of his own in the fourth quarter.

Catholic Central 0
St. Joseph 0
Saturday, October 8 at Ramona Athletic Park

In a classic battle between an irresistible force and an immovable object, Catholic Central settled for a 0-0 tie after missing a field goal with a minute remaining in its game against St. Joseph. In a game in which any kind of score could have assured victory, both teams took turns making critical stops. The scariest St. Joseph threat came late in the second quarter when left halfback Zitta broke into the open field and had nothing but green grass between him and the goal line. Milan, however, got on his horse and tackled Zitta for a 45-yard gain, 13 yards from the end zone. The Catholic Central line stonewalled St. Joseph's subsequent attempts to score.

Catholic Central had first-and-goal at the St. Joseph 8-yard line in the third quarter, with 2 ½ yards to go.

Schnur, who was playing with an infected foot, was found to be 5 inches short of the goal line after the officials pulled 21 teammates and St. Joseph defenders off the pile. Four plays later, CC returned a 20-yard punt from the St. Joseph end zone back to the 7, but netted only 2 yards on the first three plays of the fourth quarter. Confusion did the Parochials in on fourth down when no one was lined up to receive the snap from Erhardt, the center. The ball rolled all the way to the 25-yard line before St. Joseph recovered.

After getting the ball back, Mitchell completed CC's first pass of the game to Lynch, who had nothing but open field and a sure touchdown ahead of him. However, his ankle gave out before he could get going and the Blue and White still had its work cut out. Another completion, from Mitchell to Tony Annerino, a native of Venice, Italy, put CC in field-goal range, but Starr's placekick missed the mark. St. Joseph had Catholic's fans holding their breath with the game's longest pass, which probably would have resulted in a touchdown had a St. Joseph player plucked it out of the air. However, Milan again saved the day, this time with a nifty interception.

Catholic Central 6
Central 0
Saturday, October 15 at Houseman Field

The first crucial city league game of the season pitted the so-called "downtown institution of learning" against "the palace of knowledge up on the hill," otherwise known as Catholic Central and Grand Rapids Central. The winner would immediately be considered the team to beat for the mythical city title, and Houseman Field was prepared to accommodate a season-high crowd of 6,000-plus.

GR Herald Photo

Catholic Central's Martin Schnur stops a Central ball-carrier while Erhardt (r) holds off two Central players.

Catholic Central		Central H. S
Farrell	LE	Schuhart
Roach	LT	Steketee
Norman	LG	Jachnig
Erhardt	C	Gentz
Weiks	RG	Brockmeier
Starr	RT	Mee
Annerino	RE	Irwin
Milan	QB	Jones
Mitchell	LH	Gorman
Liberacki	RH	Hicks
Schnur	FB	Simpson

Catholic	0	0	6	0	6
Central	0	0	0	0	0

Touchdowns – Mitchell
Referee– Westgate, Umpire – Bensley, Head Linesman – Wrenn

More than 8,000 showed up to witness the showdown from the jam-packed stands and others watched from nearby rooftops as Catholic Central defeated Central for the first time in series history, 6-0. By ending its three-game losing streak to the Hilltoppers, CC avenged the gut-wrenching losses of 36-7, 6-0 and 13-6 over the previous three seasons.

The game wasn't as close as the score indicated, although Central remained one big play away from winning thanks to the outstanding punting of tiny Al Jones. Catholic Central had an 11-2 advantage in first downs and outgained Central in total offense, 169-70.

Milan starred for CC with his long kick returns, effective running and deft play-calling. Early in the third quarter, Milan softened up the Central defense with a sequence of off-tackle blasts into the line that moved the ball to the Hilltopper 20-yard line. Liberacki then bored through the Central defense for 8 yards and Milan powered for 9 on a sneak up the middle. Liberacki fought for 2 more yards and Mitchell finished off the drive, and the Hilltoppers, with a 1-yard plunge into the end zone.

"Cowboy" Schnur dashed two last-gasp efforts by Central with a pair of interceptions deep in CC territory in the fourth quarter. The Hilltoppers got one more chance when they blocked a Mitchell punt from his own 35, but the CC defense would not yield.

Catholic Central students and silver-haired alumni linked up to perform "delirious" celebratory snake dances all over the field where one of the greatest victories in program history had just taken place.

Traverse City 7
Catholic Central 0
Saturday, October 22 at Traverse City

The long-awaited victory over Central and a 4-0-1 record earned Catholic Central respect in city circles, but it was considered far off the pace for the state title. Such aspirations were further damaged with a 7-0 loss on the road to Traverse City High School.

Haller's first loss as the head coach couldn't have come in a more unlikely manner.

Catholic was driving in the first quarter when Mitchell fumbled and Traverse City's Frank Kucera recovered at his own 39-yard line. Two gains totaling 23 yards, and a 15-yard penalty slapped on CC for unnecessary roughness put the Black and Gold in business at the Catholic 25. Two more running plays advanced the ball 4 yards and on third-and-6, quarterback George Kucera broke free around left end and then reversed his field in the direction of the waiting arms of CC's best player and captain, Tom Roach. It appeared the giant, all-state left tackle had the Traverse City ball-carrier dead to rights, but Kucera broke the tackle and dashed 21 yards for the game-winning touchdown.

Mitchell contributed mightily to the defeat with a performance that could only be described as nightmarish. In the second quarter, Catholic drove all the way to the TCHS 15, but on fourth down, Mitchell recovered his own fumble in the backfield for possession-ending loss. Traverse City ended Catholic's second drive of the second half, which was close to midfield, by intercepting a pass thrown by Mitchell. Early in the third quarter, Mitchell's third

fumble of the game was recovered by Frank Kucera at the Catholic Central 37-line.
Redemption appeared to be headed Mitchell's way when his 15-yard pass to Milan and Schiless' 20-yard run moved the ball to the TC 15. Two more runs by Milan and Mitchell gave Catholic a first down at the Traverse 2. On the next play, Mitchell ran the ball into the end zone, but the touchdown was negated by a penalty for having only six men on the line and the ball was moved back 5 yards. Mitchell regained 2 yards and runs by Guiffre and Schiless placed the ball on the 2. But from there, the hard-luck Mitchell was smothered for no gain.

GR Herald Photo

Catholic Central Cheerleaders

(l-r) John Boyer, John Stapleton, Robert Withey and Martin Cummings

The Parochials got one more Grade-A chance in the final minute, but it ended cruelly 12 yards from the end zone when Mitchell threw his second interception, for his fifth turnover, of the game. Catholic Central dominated Traverse City statistically, including a 14-5 bulge in first downs, but the only numbers that mattered were those on the scoreboard. At 4-1-1, Catholic's dream of a state title ended, but the city championship was still within reach.

Catholic Central 0
Union 0
Saturday, October 29 at Island Park

The largest crowd ever assembled for a football game in Grand Rapids watched Catholic Central and Union push each other around between the goal lines for four solid quarters. While the 0-0 tie did little to satisfy either team, at least it didn't damage Catholic's city championship hopes. The Parochials could still capture the crown with a win against South two weeks later. South defeated Central, 6-0, in the first game of a doubleheader at Island Park field, dubbed the "world's worst football stadium" by the local press.

Catholic Central		Union H. S
Lynch	LE	Owen
Roach	LT	Cook
Norman	LG	Boiter
Erhardt	C	Russell
Weiks	RG	Brockmier
Starr	RT	Montez
Annerino	RE	Graves
Milan	QB	Hicks
Mitchell	LH	Jones
Liberacki	RH	Peck
Schnur	FB	Koets

Catholic	0	0	0	0	0
Union	0	0	0	0	0

Referee– Remmington, Umpire – Lawton, Field Judge – Vick, Head Linesman – Duncan

The theme was definitely patriotic as the red, white and blue teams lined up for the playing of the Star Spangled Banner performed by the bands of all four high schools. The 10,000-plus spectators walked away knowing they saw one of the greatest defensive battles ever waged on Furniture City turf.

Catholic made an early charge, but after it recorded its only two first downs of the game in the first quarter, the contest devolved into a stalemated scrum until the final two minutes. Union came out of its offensive shell by bashing, crashing and gashing its way into the Parochials territory before completing a 37-yard pass to the 10-yard line.

With all avenues to the end zone blocked off by stubborn CC tacklers, the West Siders decided to try to win the game with a short field goal. Quarterback Rocky Parsaca, whose talented toe had produced spectacular results in previous seasons, had recently rejoined the team after a bout with appendicitis but he hadn't kicked a ball in two months and was considered too unprepared for such a pressure-filled assignment. Union pinned their hopes on center Tony Dauksza, but his 17-yarder flew wide of the post.

But if not for the stalwart defensive play of Roach, Starr, Annerino, Norman, Lynch, Chuck Weiks and Erhardt, CC almost certainly would have suffered its first loss to Union in four seasons and dropped out of contention for city supremacy.

Catholic Central 12
South 6
Saturday, November 12 at Island Park

Coach Haller pulled a page out of Notre Dame coach Knute Rockne's book when it came to dealing with the bye that preceded the all-important game against South High. Haller not only divided the team up equally for an intrasquad game on the idle Saturday, but like Rockne, he suited up along with his players. Haller played end for the Blue team and assistant coach and former CC running back Ray Cudahy carried the ball for the White. Fans were even charged a nominal admission fee to watch the scrimmage at Island Park. Meantime, South got pasted by Jackson.

The ploy paid off for Haller and the Parochials, who avenged the bitter 9-0 defeat against South from a year earlier with a 12-6 victory. Those who weren't among the overflow crowd of more than 10,000 could listen to it on WASH radio, with Harold Roseberry providing the play-by-play.

South broke out on top first at the end of the opening quarter. Unable to move the ball against Catholic's muscular defense, the Southenders went to the air after Floyd Driscal's 30-yard punt return got them started from good field position. A few plays later, Driscal, the left half, completed a long pass to Hubbard, who was stopped at the CC 11-yard line. When a first-down run around end proved futile, Driscal lofted a pass to Hoogesteger in the end zone, but the dropkick for the extra point failed.

The Irish got the ball back from South in the second quarter when Roach knocked the ball out of Driscal's hands while planting him into the ground with all the force his 200-pound body could muster. Roach also recovered the loose ball at the South 24 and three plays later, "Cowboy" Schnur tied the game by plowing under the Southenders' defense en route to a 5-yard touchdown. Just before halftime, Mitchell completed a 32-yard pass to Schnur and a 22-yarder to Annerino to set up his own game-winning touchdown from the 1-foot line.

Catholic Central		South H. S
Lynch	LE	Hubbard
Roach	LT	Dolson
Norman	LG	Rens
Erhardt	C	Vahey
Weiks	RG	Hollard
Starr	RT	Brown
Annerino	RE	Hoogesteger
Milan	QB	Ackershook
Mitchell	LH	Driscal
Liberacki	RH	Reed
Schnur	FB	Russo

Catholic	0	12	0	0	12
South	6	0	0	0	6

Touchdowns – Mitchell, Schnur, Hoogesteger
Referee– Lloyd Olds, Umpire – Ritter, Head Linesman – Lawton, Field Judge - McCullough

Mitchell provided an encore in the third quarter with a 42-yard gain that had him avoiding tacklers and picking up blockers by running from sideline to sideline, while sometimes giving up ground. Mitchell's artful dodging drew comparisons to the way Illinois' star Red Grange zigzagged for three touchdowns in five minutes against Michigan three years earlier.

The Irish held off South the rest of the game, which ended in darkness, though the events of the final few minutes

CC/WC Archives

1927 Catholic Central First Team

Back Row (l-r) - Coach Ray Cudahy, Alex Liberacki, Martin Schnur, Tony Mitchell, Henry Milan, Coach George Haller
Front Row - Tony Annerino, Martin Starr, Chuck Weiks, Bernie Erhardt, Julius Norman, Tom Roach, Robert Lynch

remain cloaked in mystery. According to one report, CC was penalized for 15 yards for tripping and another 9 for pass interference. Another said that on the last play, the Irish tackled every South player on the field to make sure they got the one with the ball as the final whistle sounded.

Catholic Central dominated South in total offense, 285-99, and picked up 16 first downs to three, but had to share the city title with Union, which defeated South the following week.

Catholic Central 37
Cadillac 13
Saturday, November 19 at Houseman Field

Confident and on a roll, Haller delivered on his promise to give fans a preview of the 1928 Catholic Central team by starting his entire second string against Cadillac in the season finale played on snow-covered Houseman Field. The scrubs played like anything but and posted the first score in CC's 37-13 victory.

After receiving the opening kickoff, the reserves needed just three minutes to score. A 40-yard pass from Farrell to Girard Rafferty put the ball at the Cadillac 3-yard line, and Johnson hauled it from there to the end zone. It was believed that the reserves could have won easily on their own, although Cadillac tied the scored against the CC first string in the second quarter. Liberacki broke the tie just before halftime with a 15-yard touchdown run. Cadillac evened the score one more time against a defense made up of first- and second-teamers, but Schiless started a 19-0 CC run with a touchdown rush measuring 30 yards. Milan put the game out of reach with a 20-yard touchdown pass to Annerino as the Irish finished with a 6-1-2 record.

Postseason

Three of CC's five interior linemen, Roach, Erhardt and Starr joined Mitchell on the All-City First Team chosen by *The Grand Rapids Herald* while Milan and Schnur were second-team selections.

However, the coaches also picked an All-City team in conjunction with *The Grand Rapids Press*. And for the first time in state, and possibly Midwest history, the first and second teams would square off in a benefit all-star game. Led by Catholic's Roach, Starr, Erhardt, Mitchell and Schnur, the All-City First Team defeated the All-City Second Team, led by CC end Annerino, 13-7, at Houseman Field on Dec. 4.

Despite the frigid temperature that made holding onto the ball a challenge, the game was well-played and raised $2,000 for the Red Cross.

Thomas Roach
Catholic Central
1928

A three-year starter on the offensive line for Catholic Central, Roach entered the University of Michigan in the fall of 1928.

Roach won his letter at Michigan as a tackle during the 1929 season before graduating and entering the University of Notre Dames Law Schoool in the fall of 1932.

He lettered in football at Notre Dame during the 1932 and 1933 seasons and received his law degree in the spring of 1934.

Roach returned to practice law in Grand Rapids. Active in community matters, he was a member of the Grand Rapids Recreation Board in the 1940's and the first Catholic member of the Grand Rapids Board of Education during the 1950's.

Thomas Roach passed away on July 24, 1977.

GR Herald Photo

CC's Tom Roach

1927 Schedule/Results
Head Coach – George Haller

Date	Opponent	Result		Location
Sep. 17	Shelby	Won	26-0	Ramona Park
Sep. 24	Benton Harbor	Won	13-6	Benton Harbor
Oct. 1	Ottawa Hills	Won	28-7	Ramona Park
Oct. 8	St. Joseph	Tie	0-0	Ramona Park
Oct. 15	Central	Won	6-0	Houseman Field
Oct. 22	Traverse City	Lost	0-7	Traverse City
Oct. 29	Union	Tie	0-0	Island Park
Nov. 12	South	Won	12-6	Island Park
Nov. 19	Cadillac	Won	37-13	Houseman Field

	Record	Pts. Scored	Pts. Allowed
Overall	6-1-2	122	39

-1928-

Catholic Central 49
Shelby 0
Saturday, September 22 at Ottawa Hills Field

By the late 1920s, the forward pass was widely regarded as an option of last resort for teams that had difficulty moving the ball on the ground or when time was running out on deficit-reduction efforts. Neither was the case for Catholic Central as it overpowered Shelby with a 49-0 season opening victory in its first game ever played at the Ottawa Hills High School field. After all, three things can happen when a ball is thrown, and two of them are bad.

The All-City backfield tandem of fullback Tony Mitchell and left half "Cowboy" Schnur toyed with Shelby, which based on its 6-6 tie with South High two years earlier fell considerably short of expectations, while accounting for four touchdowns. Even the reserves ran roughshod over the opposition. Had the Irish operated at above 75-percent capacity, there's no telling how many points they would have scored. Catholic Central demonstrated outstanding balance, which back then meant a team could run effectively inside and outside.

Catholic Central completed its game-opening drive in just over a minute on Schnur's first of three touchdowns. Sophomore Harold Claffey, the new right half, made it 12-0 a few minutes later, and Mitchell chipped in his only tally before the first quarter ended with CC holding a comfortable 18-0 lead. In the second quarter, Mitchell's 20-yard gallop set up Schnur's 15-yard touchdown run, and Johnson, the first-year quarterback, made it 31-0 before halftime. Ed Fulgoni, a backup halfback and the younger brother of former Union great George Fulgoni, ripped off a series of long-gainers, including the only score of the third quarter. Scnhur rounded out his day with a 55-yard interception return for a touchdown and Claffey added a six-point exclimation mark after breaking several tackles along his way to the end zone.

It was the last hurrah for Mitchell in a Blue and White uniform. Based on the results of the local high school principals committee investigation into an allegation made by Union High School questioning Mitchell's age, Catholic Central informed the Michigan High School Athletic Association (which had supplanted the Michigan Interscholastic Athletic Association) that it was voluntarily removing the multi-talented halfback from further competition.

"The facts upon which the decision of the school officials was based, were not available at Catholic Central, and were uncovered only after (an) extensive search of records at other schools covering a period of several years antedating Mitchell's registration at Catholic," the school faculty said in a statement announcing the decision just prior to kickoff of CC's next game against Mount Pleasant Sacred Heart Academy. It was determined that Mitchell turned 20 years old on Sept. 18.

Catholic Central 32
Mount Pleasant Sacred Heart Academy 0
Saturday, September 29 at Ottawa Hills Field

For a quarter, it appeared the loss of star halfback Tony Mitchell, who was declared ineligible under MHSAA rules, was going to have a much more profound effect on Catholic Central than anyone could have imagined. Turns out, the Irish were simply preoccupied while playing Mount Pleasant Sacred Heart Academy to a 0-0 tie in the first quarter. Calling CC's performance "mediocre" was an understatement.

After shaking off a case of fumbleitis, Catholic Central struck for two touchdowns in the second quarter to spark a convincing 32-0 drubbing. A methodical series of runs and passes set up the first touchdown on Claffey's run and tumble into the end zone. The Irish upped the score to 12-0 on just three plays before halftime. On the first play of the drive, Johnny Farrell, who replaced Mitchell at left halfback, completed a 25-yard pass to Rafferty, the left end. The next play, a 30-yard pass from Farrell to Schnur, set up Farrell's touchdown pass to Rafferty. It came so easily the struggles of the first quarter were a distant memory.

A long pass from quarterback Johnson, to Farrell, accounted for the scoring in the third quarter, and Johnson sneaked into the end zone to give CC a 25-0 lead in the fourth quarter. With reserves from both teams playing out the final minutes, the final score seemed to come out of nowhere, much to the amazement of the fans at Ottawa Hills Field. As Sacred Heart overpowered CC's second-string line for yet another tackle behind the line of scrimmage, the ball flew out of the pile downfield to where backup right end Bernard Kiley just happened to be waiting. Whoever threw the long touchdown strike to Kiley wasn't known at the time, and it remained a mystery for the remainder of the season.

Catholic Central 33
St. Joseph 0
Saturday, October 6 at St. Joseph

Illinois had its Galloping Ghost and a few years later Catholic Central had the "Galloping Cowboy."

Schnur, the roughneck fullback from Arizona, scored three touchdowns to finish off a 33-0 victory against St. Joseph. Johnson plunged over the goal line to give CC a first-quarter lead and Rafferty returned a second-quarter St. Joe fumble 52 yards for a touchdown, but the second half was all Schnur's.

In the third quarter, Schnur intercepted a pass and ran it back 47 yards for his first score. Later in the quarter, he busted loose on an off-tackle rush for a 42-yard touchdown and he barreled into the end zone from 4 yards out in the fourth quarter.

Central 2
Catholic Central 0
Saturday, October 13 at Houseman Field

It mattered little that Catholic Central could boast its overwhelming superiority over Central High in every statistical category emanating from the fifth meeting between the two teams. The Irish dominated the battle for total yardage, 221-47, and held 12-1 mastery in first downs. However, if a team can't score a touchdown from less than a yard out, it can lose in the most heartbreaking fashion imaginable by the lowest decisive combined score possible.

Catholic Central		Central H. S
Rafferty	LE	Haskins
Milan	LT	Davis
Zanelli	LG	Rayes
Doyle	C	Plett
Paganelli	RG	Burton
Drueke	RT	Thompson
Scally	RE	Irwin
Johnson	QB	La Roche
Farrell	LH	Thwaites
Claffery	RH	Graves
Schnur	FB	Coulson

Catholic	0	0	0	0	0
Central	2	0	0	0	2

Referee– Westgate, Umpire – Van Alken, Head Linesman – Bensley

And that's exactly what happened. After Girard Rafferty was tackled 12 yards from the goal line with 25 seconds remaining, CC fell to the Hilltoppers, 2-0, at Houseman Field.

With Coach Haller in Ann Arbor attending a MHSAA hearing on the Mitchell eligibility situation, Central was the beneficiary of a generous gift hand-delivered by Catholic in the first quarter. Rugged Irish fullback "Cowboy" Schnur lined up in a two-point stance on his own 10 with the intention of passing or punting. However, Schnur had difficulty fielding the errant shotgun snap from Robert Doyle, the center, and the ball fell to the ground. After Schnur finally corralled the loose pigskin, he took a swipe at it with his foot but it traveled backward and Claffey fell on it in the end zone for a Central safety. Central then packed it in defensively, seemingly content to protect the two-point lead for as long a humanly possible against the Irish, who continued having a hard time holding onto the ball. With six minutes remaining in the second quarter, CC's punishing offense drove the ball to the Central 4-yard line. But on first-and-goal-to-go, Schnur fumbled and Halbert recovered for the Hilltoppers. Five minutes later, Schnur and Johnson pounded the Central defense with a savage series of 3-to-12-yard body blows until the ball was marked at the Gold and Black 1-yard line. On fourth down with less than a minute remaining in the half, Schnur looked for an opening between guard and tackle, but the Hilltoppers stood firm against his hurtling 175-pound body, which came to rest 12 inches from paydirt.

GR Herald Photo

Catholic Central's Joe Drueke

Regardless of what Catholic Central threw at Central, it would not relent. With less than a minute remaining, backup quarterback Chuck Ollis took the center snap at the CC 30-yard line and heaved the ball to Rafferty, who made an over-the-shoulder catch at the 40 where he fought off three Hilltopper tacklers before breaking free. Rafferty sprinted with reckless abandon down the sideline with two Central defenders in hot pursuit until, for whatever reason, he lost confidence in his speed. Apparently fearful of being run down from behind, Rafferty slowed down, spun around and faced the Black and Gold tacklers he intended to ward off while doubling back toward the end zone. The Hilltoppers were just as determined to stop him from scoring the winning TD, however, and halted the chase at 56 yards, just a dozen from city league immortality.

Observers were all but certain that had Rafferty merely maintained his stride without looking back, he would almost certainly have made it to the end zone. Catholic Central lined up with the ball twice in the final 25 seconds but again failed to crack open the Central defense. The Irish lost for the fourth time in five games against the Hilltoppers, and "even the Cowboy wept as he was led away by his followers," wrote Heinie Martin of *The Grand Rapids Herald.*

The night was about to get darker for Catholic Central and its fans. MHSAA commissioner A.W. Thompson informed the school that its football season would be suspended for a month because Mitchell was ineligible to play in the opener against Shelby. Although Thompson had warned Catholic Central before the season that Mitchell's age had been called into question, Haller testified that he was convinced the accusations against one of the city's best players lacked merit. Haller later said it was his understanding, based on a conversation with Thompson before the opener, that it would be all right to play Mitchell, who CC clearly didn't need to defeat

Shelby, as long he was convinced the player was eligible. Haller said he put his faith in a sworn affidavit from Mitchell's parents attesting to his date of birth, and the school immediately began planning an appeal.

However, if the suspension remained in force, CC would have to cancel upcoming games against Traverse City, Union, Ottawa Hills and South, and it was speculated that the final two games against Toledo and Benton Harbor would be abandoned as well.

Also at issue was Catholic Central's failure to follow MHSAA procedure by allowing Haller, who wasn't a member of the school's teaching staff or front office, to manage the football program's administrative duties such as signing contracts, arranging the schedule and documenting player eligibility.

Catholic Central 8
Union 7
Saturday, October 27 at Island Park

Catholic Central's appeal was supported by fellow city schools who would take a significant financial hit at the gate if CC couldn't play. The MHSAA rejected Catholic Central's initial appeal because it was submitted by Haller, who wasn't an official faculty representative. Action only started after Rev. R.E. Fitzpatrick, who was reinstated as CC's athletics faculty manager after a two-year hiatus, filed the paperwork. However, a special hearing before the MHSAA executive committee was convened too late to prevent the game against Traverse City from being cancelled.

Haller saved the remainder of the season by submitting his resignation while CC agreed to pay Traverse City its portion of the lost gate, minus travel expenses it didn't incur. Fitzpatrick was placed in charge of managing all aspects of the program except student-athlete eligibility, which was placed under the principal's authority. Former Catholic Central star Louis Norman was named to replace Haller prior to the Union game. Norman played center on Notre Dame's freshman team in '24 and was a Fighting Irish varsity reserve under coach Knute Rockne the following three seasons. He was considered a finalist for the head coaching position after George Fitzpatrick resigned prior to the '27 season.

The Parochials took a nine-year record of 1-6-2 against Union into the annual grudge match that stood out as much for its irony as the iron wills of both teams. Catholic's 8-7 victory was its first against the West Siders since 1923, when Norman, then a standout center, led CC to the city title. A crowd of more than 8,000 turned out for the battle of defending city co-champions in a game that was decided by Rafferty's 33-yard touchdown.

Catholic Central		Union H. S
Rafferty	LE	Zegunis
Milan	LT	Cook
Zanelli	LG	Tanis
Doyle	C	Miller
Paganelli	RG	Walker
Drueke	RT	Szczpaniak
Farrell	RE	Irwin
Johnson	QB	Bovee
Ollis	LH	Franczak
Schnur	RH	Piechocki
Claffey	FB	Brzowski

Catholic	0	2	0	6	8
Union	0	7	0	0	7

Touchdowns – Irwin, Rafferty
Referee– John Bos, Umpire – Coryell, Field Judge – Vick, Head Linesman – Bennett

Both teams were plagued by turnovers throughout the game, but a fumble by CC's Ollis actually worked in the Parochials' favor. After recovering the ball at its own 1-yard line, Union immediately tried to punt out of trouble on first down. However, Pete Zegunis inadvertently stepped out of the back of the end zone before kicking the ball, and Catholic took a 2-0 lead on the safety. However, the Red and White countered just before the end of the second quarter on left half Stan Franczak's 73-yard touchdown pass to Bob Irwin. It was the first six-pointer given up by the Parochials all season.

A scoreless deadlock ensued until the final few minutes of the fourth quarter when Ollis was once again on the throwing end of a fateful pass to Rafferty. This time, however, instead of being hauled down at the 12 as he was in the loss against Central, Rafferty hauled the ball in at the 12 and strode the rest of the way untouched for the game-winning touchdown.

GR Herald Photo
Halfback Jack Scally

Catholic Central 12
Ottawa Hills 7
Saturday, November 3 at Ottawa Hills Field

Norman's coaching honeymoon lasted barely eight days because the decision to let his reserves protect a tenuous six-point second-half lead against upstart Ottawa Hills nearly cost Catholic Central a victory.

After recovering an Indian fumble on the opening kickoff, CC grabbed an early 6-0 lead on Johnson's 35-yard sweep. Although Farrell missed the extra point, Norman apparently felt like his team had the game in the bag because he substituted liberally the remainder of the first half and into the second. The score remained unchanged, due to a rash of turnovers by both teams, until Ottawa Hills got the better of a CC defense featuring just two starters, Milan and Farrell. Walker's 35-yard pass to Wells against the Catholics inexperienced secondary tied the score and Blackford kicked the Indians into the lead, 7-6.

Norman sent his regulars back in for a key defensive series in the fourth quarter. The muscular Schnur fired up his teammates and seemed to intimidate the Ottawa Hills players when he ripped off his jersey, much the delight of the Catholic Central who roared in approval. A subsequent poor punt gave CC the ball at the Indian 42-yard line and nine plays and a 15-yard holding penalty later, Johnson powered into the end zone on fourth-and-goal at the 1.

It wasn't long before Norman's overconfidence was being called into question.

South 40
Catholic Central 7
Saturday, November 10 at Island Park

Catholic Central		South H. S
Rafferty	LE	Hubbard
Milan	LT	Laff
Zanelli	LG	Breen
Doyle	C	Ford
Paganelli	RG	Holland
Drueke	RT	Graves
Farrell	RE	Beall
Johnson	QB	Ackerschool
Claffey	LH	Nelson
Ollis	RH	Elliot
Schnur	FB	Russo

Catholic	0	0	0	7	7
South	20	7	0	13	40

Touchdowns – Nelson (2), Russo (2), Hubbard, Elliott, Scally
PAT – Russo (2), Beall (2), Johnson
Referee– Coryell, Umpire – John Bos, Head Linesman – Bennett

Norman would silence the critics if he could lead CC to victory over undefeated South High and climb back into the city championship race. With Schnur nursing a sore shoulder and Claffey ailing with an injured arm, it wasn't to be. "Lightning" Lester Nelson accounted for 416 all-purpose yards while leading the Red and Blue to an unexpected 40-7 rout that left 8,000 Catholic and South fans dumbfounded.

After his game-opening kickoff return of 70 yards, Lester, also nicknamed "The Brown Phantom" advanced the ball in yardage increments of: 3, 8, 5, 51, 32, 12 (touchdown), 90, 12, 10, 0, 10, 80 (touchdown) and 33.

Catholic's lone touchdown came on a 90-yard interception return by Jack Scally early in the fourth quarter. Nelson, who also had a 90-yard punt return for a touchdown called back because of a tripping penalty in the second quarter, was credited with the greatest individual performance in city history.

Toledo Catholic Central 26
Catholic Central 12
Saturday, November 17 at Toledo

For the second game in a row, Catholic Central was victimized by a hot running back. Toledo High's Tom Keefe didn't rack up the kind of yardage Lester Nelson did for South seven days earlier, but he scored two touchdowns, on a 90-yard kickoff return to open the second half and a 45-yard run, and passed 15 yards for another. Scally tallied twice for CC in the second half, but it wasn't enough to prevent a 26-12 defeat.

Benton Harbor 27
Catholic Central 0
Saturday, November 24 at Island Park

A season that began with so much promise, only to be disrupted by controversy, scandal and a coaching change, ended with an anticlimactic thud for Catholic Central. Unlike the previous two defeats when a single back ripped through the Parochials for spectacular gains, Benton Harbor pounded CC into submission. Catholic surrendered a touchdown in every quarter of the 27-0 loss that left it with a 5-4 record. Tackle Joe Drueke comprised CC's only first-team All-City pick, and Farrell was named to the second team.

1928 Schedule/Results
Head Coach – George Haller/Louis Norman

Date	Opponent	Result		Location
Sep. 22	Shelby	Won	49-0	Ottawa Hills Field
Sep. 29	M. P. Sacred Heart	Won	32-0	Ottawa Hills Field
Oct. 6	St. Joseph	Won	33-0	St. Joseph
Oct. 13	Central	Lost	0-2	Houseman Field
Oct. 27	Union	Won	8-7	Island Park
Nov. 3	Ottawa Hills	Won	12-7	Ottawa Hills Field
Nov. 10	South	Lost	7-40	Island Park
Nov. 17	Toledo Catholic	Lost	12-26	Toledo
Nov. 24	Benton Harbor	Lost	0-27	Island Park

	Record	Pts. Scored	Pts. Allowed
Overall	5-4	153	109
City League	2-2	27	56

-1929-

The Louis Norman coaching era spanned exactly five games at Catholic Central, which re-hired George Haller who had resigned four games into the '28 season amid the Tony Mitchell eligibility controversy. With Haller back to guide a team that went into camp 75 players strong, optimism abounded at the Sheldon Avenue school, which was picked to be in the city league title hunt come Thanksgiving Day. What wasn't given enough consideration, however, was the fact that Haller welcomed back just five letter-winners: Johnny Farrell, who was named captain; Harold Claffey; Jack Scally, Dexter Reynolds and Adolph Szczepanski. Halfback Chuck Ollis would have been a sixth veteran returnee, but he was declared ineligible. One newcomer who impressed early was George Ingraham, a towering tackle drawing comparisons to former CC All-Stater Tom Roach, who was coaching the linemen before reporting to the University of Michigan, where he was set to start for the Wolverines' varsity.

Catholic Central 6
Davis Tech 0
Saturday, September 21 at South Field

The first signs of trouble turned up in Catholic Central's narrow 6-0 victory over Davis Tech in the first game played at South High's new field. Although the defense stood tall while pitching a shutout, the offense failed to click until backup left end Melvin Kampfschulte turned a swing pass into a long touchdown with two minutes remaining in the game.

The younger brother of a former CC captain who replaced Bernard Kiley late in the game, Kampfschulte improvised his way through traffic until only 25 yards remained between him and the goal line. Kampfschulte wouldn't be denied. He broke three tackles during the stretch run and knocked the final Tech defender out of his way with a stiff-arm.

Catholic Central		Davis Tech
Kiley	LE	DeGoffau
Tarzinski	LT	Lovett
Zwers	LG	Korar
Brogger	C	Newton
Shields	RG	Jelsma
Reynolds	RT	Stearns
Purcell	RE	Cable
Balcer	QB	Thompson
Lapinski	LH	Lewis
Claffey	RH	K. Burgett
Szczepanski	FB	R. Burgett

Catholic	0	0	0	6	6
Davis Tech	0	0	0	0	0

Touchdowns - Kampfschulte
Referee– Oldenberg, Umpire – Fuller, Head Linesman – Morlan

Catholic Central 18
Shelby 0
Saturday, September 28 at Island Park

The defense continued to impress in Catholic's 18-0 victory over Shelby, and the offense finally came alive after a scoreless first quarter. Maurice Moran, the backup quarterback, capped a methodical drive with a 1-yard plung to put CC ahead 6-0 in the second quarter.

In the third quarter, Haller moved Reynolds from his right tackle position into the backfield, and he completed a 35-yard pass to Claffey. Alan Lapinski then threw passes of 18 and 35 yards to Claffey, who then ran for Catholic's second touchdown. The Parochials recovered a fumble at the Shelby 15 in the fourth quarter to set up their final touchdown which came on a 15-yard romp by Szczepanski, the burly 166-pound fullback.

Catholic Central 0
Ottawa Hills 0
Saturday, October 5 at Ottawa Hills Field

While the CC defense continued to excel, the ability to move the ball with any consistency eluded the offense in a 0-0 tie against Ottawa Hills. With neither team generating much ball-control, the game became a punting duel, which Claffey won with his exceptionally high kicks providing plenty of hang-time.

Catholic threatened late in the second quarter, but it couldn't reach the goal line before the halftime whistle sounded. The Blue and White's best chance to score came on a drive that started with a 20-yard pass from halfback Jack Scally, who missed the first two games with an injury, to Farrell. Claffey picked up 5 more on a run and another 15 on a pass from Scally. Claffey's 12-yard gain had CC sniffing the goal line, but a penalty move the Parochials back to the 20. On the next

Catholic Central		Ottawa Hills
Kampfschulte	LE	Tetro
Tarzinski	LT	Conklin
Zwers	LG	Lewis
Brogger	C	Baker
Pulte	RG	Cleveland
Reynolds	RT	VanNorman
Farrell	RE	Wells
Moran	QB	Walker
Scally	LH	Thomas
Claffey	RH	Douglass
Szczepanski	FB	Missad

Catholic	0	0	0	0	0
Ottawa Hills	0	0	0	0	0

Referee– Baker, Umpire – Knutson, Head Linesman – Oldenberg

play, Ottawa's Douglas was so driven to win the game on his own, he picked up Claffey, the miniature running back, as if he was going to carry him 80 yards and deposit him in the opposite end zone for the decisive safety. With the aide of Douglas' subsequent roughing penalty, CC advanced to the Indian 2, but fumbled the ball away before it could score.

Central 6
Catholic Central 0
Saturday, October 12 at Houseman Field

It was known simply as "The Jinx." Since 1924, although Catholic Central usually went into its annual game against city rival Central listed as the favorite, the Parochials came out as losers on five of six occasions. The scenario repeated itself in 1929 when the Hilltoppers upset CC, 6-0.

For the first time all season, the CC defense cracked under the pressure of needing to blank the opponent to have a chance to win. Well, that, and the constant pounding of "Thunderbolt" Davis, Central's 200-pound fullback.

GR Herald Photo

CC's Adolph Szczepanski (far right) attempts to get outside against Central.

The Hilltoppers' opportunity to break the scoreless deadlock came in the third quarter when Ike Whan fielded Claffey's punt at the 50 and returned it 20 yards. Davis then did most of the heavy lifting with consecutive smashes into the line of 12, 18 and 10 yards to set up a 3-yard plunge by Hughes for the game-winner. Catholic made one more bid to pull out the victory late in the fourth quarter, but right after penetrating Central territory, Claffey fumbled the ball away as though required to by the jinx. Bad karma or not, CC's offensive deficiencies were glaringly evident in Central's 255-134 advantage in total yardage.

Union 7
Catholic Central 0
Saturday, October 26 at Houseman Field

Catholic Central's lack of scoring punch became so evident, the team once favored to be in the title hunt to the very end of the season was listed as an underdog against archrival Union. And true to form, the West Siders avenged their 8-7 loss to CC a year earlier with a 7-0 victory that gave them the upper hand in the city race.

The physically superior Red and White got all the scoring it in the third quarter, after Claffey's punt from the CC 5-yard line traveled just 20 yards before being downed. After a short gain on first down, Union's Alex Yurgalitis lobbed a pass to fullback George "Bozo" Brzowski, who hauled the ball in at the 10 and barreled his way into the end zone for the game's only touchdown.

Catholic Central		Union H. S
Kampfschulte	LE	Jablonski
Ingraham	LT	Tuma
Zwer	LG	Burgess
Brogger	C	Druker
Tarzinski	RG	Walker
Reynolds	RT	Falicki
Pease	RE	Simapski
Moran	QB	Tanis
Claffey	LH	Piechocki
Scalley	RH	Yurgaitis
Szczepanski	FB	Brzowski

Catholic	0	0	0	0	0
Union	0	0	7	0	7

Touchdowns – Brzowski
PAT - Brzowski
Referee– Hoeker, Umpire – Coryell, Field Judge – Vick, Head Linesman – Lightner

Things might have gone differently for CC had it only been able to get something going offensively early on. Two minutes after the opening whistle, Scally swept around right end for what appeared to be a 70-yard touchdown. However, the officials ruled that Scally had touched the sideline with his right foot while using a stiff-arm to fend off a Union tackler and the ball was placed at the Red and White 27. Union's "Lefty" Piechocki knocked the Parochials out of scoring position when he dropped Szczepanski for a 10-yard loss.

GR Herald Photo
Center John Brogger

Creston 19
Catholic Central 0
Saturday, November 2 at Ottawa Hills Field

Catholic Central's touchdown drought officially became a crisis when it failed to score for the fourth consecutive game. The first-ever meeting between CC and Creston ended in a 19-0 decision that was all but wrapped up in the first quarter. When the Parochials failed to counter despite reaching the Polar Bear 13-yard line, most hope for a comeback was lost. Injuries had ravaged CC to the point that Haller had more reserves in the starting lineup than regulars, so a losing outcome wasn't totally unexpected. The inability to score, however, was getting ridiculous, and it was about to get worse.

South 7
Catholic Central 0
Saturday, November 9 at Island Park

The Parochials string of scoreless quarters reached 20 after a 7-0 loss to South High. Catholic's frustration became palpable in the second quarter when Moran's 20-yard reception placed the ball at the South 12-yard line. A third-down pass intended for Kampfschulte appeared destined to end the Catholic Central's points famine, but South's Elliott reached up and batted it to the ground at the last second. On fourth down, Scally tried to scamper for the remaining yards, but he was tackled behind the line of scrimmage for a big loss.

South drove nearly the length of the field to score all the points it needed on a 20-yard pass from Elliott to Heintzelman. The rest of the listless game was poorly played mishmash of penalties, substitutions, interceptions by both teams and delay tactics.

Catholic Central		South H. S
Kampfschulte	LE	Huntington
Ingraham	LT	Brown
Zwers	LG	Graves
Brogger	C	Ford
Shields	RG	Breen
Tarzinski	RT	Nelson
Farrell	RE	Joslin
Moran	QB	Elliot
Scalley	LH	McGee
Claffey	RH	Heintzelman
Purcell	FB	Zylstra

Catholic	0	0	0	0	0
South	0	7	0	0	7

Touchdowns – Heintzelman
PAT – Heintzelman
Referee– Miller, Umpire – Hyames, Head Linesman – Hoeker

Catholic Central 6
Toledo Central Catholic 0
Saturday, November 16 at South Field

After 20 scoreless quarters, CC finally broke through a touchdown in the first quarter against Toledo Central Catholic, and then held on for a 6-0 victory. The win snapped a five-game winless streak that began with a 0-0 tie against Ottawa Hills.

More important than the win over TCCHS, which brought

GR Herald Photo

Running Back Harold Claffey

a three-season unbeaten streak to Grand Rapids, was the way Catholic played. Haller's players regained the spunk they had earlier in the season when hopes were still high. The Parochials' confidence got a boost on their first play from scrimmage when Claffey went around right end for 20 yards. Szczepanski bulled through the Toledo CC defense for good gains before the drive ran out of steam. As CC continued to gain chunks of yardage later in the first quarter, Toledo CC replaced its line with its second unit, but Scally's sweep around right end set up Szczepanski's decisive touchdown. Catholic Central's much-maligned line played brilliantly while repeatedly stifling Toledo CC attacks, but never more than late in the fourth quarter. The visitors, clad in bright red jerseys, had first-and-goal at the Catholic Central 6-yard line with but a few minutes remaining. On first down, Toledo CC had a touchdown nullified by an offside penalty. A fumble on the next play backed Toledo CC up another 8 yards, and on third down from the 19, what would have been a touchdown pass was caught out of bounds. Catholic held fast on fourth down for its third win of the season.

Holland 7
Catholic Central 6
Saturday, November 23 at Holland

With a bitter Lake Michigan wind blowing over the frozen field, Catholic Central scored first but a missed extra point proved costly in a 7-6 season-ending loss to Holland. The Parochials took a 6-0 lead just before halftime on Scally's 40-yard touchdown pass to Kampfschulte. Although Catholic gobbled up chunks of yardage on a regular basis between the goal lines, including a 30-yard run by Caffey, it couldn't pad its lead.

Holland scored its touchdown on a 35-yard pass play in the third quarter, and successfully executed a fake kick to score the difference-maker. The Dutch threatened one last time, but lost a fumble at the CC 12-yard line.

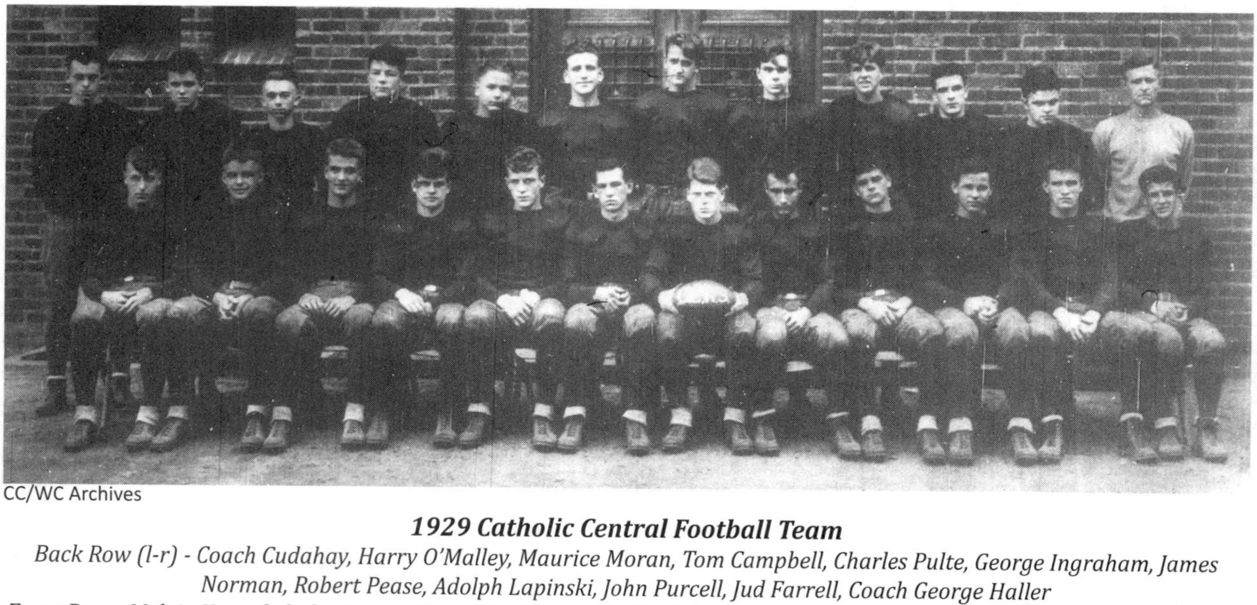

CC/WC Archives

1929 Catholic Central Football Team

Back Row (l-r) - Coach Cudahay, Harry O'Malley, Maurice Moran, Tom Campbell, Charles Pulte, George Ingraham, James Norman, Robert Pease, Adolph Lapinski, John Purcell, Jud Farrell, Coach George Haller

Front Row - Melvin Kampfschulte, Dexter Reynolds, George Shields, John Brogger, Frank Zwers, Roman Tarzinski, John Farrell, Gerald Kiley, Al Balcer, Adolph Szczepanski, Jack Scally, Harold Claffey

Catholic Central had to endure one more indignity before closing the book on its disappointing 3-5-1 season. Scally was the only CC player to earn All-City honors, and he was a second-team selection.

1929 Schedule/Results
Head Coach – George Haller

Date	Opponent	Result		Location
Sep. 21	Davis Tech	Won	6-0	South Field
Sep. 28	Shelby	Won	18-0	Island Park
Oct. 5	Ottawa Hills	Tie	0-0	Ottawa Hills Field
Oct. 12	Central	Lost	0-6	Houseman Field
Oct. 26	Union	Lost	0-7	Houseman Field
Nov. 2	Creston	Lost	0-19	Ottawa Hills Field
Nov. 9	South	Lost	0-7	Island Park
Nov. 16	Toledo Catholic	Won	6-0	South Field
Nov. 23	Holland	Lost	6-7	Holland

	Record	Pts. Scored	Pts. Allowed
Overall	3-5-1	36	46
City League	1-4-1	6	39

-1930-

Catholic Central 7
Davis Tech 0
Saturday, September 20 at Ottawa Hills Field

Catholic Central started the season slowly against Davis Tech, but all hard-nosed first-year coach Tony McCracken cared about was the way his team, which was referred to in print as the "Cougars" for the first time, finished off the punting duel with a 7-0 victory. McCracken, a noted taskmaster espousing the philosophies of University of Illinois coach Bob Zuppke, coached previously at Toledo Libby High.

McCracken put slippery quarterback Rudolph Boggiano, who was arguably the smallest player in the city league, in charge of running the offense, but the momentum shifted CC's way when Harold Claffey finally entered the game late in the first half. In the third quarter, Claffey and fellow co-captain Jack Scalley teamed up for a couple of 15-yard pass plays, but the drive ended with a fumble on the Tech 10-yard line. The Cougars made better use of their next possession, which Scally capped with a 2-yard touchdown run. Catholic was awarded the extra point after the Techmen were flagged for being offside.

The Cougars took their first step toward winning one of the three silver cups donated by Herpolsheimer's department store for the city's first-, second- and third-place finishers. The larger championship trophy was valued at $150.

Catholic Central 27
Ionia St. Peter and Paul Academy 6
Saturday, September 27 at South Field

Although he was said to be smaller "than a pint of cider," Boggiano proved to be too much for Ionia St. Peter and

FOOTBALL BROADCAST TONIGHT AT 7

Herald-Zenith Sports Hour of Gridiron Thrills Over WASH

The 1930 football season is on today 'mid cheers of thousands. Every Grand Rapids high school eleven swings into action against worthy opponents.

The first battles are being waged on college fields.

Thrills and heroes are in the making.

By special arrangement The Herald-Zenith Sports Hour over station WASH, Grand Rapids, starts at 7 o'clock. This broadcast will be given every Saturday night through the football season.

Stories of Local Games

Promptly at 7 o'clock tonight The Herald-Zenith broadcast will give the scores and highlight features of the local games, visualizing the thrilling plays and telling how victory was won. These radio stories will be prepared by trained football reporters covering each game.

The scores of college games the country over will be given to the radio audience as they come over The Associated Press special sports wires.

The whole football picture of the day will be vividly laid before you.

Tune in tonight at 7 on WASH (1270 kilocycles) for The Herald-Zenith Sports Hour.

This broadcast will whet the appetites of football fans for complete and colorful stories of the games in The Sunday Herald. These stories will be accompanied by action pictures of plays and the individual stars snapped on the field by Herald staff photographers.

TONIGHT AT 7 OVER WASH

GR Herald Photo

Advertisement from the September 20, 1930 GR Herald.

Paul to handle during Catholic Central's 27-6 victory. With the remnants of a nor'wester that sank two boats on Lake Michigan buffeting South Field, Catholic scored first after an Ionia punt from its 18-yard line was blown backward minus-3 yards. Three plays later, Tom Fennell busted off left tackle for the touchdown, but CC missed the extra point. The Cougars took the ball back a few minutes later when Academy fumbled at its own 40, and after taking the pass from center on the next play, Boggiano darted around left end, bobbing and weaving his way through numerous Academy tacklers while covering the distance for the game-winning touchdown. Boggiano then passed to Jack Purcell for the extra point. Purcell added another touchdown in the first quarter to give CC a 20-0 lead.

Academy scored against the Catholic Central second string in the second quarter, and L. Burrows tacked on an exclamation point for the Cougars in the fourth quarter.

Ottawa Hills 31
Catholic Central 6
Saturday, October 4 at Ottawa Hills Field

Three turnovers, a blocked punt and difficulty picking up first downs spelled doom for Catholic Central, which suffered its first loss of the season against Ottawa Hills by a score of 31-6. The Cougars took the fight to the Indians in the first quarter, but were outscored 13-0 in the second and 18-0 in the third.

With the time of possession tipped heavily in Ottawa's favor, the lone bright spot for CC was a 50-yard touchdown reception by backup running back Howard Konkle in the fourth quarter.

The Cougars were still in it after Douglass ran off tackle for a short touchdown early in the second quarter. But on its next possession, CC fumbled the ball back to the Indians and halfback Ed Kalawart's 15-yard pass set up their second score. Kalawart put the game out of reach with his 65-yard touchdown run in the third quarter.

Catholic Central		Central H. S
Everhardt	LE	Guest
Tarzinski	LT	Veltman
Brogger	LG	Bayes
Skar	C	Hughes
Oshinski	RG	Connors
Earle	RT	Whitney
Schmidt	RE	L. Graves
Boggiano	QB	I. Graves
Konkle	LH	Fuller
Fennell	RH	Pillinger
Grezkowski	FB	Behrens

Catholic	0	0	0	0	0
Central	0	14	0	7	21

Touchdown – Thwaites, Pillinger, Guest
PAT – Hughes (3)
Referee– Van Aiken, Umpire – Bowbier, Head Linesman – Jones

Central 21
Catholic Central 0
Saturday, October 11 at Houseman Field

It wasn't a jinx that cost Catholic Central a 21-0 loss to Central. It was the Hilltoppers' relentless smash-mouth defense and fundamentally sound blocking, taught by head coach Harold Steele who played under Fielding Yost at Michigan, that made all the difference. The Cougars never really sniffed the goal line and were outgained, 231-151, and had just seven first downs to Central's 15.

Union 20
Catholic Central 0
Saturday, October 25 at Island Park

The Cougars' dreams of winning one of the Herpolsheimer's silver cups were all but dashed by a 20-0 loss to Union. The Red and White, meantime, continued its march to a state championship on the dusty Island Park field. The CC defense stood out for continuing to fight despite a 14-0 halftime deficit, and keeping the game from becoming a runaway. Boggiano was a Tazmanian devil in the defensive secondary where he had several pass-breakups and a couple of interceptions.

Creston 6
Catholic Central 0
Saturday, November 1 at Island Park

After being victimized by Union's and Central's running attacks in the previous two games, Catholic Central fell prey to Creston's aerial assault in a 6-0 loss. The quick-hitting Polar Bears moved into scoring position with passes of 30 and 15 yards, and fullback Charles Kunkle powered in for a 6-yard touchdown. Creston had more passing yards, with 74, than CC had in total offense, with 73.

South 13
Catholic Central 0
Saturday, November 8 at South Field

The Cougars' offensive power outage continued for a fifth straight game when they lost to South, 13-0. Catholic ended city competition with a 1-5 record and was outscored 91-13 by its Furniture City rivals.

Interestingly enough, CC received credit

GR Herald Photo
Rudolph "Duff" Boggiano (left) and Roman Tarzinski

Catholic Central		South H. S
Everhardt	LE	McGee
Earle	LT	Brown
Tarzinski	LG	Nelson
Brogger	C	Ford
Oshinski	RG	Ross
Stoddard	RT	Bouwman
Zenella	RE	Dood
Saunders	QB	Elliot
Boggiano	LH	Cooley
Claffey	RH	Heintzelman
Purcell	FB	Zylstra

Catholic	0	0	0	0	0
South	0	6	7	0	13

Touchdowns – Elliot, Brown
PAT – Heintzelman
Referee– Daane, Umpire – Lightner, Head Linesman – Conger

for playing its best game of the season while making things difficult for South, which center and future University of Michigan All-American Gerald R. Ford had headed to a showdown with undefeated Union for the city title. The Cougars were undaunted after losing Boggiano to injury in the first quarter and giving up a 30-yard touchdown run in the second quarter. Catholic continued to fight for all it was worth even after falling behind by two scores in the third. The most heartening development of the game for CC was the emergence of sophomore halfback Casmir Pobojewski. The stocky pile driver served notice that they'd be dealing with him for years to come while onlookers predicted all-state honors were in his future.

Saginaw Eastern 18
Catholic Central 6
Saturday, November 15 at Saginaw

Catholic Central was the better team in its road game against Saginaw Eastern for all but five minutes. But oh, what a horrific five minutes they were. Theron Fager, of Saginaw Eastern, broke the scoreless tie with a 90-yard punt return. On SEHS' next possession, Fager threw a 20-yard touchdown pass to Elmer Potts. John Ikner returned an interception 50 yards to finish the scoring frenzy.

Fager also figured into the final score of the day when his punt was blocked by Catholic's Fred Schmidt, who also fell on the ball in the end zone.

Holland 6
Catholic Central 0
Saturday, November 22 at Island Park

Despite losing their season finale to Holland, 6-0, the Cougars felt like they finished the year on a high note while turning toward 1931. Catholic Central took comfort in knowing they played even with the team that held South to a single touchdown and beat Davis Tech by four touchdowns. The Cougars didn't yield the goal line until Holland scored on a 1-yard run in the third quarter, and after recovering a fumble at the Dutch 25, had a chance to win or tie on the final play of the game.

GR Herald Photo
A host of CC defenders chase Holland's Beekman.

Showalter recovered three fumbles for CC and Boggiano and Pobojewski again starred for the Cougars but couldn't get an offense, which scored just 12 points in seven season-ending losses, into the end zone. Thanks to its 2-7 record, Catholic had no players named to the All-City first team, anchored by Ford, who 44 years later would become the 38th president of the United States. Cougar center John Brogger and left guard Roman Tarzinski earned second-team honors, however.

1930 Schedule/Results
Head Coach – Tony McCraken

Date	Opponent	Result		Location
Sep. 20	Davis Tech	Won	7-0	Ottawa Hills Field
Sep. 27	St. Peter & Paul	Won	27-7	South Field
Oct. 4	Ottawa Hills	Tie	0-0	Ottawa Hills Field
Oct. 11	Central	Lost	0-21	Houseman Field
Oct. 25	Union	Lost	0-20	Island Park
Nov. 1	Creston	Lost	0-6	Island Park
Nov. 8	South	Lost	0-13	South Field
Nov. 15	Saginaw Eastern	Lost	6-18	Saginaw
Nov. 22	Holland	Lost	0-7	Island Park

	Record	Pts. Scored	Pts. Allowed
Overall	2-7	46	121
City League	1-5	13	91

-1931-

Davis Tech 6
Catholic Central 0
(Forfeited)
Saturday, September 19 at South Field

The score looked vaguely familiar, but the outcome was different by 180 degrees. With its 6-0 victory in a steady drizzle that made ball-handling difficult, Davis Tech snapped a two-game losing streak against Catholic Central, which won the previous meetings by scores of 6-0 and 7-0.

The Green and White drove to Catholic's 11-yard line in the first quarter, but the Cougar defense stiffened and Milito's 20-yard field-goal attempt was low and wide. A long pass from Milito to Wisinski set South up for Milito's 3-yard touchdown plunge in the second quarter. Tech drove all the way to CC's 4-yard line late in the second quarter, but CC again stood firm and regained possession of the ball on downs just before time expired. While the Cougars put up a good defensive battle, they were outgained 146-35.

However, CC's loss on the field wasn't reflected in city standings because Tech voluntarily forfeited the game after it determined it had played an ineligible player. Backup quarterback Ed Rettig transferred to Tech from Sacred Heart school, where he went for two semesters. However, Rettig, unbeknownst to Tech officials, attended St. Joseph Seminary for one year as a freshman. Consequently, he was in violation of the eight-semester rule by one semester.

GR Herald Photo
Team Captain Tom Fennell

GR Herald Photo

Advertisement from the September 26, 1931 GR Herald.

Catholic Central 19
Ionia St. Peter and Paul Academy 6
Saturday, September 26 at Ionia

An angry cold wind may have made for miserable conditions, but it helped jump-start Catholic Central to a much-needed 19-6 victory over Ionia St. Peter and Paul Academy. The win snapped an eight-game CC losing streak (including the game Davis Tech forfeited) dating back to its 27-6 triumph over Academy in the second game of the '30 season.

In the second quarter, the Cougar defense stopped Academy deep in its own territory and team captain Hadley came on to punt. However, in his effort to drive the ball low into the wind, Hadley hit one of his own teammates in the back. George Ingraham, the huge CC tackle, fell on the ball. On the next play, Jerry Weshalski, the Cougars' good-looking new halfback, scored from 4 yards out on a cross-buck.

Although Weshalski broke loose for a number of good gains, Catholic was more effective at stopping itself with fumbles and penalties than the Academy defense was. In the third quarter, however, Frank Hartnacke, who replaced George Brogger at quarterback, pulled off a perfect fake shift and ran 50 yards for CC's second score. Academy made things interesting in the third quarter with a touchdown that cut Catholic's lead to 13-6, but Al Healy, who replaced Weshalski, topped off a 70-yard drive with a 2-yard touchdown run in the fourth quarter.

GR Herald Photo

Dick Zanella

Ottawa Hills 6
Catholic Central 2
Saturday, October 3 at Ottawa Hills Field

The CC defense held All-City quarterback Ed Kalawart in check for most of the game, but the Cougars couldn't overcome a mistake that led to Ottawa Hills' game-winning touchdown. With Catholic lined up to punt on the final play of the first quarter, Bernard Hoogterp, who was playing center with an injured hand, snapped the ball over Tom Fennell's head. Fennell recovered at the CC 35-yard line, but Kalawart drove the Indians the distance in seven plays, with Kress going over from the 3.

Early in the third quarter, CC right end Fred Schmidt recovered a blocked punt at the Ottawa Hills 18-yard line and the Cougars could feel the momentum changing. The Cougars charged to the 5, where they had first down. Healey picked up 3 yards and fullback Bernard Grezcowiak carried to the half-foot line. The Indians piled up Healy for no gain, and on fourth down and inches to goal, Grezcowiak was again sent into the jaws of the beast. When the referees removed the humanity from Grezcowiak's back, however, the ball was still 2 inches from the goal line and Ottawa Hills took over. Kalawart went in to punt on first down, but he fumbled the snap and recovered in the end zone to concede the safety to CC.

Catholic made one more strong bid to win in the fourth quarter, but it ended on a fumble at the Indians' 15-yard line.

Catholic Central 20
Central 0
Saturday, October 10 at Houseman Field

The curse Central High School held over the Cougars for seven years was finally broken by Fennell's accurate left arm and a crushing CC defense. With Fennell doing most of the passing, Catholic completed 7 of 11 passes for 79 yards, two touchdowns and one interception en route to the 20-0 victory.

Meantime, the Cougar defense limited Central to just 36 yards of total offense and one first down.

Catholic unleashed its passing attack after recovering a fumble at the Central 44-yard line midway through the first quarter. From 8 yards out, Fennell hit end Dick Zanella in stride as he crossed the goal line, and Casmir Pobojewski's dropkick for the extra point gave CC a 7-0 lead. In the second quarter, after John Shada recovered a blocked Hilltopper punt at the 10-yard line and Healy ran for 6 yards, Fennell tossed a 4-yard scoring strike to quarterback Hartnacke, and CC left the field at halftime with a 14-0 lead.

As a driving rain fell during the third quarter, Fennell threw a 14-yard pass to Hartnacke to set up his own 7-yard touchdown run. It was Catholic's sweetest win in years because it snapped Central's three-game series win streak and improved CC's all-time record against the Hilltoppers to 2-6.

Union 19
Catholic Central 6
Saturday, October 17 at Island Park

Union continued its two-year domination of city foes by staying unbeaten with a 19-6 victory over the Cougars. There wasn't much shame in losing to the Red and White, which piled up a 276-84 advantage in total yards and 18-6 bulge in first downs.

For the second straight game, the Cougars were most effective on offense when Fennell threw the ball. Catholic

GR Herald Photo

Catholic's Tom Fennell (left) attempts to run past the right side of the Union line.

gained 59 of its yards through the air and Fennell's 10-yard touchdown pass to Healy cut Union's lead to 13 points in the fourth quarter. Fennell, a true triple-threat, averaged 44.5 yards per punt.

GR Herald Photo

Right End Fred Schmidt

Catholic Central 6
Creston 0
Saturday, October 24 at Ottawa Hills Field

A steady autumn rain grounded Catholic Central's vaunted passing attack, but caused even more havoc with Creston's ball-carriers, who fumbled frequently and picked up yards sparingly. The 6-0 victory kept the Cougars in contention for the city championship.

Catholic showed its versatility by relying heavily on its rushing game in the soggy conditions. The Cougars ran for 138 of their 198 yards. Meantime, the Polar Bears could manage just 15 yards on the ground.

Nevertheless, it was a long pass from Fennell to Zanella, who was brought down at the Creston 20, that set up the game's only score, on a 5-yard run by Fennell in the second quarter. The Fen-Zan combination connected for another big gain in the fourth quarter, but CC turned the ball over on downs at the 4.

GR Herald Photo

Ray O'Malley heads up field while teammate John Shada blocks Creston's Lamphere (#60).

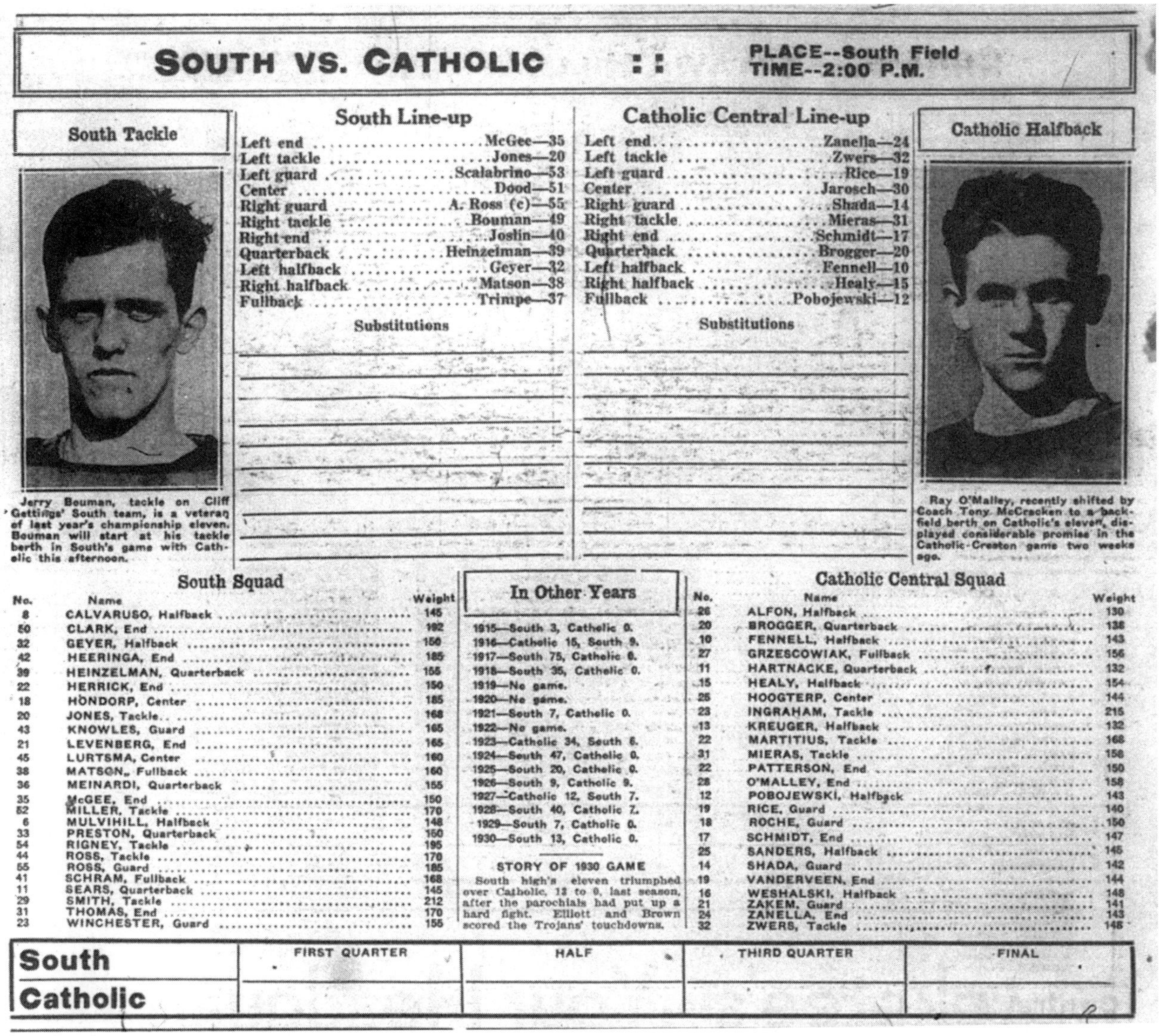

SOUTH VS. CATHOLIC

PLACE--South Field
TIME--2:00 P.M.

South Tackle

Jerry Bouman, tackle on Cliff Gettings' South team, is a veteran of last year's championship eleven. Bouman will start at his tackle berth in South's game with Catholic this afternoon.

South Line-up

Left end	McGee—35
Left tackle	Jones—20
Left guard	Scalabrino—53
Center	Dood—51
Right guard	A. Ross (c)—55
Right tackle	Bouman—49
Right end	Joslin—40
Quarterback	Heinzelman—39
Left halfback	Geyer—32
Right halfback	Matson—38
Fullback	Trimpe—37

Substitutions

Catholic Central Line-up

Left end	Zanella—24
Left tackle	Zwers—32
Left guard	Rice—19
Center	Jarosch—30
Right guard	Shada—14
Right tackle	Mieras—31
Right end	Schmidt—17
Quarterback	Brogger—20
Left halfback	Fennell—10
Right halfback	Healy—15
Fullback	Pobojewski—12

Substitutions

Catholic Halfback

Ray O'Malley, recently shifted by Coach Tony McCracken to a backfield berth on Catholic's eleven, displayed considerable promise in the Catholic-Creston game two weeks ago.

South Squad

No.	Name	Weight
8	CALVARUSO, Halfback	145
50	CLARK, End	192
32	GEYER, Halfback	150
42	HEERINGA, End	185
39	HEINZELMAN, Quarterback	155
22	HERRICK, End	150
18	HONDORP, Center	185
20	JONES, Tackle	168
43	KNOWLES, Guard	165
21	LEVENBERG, End	165
45	LURTSMA, Center	160
38	MATSON, Fullback	160
36	MEINARDI, Quarterback	155
35	McGEE, End	150
52	MILLER, Tackle	170
6	MULVIHILL, Halfback	148
33	PRESTON, Quarterback	150
54	RIGNEY, Tackle	195
44	ROSS, Tackle	170
55	ROSS, Guard	185
41	SCHRAM, Fullback	168
11	SEARS, Quarterback	145
29	SMITH, Tackle	212
31	THOMAS, End	170
23	WINCHESTER, Guard	155

In Other Years

1915—South 3, Catholic 0.
1916—Catholic 15, South 9.
1917—South 75, Catholic 6.
1918—South 35, Catholic 0.
1919—No game.
1920—No game.
1921—South 7, Catholic 0.
1922—No game.
1923—Catholic 34, South 6.
1924—South 47, Catholic 0.
1925—South 20, Catholic 0.
1926—South 9, Catholic 9.
1927—Catholic 12, South 7.
1928—South 40, Catholic 7.
1929—South 7, Catholic 0.
1930—South 13, Catholic 0.

STORY OF 1930 GAME

South high's eleven triumphed over Catholic, 13 to 0, last season, after the parochials had put up a hard fight. Elliott and Brown scored the Trojans' touchdowns.

Catholic Central Squad

No.	Name	Weight
26	ALFON, Halfback	130
20	BROGGER, Quarterback	138
10	FENNELL, Halfback	143
27	GRZESCOWIAK, Fullback	156
11	HARTNACKE, Quarterback	132
15	HEALY, Halfback	154
25	HOOGTERP, Center	144
23	INGRAHAM, Tackle	215
13	KREUGER, Halfback	132
22	MARTITIUS, Tackle	168
31	MIERAS, Tackle	156
22	PATTERSON, End	150
28	O'MALLEY, End	158
12	POBOJEWSKI, Halfback	143
19	RICE, Guard	140
18	ROCHE, Guard	150
17	SCHMIDT, End	147
25	SANDERS, Halfback	145
14	SHADA, Guard	142
19	VANDERVEEN, End	144
16	WESHALSKI, Halfback	148
21	ZAKEM, Guard	141
24	ZANELLA, End	143
32	ZWERS, Tackle	148

	FIRST QUARTER	HALF	THIRD QUARTER	FINAL
South				
Catholic				

Game Program from The Grand Rapids Herald.

Catholic Central 12
South 6
Saturday, November 7 at South Field

Another losing streak came to an end when Catholic Central defeated defending city champ South, 12-6. The red and blue Trojans had beaten the Cougars in three straight, and in five of the previous seven meetings with one game ending in a tie.

In the second quarter, CC center Bob Jarosch set up the Cougars' first score when he intercepted a pass and ran it back 35 yards before tripping and falling at the South 35. Fennell's long fourth-down pass intended for Schmidt at the 6-yard line fell incomplete, but the officials called a penalty on the Trojans for "roughing the receiver" and awarded CC with a 29-yard gain. After an offside penalty moved the ball to the 1, Fennell funneled into the end zone for a 6-0 lead. Catholic made it back to the South 5 in the third quarter, but turned the ball over on downs.

Fennell's 22-yard punt return set up Pobojewski's touchdown that came on back-to-back runs from the 5. The Cougars had a 12-point lead, but it was anything but safe, especially after Fennell fumbled at midfield in the

GR Herald Photo

1931 Catholic Central Team

Backfield (l-r) - Tom Fennell, Bernard Grey, Al Healy, Frank Hartnacke, Casimir Pobojewski, George Brogger
Line - Fred Schmidt, Ray Mieras, John Shada, Bob Jarosch, Art Rice, George Ingraham, Richard Zanella

fourth quarter. South's Heinzelman covered the distance with a 36-yard pass to McGee and a 14-yard touchdown pass to Wisner. South made a frantic bid to rally in the final two minutes after a 40-yard punt return gave the Trojans the ball at the CC 25. A pushing penalty moved South back 15 yards, but the Trojans advanced to the 6 on just two plays. However, the Cougars defense rose to the occasion and kept South from getting any closer before taking over on downs and running out the clock.

Catholic Central 8
Saginaw Eastern 0
Saturday, November 14 at Houseman Field

A late-season monsoon turned the turf at Houseman Field into a quagmire that favored Catholic Central in a 8-0 victory over Saginaw Eastern. Early in the second quarter, SEHS quarterback Speer lost the handle on the ball, and by the time he discovered it in the muddy end zone, the only thing he could do was belly-flop on it for a safety and a 2-0 CC lead.

Catholic already had enough points to win, but sealed the deal a few minutes later after Fennell nailed a 60-yard punt that pinned Saginaw Eastern down at its own 10. Unable to move the ball, Speed tried to punt out of trouble, but Popojewski fielded his wounded duck of a kick on a dead run and returned it for a touchdown.

The rest of the game was a monotonous series of punts and both teams combined for just five first downs. Fortunately for the few fans who remained to the bitter end, the game was finished in less than 90 minutes, including halftime.

Bay City Central 6
Catholic Central 0
Thursday, November 26 at Bay City

Catholic Central set up its gymnasium to resemble a mini-football stadium where fans could gather to listen to the radio broadcast of the Cougars season finale at Bay City Central High School. The band and cheerleaders were on hand to entertain the fans, who were charged 25 cents for admission.

The CC faithful left in disappointment, however, after a 6-0 loss.

The Cougars more than held their own against BCCHS, and Fennell dictated field position with his brilliant punting, including several kicks that traveled at least 60 yards. Bay City scored its decisive touchdown after traveling more than 90 yards on a drive that would have stalled at the CC 1-foot line if not for a penalty.

Faced with first-and-goal-to-go at the 9, Bay City ran for 4 yards on first down, 1 on second and 3 on third. BCCHS captain Wildman tested the middle of the CC defense on fourth-and-2, but the Cougars stopped him a foot short of the goal line. However, the officials penalized Catholic for unnecessary roughness, and after a 6-inch walkoff, Wildman plunged over on the replay of fourth down. Fennell tried to rally CC in the final minute, and his pass to Healy put the Cougars at the Bay City 40. Unfortunately, his next pass was intercepted.

Fennell represented CC on the All-City first team and Jarosch earned second-team recognition.

1931 Schedule/Results

Head Coach – Tony McCraken

Date	Opponent	Result		Location
Sep. 19	Davis Tech	Won*	2-0	South Field
Sep. 26	St. Peter & Paul	Won	19-6	Ionia
Oct. 3	Ottawa Hills	Lost	2-6	Ottawa Hills Field
Oct. 10	Central	Won	20-0	Houseman Field
Oct. 17	Union	Lost	6-19	Island Park
Oct. 24	Creston	Won	6-0	Ottawa Hills Field
Nov. 7	South	Won	12-6	South Field
Nov. 14	Saginaw Eastern	Won	8-0	Houseman Field
Nov. 26	Bay City Central	Lost	0-6	Bay City

	Record	Pts. Scored	Pts. Allowed
Overall	6-3	75	43
City League	4-2	48	31

*Won by forfeit

-1932-

With star halfback Tom Fennell headed to Michigan State and Al Healy and Dick Zanella off to Ypsilanti Normal University (Eastern Michigan), Catholic Central had to deal with a significant depletion of talent but was picked to have its best team in nine years, nonetheless. All city schools would have to adjust to new rules designed to lower the football-related death toll, which soared to 49 nationally in 1931. The "flying wedge," formed by blockers locking arms on kickoff returns, was curtailed. In an effort to prevent piling on, play was to be whistled dead as soon as any part of the ball-carrier's body, with the exception of feet and hands, touched the ground. Plank-like shoulder pads were abolished and padding was required to cover hard-surfaced equipment.

GR Herald Photo

Bernard Grezcowiak

Catholic Central 68
Ionia St. Peter and Paul Academy 0
Saturday, September 17 at South Field

Newly named captain Casmir Pobojewski led the Cougars, who came out with white-winged helmets long before the University of Michigan adopted the look, to a resounding 68-0 thumping of St. Peter and Paul Academy in the season opener. CC led by 19 points at the end of the first quarter and 39 at halftime in one of the biggest mismatches in years. Catholic outgained Academy 308-16 and had a 17-0 advantage in first downs. The Cougars scored a touchdown on each of their possessions and two of Academy's with a safety and a fumble recovery in the end zone. Bernard Grezkowiak and Jerry Weshalski score two touchdowns apiece.

Catholic Central 20
Flint Northern 0
Saturday, September 24 at Flint Atwood Stadium

The Cougar backfield quartet of Pobojewski at fullback, halfbacks Grezcowiak and Weshalski and Frank Hartnacke at quarterback combined with smothering special teams play to score all three touchdowns of a 20-0 victory at Flint Northern in the second quarter.

Catholic Central's first scoring drive started at the Flint Northern 47-line thanks to a poor punt. Grezcowiak passed to Joe Zwers for a 7-0 lead, and then Grezcowiak completed a 26-yard scoring toss to Hartnacke. Zwers fell on a blocked punt in the end zone to complete the scoring.

Catholic Central 0
Ottawa Hills 0
Saturday, October 1 at Ottawa Hills Field

After two easy victories, things got considerably tougher for CC in city play. The Cougar defense earned its third shutout of the season, but the offense failed to score in a 0-0 tie against Ottawa Hills.

Catholic Central fans thought the Cougars had scored in the second quarter when Grezcowiak got up with an Ottawa fumble and galloped 45 yards to the end zone, but the officials ruled the play dead before the return. In the fourth quarter, the Indians drove all the way to the CC 15 on one drive, but the Catholic defense wouldn't let them get any closer. The Cougars met a similar fate a few minutes later after Hartnackne intercepted a throw by Ottawa's Payne. Catholic Central passed its way to the Indians' 13-yard line but lost the ball on an interception.

The Cougars outgained the Indians by more than 100 yards, but that was a meaningless statistic given the score.

Central 7
Catholic Central 0
Saturday, October 8 at Houseman Field

The Cougars were favored to win six of their eight previous games against Central, but held a 2-6 series record. No one at the Sheldon Avenue school seemed to mind, therefore, that the 1932 meeting between CC and the Hilltoppers was considered a tossup.

Not that it mattered. The Central jinx reared its head again as CC fell, 7-0. The game could have gone either way until with two minutes remaining, the Hilltoppers lined up in a "spread formation" at the Catholic 10. Central's Sandy Farrell waited until the last possible instant against a relentless CC pass rush to loft a desperation throw toward the end zone. The ball floated down to the hands of Pete Lebanowski, who was surrounded by four Cougar defenders, just as he crossed the goal line. Catholic got the ball back with a minute remaining, but Lebanowski's interception sealed the defeat.

GR Herald Photo

Bernard Grezcowiak is stopped by a Central defender.

Catholic Central 6
Union 0
Saturday, October 15 at South Field

Frank Hartnacke starred as a pass receiver and a pass interceptor to lead Catholic Central to a 6-0 victory over Union. The Cougar victory ended the defending city and co-state champion's unbeaten streak dating back to 1927. Catholic's third win in 14 series games ended three-game losing streak to the West Siders.

Hartnacke was the difference in the game from the quarterback position. Weshalski's 12-yard pass to Pobojewski went to the Union 20-yard line with just over a minute remaining. On third down, Dubridge, who replaced Pobojewski at fullback, dropped back 5 yards – as required by the rules of the game at that time - and flung the ball to the well-covered Hartnacke. The slender Hartnacke came down with it in the end zone with 56 seconds remaining, but his work was far from over.

GR Herald Photo

CC's Jerry Weshalski rambles around Union's right end.

Catholic Central		Union H. S
Zwers	LE	Abromitis
Ingraham	LT	Zindel
Roche	LG	Mangas
Furman	C	King
Shada	RG	Olman
Mieras	RT	Szczepaniak
Vanderveen	RE	Gronko
Hartnacke	QB	Burns
Grezcowiak	LH	Vander Lind
Weshalske	RH	Kelly
Pobojewski	FB	Eaveld

Catholic	0	0	0	6	6
Union	0	0	0	0	0

Touchdowns – Hartnacke
Referee– Churm, Umpire – Hicks, Head Linesman – Roper

After the ensuing kickoff, Union made one last bid with a deep throw to the 50-yard line. At the last instant, Hartnacke stepped in front of what had been a wide-open receiver and picked off the ball to keep CC in contention for the city title.

Catholic Central 13
Creston 0
Saturday, October 29 at Ottawa Hills Field

The Cougars completed just one of its six passes, but it resulted in the touchdown they needed to defeat Creston. Catholic Central added an insurance marker in the final quarter to send the Polar Bears back to their north-end home with a 13-0 defeat.

Hartnacke set up CC's first scoring drive with a punt return to the Creston 43-yard line. After an incomplete pass, Hartnacke was the "spinner buck" on a running play and broke free for 17 yards. On the next play, Hartnacke sprinted upfield as Grzeskowiac dropped back and let loose with a strike. Hartnacke snagged the ball without breaking stride and glided into the end zone for a 26-yard touchdown. Grzekowiac dashed 30 yards before slipping to the ground to set up Pobojewski's 1-yard dive that put the game out of reach.

Catholic Central 7
Davis Tech 0
Saturday, November 5 at South Field

No team was throwing the ball as effectively as Catholic Central was with the end of the season drawing near. The Cougars came out passing against Davis Tech, and though outplayed in the first quarter, stuck with it to pull out a 7-0 win.

The Wildcats were driving deep into CC territory late in the first quarter when Hartnacke intercepted a pass at his own 22-yard line and returned it 16 yards to set up a 10-play possession that was a perfect blend of passes and runs. The Cougars ended the period on a 10-yard pass from Weshalski to Zwers to the 48. The chance to switch ends seemed to energize Catholic, and on the first play of the second quarter, Grezcowiak completed an 18-yard pass to Weshalski to the Tech 34. Weshalski then ran for 5 and completed a 7-yard flat pass to Zwers. Weshalski plunged for 4, Hartnacke swept around end for 4 and Pobojewski dove for 2. Hartnacke was dropped for a 7-yard loss, but Grezcowiak recovered those yards on a short pass from Weshalski to the 13. On the final play of the drive, the ball ended up in Hartnacke's hands after a criss-cross in

GR Herald Photo

Frank Hartnacke sweeps the right end against Davis Tech.

the backfield. From that vantage point, Hartnacke found lanky end Don "Dutch" Vanderveen standing alone in the end zone and put the ball on target.

The Wildcats tried to pass their way into a tie, but CC intercepted four of their next five passes, including one each by Hartnacke and Ed Furman in the final three minutes of the game. The Cougars completed 8 of 17 passes for 82 yards, one touchdown and one interception.

Meantime, Central defeated Creston, 14-0, to clinch its first city championship in 11 years.

GR Herald Photo

All-City Lineman Joe Zwers and George Ingraham

Catholic Central 28
South 0
Saturday, November 12 at South Field

A muddy field slowed "Air" Catholic, but the Cougars found other ways to defeat South High 28-0 and wrap up second place in the city league. Early in the first quarter, Ray Mieras blocked a South punt that Pobojewski recovered at the 12-yard line. Pobojewski then had back-to-back runs of 9 and 2 yards and Hartnacke went over from the 1 thanks to a big push by the offensive line led by giant tackle, George Ingraham.

Weshalski dictated field position when with the wind at his back pinned South down with a 40-yard punt that rolled out of bounds at the 2. The Trojans immediately tried to kick their way out of trouble, but their punt only made it to the 32 for a CC net-gain of 10 yards. The Cougars used two passes to move the ball to the 16. Then, faced with fourth down with inches to go to goal, Hartnacke

Joe Zwers
Catholic Central
1933

An All-City end for Catholic Central in 1932, Zwers went on to letter in football at Notre Dame from 1935-1937 and served as captain of the 1937 Fighting Irish.

A Chicago area resident after his graduation from Notre Dame, Zwers passed away on January 18, 1998

CC/WC Archives

Notre Dame's Joe Zwers

pushed the ball over. Weshalski put the game out of reach with a 75-yard interception return in the fourth quarter. Catholic Central added another touchdown and a safety.

The Cougars finished the season with a 6-1-1 record and Grezcowiak, Zwers and Ingraham were named first-team All-City to complete CC's best season in nearly a decade.

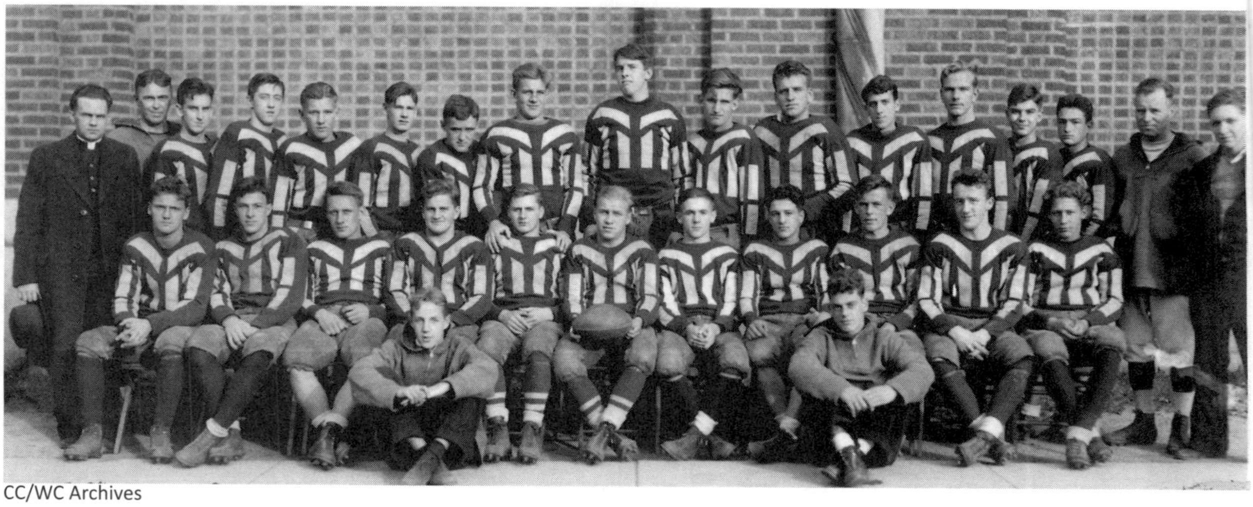

CC/WC Archives

1932 Catholic Central Team

Standing (l-r) - Fr. Sweeney, Coach McCracken, Frank Hartnacke, John McCormick, George Garcheski, Flinton Dubridge, Ed McPhilamy, George Topolski, Dave Pike, "Red" Novakoski, George Ingraham, Joe Nabkey, Wysocki, Stan Hoffman, Romeo Viventi, Asst. Coach Norm Bowbier, Asst. Jim Sweedyk

Seated - Don Vanderveen, Ray Mieras, Jerry Weshalski, Bernie Grezcowiak, Stuart Roach, Casimir Pobojewski, Ray O'Malley, John Shada, Ed Furman, Joe Zwers, Joe Godleski

1932 Schedule/Results

Head Coach – Tony McCraken

Date	Opponent	Result		Location
Sep. 17	Ionia St. Peter & Paul	Won	68-0	South Field
Sep. 24	Flint Northern	Won	20-0	Flint
Oct. 1	Ottawa Hills	Tie	0-0	Ottawa Hills Field
Oct. 8	Central	Lost	0-6	Houseman Field
Oct. 15	Union	Won	6-0	South Field
Oct. 29	Creston	Won	13-0	Ottawa Hills Field
Nov. 5	Davis Tech	Won	7-0	South Field
Nov. 12	South	Won	28-0	South Field

	Record	Pts. Scored	Pts. Allowed
Overall	6-1-1	142	6
City League	4-1-1	54	6

-1933-

Rebuilding the offensive line to an acceptable level was listed as the key to Catholic Central having a consecutive successful season. Ed Furman, John Shada and Ray Mieras were back, but who would replace George Ingraham, the giant 200-pound All-City tackle, All-State end Joe Zwers who enrolled at Notre Dame and Stewart Roche, an outstanding guard?

Catholic Central 60
Ionia St. Peter and Paul Academy 0
Saturday, September 23 at South Field

Replacing their stars didn't seem like much of an issue in the Cougars' 60-0 season-opening romp over St. Peter and Paul Academy. Then again, CC outscored the undersized Ionia eleven by 128-0 in the two most recent meetings.

Quarterback Frank Hartnacke and Johnny McCormick ran for two touchdowns each as Catholic appeared to have added speed around the flanks and inside power to its vaunted passing attack of the previous season.

Flint Northern 14
Catholic Central 7
Saturday, September 30 at Ottawa Hills Field

Scheduling a light-weight opponent for Homecoming apparently was still an undeveloped concept at Catholic Central, which lined up traditional state power Flint Northern for its first gathering of alumni.

Thousands, including numerous former players from CC's first teams, turned out to see the Cougars fall to FNHS, 14-7. Hartnacke started Catholic's 60-yard scoring drive with a 13-yard sweep and Jerry Weshalski's 9-yard dash around end resulted in a 7-0 lead. Flint Northern unleashed a relentless aerial attack to tie the score before halftime.

The Cougars' dobbers plummeted after standout left guard Edward McPhilamy suddenly staggered about the field and collapsed at midfield late in the second quarter. A police ambulance drove right onto the field to collect McPhilamy, who suffered a concussion and fractured vertebrae, and sped off with lights flashing and siren blaring.

Flint Northern came out in the second half intent on attacking McPhilamy's replacement, Stan Huffman, and drove down the field against the dispirited Cougars for the game-winning 3-yard touchdown.

GR Herald Photo

Catholic Central Alumni following the Flint Northern game.

GR Herald Photo

Grezcowiak punting the ball during the Central game.

Central 6
Catholic Central 0
Saturday, October 7 at Houseman Field

A key early season matchup that would play a part in determining the city championship may have started with high hopes for Catholic Central and arch-nemesis Central on an idyllic sun-bathed autumn afternoon. But it became a battle of survival after a steady rain arrived to turn Houseman Field into a mud pit.

The Cougars and Hilltoppers fought to a standstill until Catholic was duped by a fake punt with five minutes remaining in the game. Faced with third down at the CC 28-yard line, Central halfback Sandy Farrell dropped back as if to punt – a common strategy designed to affect field position. The Cougars dropped back off the line of scrimmage to keep the ball in play and away from their own goal line, and Farrell even swung his leg in a kicking motion.

Catholic Central		Central H. S
Mieras	LE	Hultman
Topolski	LT	Koning
Hoffman	LG	Downing
Furman	C	Melcher
Shada	RG	Wiersma
Novakoski	RT	Osmun
Godleski	RE	Camburn
Viventi	QB	Buth
Grezcowiak	LH	Ferrell
Weshalski	RH	Roose
McCormick	FB	Halbert

Catholic	0	0	0	0	0
Central	0	0	0	0	6

Touchdown – Koning
Referee– Speelman, Umpire – Greenbach, Head Linesman – Feller

GR Herald Photo

Catholic Central and Union battling to a stand-off in the mud at Island Park.

However, instead of booting the waterlogged ball, Farrell heaved it to Howard Koning, who gathered it between two CC defenders at the 5-yard line and trotted through the slop for the game's only score. The Cougars suffered their second consecutive heartbreaking loss in the waning moments at the hands of Farrell and the Hilltoppers. Catholic's highlights came in the third quarter when it put up a goal-line stand to keep Central out of the end zone, and then saw Farrell miss a short field-goal try on its ensuing drive.

Catholic Central 0
Union 0
Saturday, October 21 at Island Park

Catholic Central		Union H. S
Topolski	LE	Gronko
Mieras	LT	Hank
Hoffman	LG	Mangus
Furman	C	Miknavitch
Shada	RG	Olman
Novakoski	RT	Szczepaniuk
Godleski	RE	Schaubel
Viventi	QB	Burns
Grezcowiak	LH	Jurewic
Wisniewski	RH	Kelly
McCormick	FB	Olenczak

Catholic	0	0	0	0	0
Union	0	0	0	0	0

Referee– Strom, Umpire – Brady, Head Linesman – Walters

Health woes continued to mount for Catholic Central, which learned that Weshalski, its star halfback, suffered an appendicitis attack prior to playing traditional rival Union High. Two days later, Shada sustained a sprained collarbone in practice. The Cougars had already been playing without McPhilamy, who suffered a season-ending neck injury in the second game.

Consequently, the monsoon that swamped Island Park for the game against the West Siders could be counted as a blessing. Union out-gained CC 214-42 and had 12 first downs to two but couldn't get the ball over what was left of the goal line. Union had several scoring chances but missed field-goal attempts in the first and fourth quarters, and was turned back seven times deep in Catholic Central territory by the stubborn Cougar defense led by Shada, Viventi and Furman. The best opportunity came in the first quarter when the Cougars put up a goal-line stand that stopped Union a foot short of the end zone on fourth down.

GR Herald Photo

Leo Wisneski tries to shake a Polar Bear during the Creston game.

Catholic Central 35
Creston 0
Saturday, October 28 at South Field

Catholic Central shrugged off the doldrums that saw it score just seven points in the previous three games by flexing its offensive muscle in a 35-0 victory over Creston.

The Cougars gained 120 of their 193 yards and had six first downs in the first quarter. Grezcowiak started the scoring splurge with a 2-yard touchdown plunge. Hartnacke provided the game's big highlight with a 73-yard touchdown run in the third quarter, and Viventi, Leo Wisneski and McCormick also toted the ball across the goal line.

Catholic Central 6
Davis Tech 2
Saturday, November 4 at South Field

The offensive fireworks died down for CC a week after putting 35 on the board against Creston.

The Cougars fell behind Davis Tech 2-0 early on a bizarre officials error that actually worked in their favor after they finally showed they were capable of scoring the game-winning touchdown in the second half. The Wildcats moved into scoring position in the first quarter on a long pass. Faced with third-and-goal at the CC 9, Pete Milito's pass into the end zone fell incomplete. The officials, however, ruled that Hartnacke interfered with the receiver and awarded a safety to Davis Tech. The correct call, referee John Bos explained after the game, would have been to give the Wildcats a first down at the Catholic 1-yard line.

GR Herald Photo

Right End Joe Godleski

Still, the two points appeared to be enough to beat the Cougars, who were struggling offensively. However, late in the third quarter, Hartnacke threw to fullback Bernard Grezcowiak in the flat, and he did the rest by weaving in and out of traffic, while taking advantage of outstanding blocking, for a 33-yard touchdown reception. After the game, both coaches said they would have preferred that the officials would have made the correct ruling in the first quarter. Catholic Central coach Tony McCracken said he was confident his defense would have held Davis Tech out of the end zone on four tries from the 1, while Tech coach Cullberson was certain Milito would have been able to bust through for a touchdown.

Catholic Central 6
South 0
Saturday, November 18 at South Field

Soon after Catholic Central defeated Davis Tech, the school's administration announced that McCracken would resign at the end of the season and would be replaced by Ed Killoran, a former three-sport star at Central State Normal (Central Michigan University). Meantime, the Cougars' game scheduled for Nov. 11 against Ottawa Hills was postponed because of a snowstorm and rescheduled for Thanksgiving Day.

Catholic Central retook the field, or what was left of it after supposedly being cleared of snow, 14 days after beating Tech. The time off and wet conditions must have caused considerable rust, because the Cougars didn't pull out a 6-0 victory until the final five minutes.

Two CC drives stalled inside the Trojans' 20-yard line in the first quarter, and the Cougars were turned back after driving inside of the 5 in the third. Catholic Central finally found its scoring touch after Joe Godleski blocked a punt and recovered the loose ball at the South 20-yard line. Viventi picked up 6 yards on first down, and a 4-yard pass from Grezcowiak gave CC a first down at the 10. McCormack went through center for 5 and Weshalski plowed to the 3. On third down, Grezcowiak ran wide to the left and strung out the South tacklers before tucking the ball just inside the flag for the game-winning touchdown.

Catholic Central 7
Ottawa Hills 6
Thursday, November 30 at Ottawa Hills Field

Catholic Central sewed up second place in the city league with a 7-6 victory over Ottawa Hills on the same day Union beat Central, 13-0, to finish undefeated, unscored upon and atop the standings.

It was John Shada's birthday, but he was the one giving out gifts.

Catholic fell behind, 6-0, when Indians fullback Bernard Jefferson scampered 60 yards for a touchdown in the second quarter. Cougar passers had trouble finding their targets after halftime and threw two interceptions in the third quarter.

They weren't much more accurate in the final quarter, but Godleski set up Catholic's trying touchdown with a spectacular one-handed catch at the Ottawa Hills 16. Two plays later, Grezcowiak swept around left end for a 6-yard touchdown to set the stage for Shada with four minutes remaining.

The CC contingent included in the crowd of 3,500 fell silent as Hartnacke, the holder, smoothed a patch of grass for the all-important extra point. With Indian fans chanting, "Block that kick! Block that kick!", Shada's toe connected with the sweet spot and the ball sailed over the center of the crossbar for the winning point.

CC/WC Archives

John Shada with Ottawa Hills game ball.

CC/WC Archives

All-City Linemen Ray Mieras

Shada, Mieras and Grezkowiak represented Catholic Central on the All-City first team and Godleski was a second-team selection.

Leo Wisneski
Catholic Central
1934

Though not a star for Catholic Central during his high school football career, Leo Wisneski made a name for himself in the collegiate ranks as a three-sport athlete for Central Michigan University.

Wisneski earned 10 letters during his four-year stay at Central Michigan University - four in baseball and three each in football and basketball.

Wisneski had a career batting average above .400 in four seasons for the CMU baseball team, setting a single-season record of .486 in 1941.

He started three years in basketball, leading the Chippewas to a 40-12 record and averaging 10.8 points per game as a senior in 1941.

Quarterbacking the frosh team to an 8-0 mark in 1937, Wisneski guided the Chippewas to a 18-5-1 during his three varsity seasons and was named CMU's first football All-American in 1939.

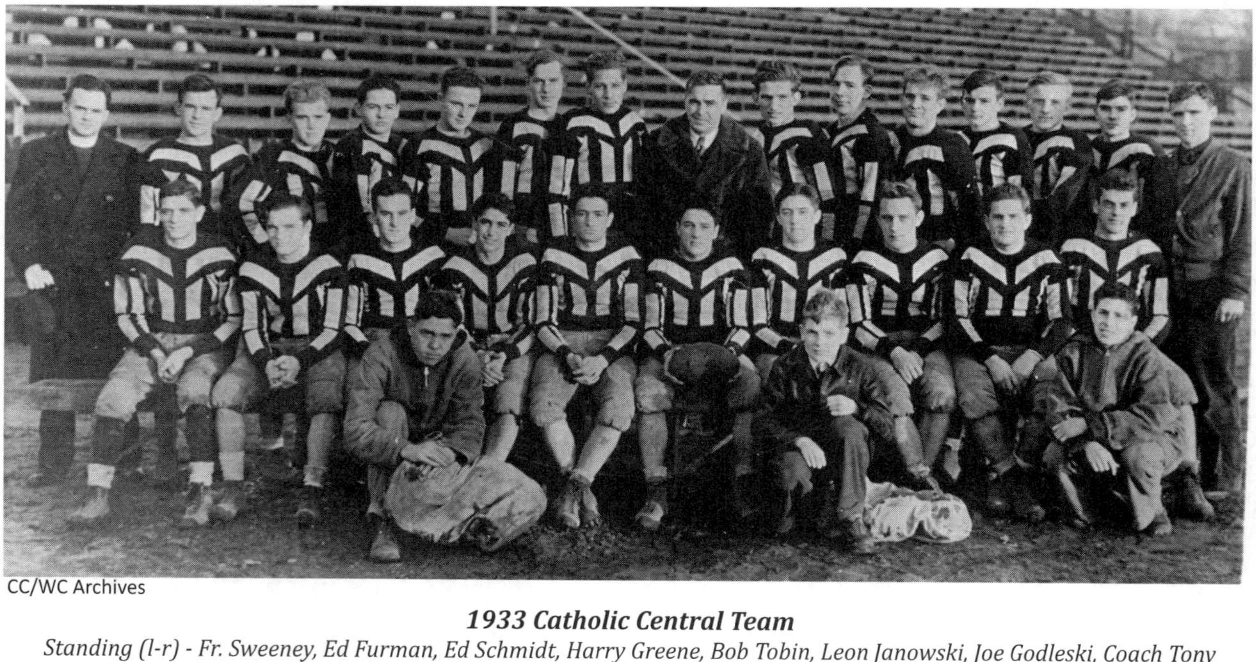

CC/WC Archives

1933 Catholic Central Team

Standing (l-r) - Fr. Sweeney, Ed Furman, Ed Schmidt, Harry Greene, Bob Tobin, Leon Janowski, Joe Godleski, Coach Tony McCracken, "Red" Novakoski, Mucynski, George Topolski, Leo Wisneski, Ted Kusto, Stan Hoffman, Ed McPhilamy
Seated - Mike Marsiglia, Bob Davidson, Frank Hartnacke, Romulus Romani, Romeo Viventi, John Shada, John McCormick, Garry Weshalski, Bernie Grezcowiak
Managers - Tom Fox, Jack Sweedyk, William Crinzi

1933 Schedule/Results
Head Coach – Tony McCraken

Date	Opponent	Result		Location
Sep. 23	Ionia St. Peter & Paul	Won	60-0	South Field
Sep. 30	Flint Northern	Lost	7-14	Ottawa Hills Field
Oct. 7	Central	Lost	0-6	Houseman Field
Oct. 21	Union	Tie	0-0	Island Park
Oct. 28	Creston	Won	35-0	South Field
Nov. 4	Davis Tech	Won	6-2	South Field
Nov. 18	South	Won	6-0	South Field
Nov. 30	Ottawa Hills	Won	7-6	Ottawa Hills Field

	Record	Pts. Scored	Pts. Allowed
Overall	5-2-1	121	28
City League	4-1-1	54	14

CHAPTER 4
The Ed Killoran Years
1934-1942

Changes that would affect the Catholic Central football program for decades to come were afoot. Island Park, the Cougars' practice site and the location of so many memorable city league games, was in danger of being crowded out by the expanding City Market. Fearful of losing its practice grounds, the Catholic Central administration appealed to the Grand Rapids City Commission for permission to practice at Rumsey Park. Meanwhile, Y-Industrial Baseball League officials asked the city to delay tearing down the bleachers and grandstand at Island Park until after the 1934 baseball season was completed. Although the city's Committee on Public Service recommended that Island Park land be given over to the growing City Market, the existing stadium wouldn't be razed until the following year because work on the new baseball facility at the corner of Valley Avenue and Fourth Street NW – Valley Field – wouldn't be completed in time. Consequently, Catholic Central would be able to conduct practices and play games at Island Park for one more season. Nevertheless, the CC varsity football team never played another game there.

The impending demise of Island Park wasn't considered much of a loss because it was universally regarded as one of the worst high-school venues in the state and a $100,000 remodeling of Houseman Field, the home of Central High School's football team, was nearing completion. Capacity was increased to 7,200, equally divided amongst the north and south seating areas. A pressbox was erected over the south stands and a giant football-shaped scoreboard was put up behind the east end zone. Goalposts were bolted to concrete anchors for easy removal to accommodate other events. The newly re-sodded field was surrounded by a quarter-mile track covered with a state-of-the-art cinder surface. Work on the new "modern" field house at the northwest corner of the field was going slowly due to a lack of funds and parking was an issue, although spectators were accustomed to parking on surrounding streets. The Hilltopper football team practiced on a field adjacent to the north stands, and it was thought that could also be used for parking. The facility was lauded as the best in the state and the possibility of playing at night came with the installation of lights in 1935.

Central, which began preseason football practice with 100 candidates, opened the new Houseman Field on Sept. 15 with a game between the varsity and the alumni. The proceeds from the game were designated for the field house and ticket booths and Michigan State College coach Charlie Bachman, who tutored Knute Rockne at Notre Dame, put on a clinic for the eight city league teams.

Catholic Central was lined up to play the Hilltoppers in the formal dedication game on Oct. 6. Both schools agreed to hold joint Homecoming celebrations in conjunction with the game. New York Yankees, Detroit Tigers and Cincinnati Reds first baseman Wally Pipp, a CC grad, was named to the Homecoming Committee.

GR Herald Photo

The "New" Houseman Field

-1934-

First-year Catholic Central coach Ed Killoran put the Cougars through a crash course on the complex Notre Dame offensive system that most college imitators needed a full season to learn. Killoran, a former standout at Central State Teachers College (Central Michigan University), used the Fighting Irish attack while leading Mount Pleasant Sacred Heart to a Class C championship.

The offense was completely different from the one the Cougars learned under Tony McCracken, but with the help of assistant coach Ted Sowle, who accompanied Killoran from Sacred Heart, CC was more than ready for its opener.

Catholic Central 39
Owosso St. Paul's 0
Saturday, September 29 at Ottawa Hills Field

With only two regulars from the '33 team in the lineup, Catholic Central destroyed Owosso St. Paul's, 39-0. The Cougars left the St. Paul's players dazed and confused with their dazzling offensive display. Right halfback Lou Rademacher scored CC's first touchdown of the season, his first of three in the game, on a 6-yard sweep around left end in the first quarter. Backup fullback Romulus Romani made it 14-0 just before halftime on a 6-yard sneak up the middle.

In the third quarter, fullback Ed Kuczynski's 22-yard run set up a 12-yard touchdown dash by left half Johnny McCormick and Rademacher burst through the line for a 47-yard touchdown. Catholic got two more touchdowns in the fourth quarter on Rademacher's 24-yard burst and on a plunge by Kuczynski, who dragged three St. Paul's tacklers with him across the goal line.

The Cougars outrushed St. Paul's 242-45 and held a 384-87 advantage in total yardage.

Central 20
Catholic Central 6
Saturday, October 6 at Houseman Field

The points didn't come nearly as easily for Catholic Central in its 20-6 loss to Central in the first game played in newly renovated Houseman Field. The traditional rival fought to a 0-0 tie that stood until the fourth quarter.

GR Herald Photo

CC Fullback Johnny McCormick runs off-tackle in the Central game.

The Hilltoppers broke out on top, 6-0, with a 2-yard run by Buth early in the final period but the Cougars countered almost immediately with a 61-yard drive fueled by McCormick's sharp passing. He completed the possession with a 2-yard plunge and the score remained tied after McCormick's pass for the extra point fell incomplete.

On fourth-and-goal at the CC 10, Central took the lead on a toss sweep and put the game away on a 80-yard run by a backup quarterback named Bentley.

Catholic Central 0
Creston 0
Saturday, October 27 at Houseman Field

GR Herald Photo

McCormick throws to Godleski during the Creston game.

A defensive battle raged between Catholic Central and Creston in the rain, snow and bitter cold until Leo Wisneski replaced McCormick in the Cougars' backfield early in the second half. However, when Wisneski left the game with an injury in the fourth quarter, the momentum dissipated as quickly as it came, and the game ended in a scoreless tie.

The first time Wisneski touched the ball, he returned a punt 20 yards to the Creston 40, but that drive ended when the Polar Bears intercepted a Wisneski pass. However, Wisneski had the Cougars back in business in the fourth quarter after Kuczynski recovered a Creston fumble at the Bears' 25. Wisneski picked up a first-down with a 9-yard run to the 15. Back-to-back runs by Wisneski and Kuczynski gave CC a first down at the 5, but the Creston defense was impenetrable for four straight downs.

The Bears couldn't move the ball forward and punted, but Wisneski was injured during the 11-yard return and left the game. McCormick returned to the backfield with CC in possession of the ball at the Creston 22, but the drive stalled after a 5-yard loss and the Bears took over on downs.

Catholic Central 6
Davis Tech 6
Saturday, November 3 at South Field

If Catholic Central's 6-6 penalty-laced tie with Davis Tech had to be described one word, it would be: "Survival," and not necessarily of the fittest.

The Cougars' disastrous first possession of the game ended when Tech blocked Kuczynski's punt and recovered at the CC 15-yard line. The Wildcats made it all the way to the 1-yard line, but Catholic survived the threat thanks to a tackle 6 yards behind the line of scrimmage on fourth down. Tech got the ball back in fine field position, nonetheless, and scored from the 7 on back-to-back runs by Tibbets as the first quarter expired.

Catholic Central's second-quarter scoring drive started with a 25-yard pass interference penalty, and left end Joe Godleski's 20-yard reception moved the ball to the Tech 10-yard line. It took McCormick, who was limping noticeably, two runs to score from there, but the dropkick for the point after missed. Catholic had a golden opportunity to end the deadlock in the third quarter after Mike Marsiglia blocked a punt and recovered the ball at the Wildcat 7. But two runs into the line were stopped for no gain, a third-down pass fell incomplete and McCormick was dropped for a big loss on fourth down. Both teams passed frantically in the fourth quarter, but couldn't connect.

Ottawa Hills 12
Catholic Central 0
Saturday, November 10 at Ottawa Hills Field

After Joe Godleski dropped what would have been a 3-yard touchdown pass on fourth down in the second quarter, Catholic Central tried to gain the upper hand in the battle for field position on the raw, cold day by receiving the second-half kickoff and immediately punting it back to Ottawa Hills via a legal "return kick."

The strategy worked to perfection -- until it backfired. The Indians took over at their own 22-yard line, and two plays later, Bernard Jefferson, their African-American captain, broke lose for a sensational 77-yard touchdown run. Shortly after the fourth quarter got underway, Jefferson intercepted a pass by McCormick and returned it to the CC 20-yard line. The powerful fullback slashed off tackle for a gain to the Cougar 10, went up the middle for 9 ½ yards on the next play and plunged in from there to personally deliver a 12-0 loss to Catholic.

South 20
Catholic Central 7
Saturday, November 17 at South Field

All that stood between South High and the city championship was 0-2-2 Catholic Central. The injury-riddled Cougars put up a good fight but could never catch up after falling behind late in the second quarter and lost 20-7.

The Trojans' Platt intercepted a pass by Godleski and returned it to the CC 33-yard line. Bob Devereaux rushed for gains of 18 and 12 yards and four plays later, John Kemperman carried it in for a 1-yard touchdown and a 7-0 lead just as the first half came to an end. Knickerbocker's 5-yard touchdown reception made it 14-0 in the third quarter, and South took advantage of Cougar fumbles to score its final TD and hold of CC the rest of the way.

Union 25
Catholic Central 0
Saturday, November 24 at South Field

GR Herald Photo

Union's fullback smashes through the center of the Catholic line for a first down.

When the season began, Catholic Central and Union were considered evenly matched, but neither was given much of a chance to win the city title. The Cougars returned just two regulars from its 1933 team and Union graduated 25 seniors. But as the season went on, the Blue and White and the Red and White took radically divergent paths.

Injuries contributed to CC's winless slate going into the season finale against its archrival while Union developed nicely behind the leadership of quarterback Dickie Burns. Each team's fate was adequately summed up in Union's 25-0 victory over the Cougars.

Catholic registered zero first downs to 15 for the West Siders and at one point in the third quarter was penalized 25 yards for illegal substitution after calling a fourth time-out to remove an injured player. Burns scored the only touchdown Union needed on a 46-yard punt return in the second quarter with no Cougar coming close to laying a paw on him.

Catholic Central (0)		Union H. S (25)
Godleski	LE	Honholt
Jankowski	LT	Schuiling
McKnight	LG	Whitecavage
Furman	C	Blashklew
Smilgus	RG	Waskiewics
O'Rourke	RT	Darbinski
Marsiglia	RE	Amon
Haas	QB	Burns
Romani	LH	Kallunas
Huyge	RH	Gamble
McCormick	FB	Olenczak

Touchdown – Burns, Amon, Olenczak (2)
PAT - Burns
Referee– Bos, Umpire – Fuller, Head Linesman – Daane

Godleski was CC's lone first-team All-City selection, and center Ed Furman and Gerald Smilgus, a left guard, earned second-team honors. The Notre Dame-bound Godleski also won the Rotary Club Award as the city's top student-athlete and was named All-State.

1934 Schedule/Results

Head Coach – Ed Killoran

Date	Opponent	Result		Location
Sep. 29	Owosso St. Paul's	Won	39-0	Ottawa Hills Field
Oct. 6	Central	Lost	6-20	Houseman Field
Oct. 27	Creston	Tie	0-0	Houseman Field
Nov. 3	Davis Tech	Tie	6-6	South Field
Nov. 12	Ottawa Hills	Lost	0-12	Ottawa Hills Field
Nov. 17	South	Lost	7-20	South Field
Nov. 24	Union	Lost	0-25	South Field

	Record	Pts. Scored	Pts. Allowed
Overall	1-4-2	58	83
City League	0-4-2	19	83

-1935-

Killoran opened CC preseason practice at Rumsey Park with nearly 50 players in uniform – fewer than the 65 who showed up for Creston's first day but more than the 30-40 who turned out at the other city schools. "We'll be bigger than last year, and smarter, and that's something," Killoran said. The coaches and players were treated to a preseason clinic presented "under the lights" at Houseman Field by Michigan State coach Charlie Bachman, Harry Kipke of the University of Michigan and the University of Detroit's Gus Dorais, the legendary former Notre Dame quarterback who threw the first pass in Fighting Irish history to Knute Rockne in 1911, and was the school's first consensus All-American. Dorais and Rockne are credited with popularizing the forward pass.

Catholic Central 25
Grandville 0
Saturday, September 21 at South Field

The Cougars passed their first test of the season with a 25-0 victory over Grandville, which was considered one of the area's strongest Class C teams. Al Lemanski scored the first touchdown of the season on a 3-yard dive, then prevented Grandville from scoring off an interception by tackling Herema at the CC 40-yard line after a 40-yard return. Floyd Rademacher's fumble recovery in Grandville territory set up a long touchdown run by Norb Grezcowiak, the younger brother of former CC All-City fullback Bernard Grezcowiak. In the fourth quarter, Stapleton ran for a 25-yard touchdown and Lemanski added a 55-yarder to close out the scoring. The only negative for Catholic was its 85-0 edge in penalty yards.

Catholic Central 25
Grand Haven 0
Saturday, September 28 at Grand Haven

The Cougars lost two fumbles near the Grand Haven goal line and turned the ball over on downs while in scoring position once in the first quarter, but still won handily, 25-0, thanks to the dynamic running of right half Johnny Pattock. Finally, after Pattock put CC in another first-and-goal situation, fullback Bernie "Red" Tofel plowed into the end zone from 2 yards out and Pattock's placekick put the Cougars ahead, 7-0. In the second quarter, Pattock's 33-yard gain set up CC's second touchdown, which came on another 2-yard burst by Tofel, who scored standing up.

Pattock burned Grand Haven in the third quarter after reversing his field during a 53-yard scoring jaunt and Joe Kahnoski, a backup running back, scored in the final period.

Central 13
Catholic Central 12
Saturday, October 5 at Houseman Field

Pattock's missed extra point in the third quarter haunted Catholic Central, which failed to break the Central curse for the 10th time in 12 meetings and lost 13-12. The Hilltoppers took a 7-0 lead in the second quarter on Johnny Buth's 2-yard touchdown run – which was aided by a CC offside penalty two plays earlier – and successful placekick for the point after.

The Cougars got on the board in the third quarter on a possession that saw them converting three fourth-downs. On fourth-and-2 at the Central 45, Pattock broke through the line and averted the secondary tacklers by sprinting toward the northwest corner of the field. Just as the Hilltopper safety appeared to have the angle on Pattock, he cut back to the center of the field and scored unmolested. Pattock struck the ball well on the placekick for the point-after, but the ball hooked left at the last instant and CC trailed, 7-6. Central regained the lead after intercepting a Pattock pass and Buth bulled over for a 2-yard touchdown on the first play of the fourth quarter. Eddie Galant broke through to block Buth's extra point, and the Cougars were a touchdown and an extra point away from tying.

Catholic Central		Central H. S
Rademacher	LE	Anderson
Laskowski	LT	Christianson
Zakem	LG	Merdzinski
Galant	C	Ripmaster
Merdzinski	RG	Hudson
Jankowski	RT	Rahn
Long	RE	Stoebler
Milan	QB	Barrows
Pattock	LH	Charon
Lamanski	RH	Withrow
Tofel	FB	Buth

Catholic	0	0	6	6	12
Central	0	7	0	6	13

Touchdown – Pattock (2), But (2)
PAT - Buth
Referee– Roper, Umpire – Speelman, Head Linesman – Brady

Late in the fourth quarter, Kahonski repeatedly battered the Central defense for good gains until he reached the 13-yard line. With the Hilltopper front seven suitably tenderized, Pattock trotted through a gaping hole and covered the remaining distance to cut Central's lead to one point. Catholic elected to run for the point, but Kahonski was stuffed at the line by a committee of Hilltopper tacklers. The Cougars outgained Central by 140 yards (249-109), but "The Jinx" continued.

Just 2,000 spectators turned out for the "Battle of the Johnnies" at Houseman Field. What was considered the smallest crowds in series history was attributed to the rabid interest in the radio broadcast of the World Series game between the Detroit Tigers and the Chicago Cubs.

GR Herald Photo

Johnny Pattock misses the PAT after CC's first touchdown.

Union 7
Catholic Central 0
Saturday, October 19 at Ninth Street Field

After a bye week, CC traveled to Union's new Ninth Street Field, located in the shadows of the American Seating Co., full of optimism. The Red and White was jeered by fans a week earlier after playing poorly in a 14-0 loss to Central, which had defeated CC by a point, and morale was said to be down. The Cougars couldn't overcome their mistakes, however, and lost, 7-0, to Union.

The game developed into a punting duel from the start, and sadly for CC, that's how it ended.

With less than a minute remaining in the third quarter, Lemanski dropped back to punt from deep in Catholic Central territory. Since he hadn't faced much of a rush from Union all game long, Lemanski addressed this particular kick with deliberate patience. This time, however, Jack Amon blasted through the Cougar line and blocked the kick. Amon reached Lemanski so quickly, the ball hit him in a stomach before hitting the ground, and he fell on it at the CC 18. The Catholic defense forced Union into a fourth-and-5 situation at the 13, but Vanderlaan's pass to Amon picked up the first down by the stubby nose of the football.

After Catholic was penalized half the distance to the goal for being offside on fourth down, Vanderlaan drove into the pile and moved the ball over the goal line only by an inch or two. At least two fumbles and a couple of interceptions ended legitimate scoring chances for Catholic Central throughout the game.

Catholic Central		Union H. S
Rademacher	LE	Honholt
Laskowski	LT	VanDestinon
Zakem	LG	Zukowski
Galant	C	Newman
Merdzinski	RG	Michalak
Jankowski	RT	Drabinski
Long	RE	Amon
Milan	QB	VanderLaan
Pattock	LH	Kallunas
Lamanski	RH	Klein
Tofel	FB	Oleszczek

Catholic	0	0	0	0	0
Union	0	0	0	7	7

Touchdown – VanderLaan
PAT - Drabinski
Referee– Bos, Umpire – Churm, Head Linesman – Gunther

Catholic Central 6
Creston 0
Saturday, October 26 at Houseman Field

The Cougars vented the frustration built up by back-to-back narrow losses to Central and Union by pounding Creston. The size of the final 6-0 advantage wasn't indicative of Catholic's dominance.

Creston managed just 99 yards of total offense against the CC defense, which held the Polar Bears to 2-for-14 passing and had two interceptions. Tofel, the Catholic defensive halfback, accounted for the first pickoff – off a Meinke pass to the flat – early in the second half and returned it 25 yards for the game-winning touchdown.

GR Herald Photo
Union's Honholt caught from behind by an unidentified Catholic Central player.

The Cougar offense moved the ball to the Creston 5-yard line on its ensuing possession, but turned the ball over on downs. Catholic fans got nervous over the prospect of seeing another win slip away in the final moments when Creston advanced to the CC 20 with under five minutes to play. However, Tofel intercepted Meinke for the second time to end the threat. Catholic Central amassed 186 yards of total offense in its first city victory of the season.

Catholic Central 0
Davis Tech 0
Saturday, November 2 at South Field

Davis Tech was credited with a mild upset when it recovered six of eight Catholic Central fumbles and forced the Cougars to settle for a 0-0 tie. It was a bad day all around for CC, which also threw three interceptions and had a 51-yard touchdown run by Lucien Bartnick nullified by a clipping penalty in the second quarter. A minute later, Bartnick broke into the open from his own 16-yard line and seemingly headed for an uncontested touchdown, but after sprinting by the last Tech defender, slipped and fell at midfield.

GR Herald Photo
CC's Johnny Pattock breaks off a big run in the Creston game.

The debacle started when Tofel fumbled the ball away at the Wildcat 5-yard line in the first quarter. Davis Tech never had a legitimate scoring opportunity and had just four first downs to CC's 14. And with a 224-90 advantage in total offense, it was improbable that Catholic couldn't have won the game. But the Cougars' nine turnovers told the real story.

Catholic Central 37
Ottawa Hills 0
Saturday, November 9 at Ottawa Hills Field

Catholic Central showed what it could do when it played a "clean" game. By eliminating the turnovers and penalties that plagued them in previous games, the Cougars demolished winless Ottawa Hills, 37-0. It didn't hurt that they entered the game with a chip on their shoulders left over from their mistake-plagued performance against Davis Tech.

Catholic Central looked like the best team in the city, bar none, right from the outset. After CC did its job by stopping the Indians on third down at their own seven, Pattock took the offense out of the equation with a hip-shaking, 45-yard punt return for a touchdown with barely two minutes gone in the game. On the second play of the second quarter, Pattock rumbled through the Ottawa line for a 4-yard touchdown and the game was all but decided.

The Cougars converted James McInerny's recovery of an Ottawa fumble at its own 17 into a 2-yard touchdown run by Tofel. Then, after the Cougars blocked an Indian punt and Rademacher recovered, Stapleton threw a 37-yard touchdown pass to Long for a 25-0 halftime lead. Pattock scored again on a 10-yard rush in the third quarter.

South 7
Catholic Central 0
Saturday, November 16 at South Field

Catholic Central had a chance for a last hurrah in the 1935 season. The Cougars would wreak havoc on the city championship race if they could beat South, which was in a virtual tie with Union and Central for first place.

The Cougars proved they had a championship caliber team by outgaining South, 156-127, and collecting eight first downs to two for the Trojans. But, the only numbers that mattered were on the scoreboard, and they favored South, 7-0.

If CC hadn't returned to its turnover ways, it might have played the role of the spoiler. The Cougars not only fumbled the ball on the opening kickoff – they retained possession because the ball went out of bounds before South could recover – but Lemanski coughed up the ball on their first play as well, and this time the Trojans did recover. At least Lemanski atoned for his mistake by intercepting a pass.

In the second quarter, Johnny Kemperman intercepted a CC pass and returned it to midfield. On the next play, Bob Devereaux slashed through the Cougar line, sidestepped a defensive back and ran the distance for a 48-yard touchdown. Kemperman held Catholic at bay the rest of the way with his masterful punting. The Cougars never got closer than the South 35.

Eddie Galant represented Catholic on the All-City first team and Lemanski and Chester Laskowski earned second-team notice.

Catholic Central		South H. S
Zwers	LE	Hubbard
Ingraham	LT	Ross
Roche	LG	Knowles
Furman	C	McPhilamy
Shada	RG	Calabrino
Mieras	RT	Lubdell
Vanderveen	RE	Spears
Hartnacke	QB	Reynolds
Grezcowiak	LH	Wisner
Weshalske	RH	Burns
Pobojewski	FB	Sheets

Catholic	0	0	0	0	0
South	0	7	0	0	7

Touchdowns – Devereaux
PAT – Devereaux
Referee– Conger, Umpire – Coryell, Head Linesman – Waters

GR Herald Photo

CC's Al Lemanski runs for daylight against South.

1935 Schedule/Results
Head Coach – Ed Killoran

Date	Opponent	Result		Location
Sep. 21	Grandville	Won	25-0	South Field
Sep. 28	Grand Haven	Won	25-0	Grand Haven
Oct. 5	Central	Lost	12-13	Houseman Field
Oct. 19	Union	Lost	0-7	Ninth Street Field
Oct. 26	Creston	Won	6-0	Houseman Field
Nov. 02	Davis Tech	Tie	0-0	South Field
Nov. 9	Ottawa Hills	Won	37-0	Ottawa Hills Field
Nov. 16	South	Lost	0-7	South Field

	Record	Pts. Scored	Pts. Allowed
Overall	4-3-1	105	27
City League	2-3-1	55	27

-1936-

Catholic Central 37
Reed City 0
Saturday, September 26 at Ottawa Hills Field

Left halfback Lucien "Lu" Bartnick scored all of Catholic Central's points in a 37-0 season-opening romp over Reed City. The six-touchdown performance was so impressive, Bartnick was dubbed the "Galloping Ghost" in deference to former Illinois great Red Grange. The Reed City defense had little success at tackling the phantom speedster recruited from the CC track and field team.

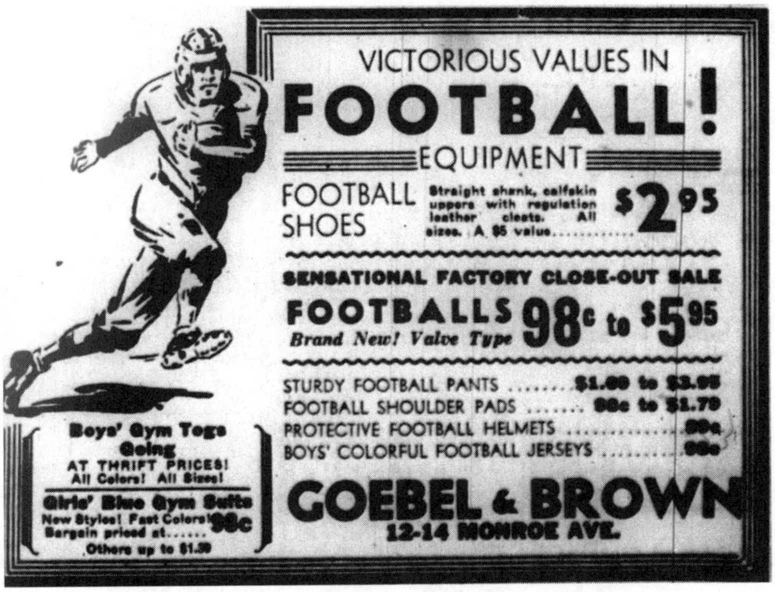

GR Herald Photo

Goebel and Brown Ad in The Grand Rapids Herald.

A CC fumble recovery at the Reed City 26-yard line on the first play of the game led to Bartnick's 2-yard touchdown run. On Reed City's next possession, Merslo Patterson blocked a punt and Bartnick ran the ball in from 14 yards out.

Bartnick completed a 25-yard pass to Patterson to set up his third score, which came on a 20-yard burst in the second quarter. After a Reed City punt and runs by Charles Pobojewski and Patterson, Bartnick made the score 23-0 with a 13-yard trot into the end zone and his only successful kick for the point after. Norb Grezcowiak raced 30 yards to set up Bartnick's fifth touchdown, which covered 36 yards in the third quarter. He added a 9-yarder later in the period

Catholic Central 21
Grand Haven 13
Friday, October 2 at Houseman Field

Catholic Central came back from a two-touchdown deficit in the third quarter to defeat Grand Haven, 21-13, in the first night game in school history. Grand Haven struck quickly in the first quarter after Riemersma returned a Roman Kaman punt 25 yards and then picked up another 25 on the first play from scrimmage. Two plays later, Nietring put GHHS ahead 7-0 with an 11-yard touchdown jaunt and his kick for the PAT.

GR Herald Photo

Lucien Bartnick on one of his six touchdown runs versus Reed City.

What had become a punting duel went bad for CC in the third quarter when Kaman's punt was blocked and Nietring recovered the ball in the end zone for a touchdown and a 13-0 lead.

Bartnick kick-started the Cougars with a good kick return and 33 rushing yards on their next three plays. The drive ended on a 13-yard run by Bartnick, Kaman's 9-yard plunge and Gresczcowiak's 1-yard dive into the end zone. Catholic took its first lead, 14-13, later in the quarter on a 24-yard touchdown pass from Bartnick to Patterson, the left end. Bartnick completed the greatest comeback in school history with a 20-yard touchdown run.

Catholic Central 12
Creston 6
Saturday, October 10 at Ninth Street Field

Bartnick continued to run wild for Catholic Central, and his two touchdowns were the difference in a 12-6 city league-opening victory over Creston. The game wasn't as close as the score indicated, as CC failed to cash in on five or six other legitimate scoring opportunities.

After the Cougars returned a partially blocked punt to the Creston 3-yard line, Bartnick ran the ball in from there for a 6-0 first-quarter lead. Bartnick lined up to kick the extra point, but when the ball got away from the holder, he picked it up and tried to improvise but his dropkick just missed. Another break led to CC's second score. On the fifth play after Catholic recovered a fumble at the Creston 22, the Cougars ran a criss-cross fake in the backfield with dizzying precision and Bartnick sped 5 yards for a touchdown before the Bears knew he had the ball.

Later in the quarter, Creston used a couple of long passes to set up Morse's 11-yard touchdown run off a reverse. James McInerny thwarted the Bears' final opportunity to win with an interception in the fourth quarter.

Union 15
Catholic Central 0
Saturday, October 24 at South Field

The difference in the highly anticipated showdown between Cougar sensation Lucien Bartnick and Union High dynamic quarterback Kozlowski was an inch, maybe two, in CC's disappointing 15-0 loss.

Catholic suffered a relapse of "fumbleitis," the malady that sabotaged its success in '35, in the first half. The Cougars put the ball on the ground twice in the first quarter, and in the second, Bartnick mishandled a snap while attempting to punt from the CC end zone. He covered the ball for a safety and Union led, 2-0. Meantime, on Union's possession following the free kick, Kozlowski churned for good yardage on three carries to the CC 5-yard line. The Cougars held until fourth down when Kozlowski charged into the line, fumbled the ball into the end zone and recovered for the touchdown giving the Red and White a 9-0 lead.

Catholic Central		Union H. S
McInerny	LE	Kurtyka
Ocak	LT	Bailis
Freeman	LG	Vanderlaan
Brogger	C	Miller
Naplepalski	RG	Michalak
Muczynski	RT	Kelzeski
Patterson	RE	Newman
Cebelak	QB	Jackin
Bartnick	LH	Gregory
Grezcowiak	RH	Amon
Kaman	FB	Mercer

Catholic	0	0	0	0	0
Union	0	9	0	6	15

Touchdown – Kozlowski, Miller
Referee– Churm, Umpire – Daane, Head Linesman – Knutson

Bartnick, a threat to score on any play, appeared to have tightened up the game with an 80-yard sprint for a touchdown, but an official ruled his toe touched the sideline at the Union 47. Catholic Central desperately tried to pass its way back into contention, but that strategy backfired when a pass by Greszcowiak was deflected at the line. Union defensive center Miller plucked the wobbling ball out of the air and ran it back 51 yards for the game-clinching score.

Catholic Central 20
Ottawa Hills 20
Friday, October 30 at Houseman Field

In response to complaints from neighboring residents regarding late-night rowdiness following games at Houseman Field, the Grand Rapids Board of Education moved kickoff for the Catholic Central-Ottawa Hills game, and all those thereafter, up an hour to 7:30 p.m. But that just reduced the wait for the duel between Bartnick and splendid Indian running back Ward Walstrom. Tickets for reserved seating went on sale at three downtown locations: Philbrick's, Goebel & Brown Sporting Goods and Joe Donahue's.

GR Herald Photo
Union's Kozlowski finds a hole in the Catholic line while Norb Grezcowiak (20) and James McInerny (8) close in.

Bartnick and Walstrom didn't disappoint in a 20-20 tie that might have left the 4,000 fans in attendance unfulfilled if not for the thrilling nature of the game. On the second play of the game, Bartnick slipped through a crease created on the right side of the Cougar line, cut back across the grain of the defense and raced 79 yards for a touchdown and a 6-0 lead. Five plays after the Indians recovered a fumble at the CC 19 in the second quarter, Walstrom tied the score with a 1-yard dive. Later in the quarter, Bartnick's 19-yard run set up Greszcowiak's 1-yard plunge for a TD, and Bartnick's PAT gave Catholic a 13-6 lead. On Ottawa's ensuing possession, Walstrom dropped back to pass but when he couldn't find an open receiver, scrambled for 35 yards to the CC 24. With under two minutes remaining in the second quarter, Walstrom tied the score with a 20-yard touchdown pass to Chatterdon.

On the second play of the third quarter, Bartnick threw deep, but Walstrom intercepted and returned it 70 yards for the go-ahead touchdown, 20-13. Kaman's 16-yard return of the ensuing kickoff and Bartnick's 44-yard dash set up Greszcowiak's 14-yard run through a big hole up the middle. Bartnick kicked the all-important extra point to tie.

The back-and-forth theme shifted to the defenses in the fourth quarter when Catholic Central stopped the Indians on downs on its 18 and Ottawa held the Cougars out from its own 22.

Catholic Central 27
Davis Tech 0
Saturday, November 7 at South Field

Davis Tech sprinter Pete Dykhouse got the better of Bartnick during the 1935 track and field season, but Bartnick exacted his revenge with two touchdowns in Catholic's 27-0 win over the Wildcats on the gridiron. On CC's first scoring drive, Bartnick completed a 35-yard pass to Patterson and then covered the final 15 yards on two runs for a 7-0 lead. Bartnick made it 14-0 when, on the third play of the third quarter, he eluded a host of Tech tacklers en route to a 52-yard touchdown.

Patterson, who batted down four of eight Wildcat passes, also got his paw on a punt in the fourth quarter. Without breaking stride, Patterson snared the wildly bouncing ball with one hand and returned about 25 yards for a touchdown. The Cougars put the game away moments later after recovering a Dykhouse fumble at his own 23.

Catholic Central		South H. S
Patterson	LE	Stellini
Brogger	LT	Eckhardt
Freeman	LG	Matson
Keating	C	Trimpe
Naplepalski	RG	Savage
Muczynski	RT	Vanderhull
McInerny	RE	Gibbs
Cebelak	QB	Stevens
Bartnick	LH	Mitchell
Grezcowiak	RH	Kemperman
Kaman	FB	Pifferella

Catholic	0	0	0	6	6
South	0	12	0	2	14

Touchdowns – Bartnick, Kemperman, Gibbs
Referee– Hoekee, Umpire – Coryell, Head Linesman – Brady

Three plays later, Bernard Friar, who replaced Bartnick at left half, threw a 10-yard touchdown pass to McInerny. Catholic Central outgained Tech, 210-41, and Patterson had the best defensive play of the game when he broke through the Wildcat front wall, batted down a lateral and recovered the fumble 15 yards behind the line of scrimmage.

South 14
Catholic Central 6
Saturday, November 14 at South Field

Bartnick returned a South fumble 99 yards for a fourth-quarter touchdown, but it wasn't enough to prevent a 14-6 defeat that knocked Catholic Central out of contention for the city championship.

The field-length dash cut the league-leading Trojans' lead to 12-6, and the CC defense stopped them cold on their next possession. However, Friar misjudged a punt, which bounced off of him at the 28-yard line, and South recovered at the Catholic 26. It looked like South was going to break the game open, but John Kemperman fumbled and the Cougars recovered at the 10. Catholic couldn't pick up a first down, and the game fell out of reach when the snap from center flew over the head of Bartnick, who was going to punt out of the end zone, and South scored a safety.

After stopping the Trojans again, the Cougars marched the ball down the field, but the game ended on Bartnick's final 3-yard run to the South 2. A touchdown and an extra point wouldn't have been enough, regardless.

GR Herald Photo

CC's Lucien Bartnick (left) approaches South's John Kemperman an instant before Kemperman's fumble and Bartnick's 99-yard return.

Central 13
Catholic Central 7
Saturday, November 21 at Houseman Field

Catholic Central		Central H. S
McInerny	LE	Anderson
Brogger	LT	Pound
Freeman	LG	Hudson
Keating	C	Gogo
Naplepalski	RG	Hastie
Muczynski	RT	Lillie
Patterson	RE	Ogren
Staskiewicz	QB	Barrows
Bartnick	LH	Idema
Grezcowiak	RH	Kock
Kaman	FB	Charon

Catholic	0	0	0	7	7
Central	7	6	0	0	13

Touchdown – Quigley, Kok, Bartnick
PAT – Barrows, Bartnick
Referee– Brady, Umpire – Speelman, Head Linesman – Roper

Even though Catholic Central could make a legitimate claim that it beat itself with mistakes, it didn't take away the stigma of losing to Central again. With a 2-2-1 city record, the Cougars appeared to be at least somewhat better than the Hilltoppers at 1-3.

However, CC played giveaway all day and lost, 13-7. In the first quarter, Central tried to give the ball back to the Cougars on successive punts, but CC was offside both times. After retaining the ball near midfield thanks to the penalties, the Hilltoppers drove all the way to the 5-yard line, where they ran out of downs. When Catholic failed to pick up a first down, Bartnick lined up to punt from his own end zone with a strong wind blowing at his back. But instead of getting the Cougars out of trouble, Bartnick shanked the kick and it came down at the CC 3, where Central's Kolk corralled it before taking credit for a football oddity, a 3-yard punt return for a touchdown.

On the ensuing drive, Bartnick threw an interception to Hilltopper halfback Charon at the Central 28. The Hilltoppers drove 72 yards and increased their lead to 13-0 on Barrows' 14-yard touchdown pass to Quigley. After an offside penalty moved the ball back to the Central 13 on Catholic's final possession of the first half, an 11-yard Bartnick-to-Cebelak pass came up 2 yards short as time expired.

Catholic staged a furious rally in the fourth quarter, and was only a touchdown and an extra point away from victory after Bartnick swept around left end for a 36-yard TD. On the Cougars' last gasp of the game, Kaman, Greszcowiak and Bartnick drove the ball down the field, with the hard-charging Kaman's 8-yard blast giving CC a first-and-goal at the Central 8 with two minutes to go. Bartnick was dropped for a 7-yard loss on first down and gained 2 on second. On third down, Bartnick threw a perfect sideline pass to Greszcowiak, who started running before securing the ball and crossed the goal line without it. A fourth-down incompletion ended Catholic's hope for a comeback and winning city record.

Bartnick was a cinch All-City pick and Patterson joined him on the first team. End Bob Anderson and guard Chuck Freeman were second-team picks. Meantime, former Cougar end Joe Zwers started every game at Notre Dame.

Lucien Bartnick
Catholic Central
1937

After an outstanding senior season on the gridiron and a city championship in the 100-yard dash the following spring, Lucien Bartnick moved on to Central Michigan University to continue his athletic and acdemic career.

An honor student at CMU and a four-year letterwinner in football, Bartnick also excelled in basketball, track and gymnastics for the Chippewas.

After coaching the Mt. Pleasant Sacred Heart football team in 1942, Bartnick returned to Catholic Central in the spring of 1943 to coach baseball. He was to assist with the football and basketball teams during the 1943-44 season but passed away unexpectedly with a heart attack on June 30, 1943.

1936 Schedule/Results
Head Coach – Ed Killoran

Date	Opponent	Result		Location
Sep.26	Reed City	Won	37-0	Ottawa Hills Field
Oct. 2	Grand Haven	Won	21-13	Houseman Field
Oct. 10	Creston	Won	12-6	Ninth Street Field
Oct. 24	Union	Lost	0-15	South Field
Oct. 30	Ottawa Hills	Tie	20-20	Houseman Field
Nov. 7	Davis Tech	Won	27-0	South Field
Nov. 14	South	Lost	6-14	South Field
Nov. 21	Central	Lost	7-13	Houseman Field

	Record	Pts. Scored	Pts. Allowed
Overall	4-3-1	130	81
City League	2-3-1	72	68

-1937-

Catholic Central 12
Jackson 6
Friday, September 17 at Jackson

An interesting rebuilding job awaited Catholic Central. Lucien Bartnick's meteoric prep career was over after just one spectacular season, but hard-charging 185-pound fullback Roman Kaman, fleet-footed backs Norb Greszcowiak and Lou Cebelak, and Charles Pobojewski, a gifted end, returned. However, second-team All-City guard Chuck Freeman was the Cougars' only returning experienced lineman.

Nevertheless, CC unleashed a powerful running attack in its opener while defeating Jackson High, 12-6. Pobojewski put the Cougars ahead 6-0 when he fell on Viking halfback Grosciewski's fumbled snap in the end zone in the second quarter. After the "Prison City Boys" tied the score in the third, Kaman capped a 60-yard drive with a 6-yard touchdown early in the fourth.

Catholic Central 38
South Bend St. Hedwig 0
Friday, September 24 at Houseman Field

Playing at Houseman Field under a new set of lights, four towers instead of three and 35-40 feet closer to the field, Catholic Central trimmed South Bend (Ind.) St. Hedwig, 38-0, in a driving rainstorm. The Cougars were dominant while scoring 19 points in each half, but St. Hedwig made things a lot easier for them by attempting a total of 20 passes in the first and second quarters and only two runs when the conditions dictated an opposite strategy.

Running the ball worked like a charm for CC. Greszcowiak rushed for four touchdowns of 16, 79, 15 and 40 yards, Staskiewicz ran one in from 14 yards and Kaman bowled St. Hedwig's over for a 3-yard score.

Catholic Central 25
Grand Haven 0
Saturday, October 2 at Grand Haven

Catholic Central completed its domination of non-league opponents with a 25-0 victory against Grand Haven High at Ferry Field. The Cougars outscored their out-of-town foes, 75-6, and appeared to be finely tuned for city competition.

It took awhile for CC to get rolling, but once it did, it turned out touchdowns like a well-oiled machine. Cebelak took advantage of outstanding blocking to get things started with a 45-yard punt return for a touchdown midway through the second quarter. Grand Haven made its best bid to tie the score with a 52-yard pass play, which included a lateral, to the CC 29, but Greszkowiak snuffed out the drive with an interception. The Cougars overcame two 15-yard penalties with 34- and 20-yard gains by Greszcowiak and Cebelak on their first drive of the second half to pave the way for Cebelak's 18-yard touchdown run.

Greszcowiak ran 56 yards for CC's third touchdown and John Dudley intercepted a pass in the fourth quarter to set up the final score which came on Kaman's 4-yard blast after the Cougars were penalized on previous plays for holding and offsides.

Catholic Central 20
Union 0
Saturday, October 9 at Ninth Street Field

The Cougars conjured up memories of their glorious 1923 city championship team with a 20-0 trouncing of crosstown rival Union before a crowd of 5,000 at Ninth Street Field. The victory was a tribute to power football and improved Catholic's record to 4-0.

Archives, Grand Rapids Public Library

CC's Norb Grezcowiak looks to turn the corner against the Redhawks.

Catholic Central		Union H. S
Patterson	LE	Kurtyka
Brogger	LT	Bailis
Freeman	LG	Vanderlaan
Keating	C	Miller
Naplepalski	RG	Michalak
Muczynski	RT	Kelzeski
Mclnerny	RE	Newman
Cebelak	QB	Jackin
Bartnick	LH	Gregory
Grezcowiak	RH	Amon
Kaman	FB	Mercer

Catholic	6	0	14	0	20
Union	0	0	0	0	0

Touchdown – Kaman, Walsh, Grezcowiak
PAT - Pobojewski
Referee– Knutson, Umpire – Bowbeer, Head Linesman – McGavin

The West Siders had a formidable passer in halfback Prominski, but he was no match for a Catholic Central backfield boasting Kaman, Greszcowiak and Cebelak, who got the Cougars started with a punt return to the 45 and runs of 25 and 10 yards. Kaman rambled for another 10 to the Union 10 and Greszcowiak swept in from there for a 6-0 lead. The feisty Cougars suffered a bad break when Tom Schoen was ejected for slugging, and the 24-yard penalty, marked off half the distance to the goal, set Union up at the CC 20. However, Catholic stopped the threat by knocking the ball loose for a fumble and Greszcowiak shook free for a 48-yard gain on the next play.

Kaman all but put the game out of reach in the third quarter when he intercepted a long Prominski pass and returned it 40 yards down the sideline for a touchdown. Union also had a player, Mikita, ejected for slugging, and after the 16-yard penalty was walked off and Pobojewski threw Prominiski for a 10-yard loss, the Red and White punted. Kaman took advantage of the good field position and his pass, Catholic's first of the day, found Walsh for a 34-yard score. It was CC's fourth victory over Union in series history.

Archives, Grand Rapids Public Library

Union's Prominski finds himself surrounded by the Catholic Central defense.

Catholic Central 32
Ottawa Hills 6
Saturday, October 16 at South Field

The spotlight shifted from Catholic Central's powerful offense to its stifling defense during its 32-6 trouncing of Ottawa Hills. All the Cougar offense did was convert blocked punts and interceptions into touchdowns.

Catholic's first score came after Bob Long blocked an Indian punt and Walsh recovered at the 10-yard line. Two plays later, CC perfectly executed a Notre Dame-style reverse and Cebelak walked into the end zone from 7 yards out. After an exchange of punts, Staskiewicz threw a 21-yard pass to Cebelak in the deep corner of the end zone to put Catholic ahead 13-0 in the first quarter. Ottawa momentarily stayed in the game when the ball popped out of Greszcowiak's hands when he tried to stiff-arm a tackler, and Les Gaunt plucked the fumble out of the air and ran it back 25 yards for a touchdown.

Kaman's interception set up his own 1-yard plunge into the end zone just before halftime, and he put the game out of reach with a 26-yard touchdown pass to Jim Walsh in the third quarter. Kaman added a 5-yard touchdown run in the fourth quarter to put the finishing touches on CC's 2-0 start in city league play and 5-0 overall record.

Creston 20
Catholic Central 13
Saturday, October 23 at Houseman Field

Catholic Central's ground-gaining trio was outshone by Creston halfback Chuck DeShane in a crushing 20-13 defeat. On the fifth play of the game, DeShane followed up a CC penalty and his own 22-yard jaunt with a touchdown. DeShane broke several tackles during his 20-yard touchdown run that put the Cougars in a 13-0 hole midway through the second quarter.

Catholic Central battled right back on the ensuing possession with a 68-yard scoring drive which Kaman capped with a 9-yard touchdown pass to Cebelak, who sidestepped a tackler on his way to the end zone. The Cougars tied the score by opening the second half with an 80-yard march. Kaman completed an 18-yard pass to Cebelak to set up the latter's 6-yard touchdown run behind a line that steamrolled the Creston defense. Undaunted, DeShane set up the Bears' winning score with a 60-yard punt that was downed at the CC 5. Catholic immediately tried to punt out of trouble on first down, but Kaman's kick from the end zone was knocked down at the line of scrimmage and DeShane needed just two plays to score from the 5.

Central 25
Catholic Central 7
Friday, November 5 at Houseman Field

Catholic Central had a good team, but it couldn't keep pace with what was being considered among the very best in Central High School history. The 25-7 loss saddled the Cougars with a two-game losing streak and all but eliminated them from the city title hunt.

Massive fullback Ed Ripmaster scored on a run of 17 yards and threw for a 16-yard touchdown pass – after fading back 20 yards in the first quarter, he pounded through the line for a 6-yard score in the second and battered the CC defense for a 49-yard rushing TD in the third before the Cougars finally got on the board. Staskiewicz averted the shutout with a 1-yard sneak with 45 seconds remaining in the game. Central blocked the kick for extra point, but Cebelak scooped up the loose ball and ran it over the goal line for the point.

Catholic Central 18
Davis Tech 0
Saturday, November 13 at Ninth Street Field

In desperate need of a victory, Catholic Central couldn't have been catching Davis Tech at a worse time. The winless Wildcats were even hungrier for a win, and it was their Homecoming. "Hammering" Roman Kaman wasn't about to be done-in by sentiment, however, and ran for two touchdowns and passed for another to lead the Cougars to an 18-0 win.

Catholic Central right tackle Roman Snow recovered a fumble at the Tech 20-yard line to set up Kaman's bronco-busting 16-yard touchdown in the first quarter. Snow's third fumble recovery of the first half, at the Wildcat 26, opened the door for Kaman's 22-yard touchdown romp, and in the fourth quarter, Kaman threw a 45-yard touchdown pass to Jim Walsh. Kaman was all over the field during the game. He also recovered a fumble and batted down a fourth-down pass to end one Tech possession.

Catholic Central 14
South 0
Saturday, November 21 at South Field

The Cougars may have been out of city league title contention, but they had a say in who would win the championship. The Trojans entered the game in a virtual tie with Central for the league lead. South had a 3-0-1 record, including a 6-6 tie against the Hilltoppers, who were 3-0-2. Catholic Central's 14-0 victory over the Trojans, combined with Central's victory over Davis Tech, settled the debate regardless of the outcome of South's finale against Union.

South entered the game minus star punter Pete Mitchell, but CC was without the services of standout guard Chuck Freeman, who missed most of the season with an injury, and suited up one last time only for a ceremonial starting assignment.

GR Herald Photo

Norb Grezcowiak negotiates the snowy field and South's defense.

South gambled twice against the Cougars, and lost both times. After Dood of the Trojans thwarted a second-quarter CC threat with an interception at their own 18, they tried to pass out of the shadow of their own goalpost and Staskiewicz intercepted right back, returning the ball to the 15. Three plays later, Cebelak tip-toed over the snow and through the South defense for a 14-yard touchdown and a 7-0 lead.

The Trojans must have been overcome by amnesia in the fourth quarter because after getting the ball back on downs at their own 20, Gibbs attempted a pass which was intercepted by Kaman, who ran it back for a touchdown. The Cougars held a 178-69 advantage in total offense and finished the season with a 4-2 city mark and 7-2 overall record.

Cebelak earned first-team All-City honors but Kaman was relegated to the second team, behind Central's Ripmaster, along with Cougar end Jim Walsh.

1937 Schedule/Results

Head Coach – Ed Killoran

Date	Opponent	Result		Location
Sep. 17	Jackson	Won	12-6	Jackson
Sep. 24	South Bend St. Hedwig	Won	38-0	Houseman Field
Oct. 2	Grand Haven	Won	25-0	Grand Haven
Oct. 9	Union	Won	20-0	Ninth Street Field
Oct. 16	Ottawa Hills	Won	32-6	South Field
Oct. 23	Creston	Lost	13-20	Houseman Field
Nov. 5	Central	Lost	7-25	Houseman Field
Nov. 13	Davis Tech	Won	18-0	Ninth Street Field
Nov. 24	South	Won	14-0	South Field

	Record	Pts. Scored	Pts. Allowed
Overall	7-2	179	57
City League	4-2	104	51

-1938-

Catholic Central 13
Coopersville 0
Saturday, September 24 at Houseman Field

With battering-ram fullback Roman Kaman off to Michigan State and All-City halfback Lou Cebelak, running mate Norb Greszcowiak and quarterback Staskiewicz also graduated, Catholic Central had to completely overhaul its backfield. Coach Ed Killoran was even considering converting some of his more experienced linemen into running backs. Plagued by penalties and so-so blocking, the Cougars finally broke through in the second half to beat Coopersville, 13-0, in their season opener.

Fullback Ed Miedzielec blocked two Coopersville defenders out of the way and left half James Farage toted the ball 9 yards for a touchdown that put CC ahead 7-0 in the third quarter. Backup half John Irwin displayed outstanding broken-field running during a 41-yard gain in the fourth quarter, and pushed the ball over from 1 yard on the next play.

Catholic Central 6
Grand Haven 0
Friday, September 30 at Houseman Field

James Brogger, the fourth in a line of brothers (John, George and Charles) who played football for Catholic Central, played a starring role as a punter in the Cougars' 6-0 victory against Grand Haven. After CC recovered a fumble at the Havenite 35-yard line in the game's opening moments, Brogger was called upon to enact a strategy typical of the day. He punted on first down and the ball was downed at the 3-yard line. Grand Haven lined up immediately to punt the ball out of trouble on first down, but Catholic co-captain Jack Hart blocked Miller's kick and right end Austin Ruth pounced on it in the end zone for the touchdown.

Brogger set up a similar scoring opportunity for the Cougars in the second quarter. Although Grand Haven successfully punted from the 3, their ensuing drive ended on downs at the 2. Defense came to Catholic's rescue in the third quarter when Tom Schoen recovered a Grand Haven fumble at the CC 4-yard line. Brogger again lined up to punt on first down, but after fumbling the snap picked up the ball and ran it back to the 4. He kicked the ball out of the end zone on second down, and Grand Haven took over at the 35. The Cougars got the ball back on Carl Milito's interception at the 17 and Brogger again dictated field position with a punt to the Havenite 45.

Counting on Brogger to bail out the offense one last time nearly cost Catholic the game after fumbling at its own 30. Grand Haven advanced the ball only to the 19, where it surrendered the ball back on down, but with a minute to play, Brogger again punted on first down and the Havenites took over at the 40. Grand Haven completed two quick passes, but time ran out with the ball at the CC 26.

Catholic Central 14
Davis Tech 7
Saturday, October 8 at Houseman Field

A dazzling array of rushes off "spinners" and reverses, and Brogger's talented toe, staked Catholic Central to a 14-7 victory over Davis Tech. The Cougars took a 7-0 lead in the second quarter with a 61-yard drive, highlighted by fullback John Dudley's 25-yard rush and 12-yard touchdown run.

Brogger, who had been booting CC out of trouble all game long with 50- to 60-yard punts, ended a Tech scoring chance in the third quarter and began one for Catholic when he intercepted a pass and returned it 3 yards to his own 38. Farage started the Cougars' ensuing possession with a 16-yard rush up the middle and Brogger picked up 11 more off a spinner. After taking the ball off a reverse, John Markus cut upfield behind the center and carried the ball to the Tech 24, and on the following play went the distance on a dive up the middle. The Wildcats scored a few minutes later on a 3-yard pass, but Catholic's defense was impenetrable in the final quarter.

Archives, Grand Rapids Public Library

CC's John Markus tries to outrun the South defense.

South 26
Catholic Central 0
Saturday, October 15 at South Field

The Cougars had to like their chances against South after finding out that one-man team Pete Mitchell wasn't available to play because of illness. It turned out the Trojans' committee of running backs was just as good in a 26-0 defeat marred by CC turnovers.

Although South took a 7-0 lead in the first quarter with no assistance from Catholic, the Cougars were all-too helpful the rest of the way. One play after CC recovered a Trojan fumble at their own 30, Farage fumbled it right back to kill a Grade-A scoring chance. Another Catholic Central drive ended in South territory in the third quarter and in the fourth quarter, Fred Veenkamp intercepted a Farage pass and returned it 40 yards for a touchdown.

Archives, Grand Rapids Public Library
CC's Tom Schoen (44) makes a futile lunge for South's Fred Veenkamp.

Ottawa Hills 20
Catholic Central 6
Saturday, October 22 at Houseman Field

For two quarters, Catholic Central figured out ways to stop Ottawa Hills fullback Burgess "Toots" Lawson, and even stymied the 210-pound pile driver on fourth-and-goal from the 2. The Cougars ran out of answers in the second half, however, and lost 20-6.

Lawson and shifty halfback Ed Breen gave the Indians a potent Mr. Inside-Mr. Outside attack. In the third quarter, they traded carries until Breen capped the 55-yard drive with his first of two touchdowns. After Ottawa got the ball back on an interception, Lawson started the drive from the CC 34 with a 4-yard pass to Breen, who covered the remaining distance with runs of 20 and 14 yards.

The Cougars looked good during a four-play, 73-yard scoring drive in the fourth quarter. John Zakem, the CC fullback, started the possession with an 18-yard pass to Ruth, carried the ball for 25, passed to Farage for 6 and completed a 24-yard touchdown pass to Ruth. However, the jaws of the 3,500 in the stands dropped when Lawson received the ensuing kickoff and rumbled, bumbled and stumbled his way to 78-yard touchdown to complete the scoring for the undefeated Indians.

Kalamazoo St. Augustine 27
Catholic Central 0
Friday, October 28 at Kalamazoo College Field

Perhaps softened up by the pounding inflicted by bruising Ottawa Hills fullback "Toots" Lawson six days earlier, Catholic Central proved to be no match for Kalamazoo St. Augustine brute Chet Jurwiak, who ran for two touchdowns, including a 50-yarder, in CC's 27-0 defeat.

Catholic Central 6
Central 0
Saturday, November 5 at Houseman Field

Catholic Central earned a reprieve from the so-called jinx it had endured for years in the series against Central with a 6-0 victory that prevented the Cougars from falling into a last-place tie with the Hilltoppers. The Cougars scored the game-winning touchdown on a 60-yard reverse by Markus, who had a clear path to the goal line thanks to quarterback Dudley's blocking on Central defensive backs.

It appeared the Hilltoppers might break CC's heart once again after mounting a goal-line stand that prevented the Cougars from scoring an insurance touchdown in the fourth quarter. But the Catholic Central defense preserved the shutout.

Creston 19
Catholic Central 0
Saturday, November 12 at Ninth Street Field

Handicapped by the loss of Markus and Dudley to injuries sustained a week earlier in the win over Central, Catholic Central couldn't keep pace with Creston in a 19-0 defeat. The Cougars never mounted much of an offensive attack until the end of the game when it was too late. They also struggled defensively, and in the fourth quarter gave up a 60-yard touchdown run by Polar Bear captain Elton Harris.

Catholic Central 0
Union 0
Saturday, November 19 at Ninth Street Field

Listless play and missed opportunities were the main ingredients in a 0-0 tie in Catholic's season finale against Union. The West Siders, now known as the Redhawks, had the best opportunity to score in the first half, but Straub's 32-yard field goal attempt went wide on the final play of the second quarter.

Brogger's punting created the most interest in the second half until Irwin completed a 25-yard pass to Coffey, who was tackled at the Union 15-yard line with a minute remaining in the game. Coffee ran for 12 yards on the next play, and Irwin gained 2 more on first and goal. However, Irwin's second-down plunge was stopped 6 inches short of the end zone as time expired.

On Thanksgiving Day, the Redhawks pulled off a stunning upset of previously unbeaten South, which resulted in Ottawa winning its first city championship. Catholic's only postseason award recipients were center Bob Long and John Markus, who were named second-team All-City.

1938 Schedule/Results
Head Coach – Ed Killoran

Date	Opponent	Result		Location
Sep. 24	Coopersville	Won	13-0	Houseman Field
Sep. 30	Grand Haven	Won	6-0	Houseman Field
Oct. 8	Davis Tech	Won	14-7	Houseman Field
Oct. 15	South	Lost	0-26	South Field
Oct. 22	Ottawa Hills	Lost	6-20	Houseman Field
Oct. 28	Kalamazoo St. Augustine	Lost	0-27	Kalamazoo College
Nov. 5	Central	Won	6-0	Houseman Field
Nov. 12	Creston	Lost	0-19	South Field
Nov. 19	Union	Tie	0-0	Ninth Street Field

	Record	Pts. Scored	Pts. Allowed
Overall	4-4-1	45	99
City League	2-3-1	26	72

-1939-

Catholic Central 31
Kalamazoo St. Augustine 12
Saturday, September 23 at Houseman Field

Halfback Tommy Sullivan burst onto the Catholic Central football scene much like his namesake and boxer, John L., did as America's national sports hero a half-century earlier. The Cougars' Sullivan scored four touchdowns and delivered the knockout punch in a 31-12 season-opening victory over Kalamazoo St. Augustine.

Sullivan, who put on a clinic for open-field running, made his CC scoring debut with a 32-yard scoring run up the middle in the first quarter. In the second, behind the blocking of fullback Ed Miedzielec, Sullivan scored from 13 yards out on a reverse. Catholic took a 19-0 lead in the third quarter on Austin Ruth's 25-yard interception return for a touchdown, but St. Augustine rallied for two unanswered scores to make it a seven-point game.

However, Sullivan put the game away with a one-two punch in the final five minutes. Another block by Miedzielec sprung Sullivan, who did the rest with a breathtaking 62-yard touchdown scamper. He finished off the visitors a minute later with a 26-yard burst up the gut.

Catholic Central 13
South Bend Catholic Central 7
Saturday, September 30 at Ottawa Hills Field

Having kickoff delayed for two hours by late-arriving South Bend (Ind.) Catholic Central didn't cause the Cougars to lose their edge. In fact, they scored early in the first quarter and again in the second, and then held on for a 13-7 victory against the school with an enrollment of 1,500.

Grand Rapids Catholic started its first possession after forcing South Bend to punt and a series of tackle-breaking runs by Miedzielec put the Blue and White into scoring position. A 26-yard touchdown pass from quarterback John Zakem to left end Bob Long gave the Cougars a 6-0 lead. James Brogger effected field position with his punting in the second quarter, and after pinning South Bend down at its 10, the Cougars came out of the kicking exchange with good field position. Miedzielec completed the short drive with a 2-yard touchdown plunge. The Cougars gave up a 28-yard touchdown pass in the fourth quarter, but after South Bend reached the Grand Rapids Catholic 20-yard line in the waning moments, they batted down three passes and forced a fumble on fourth down to secure the win.

Catholic Central 7
Union 0
Saturday, October 7 at Houseman Field

Catholic Central scored one the hard way, but it was enough to come away from Houseman Field with a well-earned 7-0 victory over Union High School. The Cougar defense spent the better part of three-plus quarters repulsing enemy forays deep into their own territory, including one that stalled out after four successive Redhawk running plays from the 10-yard line, and James Brogger was often called on to punt from the vicinity of his own goal line.

Meantime, CC's offensive attacks failed to produce points, including Sullivan's scintillating 61-yard TD run that was nullified by a clipping penalty. However, Sullivan kept the drive alive with a run to the Union 34, and on the next play the ball was snapped to a short receiver who lateralled to Miedzielec, who threw downfield to Don Long.

However, the play grew in complexity when Redhawk defensive back Canfield broke on the ball to make an interception. Canfield couldn't haul the ball in, however, and his deflection went right to Long, who snagged it with his condor-light wingspan while standing on the goal line.

GR Herald Photo

Ed Miedzielec (55) grabs the Creston ball-carrier in their game at South Field.

Creston 6
Catholic Central 0
Saturday, October 14 at South Field

Catholic Central fumbled away at least six bona fide scoring opportunities and an interception led to the touchdown that cost it a 6-0 defeat against equally mistake-prone Creston. The game wasn't decided until the fourth quarter when Polar Bear defensive back Bailey picked off a pass that slipped through Zakem's fingers, and returned it to the CC 30. On its second play of the drive, Creston ran a "Statue of Liberty" – which was considered ancient even by prevailing standards – for a 20-yard gain to the 1, and the Bears drove in from there.

Sullivan returned the ensuing kickoff all the way to the Creston 40, and the Cougars picked up 17 yards on the next two plays. Catholic Central had all the momentum going for it until it was afflicted with yet another fumble. Although the Cougars recovered this one, it was marked for a 5-yard loss and they eventually turned the ball over on downs. Catholic had one more chance after moving the ball to the Bear 20 with 30 seconds remaining, but a pass fell incomplete in the end zone as time ran out.

Catholic Central 0
Ottawa Hills 0
Saturday, October 21 at South Field

Both Catholic Central and Ottawa Hills had journeyed inside their enemy's 10-yard line at least once. The Cougars' highlight came on a 60-yard run by Zakem, and the Indians featured a 54-yard gain by Tom Blackburn. However, neither team was able to get the ball across the goal line in an entertaining 0-0 tie.

Catholic kept the Indians from scoring in large part because it recovered three of their eight fumbles and backup Strutzel's game-saving tackle of Blackburn at the 8-yard line in the third quarter. The Cougars had one final chance to pull out a victory after Tom Schoen recovered a fumbled punt at the Ottawa 20. On first down, Zakem passed to Long, who lateralled to Miedzielec, but Indian defenders hauled him down 16 yards from paydirt and there wasn't enough time left to run another play.

GR Herald Photo

Ottawa's Tom Blackburn breaks off an 54-yard run blowing by Miedzielec (left), Ferguson (60) and Ruth (47).

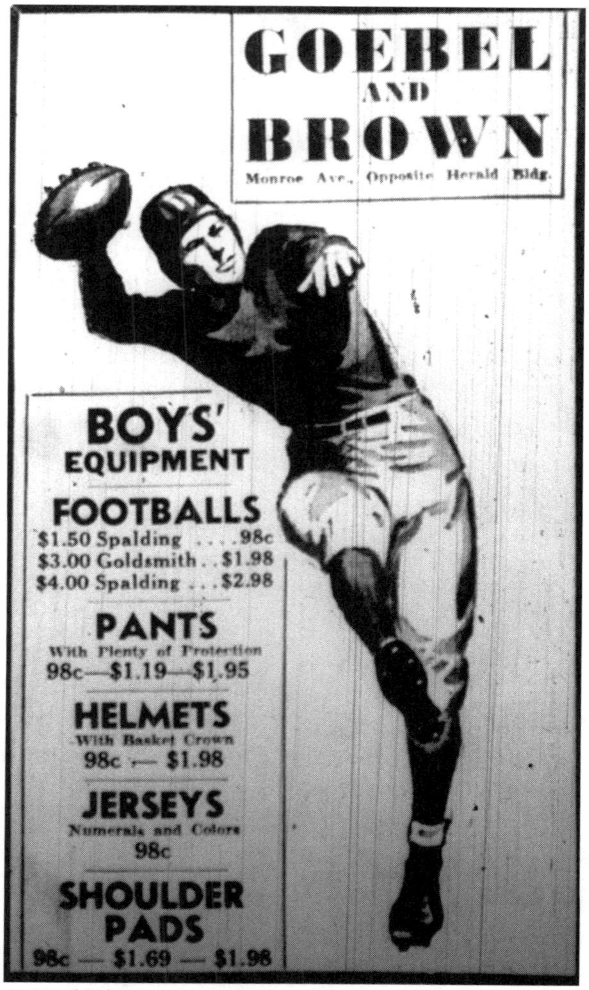

GR Herald Photo

Advertisement in The Grand Rapids Herald.

Davis Tech 7
Catholic Central 6
Friday, October 27 at Houseman Field

The late-game heroics that eluded Catholic Central in its previous two games played out for Davis Tech in a 7-6 loss. After a scoreless first half, the Cougars made their own breaks by putting an all-out rush on Wildcat punter Krajewski, whose kick traveled only 10 yards to the 25. A pass from Zakem to Long, who lateralled to Sullivan, covered 22 yards. Catholic took a 6-0 lead two plays later on a 1-yard dive by Miedzielec, but his PAT kick went wide.

Nevertheless, the Cougars appeared to be destined for victory until Sullivan fumbled a punt at his own 19 and Edward Svoboda recovered for Tech with less than five minutes remaining. Coach Killoran said his players were uninspired.

South 20
Catholic Central 7
Friday, November 3 at Houseman Field

The losses to Creston and Davis Tech left Catholic Central in the spoiler's role going into the game against undefeated and untied South High. The Trojans had yet to beat a city league opponent by more than seven points, so it seemed like a reasonable goal.

Even after Merle Swann put South ahead 7-0 with a 60-yard sweep around end on the third play of the game, Catholic was up for the challenge. Later in the first quarter, Sullivan carried the ball from CC territory to the Trojan 40, where he was separated from the ball by a jarring hit. However, Austin Ruth, who was trailing on the play, picked up the fumble at the 25 and without breaking stride went the distance for the tying score.

A South punt to the Catholic Central 2-yard line and a subsequent CC punt from its own end zone in the third quarter led to the short 36-yard drive Swann capped with a 2-yard touchdown sweep. The Trojans scored their final touchdown later in the third, after a similar exchange of punts. Catholic made a comeback bid in the fourth, but it fizzled when a 60-yard drive ended on an unsuccessful fourth-down play.

Catholic Central 12
Central 7
Friday, November 10 at Houseman Field

The Cougars played well enough in the brutally cold and muddy conditions to beat any team in the city, but were satisfied with a 12-7 victory that gave them back-to-back wins over Central for the first time in the series' long history. Midway through the first period, Catholic Central staged a 65-yard drive that ended on a Sullivan's 2-yard touchdown run.

Catholic took advantage of great field position to put the game out of reach in the third quarter. First, a punt by Central's Afendoulis hung up in the wind and was downed at the Hilltopper 18-yard line. The Cougars made it to the 10, but the drive ended with an interception. Afendoulis' next punt made it to the 25, but Miedzielec picked up 12 yards on CC's first play and Sullivan gained another 3 on its second. The third was quite charmed as Brogger passed to Long, who caught the ball at the 5 and before being dragged to the ground, lateralled to Sullivan, whose touchdown gave the Cougars a 12-0 lead.

Central scored a touchdown late in the fourth quarter, but once Catholic Central regained possession, it not only killed the clock, but the storied "Central Jinx" along with it. The Cougars finished the season with a 4-3-1 record and Sullivan and Ruth were named first-team All-City while Miedzielec and Schoen were second-team picks.

1939 Schedule/Results

Head Coach – Ed Killoran

Date	Opponent	Result		Location
Sep. 23	Kalamazoo St. Augustine	Won	31-12	Houseman Field
Sep. 30	South Bend Catholic Central	Won	13-7	Ottawa Hills Field
Oct. 7	Union	Won	7-0	Houseman Field
Oct. 14	Creston	Lost	0-6	South Field
Oct. 21	Ottawa Hills	Tie	0-0	South Field
Oct. 27	Davis Tech	Lost	6-7	Houseman Field
Nov. 3	South	Lost	7-20	Houseman Field
Nov. 10	Central	Won	12-7	Houseman Field

	Record	Pts. Scored	Pts. Allowed
Overall	4-3-1	76	59
City League	2-3-1	32	40

-1940-

Muskegon 22
Catholic Central 0
Friday, September 20 at Hackley Field

It was an ambitious request: beat a traditional lakeshore powerhouse in its first ever home night game with a rebuilding team made up primarily of inexperienced players. Considering the circumstances, Catholic's 22-0 defeat before a Hackley Field opening-game record crowd of 7,500 wasn't unexpected. That the young Cougars fought well enough to keep the score from become a complete blowout was something of a surprise.

Catholic Central 7
Central 7
Friday, September 27 at Houseman Field

Fullback Jack Milito, one of Catholic Central's few veteran players, rallied the Cougars back from their disappointing opener with his passing arm and a 6-yard touchdown run that resulted in a 7-0 halftime lead against Central. Catholic held its ground until it no longer could late in the fourth quarter when the Hilltoppers pulled off a 91-yard drive for the game-tying touchdown with four minutes remaining.

Lansing Eastern 19
Catholic Central 0
Friday, October 4 at Lansing

When your star player is the punter, you know you've had a rough night. James Brogger did a fine job of kicking the ball against Lansing Eastern, but the rest of the Cougars struggled during a 19-0 road loss. The disparity in rushing yards told the story. The Quakers outgained CC on the ground, 351-32. Brogger also accounted for Catholic Central's lone offensive highlight with a 40-plus yard reception in the third quarter.

Catholic Central		Union H. S
Schmidt	LE	Waivio
Christopher	LT	Gooseman
McArdie	LG	Cowell
Gorski	C	Sherwood
Walsh	RG	Grey
Delaney	RT	Grudzinskas
Edgerle	RE	Dykstra
Brogger	QB	Kiehle
Froman	LH	Roseman
C. Milito	RH	DeGraw
J. Milito	FB	Czuhai

Catholic	0	6	0	6	12
Union	0	0	0	0	0

Touchdown – C. Milito, J. Milito
Referee– Beatty, Umpire – Roper, Head Linesman – Peterson

Catholic Central 12
Union 0
Saturday, October 12 at Houseman Field

Despite two lopsided non-league losses, Catholic Central remained in city league championship contention thanks to a 12-0 victory over archrival Union. All of the Cougars' points were scored by the Milito brothers, Jack and Carl, on 3-yard touchdown runs.

Jack finished off a 9-play, 45-yard scoring drive, sparked by Walt Froman's 20-yard rush to the Redhawk 18, in the second quarter. Carl's TD came on the first play of the fourth quarter after the Cougars advanced the ball from their own 18-yard line with a methodical drive which included an 18-yard run by Jack, a 16-yarder by Carl and one for 12 yards by Froman off a reverse. With less than three minutes to play, Union muffed a punt and Thomas Edgerle recovered for CC at the 7. After an illegal motion penalty moved the Cougars back on third down, Jack's 8-yard touchdown run was negated by an offside penalty.

GR Herald Photo

An unidentified Catholic player pulls down Creston quarterback Noorthoeck while Jim Christopher (42) moves in to assist.

Creston 20
Catholic Central 0
Saturday, October 19 at Briggs Field

Jack Milito's bid to give Catholic Central the upper hand against Creston ended when Eardley dropped his pass with no one around him at the Polar Bear 33-yard line in the second quarter. After the first half ended in a 0-0 draw, Creston blocked three punts, including two on the same drive, to saddle CC with a 20-0 defeat.

In the third quarter, Creston's Klomparens, who had already blocked one punt by Brogger, broke through the Cougar line to knock down another. The ball rolled out of bounds at the 1-foot line, and after several minutes of arguing by both coaches with the officials, it was ruled CC's ball. Brogger again punted, and Klomparens again got a hand on the ball, which made it to the

Catholic 29. The Bears scored six plays later on a 7-yard reception by Klomparens, and added two touchdowns in the fourth, including one on a 38-yard interception return.

Ottawa Hills 7
Catholic Central 0
Saturday, October 26 at Ottawa Hills Field

Catholic Central was its own worst enemy in a 7-0 loss to Ottawa Hills. The Cougars got the break they needed early in the first quarter when they recovered a fumble on their own 5-yard line. But they fumbled the ball back on the very next play, and three plays later, Indian fullback Tom Blackburn barreled over from the 1-yard line.

The Cougars had trouble running the ball because Jack Milito was sidelined by an injury. His absence was felt in the third quarter when CC had first-and-goal at the 1-yard line, but Froman, the pint-sized halfback, was stopped for no gain on four straight plunges in to the line. Ottawa center Sterkenberg dropped Froman for a 4-yard loss on fourth down and the Indians held on the rest of the way.

Catholic Central 13
Davis Tech 7
Saturday, November 2 at Houseman Field

The game had a pronounced ebb and flow, and by dominating the second and third quarters, Catholic Central

GR Herald Photo

CC's Carl Milito fights off an Ottawa defender while teammate Don Lennon tries to throw a block.

snapped a two-game losing streak with a 13-7 victory over Davis Tech. The Wildcats were clearly superior in the first quarter when they controlled the ball for 23 of 25 plays. Their scoring drive, which started with the recovery of a Carl Milito fumble, featured five consecutive first downs.

However, once the Cougars decided to assert themselves, they could not be denied. Four of their 10 first downs came in the second period, and although they didn't score – one drive ended on a fumbled snap at the Tech 5-yard line and another at the 12 on an interception – neither did the Wildcats. Catholic reset the down marker five times in the third quarter, which is also when it also took control of the scoreboard.

The Cougars wasted no time tying the score after a 14-yard Tech punt gave them the ball just 40 yards from the end zone. A 20-yard pass, from Jack Milito to end Eaderly, who lateralled to Brogger, gave CC a first down at the 10, and two plays later the Jack Milito-Eaderly-Brogger connection connected the dots for a 5-yard TD. Catholic Central started its next possession on the Wildcat side of midfield after another poor punt, and drove smartly to the 13-yard line on the final play of the period. On the third play of the final stanza, Jack Milito dove in from the 2. The teams played to a draw the rest of the way, but CC breathed a huge sigh of relief when Tech's Telman ran free behind the secondary and got his hands on a perfectly thrown deep ball, only to juggle it before dropping it to the ground.

South 26
Catholic Central 0
Friday, November 8 at Houseman Field

By the end of a long season, Catholic Central was still a rebuilding team when it met South, an established powerhouse and the disparity was defined not only by score, but by the way the Trojans won, 26-0. The Cougars could have played a perfect game and still not had a chance.

South, which successfully defended its 1939 city title with a 4-0-1 mark, scored its first touchdown six minutes into the game and never let up. It even scored a touchdown in the third quarter despite fumbling twice, and

CC/WC Archives

1940 Catholic Central Team

Front Row (l-r) - Ed Symanski, Long, Edgerle, Prangley, Ruth, Sullivan, Miedzielec, Golembeski, C. Milito
Middle Row - Walsh, E. Farrell, Longstreet, Zakem, Zielinski, Ferguson, Gillespie, Levandoski, Gorski, J. Milito
Back Row - Coach Ed Killoran, Assitant Coaches Zwers and Szymanski, Managers Stein, Green, Hickey, Barofsky

recovering both times, on the same drive. Catholic picked up just two first downs, and its best chance to score ended on three long incomplete passes from Trojan 45. Cougar center Ed Gorski was named first-team All-City and the Milito brothers, Brogger and tackle Don Delaney were honorable mentions.

1940 Schedule/Results

Head Coach – Ed Killoran

Date	Opponent	Result		Location
Sep. 20	Muskegon	Lost	0-22	Hackley Field
Sep. 27	Central	Tie	7-7	Houseman Field
Oct. 4	East Lansing	Lost	0-19	Lansing
Oct. 12	Union	Won	12-0	Houseman Field
Oct. 19	Creston	Lost	0-20	Briggs Field
Oct. 26	Ottawa Hills	Lost	0-7	Ottawa Hills Field
Nov. 2	Davis Tech	Won	13-7	Houseman Field
Nov. 8	South	Lost	0-26	Houseman Field

	Record	Pts. Scored	Pts. Allowed
Overall	2-5-1	32	108
City League	2-3-1	32	67

-1941-

Muskegon 21
Catholic Central 0
Friday, September 19 at Hackley Field

The Cougars had reason to be cautiously optimistic when they opened preseason camp. Ed Gorski, the 175-pound All-City center, was returning along with five other regulars and nine lettermen in all. "We'll be better this year than last season," Coach Ed Killoran told *The Grand Rapids Herald*. "We had a green team in 1940 which learned a lot of football and most of the boys are back to have another whirl at those same foes."

Archives, Grand Rapids Public Library

Coach Ed Killoran and an unidentified Catholic Central player.

Catholic Central still wasn't in perennial powerhouse Muskegon's league, however, and lost its opener, 21-0. The Cougars fumbled the opening kickoff at their own 20, which led to the Big Reds' first touchdown, and had just two first downs to 18. Trailing by three touchdowns, Catholic didn't make a bid to score until the final quarter. A pass from fullback

GR Herald Photo

All-City Tackle Jim Christopher

Jack Milito to Gene "Davey" Wojtaszek picked up 20 yards, and Milito ran another 11 to the Muskegon 17. Backup halfback Gordon Zielbeck's 2-yard gain gave CC a first down, but Milito fumbled the ball away on the next play.

"This year's Muskegon team is the strongest I've ever seen and that includes those I played against in the days of (then-future Michigan star and coach Bennie) Oosterbaan and other Muskegon stars," said Killoran, who prepped at Lansing Central High, said afterward. "We simply were not good enough."

Catholic Central 7
South 7
Saturday, September 27 at Houseman Field

A knee injury sustained by Don Delaney meant Catholic Central would be without its standout 200-pound tackle for at least a month. Nevertheless, buoyed by how they stood up to the physical challenge presented by Muskegon a week earlier, the Cougars battled two-time defending city champ South to a 7-7 tie.

The hotly contested game could have gone either way in the first quarter. Twice Milito punted to switch field position, and the Trojans fumbled both times. Catholic couldn't convert the first turnover recovered at midfield, but end Carl McKnight and left tackle James Christopher jumped on the second loose ball at the South 27. Two plays later, left halfback Walt "Bud" Froman followed Milito's blocking to the open field, and then broke Ken Throckmorton's attempted tackle at the 5 to score a 27-yard touchdown.

South played like the champion it was in the fourth quarter after recovering Zielbeck's fumble at the CC 27 to set up Pete Mitchell's 11-yard touchdown with three minutes to play. The Trojans outgained Catholic Central, 148-79, and completed 3 of 6 passes for 50 yards while all seven Cougar passes fell incomplete.

Catholic Central 34
Central 0
Friday, October 3 at Houseman Field

Decades of frustration and irritation came to an end when Milito scored three touchdowns to lead Catholic Central to a 34-0 drubbing of Central. Cougar wins were hard enough to come by in the series, and none came close to being this emphatic. If not for an inordinate number of penalties – two fourth-quarter touchdowns were called back – CC's margin of victory would have been even greater.

A 15-yard holding penalty that backed the Cougars up midway through the first quarter ignited their 20-point second quarter. Right half Norm Wiersing's 24-yard romp on first down all but wiped out the negative yardage and left CC 1 yard short of a first down. He picked that up, and more, with an 8-yard gain. Two plays later, Joe "Wojie" Wojciakowski gobbled up 13 yards, and with the Central line buckling from a relentless pounding, Froman broke two tackles to score on fourth-and-4 early in the second quarter.

Another holding penalty wiped out a long gain to the Hilltopper 5, but Milito dodged one tackler after another en route to a 48-yard touchdown. Zielbeck returned an interception 45 yards for a touchdown, and CC led 20-0 at halftime. Milito set up his second touchdown, from the Central 1 in the third quarter, with a 20-yard gain, and his final score covered 20 yards in the fourth quarter and was reminiscent of the way Michigan's Tom Harmon read blocks and maneuvered through traffic.

Union 7
Catholic Central 0
Friday, October 17 at Houseman Field

Catholic Central		Union H. S
McKnight	LE	Albers
Christopher	LT	Goldis
McArdie	LG	Nelson
Gorski	C	Hausser
O'Rourke	RG	Waivio
Bernard	RT	Goosman
Wojtaszek	RE	Tebean
Skouras	QB	Kiehle
Milito	LH	Czuhai
Wojciakowski	RH	Simoncini
Froman	FB	Roseman

Catholic	0	0	0	0	0
Union	0	0	0	7	7

Touchdown – Roseman
PAT - Goldis
Referee– Beatty, Umpire – Wheeler, Head Linesman – Breen

With an overflow crowd of 9,000 watching Catholic Central and Union do battle for more than an hour, Jack Milito dropped back for one fateful pass he hoped would decide the game on the final play of the game. It did, but not in the Cougars' favor. Milito's toss from the CC 25-yard line was intercepted by Red Hawk back Rex Roseman, who sprinted the distance for the victorious touchdown.

The Catholic Central fans standing two-deep outside the fences surrounding Houseman Field walked away in stunned silence while the Union faithful danced jubilantly in their midst. It was a mind-numbing defeat, given the fact the Cougars squandered at least five prime scoring opportunities, while Union failed to capitalize on two such chances.

Catholic Central 13
Creston 6
Thursday, October 23 at Houseman Field

A goal-line stand in the first quarter against Gordon Hunsberger-led Creston was all Catholic Central needed to rid itself of the bad feelings left over from its heartbreaking loss to Union six days earlier. First, the Cougars punted out of danger, and then, after getting the ball back, took advantage of a Polar Bear penalty to score first in a 13-6 victory that preserved their chance at a city championship.

Near the end of the first quarter, the officials whistled Creston for piling on and moved the ball 15 yards to midfield. On the next play, Wojciakowski carried the ball to the Bear 21, and Froman, the nimble little halfback, covered the remaining distance on the first play of the second quarter.

Quarterback Chris Skouras, who called the fateful pass play that cost CC the game against Union, earned a measure of redemption when he recovered a Creston fumble at the 43-yard line in the third quarter. In a cruel twist, Skouras returned the ball for a touchdown, but was ruled down at the point of the recovery. Five plays later, on fourth-and-1 at the 27, Skouras again called for Milito to pass the ball, which he did. Skouras' heart must have sunk when he saw Bear defender Joe Noorthoek get a hand on the ball. However, instead of intercepting it or knocking it down, Noorthoek deflected it to Wojciakowski, who made a brilliant circus catch before scampering into the end zone for what would stand as the decisive score.

With their second dramatic goal-line stand of the game, the Cougars stopped Creston six inches short of the goal line in the fourth quarter. The Bears finally scored with two minutes to go, but CC successfully ran out the clock to drop them from the ranks of the unbeaten in city play. Creston left the game with a 3-1 record while the Cougars improved to 2-1-1.

Catholic Central 18
Ottawa Hills 7
Tuesday, November 4 at Houseman Field

Heavy rains caused Catholic Central's game against Ottawa Hills to be postponed from Saturday to the following Tuesday, but the Cougars held their edge. Catholic never let the Indian offense get closer than the 35-yard line until victory was safely in hand to win 18-7.

Catholic took control of the game immediately by gashing the Ottawa defense for hefty gains on its first possession. Milito polished off the eight-play, 70-yard drive with a 3-yard touchdown run. "Flash" Froman's 17-yard dash got a 74-yard CC drive started in the third quarter, and Zielbeck converted on fourth down with a 7-yard TD waltz around end on the first play of the fourth quarter to increase the Cougar lead to 12-0.

Greg Kurkjian's punt return to the Indian 39 led to Milito's 9-yard scoring run, and CC was comfortably ahead even after Phil Montgomery's 70-yard touchdown reception put the Indians on the board.

Catholic Central 0
Davis Tech 0
Friday, November 8 at Houseman Field

Snow and mud conspired to keep play between Catholic Central and Davis Tech near midfield until the final possession. The Wildcats got the break both teams had been angling for when Froman fumbled a punt and Don Nixon recovered at the CC 20-yard line for Tech.

The Wildcat drive stalled at the 14 when the Cougars sniffed out a fake field goal on fourth down, but CC couldn't move the ball either and punted again. Tech drove from the 32 to the 2, but on fourth down, the Cougars stuffed Gamble 12 inches short of the goal line to prevent losing on the final play of the game for the second time. The 0-0 tie left Catholic (3-2-2 overall) with a 3-1-2 mark in city play, just behind Union (5-0-1) and South (4-0-2) in the final standings. The Red Hawks secured the title outright with a 6-6 tie against South before a record crowd of 13,000 at Houseman Field.

Milito, Gorski, right guard Bob McArdle and right tackle James Christopher earned first-team All-City designation from *The Grand Rapids Herald*. Skouras was a second-team selection along with Wojtaszek, Wojciakowski, McKnight and guard Charles O'Rourke,

Archives, Grand Rapids Public Library

Catholic Central's Backfield
(l-r) Walt Froman, Jack Milito, Joe Wojciakowski and Chris Skouras

1941 Schedule/Results
Head Coach – Ed Killoran

Date	Opponent	Result		Location
Sep. 19	Muskegon	Lost	0-20	Hackley Field
Sep. 27	South	Tie	7-7	Houseman Field
Oct. 3	Central	Won	34-0	Houseman Field
Oct. 17	Union	Lost	0-7	Houseman Field
Oct. 23	Creston	Won	13-0	Houseman Field
Nov. 4	Ottawa Hills	Won	18-7	Houseman Field
Nov. 8	Davis Tech	Tie	0-0	Houseman Field

	Record	Pts. Scored	Pts. Allowed
Overall	3-2-2	72	41
City League	3-1-2	72	21

-1942-

Catholic Central 6
Battle Creek Central 6
Friday, September 18 at Battle Creek

A storm had been brewing at Catholic Central during the previous two seasons. How close it would come to being perfect couldn't have occurred to the Cougars while tying Battle Creek Central, 6-6, in the season opener.

New end Edward Baes put on a pass-catching show and Catholic Central took a 6-0 lead on a run up the middle by Greg Kurkjian early in the third quarter. However, the extra point failed when Joe Soboleski, the holder, couldn't handle a bad snap from center. First he considered dropkicking for the point, but then decided to run for it and was stopped short of the goal line. A 30-yard pass play set up Central's 1-yard touchdown late in the third quarter, but the PAT kick was wide. Central had one last chance to win, but its 16-yard field-goal attempt sailed wide as time expired and the Cougars left the Cereal City still undefeated.

Catholic Central 7
Davis Tech 6
Monday, September 28 at Houseman Field

After falling behind 6-0 on a blocked punt, Catholic Central made good on two critical second chances, one unfortunate and the other fortuitous, to pull out a 7-6 victory over Davis Tech in its city league opener.

The game played out like a chess match in the first half, but the Cougars were winning the punting duel until they lined up to punt from their own 18 midway through the second quarter. Karczewski, the hard-nosed Wildcat tackle, bull-rushed through the CC line, and batted Soboleski's kick backward high into the air, and Gamble fielded it in the end zone for the touchdown. Tech captain Frank Nawara missed the extra point, however, and Catholic was only a touchdown and an extra point away from taking the lead a low-scoring game.

Unfortunately, the Cougar offense was handicapped by turnovers and dismal punting. Finally, the defense took matters into its own hands midway through the fourth quarter when fullback Dick Mysliewiec blitzed through the Wildcat line, picked off Gamble's lateral and raced 44 yards for an apparent touchdown. Unfortunately, the officials ruled they inadvertently blew the play dead with a quick whistle and gave CC the ball where Mysliewiec snatched the ball. Mysliewiec made up nearly all the distance taken away from him with a 41-yard pass to Baes and two plays later, Bob VandenBerg tied the score with a 1-yard smash into the end zone with less than three minutes to play.

Mysliewiec's kick for the game-winning extra point went wide, but fortuitously, Tech was called for offside and this time VandenBerg plowed up the middle for the score.

Catholic Central 13
South 6
Friday, October 2 at Houseman Field

Thanks to the blocking of center and captain John Bernard, the hard running of halfback Bob Fron and the alert play of VandenBerg, Catholic Central manufactured a 13-0 first-half lead and then hung on despite a rash of injuries and fatigue to defeat South, 13-6.

In the opening quarter, Fron set up CC's first score with a first-down run of 25 yards around left end from the Trojan 40. VandenBerg added 4 off a delayed crossbuck to the 11 and Fron picked up 7 on the next two downs for a first-and-goal-to-go at the 4. Bigford dropped Fron for a 4-yard loss on the next play, but Fron cruised in for an 8-yard touchdown with one minute remaining in the period. South smothered the extra-point try before Greg Kurkjian could even get a foot on the ball.

In the second quarter, VandenBerg intercepted a pass that glanced of the hands of Trojan receiver Frank Mitchell and ran it back 62 yards for a touchdown, and this time Kurkjian's kick was true. Just before halftime, Soboleski, the CC guard, broke his left ankle when he tackled Mitchell during a punt return and was taken to St. Mary's Hospital for treatment. After a scoreless third quarter, the Trojans had the tiring Cougars on the ropes and scored easily on a drive they completed with Bosma's 6-yard scoring run. Catholic rose up to block Art Jackson's extra point, however. Later South drove to the CC 27, but its bid to tie the score ended when the Cougars got the ball back on downs with a minute to play.

Archives, Grand Rapids Public Library
Quarterback Louis Bernard and his brother, center John Bernard.

Catholic Central 13
Central 13
Saturday, October 10 at Houseman Field

Nothing was coming easy for Catholic Central, and that theme continued in the battle for first place against equally undefeated and untied Central. Although the Hilltoppers entered the game as a slight favorite, CC forged a 13-13 tie in what *The Grand Rapids Herald*

Archives, Grand Rapids Public Library

An unidentified back follows the block of quarterback Louis Bernard (45) during the Central game.

sportswriter K.C. Clapp described as "ding-dong scrap all the way."

A long pass from classy Central halfback Gust Afendoulis to quarterback Maloley set up the game's first score midway through the first quarter. After the Hilltoppers advanced to the CC 12, Jimmy De Boer set up several yards behind center as if to kick and after taking the snap, dropped the ball on the ground, picked it up and raced into the end zone. The Cougars blocked his extra-point attempt, but trailed, 6-0. Catholic countered quickly to take a 7-6 lead on its ensuing drive. After pounding the ball to the Hilltopper 35, VandenBerg swept around end for a 28-yard gain and fullback Mysliewiec slithered through a crease to find the end zone three plays later. VandenBerg's run up the middle for the extra point gave CC a 7-6 lead with two minutes remaining in the first quarter.

Midway through the second quarter, Central got the ball back on a fumble and then took advantage of two 15-yard penalties assessed against Catholic for unnecessary roughness and holding to forge a 13-7 lead on Chamberlain's plunge from less than 1 yard out. Kurkjian came through for the Cougars in the fourth quarter when he intercepted a pass thrown by Afendoulis and returned it to the CC 40-yard line. Fourteen yards and two plays later, Mysliewiec lofted a long pass, which Baes hauled in at the Central 15. Baes eluded two Hilltoppers to complete the dramatic 46-yard scoring play, but Mysliewiec was stopped short of the goal line on his run for the point-after, and Catholic Central had to be content with a tie that kept it undefeated in league play.

Catholic Central 32
Lansing St. Mary's 12
Saturday, October 17 at South Field

Catholic Central enjoyed a respite from rugged league play with an easy 32-13 victory over Lansing St. Mary's in a game that featured a coaching duel between CC's Ed Killoran and his brother Frank, the coach of St. Mary's.

The Cougars' first possession began 45 yards away from the goal line after a St. Mary's punt, and VandenBerg covered the distance on runs of 18, 17 and 10 yards for a 6-0 lead. VandenBerg added a 30-yard touchdown a few minutes later and reserve back Jerry Bockheim's 5-yard plunge made the score 20-0 just before halftime. Don O'Hearn's 70-yard gallop set up VandenBerg's third touchdown, which came on a 1-yard plunge and resulted in a 26-0 lead. Mysliewiec's interception late in the third quarter set up Bockheim's 28-yard touchdown for an insurmountable 32-0 advantage.

Despite playing an out-of-league opponent, Catholic (2-0-1) took over sole possession of first place when lowly Creston tied prohibitive favorite Central (2-0-2).

Catholic Central 19
Union 13
Friday, October 23 at Houseman Field

An inspired Union team struck first against its ancient rival, but Catholic Central roared back for three unanswered touchdowns to pick off a 19-13 victory vital to its championship aspirations.

Redhawks coach Milo Sukup, the former University of Michigan regular, had his team ready to play. Union's first advance reached the CC 40, and Carl Waivio's punt was fielded by Fron at his own 12. The Cougars failed to pick up the first down in three plays, and the Redhawk rush converged on Mysliewiec and blocked his punt in the end zone, where Ed Timmerman recovered for Union's first touchdown and a 7-0 lead.

The Cougars struck back immediately after starting their ensuing drive at the 35. After picking up three consecutive first downs, VandenBerg flew around right end for a 36-yard touchdown. Kurkjian's kick was wide and Union still led, 7-6. Neither team scored on its next possession, but one play after getting the ball back via a Redhawk punt, Baes put CC ahead to stay with a nifty 56-yard end-around.

The Cougars kept the pressure on in the third quarter, and on third down at Union's 45, Mysliewiec evaded a fierce rush and completed a long pass to Baes, who was dragged down at the 3-yard line. Catholic failed to advance the ball on three runs into the line and was backed up 5 additional yards because of an illegal procedure penalty. But on fourth down, Mysliewiec dropped back to pass and threw a dart to Gene Wojtaszek, who scored standing up for a 19-6 lead. Union's Jarvis ran back the ensuing kickoff 62 yards to the Catholic 24 and Canfield scored from close distance on the sixth play of the drive, and the third play of the fourth quarter. The Cougars controlled the ball the remainder of the period to secure the win.

Catholic Central 19
Creston 0
Monday, November 2 at Houseman Field

Coach Killoran went into Catholic's game against Creston full of trepidation. Although the Polar Bears sported a 1-1-1 city record, Killoran pointed out they tied league-leading Central, as CC had, and defeated Davis Tech by a single point, as did his 3-0-1 Cougars. "I'm at a loss to understand why everyone figures Creston to be the underdog in this game," he said.

It took awhile on the mud-covered Houseman Field plain, but Killoran finally knew the answer after the Cougars closed in on the city championship with a 19-0 victory. Catholic capitalized on an early opportunity after Creston's Harrison fumbled the opening kickoff and the Cougars recovered at the 37. Mysliewiec came out throwing, and his 19-yard pass to VandenBerg, who slipped and fell, gave CC first-and-goal at the 8. VandenBerg plodded for 7 on the next play, and quarterback Louis Bernard flooded through a hole up the middle for the only points the Cougars would need, though Kurkjian's pass off a fake-extra point to Baes made it 7-0.

VandenBerg finally provided an insurance marker with a 43-yard touchdown off a reverse on the first play of the fourth quarter. After the Cougars got the ball back on a Joe McGee fumble at his own 35 a few minutes later, Killoran called for another reverse for VandenBerg. Although the Bears appeared to have him cornered at the 15, he bounced the play outside and scored to seal the deal.

In a testament to the role faith played on CC's team, Killoran said Creston had the great misfortune of playing the Cougars on All Souls Day. "We were so keyed up I believe we could have taken the Notre Dame varsity that night."

Catholic Central 27
Ottawa Hills 0
Saturday, November 7 at Houseman Field

Catholic Central completed its near-perfect storm with a statement-making 27-0 victory against Ottawa Hills. The Cougars finished with a 5-0-1 city league record (6-0-2 overall) for their first undisputed championship in school history. It was CC's first title since 1926 when it tied Central for first place, and the best showing since its storied 1923 season, when it didn't face the Hilltoppers.

Catholic, with do-it-all halfback VandenBerg leading the way, didn't need to play flawless football to beat the Indians, but it did. Its first drive featured runs of 23 yards by Kurkjian and 26 by VandenBerg and ended on Bockheim's 10-yard touchdown run. A fake punt in the third quarter, with VandenBerg taking a deep handoff from Mysliewiec, covered 26 yards and set up VandenBerg's 7-yard score for a 13-0 lead. One play after VandenBerg returned an interception 28 yards, he scored on a 35-yard run that put CC ahead 20-0 in the third quarter. Baes put the exclamation mark on the win and the season when he picked off Ottawa halfback Lily's two-handed jump pass and ran it back 40 yards for the final score.

Louis (quarterback) and John (center) Bernard, VandenBerg (halfback) and tackle Richard Stoddard were named first-team All-City and Mysliewiec and Eugene "Davey" Wojtaszek were put on the second team. Baes, Fron and guard Richard Gallagher were

GR Herald Photo

Bob Fron looks to get outside against Ottawa Hills.

Joe Soboleski
Catholic Central
1943

Though never named to an All-City team, Joe Soboleski became the first Catholic Central football player to play in the National Football League.

After graduating from high school, Soboleski spent 18 months in the United States Navy, including eight months in the Pacific Theater during World War II.

He played college football at the University of Michigan as a defensive lineman from 1945 to 1948. He was a starting defensive lineman on Michigan's undefeated 1947 and 1948 national championship teams. At the conclusion of his college career, Soboleski was selected to play in the 1949 College All-Star Game in Chicago.

Selected in the ninth round of the 1949 NFL Draft by the New York Giants, Soboleski instead signed with the Chicago Hornets of the All-America Football Conference. Soboleski played four years of professional football for five teams: Chicago Hornets (1949), Washington Redskins (1949), Detroit Lions (1950), the New York Yanks (1951), and the Dallas Texans (1952).

He was released by the Texans after a 24-6 loss in the 1952 season opener.

GR Herald Photo

1942 Catholic Central Football Awards Banquet

(l-r) Coach Ed Killoran, 1943 captain Ed Krupicewicz, 1942 captain John Bernard, Ed (Moose) Krause, Rev. J. P. Flannery and Rev. William J. Murphy

honorable mentions. The champions were honored by a crowd of 260 at a banquet held at St. James' Elementary School. Ed "Moose" Krause, a member of the Notre Dame coaching staff, was the keynote speaker.

Monsignor Dennis E. Malone noted how the Cougars didn't even have suitable football pants or shoes when CC started its program more than a quarter-century earlier, and thanked boosters for their financial support of the athletic department. Rev. J.P. Flannery, the Catholic Central superintendent, thanked the city public schools for recognizing the school as a full-fledged member of the city league. Messages of congratulations from Bishop John C. Plagens and Governor-elect Harry F. Kelly were read. Team captain John Bernard presented Coach Killoran with a beautiful Catholic Central blue blanket to commemorate the title, and members of the Cougars' city reserve championship team, known as the "Peanut Squad," did the same for their coach, Ted Sowle.

It was all a harbinger of even greater things to come for the Catholic Central football program.

1942 Schedule/Results

Head Coach – Ed Killoran

Date	Opponent	Result		Location
Sep. 18	Battle Creek	Tie	6-6	Battle Creek
Sep. 28	Davis Tech	Won	7-6	Houseman Field
Oct. 2	South	Won	13-6	Houseman Field
Oct. 10	Central	Tie	13-13	Houseman Field
Oct. 17	Lansing St. Mary's	Won	32-12	South Field
Oct. 23	Union	Won	19-13	Houseman Field
Nov. 2	Creston	Won	19-0	Houseman Field
Nov. 7	Ottawa Hills	Won	27-0	Houseman Field

	Record	Pts. Scored	Pts. Allowed
Overall	6-0-2	136	56
City League	5-0-1	98	38

CHAPTER 5

Catholic Plays with Sowle
1943-63

Theo (not Theodore) James "Ted" Sowle had a knack for being in the right place at the right time. In his previous coaching stops, he had always inherited a program that had won a championship the previous season. The situation was no different in 1943 when he was promoted from the Catholic Central reserve squad, which had won the city league junior varsity title the previous season, to replace Ed Killoran, who was called up by the Navy for active duty during World War II and temporarily bowed out as the Cougars' varsity coach with a city championship of his own. When Killoran returned from the war and resumed his CC coaching duties in 1946, Sowle spent that season coaching in Erie, Pa.

Nevertheless, although Sowle claimed his first state title with the Cougars right out of the gate, he could never be accused of winning with someone else's players before moving on to the next program, as he showed for two legendary decades at CC.

The Mount Pleasant native prepped at Sacred Heart Academy before going on to play center for Central State Teachers College, the forerunner of Central Michigan University. Although Sowle made his name in football, his favorite sport was track and field and he starred as a high jumper and javelin thrower.

-1943-

GR Herald Photo

First Day of Practice at Buckley Field

(l-r) Bob Lang, Dave Howe, Coach Bob Young, Don Patterson, Greg Kurkjian, Coach Ted Sowle, Joe Ruschmann

Catholic Central 6
Muskegon 0
Friday, September 17 at Hackley Field

Bad news greeted Catholic Central before the season even started when standout fullback Dick Mysliewiec suffered a wrist injury and was sidelined for the foreseeable future. Fortunately, new head coach Ted Sowle inherited a full stable of capable ball-carriers, and Bob VandenBerg, the defending city league track and field champion in the 100- and 220-yard dashes, made a seamless transition from halfback to fullback heading into the opener at Muskegon High School.

However, it was little Joe Klocko, in his first start at left halfback, who provided the fireworks in the Cougars' 6-0 upset over the Big Reds. The prevailing perception that CC was being outplayed dissolved early in the third quarter when Klocko returned a punt 82 yards for the game's only score. "Boy, I had some good blocking," Klocko said afterward. Klocko also provided the first tangible evidence of the Sowle touch. Discouraged by his lack of progress on the reserve team in '42, Klocko was on the verge of quitting football until a heart-to-heart talk with Sowle convinced him to give it one more try.

The Catholic Central defense demonstrated a propensity for rising to the occasion. In the first quarter, CC stopped the Big Reds on downs at its own 5-yard line. VandenBerg ended a Muskegon threat at the 14 with an interception in the second period and the Cougars forced another turnover on downs at their own 12 late in the third quarter. It was the city league's first victory over Muskegon since Union pulled one out 10 years earlier.

Catholic Central 31
Ottawa Hills 0
Saturday, September 25 at Houseman Field

The Cougars scored at will while winning their city league opener against Ottawa Hills, 31-0. Klocko and backup fullback Art Bartnick took turns mining touchdowns in the first three quarters to break the game open. Klocko went over from 2 yards out in the opening stanza and Bartnick plowed in for a short score a few minutes later. Klocko snapped off a 23-yarder in the second quarter and Bartnick rushed for a 10-yard score in the third. The Indians couldn't stop CC's second string either, and backup Don O'Hearn took a reverse 11 yards for the final TD.

Catholic Central 31
Davis Tech 6
Friday, October 1 at Houseman Field

The Cougars came out flat against lightly regarded Davis Tech and trailed 6-0 late in the second quarter. Catholic Central saved face just before halftime when VandenBerg, who had a 45-yard touchdown run nullified by a clipping penalty a few plays earlier, sprinted 23 yards off a reverse for the first of CC's five unanswered TDs in a 31-6 victory.

Catholic Central dismantled the Wildcats in the third quarter in quick fashion. VandenBerg gave the Cougars the lead on a 15-yard sweep and halfback Jerry Bockheim intercepted a pass on Tech's ensuing possession to set up his own off-tackle plunge into the end zone on the very next play. VandenBerg took advantage of a huge hole to close out the third quarter with a 6-yard touchdown run. Klocko's 36-yard gain to the Wildcat 4, and a 5-yard offside penalty on the next snap, put VandenBerg into position for his fourth touchdown, which came on a 9-yard run.

Catholic Central 19
South 14
Monday, October 11 at Houseman Field

Catholic Central		South H. S
Sypniewski	LE	Russell
Zarzecki	LT	Hondorp
Karas	LG	Andrus
Patterson	C	French
Howe	RG	Fessehden
Szarowicz	RT	Eabaugh
VanGessel	RE	Luccheai
Bernard	QB	Catlin
Klocko	LH	Liekteig
VandenBerg	RH	Norgrove
Bockheim	FB	Giammona

Catholic	0	12	7	0	19
South	0	7	0	7	14

Touchdowns – Sypniewski, VandenBerg (2), Swanson, Russell
PAT – VandenBerg, Russell (2)
Referee– Japinga, Umpire – Formana, Head Linesman – VanWingen

As World War II raged, the Catholic Central football program suffered a significant off-the-field loss when assistant coach Jack Young was called up for active duty by the U.S. Navy. Credited by Sowle for helping develop the Cougars into a city league powerhouse, Young was also slated to coach the CC varsity baseball team in the spring.

The blow was softened by the return of Mysliewiec, who led Catholic Central to a dramatic 19-14 victory over South before more than 8,000 fans in the city's version of Monday night football decades before it became a national treasure. VandenBerg's punt return to the Trojan 24 and 13-yard run off a reverse set up left end Joe Sypniewski's 11-yard touchdown run, giving the defending champs a 6-0 lead in the second quarter. The Cougars went back on offense a short time later, and Mysliewiec struck quickly with a 50-yard touchdown pass to VandenBerg for a 12-0 lead just before halftime. Catholic Central's strategy to avoid a long return by kicking the ball out of bounds backfired. Starting the ensuing possession where the ball crossed the sideline at the 40, South's Anthony Giammona took a lateral and threw a 60-yard scoring bomb to Swanson to cut CC's lead to 12-7 with only seconds remaining in the second quarter.

Catholic Central appeared to take control of the game late in the third quarter when the speedy VandenBerg weaved in and out of traffic while returning a Giammona punt 55 yards for a touchdown that provided a 19-7 possession. However, Giammona started picking the Cougar secondary apart in the fourth quarter, and his 30-yard touchdown pass to Tom Russell – Giammona and Russell also combined for the extra point – made it a one-possession game.

The game ended in frenzied controversy after South drove to the CC 6-yard line on the final possession. On second down, it appeared Trojan left half Lickteig powered his way into the end zone, but the officials marked the ball at the half-inch line. The stout Cougar defense yielded less than a quarter-inch on the next play, and it threw Giammona for a 2-yard loss on the next. Then, on the last play of the game, South's pass attempt over the goal line fell incomplete in the end zone, which was fortuitous because the Trojans had been awarded a fifth down.

Catholic Central 22
Central 0
Tuesday, October 19 at Houseman Field

A mid-season rule change enacted by Grand Rapids recreation director John Bos moved kickoff for city league night games up 15 minutes to 7:30 p.m. so they would end in time to abide by the 10 p.m. curfew law. Game officials were also instructed to speed up play as much as possible.

Bos needn't have bothered for what was expected to be a titanic tussle between Catholic Central and defending city league runner-up Central. The game lived up to its billing, but the Cougars scored all the points they would need to win just before halftime after Ted Karas recovered a Hilltopper fumble 19 yards away from the end zone. Ed O'Rourke took over from there, running for 4 and then 2 yards on first and second downs before passing to VandenBerg for the final 13 and what would stand as the game-winning touchdown in a crucial 22-0 victory.

Catholic Central and its longtime nemesis played to a stalemate through the third quarter and into the fourth until the Cougars blocked a Central punt for a safety that sparked a 16-point outburst. Back-to-back 20- and 10-yard rushes set up a 10-yard touchdown run by Bartnick, and O'Rourke hooked up with VandenBerg for a dazzling 35-yard scoring pass that kept CC fans' spirits high as they headed to the exits.

Catholic Central		Union H. S
Sypniewski	LE	Timmerman
Ruschmann	LT	Krause
Kurkjian	LG	Nowicki
Patterson	C	Houser
Mylar	RG	Chapel
Szarowics	RT	Moreland
VanGessel	RE	Kulhawik
Bernard	QB	VanAllsburg
Mysliwiec	LH	Lentz
VandenBerg	RH	Wysocaynski
Bockheim	FB	Canfield

Catholic	0	0	0	0	0
Union	0	0	0	7	7

Touchdown – VandenBerg (3)
PAT – VandenBerg, Klocko
Referee– Nisbet, Umpire – Pugne, Head Linesman – VanWingen

Catholic Central 20
Union 0
Friday, October 29 at Houseman Field

Union, now referred to as the Red Hawks, thought it had Catholic Central's number until No. 8 struck for three fourth-quarter touchdowns in a 20-0 victory that put the Cougars in position to secure their second consecutive city title.

Right halfback VanderBerg's unparalleled display of broken-field running took place in the final 10 minutes of the game. First, his 27-yard sweep led to a tackle-dodging 18-yard touchdown for a 7-0 lead. Bockheim's interception on Union's ensuing drive and Sypniewski's 10-yard rush set the table for a 16-yard VandenBerg scamper and his 3-yard touchdown. VandenBerg concluded a 65-yard drive by taking a handoff out of the T-formation and rambling 16 yards for his final touchdown.

CC/WC Archives

Catholic Central's Backfield vs. Union

(l-r) right halfback Bob VandenBerg, fullback Jerry Bockheim, quarterback Lou Bernard and left halfback Dick Mysliewiec.

Catholic Central 28
Creston 13
Friday, November 19 at Houseman Field

Catholic Central crushed Creston, 28-13, to end the season with a perfect 7-0 record and a mythical Class A state title it shared with Dearborn Fordson (7-0) and Ann Arbor (8-0). An overflow crowd of more than 10,000 spectators, many spilling onto the grassy banks at Houseman Field, watched CC come back from a 13-7 halftime deficit by scoring 21 unanswered points.

Cougar fans watched in horror as Creston took a 7-0 first-quarter lead on halfback Joe McGee's 12-yard sweep around right end. VandenBerg calmed things down when he used his sprinter's speed to race 36 yards to tie the score early in the second quarter. The Polar Bears, however, weren't intimidated and regained the lead when left defensive halfback Burt Brown intercepted a Mysliewiec pass and returned it 45 yards for a score.

Catholic Central asserted itself as the champion it became a year earlier when VandenBerg burst through the line and sped away from every Creston pursuer en route to a 71-yard touchdown run in third quarter. He still had enough in the tank to sweep in for the extra point that put CC ahead to stay, 14-13. As the third quarter wound down, Klocko picked up 24 yards on three consecutive rushes and VanderBerg broke loose for a 17-yarder to set up his 8-yard touchdown run.

The Bears threatened again in the fourth quarter, but Mysliewiec made up for his second-quarter turnover by picking off a pass thrown by McGee and running it back 55 yards to complete the rout.

It was no surprise that VandenBerg headed the All-City team and he was joined on the first squad by Cougar right guard Ben Myler.

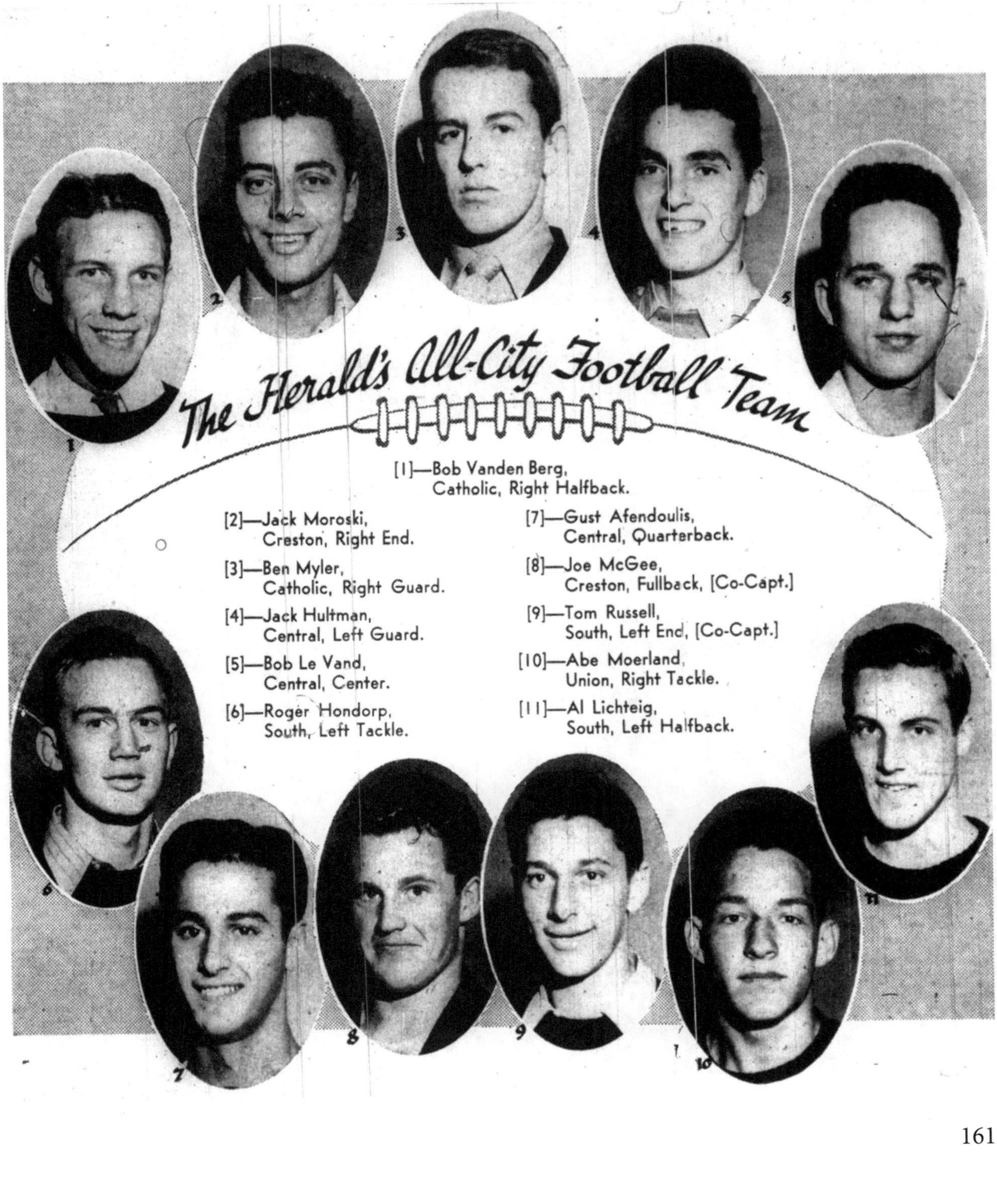
The Herald's All-City Football Team

[1]—Bob Vanden Berg, Catholic, Right Halfback.

[2]—Jack Moroski, Creston, Right End.

[3]—Ben Myler, Catholic, Right Guard.

[4]—Jack Hultman, Central, Left Guard.

[5]—Bob Le Vand, Central, Center.

[6]—Roger Hondorp, South, Left Tackle.

[7]—Gust Afendoulis, Central, Quarterback.

[8]—Joe McGee, Creston, Fullback, [Co-Capt.]

[9]—Tom Russell, South, Left End, [Co-Capt.]

[10]—Abe Moerland, Union, Right Tackle.

[11]—Al Lichteig, South, Left Halfback.

CC/WC Archives

1943 Michigan State Champions

Front Row (l-r) Greg Kurkjian, Don Patterson, Jerry Bockheim, Dick Mysliewiec, Bob VandenBerg, Gil VanGessel, Joe Sypniewski, Alex Szarowicz

Second Row - Fr. J. P. Flannery, Fr. William J. Murphy, Dick Zarzecki, Ed Kieras, Dick Prawdzik, Joe Ruschmann, Lou Bernard, Ben Myler, Dave Howe, Coach Ted Sowle

Third Row - Don Owens, George Kanoza, Bill Feutz, Bob Lang, Gerald Houseman, Bill Brunner, Bob Reagan, Student Managers Tom Carmondy and Jim Nachtegall

Fourth Row - Student Manager Tommy Bockheim, Bob Gibson, Student Managers Dan Mead and Bob Sullivan, Bob Fron, John Donnazzollo, Don O'Hearn, Stan Karas, Art Bartnick, Bob Smith, Joe Klocko, Student Manager Mike Mead

1943 Schedule/Results

Head Coach – Ted Sowle

Date	Opponent	Result		Location
Sep. 17	Muskegon	Won	6-0	Hackley Field
Sep. 25	Ottawa Hills	Won	31-0	Houseman Field
Oct. 1	Davis Tech	Won	31-6	Houseman Field
Oct. 11	South	Won	19-14	Houseman Field
Oct. 19	Central	Won	22-0	Houseman Field
Oct. 29	Union	Won	20-0	Houseman Field
Nov. 19	Creston	Won	28-13	Houseman Field

	Record	Pts. Scored	Pts. Allowed
Overall	**7-0**	**157**	**33**
City League	**6-0**	**151**	**33**

-1944-

Muskegon 13
Catholic Central 0
Friday, September 22 at Houseman Field

With only two starters – fullback Dick Mysliewiec and end Joe Sypniewski – returning from his first state championship team, Catholic Central coach Ted Sowle wasn't even hinting at a third straight city title even though 110 players showed up for the first day of practice. There wasn't enough strength in those numbers for the Cougars to avert a 13-0 season-opening loss against Muskegon.

The Big Reds intercepted several passes to snap CC's 17-game unbeaten streak – 15 wins and two ties – dating back to a 7-0 loss suffered against Union on Oct. 17, 1941. The Cougars had a chance to gain the upper hand in the game after Sypniewski recovered a fumble to end Muskegon's first possession at its 32. A fourth-down pass from Mysliewiec to Don O'Hearn resulted in a first down at the 21, and two plays later, O'Hearn's 13-yard run gave Catholic first-and-goal at the 6. Mysliewiec burrowed his way to the 1-foot line, but on second down a back-field-in-motion penalty moved the ball back 5 yards and a Mysliewiec pass fell incomplete as the first quarter ended. Catholic Central got 3 yards closer after Muskegon jumped offside, but Mysliewiec was stopped a yard short of the goal line on fourth down.

GR Herald Photo

Coach Ted Sowle diagrams a play in the sand of Buckley Field.
(l-r) Bill Feutz, John Donazzolo, Bob Smith, Coach Sowle, Joe Ruschmann, Stan Karas and Don O'Hearn

GR Herald Photo

Coach Ted Sowle immortalised by The Grand Rapids Hearld's *Ray Barnes.*

A failed fourth-down gamble near midfield set up Muskegon's first touchdown and the Cougars trailed 6-0 at halftime. Catholic Central held its own against its more experience opponent in the second half until the Big Reds turned another interception into a 16-yard reverse for a touchdown in the waning moments of the fourth quarter.

Catholic Central 19
Creston 13
Saturday, September 30 at Houseman Field

Dick Mysliewiec's 1-yard touchdown late in the fourth quarter decided a seesaw battle against Creston in Catholic Central's favor, 19-13. The Cougars took a 6-0 lead in the first quarter after Dan Pobojewski returned a punt booted from the Polar Bear end zone to their 26. Three plays after O'Hearn's 20-yard rush, Mysliewiec capped the short drive with a plunge from one foot to open the scoring.

Creston took a 7-6 lead later in the first quarter on Wes Miller's 1-yard quarterback sneak, but E.J. Owens put CC back in business early in the second quarter with a sweep. The Cougars regained the lead, 13-7, just before halftime after Mysliewiec completed a 50-yard pass to O'Hearn to the Creston 11 and tossed and 8-yard scoring pass to Sypniewski.

Bear halfback Bud Elve evened the score with a 6-yard touchdown jaunt on fourth down in the third quarter but true to form, Mysliewiec ran for what appeared to be a 59-yard touchdown on the next play from scrimmage. However, the play was nullified by a holding penalty and CC had to earn the game-winner the hard way on its next possession, which began 86 yards away from the Bear end zone. Mysliewiec got things started against Creston's fading defense with an 11-yard run. Mysliewiec then completed a 15-yard pass to Chuck Boggiano, ran for 20 yards to the Bear 40 and picked up 11 more to the 29. A 23-yard pass from Mysliewiec to Bill Feutz put the ball at the 3, and Boggiano gave Mysliewiec a breather with a 2-yard carry.

As if he hadn't already done enough to get CC's defense of its city championship off to a successful start, Mysliewiec did the rest to give the Cougars a decisive six-point lead.

Ottawa Hills 13
Catholic Central 7
Saturday, October 7 at Houseman Field

Joe Sypniewski was playing in his last game for Catholic Central before shipping off to war and the defending champs were heavily favored to defeat perennial also-ran Ottawa Hills. In other words, no one saw a monumental upset coming, and even after the Indians won, 13-7, no one believed it happened.

But it did because the Cougars failed to punch the ball into the end zone from 1 yard out before time ran out in the first half. That missed opportunity would have countered the one scored by husky Ottawa fullback Jack Zaremba, who accounted for 75 percent of his team's yardage, on a series of line plunges started at the CC 12 earlier in the second quarter.

In the third quarter, Catholic Central got the ball back at its 35 on a Zaremba fumble, but disaster struck on the first play from scrimmage when Indian quarterback Jamo stripped the ball out of O'Hearn's hands and returned it 32 yards for a touchdown. Mysliewiec did most of the damage on CC's 65-yard scoring drive in the third quarter, and the Cougars were moving toward a game-winning touchdown late in the final period. Catholic reached the Ottawa 20-yard line, but that opportunity was irreparably damaged by a holding penalty and Mysliewiec's long, fourth-down pass to Boggiano fell just short of the marker and the ball went over to the Indians on downs.

South 25
Catholic Central 0
Friday, October 20 at Houseman Field

Catholic Central passed the city championship torch to presumptive successor, South High, during the course of a 25-0 defeat. It was the Trojans' fourth decisive victory of the season and confirmation that CC was in the midst of a rebuilding year.

The Cougars went on full attack after Anthony Giammona's 6-yard touchdown run provided South with a 6-0 first-quarter lead. However, their next drive stalled out on downs at the Trojan 20 and the next ended on a fumble at the South 45. Giammona converted that turnover into a touchdown with a flip to Roger Hondorp. In his zeal to get the Cougars back into the game all by himself, CC returnman Casey Polkowski failed to secure the ensuing kickoff and the Trojans recovered his fumble at the 19 with just over a minute to play in the first half. Two plays later, Giammona passed to Baker for a touchdown and South took an 18-0 lead into the locker room at halftime.

Catholic Central		South H. S
Pasbach	LE	Baker
Jaglowski	LT	Hondorp
Smith	LG	Stormaand
Houseman	C	Woods
Donnazzolo	RG	Bergstrom
Schultz	RT	Esbaugh
Feutz	RE	Luccheai
Walenga	QB	Nelson
Mysliwiec	LH	Giammona
O'Hearn	RH	Mitchell
Boggiano	FB	Holwerda

Catholic	0	0	0	0	0
South	6	12	7	0	25

Touchdowns – Giammona, Holwerda, Hondorp, Baker
PAT – Haggai
Referee– Nesbitt, Umpire – Hinga, Head Linesman – Farnsworth

Catholic had no answer for South's potent aerial attack, which produced a 17-yard Giammona-to-Holwerda touchdown in the third quarter, until John Shutich intercepted a pass in the fourth quarter. The Cougars drove to the South 14-yard line, but Giammona intercepted a pass by O'Hearn to end the threat.

Catholic Central 12
Central 12
Saturday, October 28 at Houseman Field

Nobody leaves a tie entirely satisfied, but at least the 5,000 who watched Catholic Central play Central to 12-12 tie were entertained. The Cougars led 6-0 at halftime thanks to a 72-yard drive Pobojewski started with back-to-back runs of 17 and 29 yards and finished with a 2-yard touchdown. Catholic appeared to seize command of the game on the first possession of the second half. After a series of power runs, Pobojewski completed a 17-yard bullet pass to Boggiano, who was tackled at the 7, and Myliewiec covered the remainder of the distance with two rushes.

However, on Central's ensuing drive, halfback Doug Wicks ran up the middle for a 50-yard touchdown run to cut CC's lead in half. The Cougars moved into position to put the game away, but turned the ball over on downs near midfield with four minutes remaining. Clark Afendoulis completed a quick 20-yard pass to Post, Tommy Steele picked up 10 yards on a reverse and four plays and a Cougar offside penalty later, Wick plunged in for the game-tying touchdown. Fortunately for CC, his placekick for the point after veered off course.

Lansing Eastern 13
Catholic Central 6
Saturday, November 4 at Houseman Field

The only thing Catholic Central appeared destined to inherit by playing so meekly in the first half was a big-time whipping by highly ranked Lansing Eastern High School. However, CC out-fought the Quakers in the second half, only to see its comeback bid fall short in a 13-6 defeat.

The Cougars trailed 13-0 going into the third quarter, but Pobojewski changed the dynamic of the game instantly by sweeping around end for a 69-yard touchdown before many of the fans who visited the concession stands had a chance to return to their seats. The game almost got away from Catholic later in the third quarter when Lansing Eastern intercepted a Mysliewiec pass and returned it to midfield.

The Quakers drove all the way to the CC 9, but the Cougar defense dropped opposing ball-carriers for four consecutive losses back to the 21 and took over on downs. Pobojewski led the Catholic Central charge all the way to the Lansing Eastern 15-yard line, but another Mysliewiec pass was picked off to end the possession. The Cougars forced a punt from the 50 for one last possession, and on the final play of the game, Mysliewiec scrambled desperately before finding an open receiver. Owens made an outstanding catch, but couldn't elude a tackler at the Lansing Eastern 45 as time expired.

Catholic Central 25
Union 12
Friday, November 10 at Houseman Field

It may have been the last game of the season, but Catholic Central began its run to a 1945 city league championship with a crushing 25-12 victory against Union on a sloppy surface at Houseman Field. The Cougars pummeled the Red Hawks into submission with the one-two punch of Owens and Pobojewski.

Owens set the tone early in the first quarter with a 34-yard run to the Union 26. Pobojewski went for 14 on fourth down to the 3, and Owens steamed in from there for the game's first score. The CC defense stopped the Red Hawks cold on their ensuing possession, and Pobojewski made it 14-0 with a 69-yard romp.

Union played competitive football until the Cougar defense ripped its heart out in the second quarter with a fourth-down stop 10 yards from the end zone. The Red Hawks came back to life in the third quarter after blocking a Mysliewiec punt at the CC 42 and making it a one-possession on Krause's 4-yard rumble across the goal line. However, Owens countered almost immediately with a 43-yard gain that set up Pobojewski's 3-yard smash. Owens then made the score 25-6 after Pobojewski handed him the ball on a reverse and he scampered 40 untouched yards for a touchdown. Union scored a consolation touchdown after blocking another punt late in the game against the CC reserves.

Mylsiewiec was the only CC player named first-team All-City by a panel that included city league coaches. South High placed six players on the first team.

1944 Schedule/Results
Head Coach – Ted Sowle

Date	Opponent	Result		Location
Sep. 22	Muskegon	Lost	0-13	Houseman Field
Sep. 30	Creston	Won	19-13	Houseman Field
Oct. 7	Ottawa Hills	Lost	7-13	Houseman Field
Oct. 20	South	Lost	0-25	Houseman Field
Oct. 28	Central	Tie	12-12	Houseman Field
Nov. 4	Lansing Eastern	Lost	6-13	Houseman Field
Nov. 10	Union	Won	25-12	Houseman Field

	Record	Pts. Scored	Pts. Allowed
Overall	2-4-1	69	101
City League	2-2-1	63	75

-1945-

Coach Ted Sowle didn't quite know what to make of his team going into the 1945 season. He had a stable of fine running backs, including battle-tested scatbacks Danny Pobojewski and E.J. Owens and quarterback Chuck Boggiano. However, the untimely death of fullback Henry Milanowski was a major emotional and structural blow to the team, and aside from returning center Jerry Houseman, the line was an unknown entity. The husky Boggiano, the staring quarterback from the '44 squad, switched to fullback and former backup Bob Tietema, who Sowle once considered to play guard, took over at quarterback.

Muskegon 13
Catholic Central 7
Friday, September 21 at Hackley Field

Catholic's rubber match in the rekindled series with Muskegon High was greeted with great anticipation. A Hackley Field record crowd of more than 10,000 watched a CC team that measured up physically to the perennial lakeshore powerhouse but contributed mightily to its own demise in a 13-7 loss. It was an unsatisfying result as Owens' potential game-winning, 50-yard touchdown run was nullified by a debatable clipping penalty.

In the opening quarter, Catholic Central fumbled the ball away at its own 30, and after getting the ball back on downs, promptly fumbled it back again to set up the Big Reds' first touchdown, which came early in the second quarter. The Cougars answered in no uncertain terms on the ensuing possession, covering 65 yards in six plays as Pobojewski and Owens shredded the Muskegon defense. After Pobojewski converted on fourth-and-9 with a punishing off-tackle run, Owens blasted in from the Big Red 3-yard line and Pobojewski's extra-point run tied the score at 7-7.

Owens' third-quarter interception set up what appeared to be his go-ahead touchdown, but the play was damaging on two counts: the controversial clipping penalty cost CC a score and Pobojewski suffered a broken nose that would eventually knock him out of the game. Muskegon capitalized on back-to-back Cougar fumbles, one on a fake third-down punt that resulted in a 9-yard loss and the other on the following play when the punter fumbled the snap at the Catholic 38. The Cougars claimed they were the victims of circumstances because while most high schools were employing four officials, Muskegon-area teams were still using only three. They also claimed that the official who made the call on foul was out of position to make such a call.

Muskegon Heights 21
Catholic Central 13
Friday, September 28 at Phillips Field

Sowle stopped languishing over the clipping penalty that cost CC the game at Muskegon High the following Saturday night when he watched Muskegon Heights dismantle Creston. "To my mind, the Heights team looks better than Muskegon," Sowle said. "I'm not framing an alibi."

Sowle's words proved to be prophetic as the Cougars returned from its second consecutive trip to Muskegon in seven days with a decisive 21-13 loss. Catholic Central fell behind 2-0 early in the second quarter when the Tigers blocked a punt and Cougar Jerry McGovern covered the ball in the end zone. The Heights then took advantage of a short free kick to build a 9-0 lead. Catholic drove all the way to the Tiger 10-yard line, but couldn't get off another play before the first half expired.

CC/WC Archives

CC's E. J. Owens

Pobojewski, broken nose and all, got the Cougars right back into the game with a 60-yard punt return early in the third quarter, but the Heights, aided by a 15-yard CC penalty for unnecessary roughness, quickly countered for a 15-7 lead. Things got away from the Cougars on their next play when Pobojewski fumbled and Owens recovered for a 33-yard loss. Then, after taking a lateral at the 5, Pobjewski again lost the handle after getting hit hard and the Tigers recovered to set up the touchdown that sealed the deal.

Catholic Central 34
Creston 7
Friday, October 5 at Houseman Field

Bloodied but by no means bowed, Catholic Central showed it could take a punch in two hard-fought battles in Muskegon. The Cougars served notice to the city league it could deliver one as well with a 34-7 pummeling of Creston. The combination of Owens, who rushed for four touchdowns, and Pobojewski did most of the damage.

After turning back a Polar Bear assault

that reached its 20-yard line late in the first quarter, CC scored five unanswered touchdowns. Pobojewski started the avalanche with an 8-yard smash, and Owens, the speedster on loan from the track team, made sure Creston was good and buried.

Later in the second quarter, Pobojewski broke off a 38-yard run to set up Owens' 15-yard scoring spurt up the middle. Catholic Central ended the Bears' ensuing series by forcing a fumble and recovering at its own 49, and on a first-down reverse, Owens out-sprinted a host of pursuers en route to a 51-yard touchdown and a 21-0 halftime lead. Early in the third quarter, Owens creased Creston with a 55-yard touchdown and he added a relatively modest 1-yarder before the period ended.

CC/WC Archives

Danny Pobojewski

Catholic Central 33
Ottawa Hills 0
Friday, October 12 at Houseman Field

A punishing ground attack and stifling defense paved the way for Catholic's 33-0 victory over Ottawa Hills. The Indians reached CC territory just twice, the second time coming just before time expired, and logged four first downs to 17.

Owens set the tone by returning the opening kickoff 41 yards to the Ottawa 39-yard line, and Dick Gibson, the Cougars' mighty-mite fullback, darted 4 yards into the end zone a few plays later. Pobojewski and Owens took turns at softening up the Indians defense during sustained drives by running between the tackles. Owens scored from 6 and 3 yards out in the second quarter and he capped two drives that followed a pair of Ottawa fumbles with 12- and 14-yard scoring runs in the third.

Catholic Central 20
Central 0
Saturday, October 20 at Houseman Field

Going into his team's game against the Cougars, Danny Nameth, coach of the Central High Hilltoppers, told *The Grand Rapids Press*, "If we could stop Owens and Pobojewski, we could play Catholic on even terms."

And if "ifs" and "buts" were candy and nuts, it would be Christmas all the time.

Central had difficulty holding Owens and "Pobo" down even with the help of a flu bug that kept the dynamic duo, along with starting quarterback Bob Tietema, on the sidelines during practice and wrapped in blankets early in the game. With the anemic effort put forth by CC's substitute backfield making their condition even worse, Owens and Pobojewski not only sought a cure, they were the cure.

After the stout Cougar defense forced a Central punt downed at the CC 35-yard line late in the first quarter, Owens sucked it up for a 12-yard gain. Pobojewski rumbled for 4, Gibson tacked on 5 and Owens broke loose for 17 more. Pobojewski barreled for 12 to 15 and 10 to the 5, and Owens completed a 65-yard drive from there in one try. The Hilltoppers had reason to believe CC's recovery was only temporary because they immediately charged to the Cougar 46 on their ensuing possession. However, Catholic halfback Larry Pojeski ended the threat with an interception and on the next play, Owens rambled 35 yards to the Central 10. Pobojewski was only

CC/WC Archives

CC Linebackers Casey Polkowski (left) and Larry Pasbach

strong enough to lug the ball 9 yards and then fumbled the ball away on his next attempt.

Central failed to get out of the hole and punted only to its own 22. Owens got 15 yards back on one try, Pobojewski burrowed to within 6 inches of the goal line, Boggiano sneaked it in from there and the Cougars took a 14-0 lead into the locker room at halftime. Pobojewski had a 55-yard touchdown run nullified by an offside penalty in the third quarter, but Catholic kept the drive alive and Owens' 15-yard run to the Hilltopper 2 to set up Gibson's TD plunge.

Catholic Central 40
Union 14
Friday, October 26 at Houseman Field

Catholic Central held a 14-0 lead before running a single play on offense and then went on to devastate Union, 40-14, for a fourth straight city league triumph. Back at full strength after a bout with the flu, Pobojewski returned the game-opening kickoff 85 yards for the first touchdown. He also kicked the extra point.

The Red Hawks moved the ball to midfield on their first possession, but the ball popped out of fullback VanderLaan's hands as he tried to pick up yardage up the middle. Catholic Central center Jerry Houseman plucked the ball out of midair and returned it 41 yards for a touchdown before the game reached the three-minute mark. Pojeski's interception set up Owens' 39-yard touchdown run and CC held a 20-0 first-quarter lead.

In the second quarter, Owens' 50-yard dash led to Gibson's 5-yard touchdown. Benny Battenberg scored for Union to cut the CC lead to 27-7 just before halftime. Owens converted another Cougar fumble recovery, by Larry Pasbach, into a 37-yard touchdown and his 4-yard touchdown put Catholic ahead 40-7 in the fourth quarter. The Cougars were one win away from clinching the undisputed city title.

Catholic Central 34
South 14
Saturday, November 3 at Houseman Field

A record 17,000 tickets were sold for the heavily anticipated title clash between Catholic Central and defending state champion South High, and portable bleachers were installed wherever they could fit at Houseman Field. Tickets were sold at: Goebel & Brown Sporting Goods, Lehman's Drug Store at Madison Avenue, Burton Heights Pharmacy, the Seymour Drug Store, Riordan's Drug Store, Schichtel's Confectionery and Donahue's Cigar Store.

Although the Trojans brought a 15-game win streak dating back to 1944 into the game and Catholic Central sported a 4-2 overall record, the battle of the city league unbeatens was rated as "a tossup" in the papers. The standing-room-only-crowd didn't think much of the prognosticators after South marched 78 efficient yards on the game-opening drive and took a 7-0 lead on Hoppy Van Zoeren's 1-yard dive into the end zone.

While CC's fans were stunned, the early deficit only whetted the Cougars' appetite. On Catholic's first play from scrimmage, Owens elegantly maneuvered 62 yards for the touchdown that ignited a 34-14 rout. The Trojans responded like the champions they were and drove right back to the CC 13, but with the previous season's 25-0 drubbing still fresh on its mind, the Catholic defense got the ball back on downs and Pobojewski's 33-yard gain provided some breathing room. Three plays later, the slippery Owens, whose initials were now interpreted as "Easy Jogging", dazzled the crowd again with a breathtaking 44-yard touchdown run.

Whatever hope the Trojans had of getting back into the game in the second half evaporated when Pobojewski and Owens took turns battering their defense with thunder and lightning. On the first play of the third quarter, Owens struck for 17 yards to the 50. Two power runs by the 175-pound Pobojewski put the ball at the South 34, and finally he dragged nearly the entire Trojan defense with him for an 11-yard touchdown and a 21-7 lead. A few minutes later, Pobojewski put the game out of reach with a 48-yard scoring run up the sideline, and this time, not one South defender laid a hand on him.

Gibson finished the Trojans off with a 35-yard TD in the fourth quarter, and while South countered that one, CC was in position to score again as time expired. The Cougars left no doubt they were the city champs and the game caused so much excitement talk turned to how the city needed to expand Houseman Field to 20,000 seats.

CC/WC Archives

The Crowd at Houseman Field for Catholic Central vs. South

Lansing Sexton 13
Catholic Central 12
Friday, November 9 at Lansing

Although Catholic Central was declared the equal of any team in Michigan the night it defeated defending state champ South High, 34-14, for the undisputed city league title, the Cougars knew they had to match that performance to beat a rugged Lansing Sexton team on its own turf. Catholic Central dominated statistically, but committed too many miscues in a 13-12 season-ending loss.

Catholic Central got off to a stumbling start in the first quarter when Owens was dropped for a 3-yard loss on fourth down at the Sexton 10-yard line. The Cougars finally got back on track thanks to Pobojewski's punt return to Sexton's 47-yard line. Catholic picked up three straight first downs and Boggiano plowed in from the 5 for a 6-0 lead, but Owens was stopped short of the goal line while trying to run for the extra point. For an instant, it appeared CC was going to break the game open in the second quarter when end Casey Polkowski blocked a punt, scooped up the ball at the Sexton 25 and had clear sailing ahead. But, he tripped and fell short of the end zone and the Cougars fumbled the ball back to the hosts a few plays later.

Energized by Catholic's inability to convert, Lansing Sexton drove 65 yards to tie the score, and then took advantage of a short CC punt to its own 31-yard line to build a 13-6 halftime lead. The Cougars ran roughshod over Lansing Sexton in the second half, but failed to reach the end zone until Owens scored on a 1-yard plunge on the first play of the fourth quarter. However, Boggiano's quarterback sneak for the game-tying extra point was stuffed and CC's five-game win streak was over despite picking up all 285 of its yards on the ground to Lansing Sexton's 140 yards of total offense, and holding a 12-5 advantage in first downs.

Owens and Pobojewski were shoe-ins for first-team All-City honors, and they were joined by Polkowski and tackle Jerry McGovern. Cougar tackle Jim Schultz and guard Jack Alberts were second-team selections. Owens also made the All-State team. However, with Ed Killoran returning from WW II, Sowle's tenure as Catholic Central's head coach was placed on hold for one season. Sowle left CC to take the head coaching job at Cathedral Prep in Erie, Pa.

CC/WC Archives

1945 City Champions

Front Row (l-r) Chuck Boggiano, E. J. Owens, Roman Boruta, Jack Alberts, Casey Polkowski, Richard Lang, James Schults, Jerry McGovern, Larry Pasbach, Danny Pobojewski, Richard Gibson, Mike Mead (Manager)

Second Row - Assist. Coach Casimer Pobojewski, Lyle Morrison, James Schmidt, Joseph Ogg, Robert Tietema, Gerald Houseman, Peter Weldon, Larry Pojeski, John Jendrasiak, Gerald Meike, Donald Rice, Raymond Erazmus (Manager), Fr. William J. Murphy, Coach Ted Sowle

Third Row - Albert Klingemire, and Jim Nachtegal (Managers), Alfred Szarowicz, Robert Noll, Dean Eister, Richard Dutkiewicz, Robert Konkle, Robert Tebean, Gerald Jeleniewski, Donald Walenga, Chuck Braniff, Bert Leatherman, Robert Setterson (Manager)

1945 Schedule/Results
Head Coach – Ted Sowle

Date	Opponent	Result		Location
Sep. 21	Muskegon	Lost	7-13	Hackley Field
Sep. 28	Muskegon Heights	Lost	13-21	Phillips Field
Oct. 5	Creston	Won	34-7	Houseman Field
Oct. 12	Ottawa Hills	Won	33-0	Houseman Field
Oct. 20	Central	Won	20-0	Houseman Field
Oct. 26	Union	Won	40-14	Houseman Field
Nov. 3	South	Won	34-14	Houseman Field
Nov. 9	Lansing Sexton	Lost	12-13	Lansing

	Record	Pts. Scored	Pts. Allowed
Overall	5-3	193	82
City League	5-0	161	35

-1946-

After completing his obligation to the U.S. Navy during WW II, Ed Killoran he came back to Grand Rapids and resumed his job as Catholic Central's head football coach in addition to adding the title of athletic director. It was as though he never left. Before leaving for the Pacific, Killoran had led the Cougars to the 1942 city crown, and he inherited a city league champ loaded with talent upon his return. Killoran named fellow WW II veterans Joe Godleski, a former CC All-City end, and Jack Young as assistant coaches. Killoran would also coach track and field in the spring, Godleski would guide the baseball team and Young, who coached the baseball team in the spring of '43, took over the basketball program.

A school-record and league-high 165 candidates showed up for the first day of CC practice in '46, but three senior running backs stood head and shoulders above the rest, if not in stature than in achievement and reputation: Eddie "E.J." Owens, Danny "Pobo" Pobojewski and Dick Gibson operating out of the T-formation. What the Cougars lacked was experience in the line.

"We have the makings of a good club, but the question in our minds is how long it will take the boys to acquire the experience necessary to play championship football," Killoran said. "In a scrimmage Friday night against East Grand Rapids out at Bigelow Field, the line looked surprisingly good for so early in the season, but there were obvious mistakes which we will have to iron out if we hope to give Muskegon a fight."

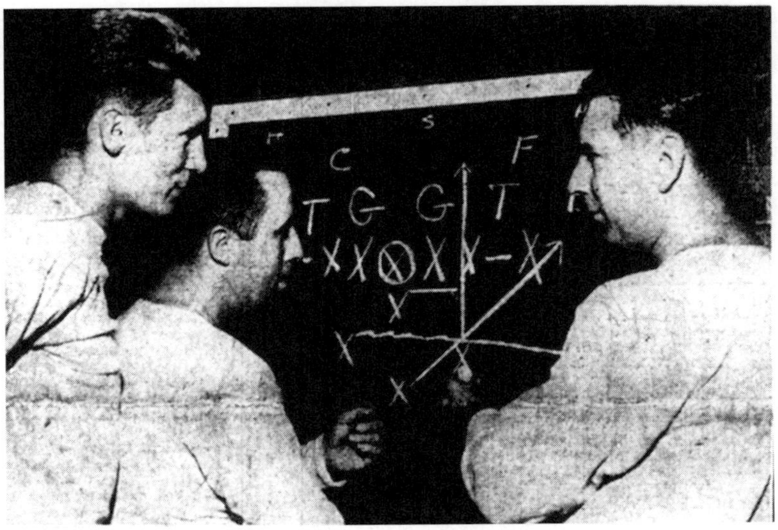

GR Herald Photo

Catholic Central's Coaching Staff

(l-r) Joe Godleski, Ed Killoran and Jack Young

Archives, Grand Rapids Public Library

An Early Season Practice at Buckley Field

(l-r) Bob Tietema, E. J. Owens, Dan Pobojewski, Tom Bieszka and Dick Gibson

Muskegon 26
Catholic Central 19
Friday, September 20 at Bigelow Field

The Cougars gave the Big Reds a fight in their opener, but only after falling behind 20-6 in the first half before 15,000 fans. Catholic Central couldn't complete its rally in the final two quarters and lost, 26-19. Pobojewski scored CC's first touchdown in the second quarter to cut the deficit to 13-6, but Muskegon quickly countered before time ran out. After falling behind 26-6 in the third quarter, Owens ran for 6- and 18-yard touchdowns in the final quarter, but the Cougars never got the ball back before time expired.

Muskegon Heights 13
Catholic Central 0
Friday, September 27 at Bigelow Field

Things didn't get any easier for Catholic Central, which welcomed defending state champion Muskegon Heights to Bigelow Field. Led by All-State quarterback, future Michigan State Spartan and Detroit Lion Everett "Sonny" Grandelius, the Tigers scored twice in the second half to saddle CC with a 13-0 defeat.

The Cougars reached the Heights 11-yard line in the first quarter, but lost the ball on downs. The Tigers scored on a methodical 60-yard drive in the third quarter and converted a fumble by Pobojewski at the Catholic Central 20 in the fourth. The loss was even more damaging because Owens suffered a leg injury that would prevent him from playing against Creston in the city league opener.

Catholic Central 19
Creston 13
Saturday, October 5 at Houseman Field

Eighty-two yards stood between Catholic Central and the first successful defense of its city title. The Cougars appeared to be in championship form while building a 12-0 lead against Creston in their league opener. Pobojewski scored on a 48-yard run in the first quarter, and he and Gibson chewed up big chunks of real estate during an 83-yard drive that ended with his 1-yard plunge in the second period.

But the Cougars lot their edge in the second half. The Polar Bears blocked a punt and recovered it at the CC 1-yard line and plunged in for their first TD. They later recovered a fumble at the CC 28 and took a one-point lead on Tom Van Wingen's 9-yard touchdown run and dropkicked extra point.

However, just as they did on their long scoring drive in the second period, Pobojewski and Gibson battered the Creston defense during a sustained downfield march, and Ed Lozon, Owens' backup, ran the ball into the end zone from 5 yards to pull out a dramatic 19-13 victory for Catholic Central.

Catholic Central 33
Ottawa Hills 13
Saturday, October 12 at Houseman Field

A week after narrowly averting a serious blow to their championship hopes, the Cougars maintained frontrunner status with a 33-13 drubbing of Ottawa Hills. The victory didn't come as easily as the final score would seem to indicate thanks to a leaky pass defense.

Catholic needed just five plays to cover 91 yards after stopping the Indians' first threat on downs. The drive was highlighted by Owens' 40-yard run through heavy traffic and Larry Pojeski's 1-yard smash for a 7-0 lead. The Cougars scored on their next drive as well after recovering an Ottawa fumble at its own 42. Quarterback Bob Tietema threw for 37 yards to Pobojewski, who three plays later dove in for a 2-yard TD. However, the Indians passed their way down the field and Jim Eaddy's 11-yard touchdown burst forced CC to settle for a 13-7 halftime lead.

After taking the second-half kickoff, Catholic wasted no time driving 76 yards; 73 came on runs of 18 by Owens, 23 by Gibson and 14 and 18 by Pobojewski who scored from 2 yards out, for a 20-7 lead. However, the Indians picked up 40 yards on two passes on the ensuing drive and cut CC's lead back down to seven on Dave Grant's 7-yard rip up the middle. The Cougars finally put the game away in the fourth quarter with a 60-yard scoring drive that ended on Pobojewski's 2-yard blast and 71-yard possession that concluded on Lozon's 5-yard tackle-breaking run. Catholic ended up with a 17-12 advantage in first downs but Ottawa completed 7 of 15 passes for 146 yards.

Central 18
Catholic Central 14
Friday, October 18 at Houseman Field

Sporting a 2-0 city league record and tied with South and Union atop the standings, Catholic Central was staring a trap game against 0-2 Central, which was respected as a preseason favorite to win the title, right in the face. Unfortunately, the Cougars flinched and the result was a devastating 18-14 loss. The fact that Killoran pointed out in the papers earlier in the week that his team wasn't looking ahead to meetings with the Trojans and Red Hawks was an indication that their focus may have been aimed in the wrong direction.

Catholic Central		Union H. S
Eddy	LE	Poterack
Schmidt	LT	Heald
Melke	LG	Ungrey
Bleszka	C	DeBoer
Bissot	RG	Burkholder
Jendrasiak	RT	Shusta
Weldon	RE	Kslelewske
Tietsma	QB	Krause
Gibson	LH	Reynders
Owen	RH	Wiest
Pobojewski	FB	Battenberg

Catholic	0	0	0	0	0
Union	0	0	6	0	6

Touchdown – Krause
Referee– Spurgeon, Umpire – Tillotson, Head Linesman – Horn

The Hilltoppers seized the momentum after receiving the opening kickoff and never really relinquished it. Tommy Steele's 40-yard sweep around left end set up Nordstrom's 5-yard touchdown for a 6-0 Central lead. Catholic stormed right back after Gibson's 50-yard run to the Hilltopper 3 set up Owens' touchdown and Gibson's go-ahead extra-point sweep, but Central was unfazed. The Hilltoppers got a break when Gibson fumbled and Kuyper recovered at the CC 28. Three plays later, Van Dam powered in from the 1-foot line and Central had a 13-7 halftime lead.

Pobojewski's fumble in the fourth quarter, which was recovered by Walenga, led to Central's decisive seven-play, 37-yard drive, which ended on Steele's short TD run. The Cougars again fought from behind, and Tietema's 15-yard touchdown pass to Eddy made it a one-possession game, but the Hilltoppers used up the rest of the clock to deal a severe blow to CC's title chances.

Union 6
Catholic Central 0
Saturday, October 26 at Houseman Field

The assignment was simple: beat Union and South in back-to-back games, and Catholic Central defends its city title.

Executing such a plan proved to be much more difficult. The Red Hawks avenged the 40-14 loss they suffered at the hands of CC a year earlier with an opportunistic 6-0 victory before a standing-room-only crowd estimated at 14,000.

Catholic Central advanced to inside the Red Hawks 10-yard line in the first and third quarters, but the Union defenders stood fast and took over on downs both times. The game turned in the third quarter when Don Buzalski recovered Owens' fumble for the Red Hawks at the Cougar 45. In its only display of offense the entire game, Union chipped away at the CC defense until right halfback Don Wiest's 24-yard pass to left half Bill Reynders put quarterback Warren Krause in position to score the game's only points on a 4-yard run three plays later.

South 14
Catholic Central 6
Friday, November 1 at Houseman Field

With their championship hopes dashed by two straight losses, the Cougars entered their city finale against league co-leader South as decided underdogs. That's how they looked, too, after giving up a pair of touchdowns in the first 16 minutes of the game. When Catholic finally snapped out of it, the hole it dug on a muddy field was too deep and it ended its league campaign with a 14-6 loss.

The Trojans took an early 7-0 lead on a 27-yard touchdown play that started with a pass down the middle from quarterback Jack Nelson to Fred Pickard, who smartly lateraled to Jack Van Ess who covered the rest of the distance. Nelson set up South's second touchdown when he intercepted a pass by Lozon and returned it to the CC 45. Six plays later, Marsh opened the second quarter with a 19-yard touchdown sweep around left end.

Lozon made up for his gaffe with a dazzling 63-yard touchdown run in the third quarter, but the CC offense bogged down the rest of the way. South's victory set up a championship showdown against Union on Thanksgiving Day, and given the way the Trojans and Catholic Central played before 17,000 fans under similar circumstances a year earlier, the debate over the need for a 25,000-seat stadium in Grand Rapids started anew.

Catholic Central		South H. S
Eddy	LE	Dood
Schmidt	LT	Houtman
Melke	LG	Delong
Bleszka	C	Hondorp
Balgarella	RG	Mick
Jendrasiak	RT	Monsma
Weldon	RE	Pickard
Tietsma	QB	Nelson
Lozon	LH	VanEss
Owen	RH	Marsh
Gibson	FB	Pellerito

Catholic	0	6	0	0	6
South	7	7	0	0	14

Touchdowns – VanEss, Marsh, Lozon
PAT – VanEss (2)
Referee– Mackay, Umpire – Wheeler, Head Linesman – Kleise

Lansing Sexton 19
Catholic Central 6
Friday, November 8 at Bigelow Field

Catholic Central appeared on the verge of redemption when it held a 6-0 halftime lead over unbeaten Lansing Sexton. But the Big Reds scored three unanswered touchdowns in the second half to leave town with a 19-6 victory.

Owens served notice that the Cougars weren't about to go down without a fight when he took a reverse handoff 77 yards for a 6-0 lead in the first quarter. But, Sexton halfback Dave Crego responded with a 57-yard run in the third quarter and the extra point put the Big Reds ahead to stay. An interception set up Sexton's second touchdown and the Cougars were out of options.

Detroit Catholic Central 21
Catholic Central 13
Friday, November 15 at University of Detroit Stadium

The upset-minded Cougars gave unbeaten and once-tied Detroit Catholic Central one of its toughest games of the season before falling 21-13. The Cougars trailed 7-0 going into the second quarter, but Tom Bieszka threw a 24-yard pass to Owens, and on the next play Tietema completed a 30-yard TD toss to halfback Bob Eddy for a 7-7 tie that stood until the third quarter when the Shamrocks took a 14-7 lead.

GR Herald Photo

University of Detroit's Catholic Central Connection
(l-r) John Zakem, Line Coach John Shada and Jack Hart

The Cougars started the fourth quarter at their own 35, and a series of runs and passes took the ball to the half-foot line, from where Gibson went over. However, Bieszka's extra-point kick flew wide of the upright and GRCC trailed, 14-13. Detroit responded immediately with a seven-play scoring drive, but the Cougars weren't quite done and drove all the way to the Shamrock 25 only to have the possession end on an interception at the 10.

A five-game losing streak took the luster off a once-promising season, but Pobojewski earned first-team All-City honors before heading off to Michigan State and eventually Purdue, and Eddy, Gibson, Bieszka and tackle Jim Schmitt were second-team selections.

South defeated Union, 6-0, to win the city championship before a jam-packed Houseman Field crowd of 13,000.

1946 Schedule/Results

Head Coach – Ed Killoran

Date	Opponent	Result		Location
Sep. 20	Muskegon	Lost	19-26	Bigelow Field
Sep. 27	Muskegon Heights	Lost	0-13	Bigelow Field
Oct. 5	Creston	Won	19-13	Houseman Field
Oct. 12	Ottawa Hills	Won	33-13	Houseman Field
Oct. 18	Central	Lost	14-18	Houseman Field
Oct. 26	Union	Lost	0-6	Houseman Field
Nov. 1	South	Lost	6-14	Houseman Field
Nov. 8	Lansing Sexton	Lost	6-19	Bigelow Field
Nov. 15	Detroit Catholic Central	Lost	13-21	Un of Detroit Stadium

	Record	Pts. Scored	Pts. Allowed
Overall	2-7	110	143
City League	2-3	72	64

-1947-

For the second time in his career, Ted Sowle replaced Ed Killoran as Catholic Central's head football coach. While Killoran guided the Cougars for one season after a stint in the Navy, Sowle put together a successful season at Cathedral Prep in Erie, Pa. When Killoran stepped down after the '46 season, the CC administration brought Sowle back to the Sheldon Avenue school. Sowle, who inherited just two starters and eight regulars, promptly installed the T-formation with the Notre Dame shift on offense, and a 6-2-2-1 base defense with options of playing with a five- or seven-man line.

GR Herald Photo

Coach Ted Sowle Returns to the CC Sidelines.

"We may lose several grid tussles this season," Sowle proclaimed during preseason drills, "but the boys really have the spirit and our opponents are going to know they've been in a ballgame."

Muskegon Heights 28
Catholic Central 8
Saturday, September 20 at Phillips Field

The Cougars had difficulty living up to even those qualified expectations in the 28-8 season-opening loss on the road against Muskegon Heights. The Tigers drove 62 yards in 12 plays to take a 7-0 lead on the opening possession. But although CC answered immediately with a 75-yard drive of its own with left end Frank Woronko scoring on a 20-yard pass from quarterback Tom Bieszka to cut the lead to 7-6, it was all Muskegon Heights the rest of the way. The Tigers scored on their ensuing drive, as well, and the Cougars threatened to counter again after moving the ball to the MHHS 12-yard line mostly on Woronko receptions, but Bieszka's fourth-down toss was intercepted. The Heights broke the game open with two touchdowns in the third quarter. Right end Tony Rubleski scored CC's final two points when he tackled a Tiger ball-carrier in the end zone in the fourth quarter.

Catholic Central 25
Holland 6
Saturday, September 27 at Holland

The halfback tandem of John Shutich and Joe Jarmulowski ran roughshod over Holland High in Catholic Central's easy 25-6 victory. Shutich got things started for the Cougars with a 57-yard touchdown run off a reverse early in the first quarter. After a series of line plunges by Shutich, Jarmulowski and Terry Spielmaker softened up the Dutchmen line, Shutich swept around end for a 7-yard touchdown that gave CC a 13-0 lead in the second quarter.

Holland cut into Catholic's lead by recovering a bad pass from center in the end zone and only trailed 13-6 at halftime. But Jarmulowski took advantage of superior line blocking, led by tackle John Jendrasiak and guard Tom O'Keefe, on a 17-yard romp that put the Cougars ahead 19-6 in the third quarter. Then, on the first play after CC blocked a Holland punt at its 10-yard line, quarterback Jim Koelzer tossed a flat pass to Ron Wolf, who did the rest.

Catholic Central 19
Union 19
Friday, October 3 at Houseman Field

As ties go, Catholic Central's 19-19 deadlock with Union had to be considered a good one given the fact the Cougars battled back from a 13-point deficit to earn it before 10,000 spectators. Catholic dug itself into an early hole when Bieszka's lateral to Shutich at the Union 41-yard line went astray and Bill Clinger pounced on the loose ball for the Red Hawks. Six plays later, Ed Timmerman flipped a shovel pass on first-and-goal to Max Curtice, who put Union ahead, 7-0. Another fumble, by Shutich, on CC's next possession, led to a 27-yard touchdown pass from Jan Wegenka to Ted Proctor, and the Cougars trailed by two scores.

Shutich made up for his mistake in the second quarter when his 63-yard run set up Howard Friar's 1-yard TD dive. In the third quarter, center Dick Pins recovered a Red Hawk fumble and Shutich knotted the score with a 24-yard spurt to paydirt.

Union regained the lead, 19-13, early in the fourth quarter when Al Manne broke loose off tackle and scored standing up. Once Catholic got the ball back on the kickoff, it covered 65 yards in just four minutes to draw even with the Red Hawks. Shutich capped the drive with an 18-yard run, but Bob Fitzgerald's game-winning extra-point attempt flew wide of the upright. Union made a strong bid to regain the lead one last time by advancing to the CC 20-yard line, but the Cougars knocked a Wegenka pass down at the goal line, and Shutich intercepted a throw by Manne at the 5 and returned it 15 yards with 30 seconds remaining.

Catholic Central		Union H. S
Woronko	LE	Proctor
Bissot	LT	VanderLaan
Bulgarella	LG	Jennings
Pins	C	Herren
Jaglowski	RG	VanGilst
Jendrasiak	RT	Levanduski
Robleski	RE	Slanger
Koelzer	QB	Lammers
Schutich	LH	Manne
Friar	RH	Curtice
Olewinski	FB	Timmerman

Catholic	0	7	6	6	19
Union	13	0	0	6	19

Touchdown – Curtice, Proctor, Manne, Friar, Schutich (2)
PAT – Doornbos, Fitzgerald
Referee– VanWingen, Umpire – Gettings, Head Linesman – Horn

GR Herald Photo

An anxious crowd looks on during the South game.

Catholic Central 20
South 14
Friday, October 10 at Houseman Field

When Ted Sowle returned to Grand Rapids to coach Catholic Central prior to the season, he had no idea he would have to talk about his game plans in hushed tones at his new house at 1717 Linden Ave. SE. He quickly found out, however, that living right next door, at 1721 Linden, was South coach George Needham. Admiring each other's lawns was one thing, sharing strategies quite another, especially the week before the Cougars were scheduled to play the defending city champion, who sported a 1-2 record but whose losses came against powerful Saginaw High (7-6) and Saginaw Arthur Hill (14-0).

Despite playing without the services of four starters for all but a short period in the third quarter, Catholic Central upended the Trojans 20-14 before a crowd of more than12,000, the largest of the season in the city league. The Cougars scored all their points in the first half and then held on to stave off South's second-half comeback bid.

Catholic Central recovered Lyle Playter's fumble on the opening kickoff at the South 36-yard line, and on the fourth play of the drive, after a Trojan offside penalty wiped out a fumble recovery of their own, Shutich swept around right end for 25 yards and the game's first score. An interception by Long, Shutich's 55-yard run and a defensive stand that forced South to punt set up CC's second touchdown, which came on a 1-foot quarterback sneak by Bieszka in the second quarter. A couple of minutes later, Jurewicz's fumble recovery at the Trojan 32 put Bieszka in position to launch a first-down touchdown pass to backup end Ed McHugh, who caught the ball at the 5 and trotted into the end zone for a 20-0 lead that held up for the final 10 minutes of the first half.

The Cougars gave up touchdowns in the third and fourth quarters while the offense sputtered. Then, once CC got rolling again to the South 24, Bieszka threw a costly interception. The defense held firm, however, while knocking down three Trojan passes, including one on fourth down. The Cougars advanced the ball all the way to the South 10 when time expired. Halfback Joe Schmitt sustained a mild concussion in the fourth quarter and spent the night in St. Mary's Hospital, where he was listed in satisfactory condition.

Catholic Central		South H. S
McHugh	LE	Dood
Monks	LT	Fish
Bulgarella	LG	Elenbaas
Pins	C	W. Baker
Jurewicz	RG	Parenti
Jendrasiak	RT	Merrill
Wolf	RE	B. Baker
Long	QB	Bigford
Schutich	LH	Playter
Fitzgerald	RH	Boom
Spielmaker	FB	Lammanoca

Catholic	6	14	0	0	20
South	0	0	7	7	14

Touchdowns – Schutich, Bieszka, McHugh, Baker, Boom
PAT – Fitzgerald, Schutich, Bigford (2)
Referee– VanWingen, Umpire – Gettings, Head Linesman – Wheeler

Central 13
Catholic Central 7
Saturday, October 18 at Houseman Field

Catholic Central pushed Central, which was coming off four consecutive easy victories, to the limit during a battle for first place in the City League, but was done in by a fourth-quarter touchdown in a 13-7 loss.

Tommy Steele, who was listed as questionable because of a recurring dislocated knee, set up the Hilltoppers' first score with a 26-yard pass to his brother Dick and then ran for the final 7 yards himself in the second quarter. The Cougars made a bid for the equalizer before halftime, but they couldn't get another play off from the Central 20-yard line before time expired.

Catholic evened the score with a dominating 97-yard march, featuring the battering-ram runs of Jarmulowski and John Olewinski that started in the third quarter and ended on Shutich's 4-yard sweep over the goal line early in the fourth period. The Hilltoppers answered with a 12-play drive of their own and fullback Gordy Osmun powered in for the decisive TD from 5 yards out. The Cougars had two more shots at victory, but turned the ball over once on downs and the last time on an interception by Tommy Steele with 20 seconds remaining.

Catholic Central 32
Creston 0
Thursday, October 23 at Houseman Field

John Shutich scored two touchdowns to lead Catholic Central to an easy 32-0 victory over winless Creston. What promised to be a difficult challenge for the Polar Bears became next to impossible when star fullback and standout defender Mick Boylan sustained a dislocated shoulder on the first play of the game and didn't return.

The Cougars got rolling in the first quarter after getting the ball for the first time on a Creston quick kick that traveled only a few yards to the CC 48. Ed Gerke, a backup running back, put Catholic ahead 6-0 with a 5-yard trot into the end zone. After getting the ball back on a blocked punt late in the first quarter, the Cougars drove from the Polar Bear 37 to the 14, and six plays later, Shutich circled across the goal line for a 13-0 second-quarter lead.

In the third quarter, Shutich's 66-yard dash set up a 1-yard touchdown pass from Bieszka to Woronko. Shutich added

Archives, Grand Rapids Public Library

All-City Cougar Center Dick Pins

a 25-yard scoring jaunt in the fourth quarter and after CC got the ball back on a fumble, Friar closed out the game with a 2-yard scoring run and a victory-sealing interception.

Catholic Central 26
Ottawa Hills 6
Saturday, November 1 at Houseman Field

Catholic Central locked up second place with an effortless 26-6 victory over Ottawa Hills. The Cougars did a better job of stopping themselves than the Indians on the game-opening drive which had a touchdown called back because of a penalty and ended with a fumble at the 10-yard line. But two plays after getting the ball back on a poor punt to the Ottawa 29, Olewinski galloped 23 yards to score standing up.

Catholic Central covered 91 yards in two plays – Jarmulowski's 31-yard run behind the blocks of right guard Gene Jaglowski and right tackle George Jurewicz and Bieszka's 60-yard pass to end Leo Huizinga – to take a 13-0 lead in the second quarter. The Cougars needed just two plays to open up a 20-0 lead before halftime with Olewinski running for 2 and left tackle John "Lard" Jendrasiak springing Jarmulowski for a 45-yard run up the sideline. In the fourth quarter, Shutich intercepted a pass thrown by Ottawa's Tom Greenhoe to set up Olewinski's 16-yard exclamation mark.

Archives, Grand Rapids Public Library

CC Players Pack for the Erie Academy Game.

Catholic Central 7
Erie Academy 0
Friday, November 7 at Erie, Pa.

GR Herald Photo

CC Halfbacks
(i-r) Ed Gerke, Joe Jarmulowski and Howard Friar.

The longest road trip in school history ended with CC's 7-0 victory at Erie Academy, which was considered one of the top high school teams in the East. Coach Ted Sowle, who coached Erie Prep the previous season, saw his undersized Cougars score on their first possession and then brave raw winds and rain to upset the newly crowned Erie City champions.

Catholic's 64-yard game-winning, all-rush drive got a boost on Jarmulowski's 18-yard run that angled in over left end Woronko's block, and ended on Bieszka's tricky lateral to Olewinski, who looped around end and outraced the Lions to the corner of the end zone to score standing up. Although the conditions degenerated further in the second half, CC dominated. Prep's deepest penetration of the game came in the fourth quarter when it reached the Catholic 41. However, defensive guard Dom Bulgarella crashed through the Lions' line, knocked the ball loose with a vicious tackle and recovered the victory-clinching fumble, much to the delight of the Erie Prep cheerleaders, who came out in support of their former coach.

The Cougars, who local fans dismissed as "midgets" before the game, outgained Academy, 257-75, had 15 first downs to seven and reached the 7-yard line late in the fourth quarter only to lose 5 yards on a delay-of-game penalty before turning the ball over on a fumble.

Catholic Central 31
Detroit Catholic Central 7
Friday, November 21 at Houseman Field

The "terrors of the city," as Houseman Field public address announcer Robert C. Todish dubbed the Cougars because of their unending list of ethnic last names, clobbered Detroit Catholic Central with a display of senior power, 31-7, in their season finale, which was delayed a week because of inclement weather.

After falling behind 7-6 in the second quarter, CC struck for two touchdowns in the third quarter and a pair in the fourth to squash the traditional Motor City power. All five TDs were scored by outgoing seniors starting with Jarmulowski, who drew first blood by completing a 54-yard drive with a 13-yard touchdown off a shovel pass. The Cougars took the lead for good in the third quarter on Bieszka's 14-yard touchdown pass to Woronko, and Olewinski made the score 19-7 a short time later with a 27-yard romp through the Shamrock defense. Shutich capped off his fine career with a 48-yard scoring run early in the fourth quarter and Wolf's interception led to his 14-yard TD that topped off a fine 6-2-1 season.

Catholic Central placed four its so-called "Mighty Mites" on the All-City first team, which featured five members of Central's city championship squad. Shutich, Jendrasiak, Bulgarella and center Dick Pins earned top honors and Woronko was a second-team selection.

1947 Schedule/Results

Head Coach – Ted Sowle

Date	Opponent	Result		Location
Sep. 20	Muskegon Heights	Lost	8-28	Phillips Field
Sep. 27	Holland	Won	25-6	Holland
Oct. 3	Union	Tie	19-19	Houseman Field
Oct. 10	South	Won	20-14	Houseman Field
Oct. 18	Central	Lost	7-13	Houseman Field
Oct. 23	Creston	Won	32-0	Houseman Field
Nov. 1	Ottawa Hills	Won	26-6	Houseman Field
Nov. 7	Erie Academy	Won	7-0	Erie, PA
Nov. 21	Detroit Catholic Central	Won	31-7	Houseman Field

	Record	Pts. Scored	Pts. Allowed
Overall	6-2-1	175	93
City League	3-1-1	104	52

-1948-

If all it took to win championships was outstanding character, Catholic Central coach Ted Sowle would have had no problem picking his Cougars to capture the City League crown. However, with so many key vacancies to fill from the team that placed second, Sowle wasn't even convinced CC could produce a winning season.

"Catholic Central won't be any pushover," Sowle said, "but it won't be until after they have had a tough few games under their belts that we will be able to judge the lads under actual conditions."

Catholic Central 7
Muskegon Heights 0
Saturday, September 18 at South Field

Sowle had a better idea of what his team, with its brand new starting backfield, was capable of doing after it snapped a three-game losing streak with what was considered a staggering upset over Muskegon Heights. The Tigers had won 27 straight games over four seasons going into the contest.

With a capacity crowd of 12,000 looking on, CC built what turned out to be an insurmountable lead midway through the second quarter when quarterback Jim Koelzer lulled Muskegon Heights to sleep with a lazy dropback before lofting an 11-yard touchdown pass to right end Don Kozminski, who was uncovered in the end zone. The score came four plays after George Jurewicz recovered a Heights fumble. The Cougars dodged a bullet after George Howell, the Tigers' All-State halfback, intercepted a Koelzer pass and returned it to the CC 30. Four plays later, Howell dove in from the 2 for what appeared to be a touchdown, but the officials ruled he fumbled before he scored and the Cougars recovered the ball in the end zone for a touchback.

Catholic was in position to put the game out of reach in the second half, but Bob Fitzgerald's 23-yard field-goal try bounced off the crossbar. The victory wasn't a fluke, as CC held a 12-8 edge in first downs.

Catholic Central 13
Holland 12
Saturday, September 25 at South Field

Thoroughly outplayed in the first half, Catholic Central rallied to take the lead on Fitzgerald's extra point late in the fourth quarter and then won the battle of the clock to pull out one of the most amazing wins in school history, 13-12, over Holland High.

A 50-yard pass led to the Dutchmen's first touchdown in the first quarter, and Holland took a 12-0 lead in the second quarter after completing a 60-yard drive with a 20-yard touchdown pass from Ron Appledorn to Ken VanWieren. The Cougars finally got untracked late in the first half, and pounded the 83 yards, including the final 1 by Ed Gerke, to cut the deficit to 12-6.

After a scoreless third quarter, Catholic converted on fourth-and-18 with Joe Schmidt's desperation pass to Gerke reaching the first-down marker at the Holland 20 with only an inch to spare. Koelzer then threw the touchdown pass to Bill Jacobitz that set up Fitzgerald's game-winning kick with three minutes remaining. The game wasn't over until Dutchmen quarterback Dave Kempker was brought down after a twisting, turning, spinning 30-yard run 10 yards shy of the goal line as the final gun sounded.

Union 31
Catholic Central 0
Saturday, October 2 at Houseman Field

"Football madness has gripped Grand Rapids," blared *The Grand Rapids Herald* in advance of the traditional rivalry showdown between undefeated Catholic Central and Union, which buried its first two opponents, Traverse City and Muskegon Heights, by a combined score of 73-21. All 11,700 tickets were purchased by noon on Thursday and emotions were running high because so many players on both teams shared a Polish heritage.

"It's a tossup where the breaks will be decisive," legendary Union coach Milo Sukup predicted while boosting the hype.

However, while Sowle may have been poor-mouthing his team to stir overconfidence in the Red Hawks, he couldn't have been more prophetic when he said, "going by our past record, I don't see how we can be anything but real underdogs in the clash."

That turned out to be the understatement of the year when the Cougars lost, 31-0. The Red Hawks covered 90 yards in nine plays to take a 6-0 first-quarter lead on Ed Timmerman's 2-yard plunge and never looked back. Timmerman's second of three touchdowns covered 53 yards and put Union ahead by the score of 13-0 in the second quarter.

Archives, Grand Rapids Public Library
CC's Jim Koelzer

Catholic Central 13
South 7
Saturday, October 9 at Houseman Field

Catholic Central needed a win against South High to stay in the City League title hunt, and once again came from behind to win, 13-7. Perhaps still licking their wounds from the 31-0 beating inflicted by Union a week earlier, the Cougars fumbled the opening kickoff and promptly fell behind on Bruce Bigford's touchdown pass to Ron DeKruif.

Stymied by turnovers the remainder of the first quarter, Catholic finally got a break when end Jim Whalen recovered a Trojan fumble at the CC 46. Halfback Terry Spielmaker "charged up" the Cougars with a 42-yard masterpiece to the 10-yard line, and Koelzer tossed to Whalen for the touchdown, but Fitzgerald's extra point was wide to the left.

The CC defense saved the day when it forced South to give the ball back on downs deep in Cougar territory late in the first half. Sowle's "Destiny Kids," as they were becoming known, struck for the game-winner early in the third quarter. The 52-yard drive was aided by a 15-yard Trojan penalty and completed by Spielmaker's hard-nosed, 9-yard, off-tackle touchdown run. After Fitzgerald missed a field-goal attempt, South valiantly tried to fashion a comeback of its own, but Gerke's interception of Bigford's pass at the Catholic 10-yard line, and 25-yard return, ran out what was left of the clock.

Catholic Central 33
Central 19
Friday, October 15 at Houseman Field

The Cougars knew they needed help from their City League brethren against Union somewhere along the line, but they helped their own championship aspirations with a 33-19 victory against Central. Despite starting its fifth different backfield combination in as many games, Catholic punished the Hilltoppers with a relentless rushing attack.
The Cougars set the tone in the first quarter with a bruising 80-yard drive that culminated with Spielmaker's

GR Herald Photo

CC's Starting Backfield for the Central Game
(l-r) Ed Gerke, Terry Spielmaker, Jim Koelzer and Bob Fitzgerald

6-yard power run up the gut. Catholic Central forced four turnovers during the game and the first, a fumble recovered by James Kowalczyk at the Central 19, led to a Koelzer-to-Jim Whalen touchdown pass for a 13-0 lead.

The Hilltoppers cut into the deficit on Howard Perrin's 55-yard touchdown pass to tiny Pat Barr for the only score of the second quarter. Then, Central tied the score when Earl Whitney returned the kickoff to open the second half 85 yards for a touchdown. That just served to fire up the Cougars, and after Gene Jaglowski recovered a Barr fumble at the Central 20, Gerke regained the lead with a 1-yard touchdown run. The Hilltoppers lost another fumble, this time at their own 21, just a few minutes later and Spielmaker made them pay with a 4-yard score that put CC ahead 27-13 in the third quarter.

Catholic's goal-line stand stopped Central's ensuing drive at the 1-foot line, but the Hilltoppers converted a Catholic Central fumble into Barr's short touchdown reception anyway. CC countered that score in the fourth after Barr muffed a punt and Fitzgerald cashed in from the 1.

Catholic Central 13
Creston 0
Saturday, October 23 at Houseman Field

Creston coach Gil Powers served notice in no uncertain terms that his Polar Bears were going to have a say in the City League race by beating Catholic Central and bringing down the Union juggernaut the following week. "We're out to win that ballgame Saturday night," he said. "We're not conceding an inch and furthermore, we're pointing for this one."

Powers' powerful words held water during the scoreless first half, but then Cougars struck for two touchdowns in the third quarter to pull out a 13-0 victory and stay on the Red Hawks' heels in the standings.

The Cougars started to establish their superiority late in the first half when they reached the Creston 6-yard line, but time expired before they could run another play. Catholic opened the second half with a nine-play, 61-yard scoring drive that featured Gerke's 21-yard rush and Spielmaker's 4-yard TD run. An interception by CC's Joe Schmidt, which was followed by a Cougar fumble recovered by the Polar Bears, which was followed by Jurewicz's pickoff and return to the Creston 22, led to Fitzgerald's back-breaking 2-yard touchdown. Catholic had a 12-3 advantage in first downs over the Polar Bears, who lost star fullback Jim Gravelyn to injuries in the first quarter.

Catholic Central 21
Ottawa Hills 6
Friday, October 29 at Houseman Field

Catholic Central's anti-climactic 21-6 finish over winless Ottawa Hills started the waiting game. The Cougars were assured of second place in the City League, but if Union could just lose one of its remaining three games... .

A hard-driving rushing attack and the Indians' penchant for fumbling the ball made for an easy night's work for CC. Jacobitz scored the first Cougar touchdown in the first quarter when he recovered a fumbled Ottawa handoff in the end zone. Spielmaker capped a 62-yard drive with a 9-yard touchdown run in the second quarter, and Fitzgerald made a 17-yard field goal, the first of the season in the City League, in the third quarter. A 45-

Archives, Grand Rapids Public Library
Lineman George Jurewicz

yard touchdown romp by Indian fullback Ken Jones in the fourth quarter was countered by tiny backup Cougar running back Chuck Frodl, who followed a convoy of blockers for 9 yards to the end zone.

Catholic Central 15
Erie Academy 7
Saturday, November 13 at Houseman Field

Ed Gerke scored two touchdowns and Fitzgerald added a field goal to lead Catholic Central to a 15-7 victory and a two-game series sweep over Erie (Pa.) Academy. Catholic was forced to punt on its first series, but the Lion returnman muffed the kick and Whalen recovered the ball 40 yards from the end zone. Gerke covered 23 of the remaining yards on one run to the 5, and carried the next two times as well, scoring from the 2.

Fitzgerald's short field goal capped an 89-yard drive from the CC 6-yard line in the second quarter and Gerke's 15-yard touchdown romp in the third provided an insurmountable 15-0 lead.

Union's state-championship team placed an unmatched four players on the All-City squad named by *The Grand Rapids Herald*, but two Cougars, Jurewicz and Koelzer, the only junior, also were honored. Catholic led the City League with three second-team selections: Jaglowski, Jacobitz and Spielmaker. *The Grand Rapids Press* All-City first 11, which was selected by the City League coaches, featured Spielmaker and Jacobitz, along with six Red Hawks.

What Sowle didn't know at the start of the season obviously didn't hurt him, but the undisputable 7-1 finish was a portent of things to come.

1948 Schedule/Results

Head Coach – Ted Sowle

Date	Opponent	Result		Location
Sep. 20	Muskegon Heights	Won	7-0	South Field
Sep. 25	Holland	Won	13-12	South Field
Oct. 2	Union	Lost	0-31	Houseman Field
Oct. 9	South	Won	13-7	Houseman Field
Oct. 15	Central	Won	33-19	Houseman Field
Oct. 23	Creston	Won	13-0	Houseman Field
Oct. 29	Ottawa Hills	Won	21-0	Houseman Field
Nov. 13	Erie Academy	Won	15-7	Houseman Field

	Record	Pts. Scored	Pts. Allowed
Overall	7-1	115	76
City League	4-1	80	57

-1949-

A year, almost to the day, after Catholic Central coach Ted Sowle feigned ignorance over what kind of team he had going into the season, he made no bones about what he expected from his outfit in 1949. When asked by a reporter if he thought the Cougars should be favored to win the City League title, Sowle, barefoot, sunburned and sporting a two-day beard said after a preseason practice session, "Yes, I think you can say that." Catholic Central also had the schedule designed to produce a state championship, if the Cougars could get through it unscathed.

Catholic Central 20
Muskegon 0
Friday, September 16 at Hackley Field

Led by the All-City tandem of quarterback Jim Koelzer and halfback "Terrible" Terry Spielmaker, Catholic Central passed its first test with flying colors by throttling traditional powerhouse Muskegon, 20-0, on the road. Spielmaker scored all three touchdowns against the Big Reds, who were a preseason pick to win the state title. A crowd exceeding 12,000, one of the biggest in Hackley Field History, watched the Cougars amass 18 first downs while relying exclusively to rushing plays, to just four for Muskegon.

Paced by the hard running of fullback Bob Fitzgerald, another returnee from CC's once-beaten City League runner-ups, and Spielmaker, the Cougars efficiently covered 56 yards with a mixture of runs out of the tight T-formation and spread sets. Spielmaker's 18-yard burst set up his 1-yard plunge for a 7-0 lead in the first quarter. Spielmaker capped a 90-yard drive in the second quarter with a scoring burst from the 1-foot line and his 5-yard run punctuated a 99-yard possession in the third.

Archives, Grand Rapids Public Library

CC Defenders close in on a Muskegon Heights' runner.

Catholic Central 16
Muskegon Heights 0
Friday, September 23 at Phillips Field

Muskegon Heights had a significant size advantage but couldn't contend with Catholic Central's speed and athleticism. With Spielmaker again leading the way, the Cougars triumphed on the lakeshore for the second time in seven days, 16-0.

Catholic took advantage of three Tiger fumbles to score all of its points. In the first quarter, center Al Rice pounced on the ball at the Heights 37-yard line, and Spielmaker went on to score on a 14-yard sprint off left tackle Jim Jebb's block. The Cougars also got a break when Tiger receiver Bob Pawlak dropped what would have been a 17-yard touchdown pass on fourth down in the end zone. In the third quarter, CC end Dick Axdorf recovered a fumble at the Tiger 23 to set up Fitzgerald's 11-yard touchdown run behind Rice's blocking up the middle. Late in the fourth quarter, a fumble recovery by end Willie Wolf set up Fitzgerald's 15-yard field goal with less than a minute to play. The game was marred by chippy play and the Cougars might have scored even more points if they hadn't been penalized several times for 70 yards. However, even the Muskegon Heights fans booed the officials when they neglected to flag a Tiger tackler who blatantly twisted the neck of CC running back Pete "Butterball" Naimo.

Catholic Central 42
Toledo Scott Catholic 13
Friday, September 30 at South Field

Ohio powerhouse Toledo Scott Catholic arrived at South Field with the promise of dazzling Catholic Central with its combination of speed and size. It was the Cougars, however, who left mouths agape with their T-formation wizardry in a statement-making 42-13 drubbing.

Koelzer's tricky play fakes and the precisely synchronized blocking of the CC line would have made ordinary backs tough to stop. But with "Terrible" Terry Spielmaker, battering-ram fullback Fitzgerald and "Butterball" Naimo, described by one writer as a "baby tank," carrying the ball, the Cougars were an irresistible force.

Ron Downer's recovery of a Toledo fumble at the CC 36 set Catholic's offense into perpetual motion. The Cougars' three-pronged running attack took turns gouging the Scott defense until Naimo swept 2 yards around

GR Herald Photo

Catholic Linemen
(l-r) - Jim Jeeb, Roger Feutz, Jerry Hekker, Norm Placheski

left end behind three blockers who preceded him across the goal line. A 21-yard pass from Koelzer to Naimo set up one of Spielmaker's patented bullet runs through the line for a 2-yard TD and 13-0 lead.

GR Herald Photo
CC's Pass-catchers (l-r) Dick Axdorf and Willie Wolf

The Catholic defense gave up its first score of the season on a 36-yard Scott touchdown pass in the second quarter, but the Cougars scored all the points they needed to win on the ensuing possession. After faking two handoffs, Koelzer also threw a 36-yard TD pass to Wolf, who sauntered into the end zone untouched. Early in the third quarter, Spielmaker catapulted through the line for a 62-yard touchdown and later Fitzgerald kicked a field goal. In the fourth quarter, CC negotiated what amounted to a 114-yard touchdown drive, officially 99 yards but lengthened by a clipping penalty, with a 12-yard pass from Koelzer to Wolf, upping the score to 36-13. Reserve running back Edmund Brochu finished off the scoring with a 12-yard touchdown run.

Catholic Central 32
Union 6
Friday, October 7 at Houseman Field

In what could later be looked back upon as a symbolic passing of the torch, Catholic Central dismantled defending city and state champion Union, 32-6, as more than 10,500 fans watched in awe at Houseman Field.

Spielmaker started the Red Hawks off to their first defeat in 12 tries dating back to 1947 after Cougar tackle Norm Plachecki recovered a fumble at the Union 30-yard line. Four alternating runs by Naimo and Spielmaker moved the ball to the 1-foot line, and Spielmaker scored from there with less than two minutes gone in the first quarter. Catholic's next possession started at its own 42 after forcing a Union punt, and the drive, sparked by Spielmaker's 25-yard gain, ended on his 9-yard touchdown run. Nick Bono, the Cougars' diminutive return specialist, ran the third-quarter kickoff back 77 yards to the Red Hawk 18, and Naimo covered the remaining distance on the first play of the second half to give CC a 19-0 lead.

Roger Granzevoort scored for Union on a 9-yard touchdown reception and Naimo countered with an explosive 44-yard TD run. After Spielmaker thwarted the final Red Hawk threat by intercepting a pass by Eugene Lekenta, backup CC halfback LaVerne Wolf broke three tackles en route to a 23-yard touchdown with 47 seconds remaining.

GR Herald Photo

Willie Wolf covers a South fumble in the Cougar endzone.

Catholic Central 27
South 7
Friday, October 14 at South Field

Putting his love for trigonometry and physics to good use, Catholic Central quarterback Jim Koelzer engineered a 27-7 come-from-behind victory over South.

A fumbled handoff on the first play of the game led to a Trojan touchdown, and the Cougars trailed 7-0. South came close to doubling its lead after intercepting a pass and driving to the CC 3-yard line, only to fumble the ball into the end zone. Starting at their own 20, the Cougars starting clicking on all cylinders thanks to Koelzer's deft ball-handling. Spielmaker got the scoring drive started with a 17-yard run and finished it in the end zone with an 8-yard scamper after taking Koelzer's fancy pitchout.

Catholic opened the second half with an onside kick, which Spielmaker recovered, and Naimo broke the 7-7 deadlock by hurtling himself 6 yards to paydirt. Ron Makowski's fumble recovery led to a bronco-busting, 24-yard touchdown run by Fitzgerald, who flattened a Trojan defensive back on his way to the goal line.

Koelzer was just as tricky on defense, as South end Jack Carroll found out when Koelzer stripped the ball out of his hands in the fourth quarter. A 29-yard pass from Koelzer to Willie Wolf put the ball at the Trojan 5, and on the next play, the slick QB befuddled the Trojans by faking one way and passing the other to Axdorf, who was waiting for the ball all alone in the end zone. The Cougars racked up 17 first downs and allowed nine.

Catholic Central 27
Central 12
Saturday, October 22 at Houseman Field

An action-packed clash of unbeaten teams treated nearly 11,000 breathless fans to a display of offensive fireworks rarely seen Grand Rapids, and when the smoke finally cleared, Catholic Central was left standing with a crucial 27-12 victory over Central.

A string of jaw-dropping plays started on the opening kickoff when the Hilltoppers were unable to field the ball and Catholic's LaVerne Wolf recovered at the Central 28-yard line. Five plays later, Fitzgerald burrowed into the end zone, but missed the extra point, for a 6-0 lead.

The Hilltoppers countered CC's superior ground attack with an outstanding passing scheme, but Spielmaker snuffed out a threat later in the first quarter with an interception at the Cougar 13. With time running out in the opening period, Rice recovered a fumble by Central's Pat Barr at the Hilltopper 29, and Naimo's 14-yard run set up his 3-yard touchdown for a 13-0 lead early in the second quarter. The game was shaping up as a CC runaway until Central's Steve Kuieck intercepted a Koelzer pass and returned it to the 43, and on the next play, Earl Whitney broke loose for a 57-yard touchdown.

Leading 13-7, Catholic opened the second half with an impressive 80-yard drive that ended on Naimo's nifty

7-yard sweep for a touchdown. Central's plan to strike back quickly in the third quarter backfired when CC linebacker Bill Banaszak intercepted Jackson's first-down pass and returned it to the Cougar 44. On second down, Naimo swept around end for 33 yards to set up Spielmaker's 10-yard rushing touchdown. Central made good on its last-gasp effort when Barr scored on a 56-yard pass from Lou Mazarella, but the Cougars were once again end-zone-bound when time expired.

Catholic Central piled up a remarkable 367 rushing yards in its sixth straight win without a loss, but Central coach Chuck Irwin said the turning point of the game came at the very beginning when Wolf recovered what amounted to an unintentional onside kick.

Catholic Central 34
Creston 7
Friday, October 28 at Houseman Field

Sowle was filled with trepidation going into the Creston game. "This team has been up for six weeks," the Catholic Central coach said, "and they could suffer a letdown." However, even though "Terrible" Terry Spielmaker the touchdown maker was sidelined by a foot injury, Sowle needn't have worried. The Cougars jumped out to a 21-0 lead in the first 15 minutes and buried the Polar Bears 34-7 to stay undefeated.

On Catholic's first play of the game, Koelzer faked two handoffs to diving backs before giving the ball to Naimo, who chugged 76 yards to the Creston 8-yard line. The out-of-breath Naimo failed to gain on the next play, but LaVerne Wolf did his best Spielmaker imitation by taking a pitchout the distance for a 7-0 lead.

Wolf finished off an 85-yard drive early in the second quarter with an 18-yard scoring sweep around right end and a few seconds later, the Cougars recovered a Creston fumble at its 17. On the very next play, Koezlar faked three handoffs before playing pitch and catch with end Al Downer, who stepped easily over the goal line. Sowle substituted liberally the rest of the way, and in the third quarter, backup quarterback Ron Makowski passed to end Dick Vorenkamp who lateraled to Hal Russell for a 45-yard touchdown play, and Bono charged in for a 9-yard touchdown in the fourth quarter to complete the scoring.

Catholic Central 27
Ottawa Hills 6
Saturday, November 5 at Houseman Field

With city and state championships hanging in the balance for Catholic Central, an odd exchange of verbal sparring broke out in the newspapers prior to the Cougars' game against Ottawa Hills, which was feeling cocky following its 19-0 upset of South and unexpected victory over Holland earlier in the season.

"I think we've got the best passing game in the state and we're faster than Catholic," said Indians coach Wendy Emery. "The team is really up for this one and my boys think they can do it."

Archives, Grand Rapids Public Library

Halfback Hal Russell outruns the Ottawa defenders.

Sowle didn't try to talk his counterpart out of his bravado.

"We really want to win this one, (but) Ottawa is considerably faster than we are," Sowle said. "We'll open up with everything we've got. We're afraid of Ottawa and won't take any chances."

The Indians may have talked the talk before the game, but the No. 1-ranked Cougars walked the walk during a 27-7 thumping that came with the undisputed City League crown. After seven stellar performances, Koelzer did the unthinkable by playing even better than anyone thought possible. After receiving the opening kickoff, Koelzer masterfully guided the Cougars 88 yards in 10 plays, the last of which was a touchdown plunge by Naimo, who was now being called "Pistol Pete."

A few minutes later, Koelzer needed just five notes to orchestrate a 65-yard scoring drive which Naimo brought to a crescendo with a 31-yard sprint down the sideline to the goal line. In the second quarter, CC covered 94 yards in just five plays, including three Koelzer passes. His final strike went to LaVerne Wolf in the end zone. The Indians scored before halftime on a 6-yard reception by Don Eaddy, but Koelzer canceled that out with a 28-yard touchdown pass to Spielmaker in the third quarter.

It was 8-0 Catholic Central's 13th straight victory dating back to 1948, and no wonder that the Cougars were being called "Michigan's little Notre Dame."

Catholic Central 40
LaPorte (Ind.) High 28
Friday, November 11 at Kiwanis Field, IN

Although Catholic Central still had an intersectional game at LaPorte (Ind.) High School to play, the Associated Press named the Cougars the undisputed state champions. It was the second mythical state title for CC, state title No. 2 for Sowle, and the second in a row for the City League, which was represented at the top of the heap by Union in '48.

Sowle was intent on not tarnishing what the Cougars had accomplished by laying an egg in Indiana, and said LaPorte was even better than Toledo Scott Catholic. Although the game was in doubt until the final quarter, Catholic Central rose to the occasion, thanks to Naimo's long-distance running, with a 40-28 victory that earned it the title of one of the best teams ever to come out of Grand Rapids.

The Cougars charged out to a 14-0 first-quarter lead on Fitzgerald's 1-yard run and Naimo's 70-yard sling-shot off tackle. The Slicers answered with a 71-yard touchdown, but CC took a 21-7 lead early in the second quarter on Naimo's 2-yard run. LaPorte scored again before halftime and the Cougars led only by seven points going into the second half.

With his short legs, Naimo hardly looked the part of sprinter, but he dashed 81 yards for his third touchdown and a 27-14 third-quarter advantage. The Slicers drove 85 yards to again make it a one-possession game, but CC took control for good when it set up for what appeared to be a 20-yard field goal attempt. However, Koezlar came out throwing and his pass to Willie Wolfe increased the Cougars' lead to 33-21. Spielmaker put the game out of reach with a 12-yard touchdown and Catholic Central's 20 seniors came home with a perfect record.

To no one's surprise, Catholic Central dominated the All-City squad with six first-team and three second-team selections. Koelzer, Spielmaker, tackles Norm Plachecki and Jim Jebb, guard Gerard Hekker and end Willie Wolf earned top honors and Rice, Naimo and Fitzgerald were on the second team.

CC/WC Archives

CC's All-City PLayers
(l-r) -Jerry Hekker, Jim Jeeb, Norm Plachecki, WIllie Wolf, Allen Rice, Jim Koelzer, Terry Speilmaker, Bob Fitzgerald and Pete Naimo

1949 Schedule/Results
Head Coach – Ted Sowle

Date	Opponent	Result		Location
Sep. 16	Muskegon	Won	20-0	Hackley Field
Sep. 23	Muskegon Heights	Won	16-0	Phillips Field
Sep. 30	Toledo Scott	Won	42-13	South Field
Oct. 7	Union	Won	32-6	Houseman Field
Oct. 14	South	Won	27-7	South Field
Oct. 22	Central	Won	27-12	Houseman Field
Oct. 28	Creston	Won	34-7	Houseman Field
Nov. 5	Ottawa Hills	Won	27-6	Houseman Field
Nov. 11	LaPorte, IN	Won	40-28	Kiwanis Field, IN

	Record	Pts. Scored	Pts. Allowed
Overall	9-0	265	79
City League	5-0	157	45

-1950-

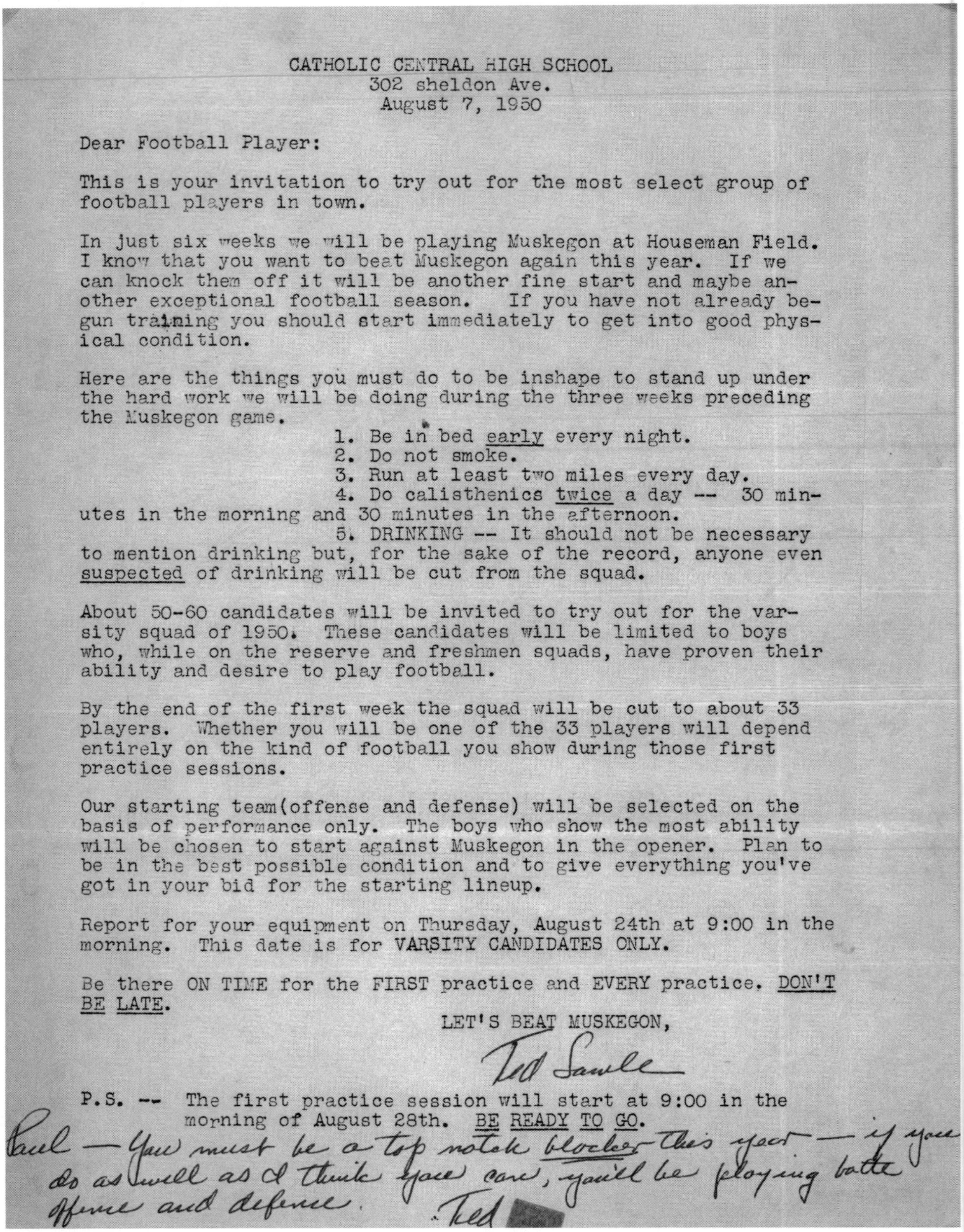

CATHOLIC CENTRAL HIGH SCHOOL
302 sheldon Ave.
August 7, 1950

Dear Football Player:

This is your invitation to try out for the most select group of football players in town.

In just six weeks we will be playing Muskegon at Houseman Field. I know that you want to beat Muskegon again this year. If we can knock them off it will be another fine start and maybe another exceptional football season. If you have not already begun training you should start immediately to get into good physical condition.

Here are the things you must do to be inshape to stand up under the hard work we will be doing during the three weeks preceding the Muskegon game.

1. Be in bed early every night.
2. Do not smoke.
3. Run at least two miles every day.
4. Do calisthenics twice a day -- 30 minutes in the morning and 30 minutes in the afternoon.
5. DRINKING -- It should not be necessary to mention drinking but, for the sake of the record, anyone even suspected of drinking will be cut from the squad.

About 50-60 candidates will be invited to try out for the varsity squad of 1950. These candidates will be limited to boys who, while on the reserve and freshmen squads, have proven their ability and desire to play football.

By the end of the first week the squad will be cut to about 33 players. Whether you will be one of the 33 players will depend entirely on the kind of football you show during those first practice sessions.

Our starting team(offense and defense) will be selected on the basis of performance only. The boys who show the most ability will be chosen to start against Muskegon in the opener. Plan to be in the best possible condition and to give everything you've got in your bid for the starting lineup.

Report for your equipment on Thursday, August 24th at 9:00 in the morning. This date is for VARSITY CANDIDATES ONLY.

Be there ON TIME for the FIRST practice and EVERY practice. DON'T BE LATE.

LET'S BEAT MUSKEGON,

P.S. -- The first practice session will start at 9:00 in the morning of August 28th. BE READY TO GO.

Paul — You must be a top notch blocker this year — if you do as well as I think you can, you'll be playing both offense and defense. Ted

CC/WC Archives

Summer Letter Written to lineman Paul Sheldon.

By a 5-1 vote, City League coaches picked Catholic Central to defend its local championship, but the lone dissenter, Cougar Coach Ted Sowle, questioned the contender status given the number of players he had to replace from his undefeated and undisputed 1949 state title team. Halfback Pete Naimo was the only returning starter on offense and linebacker Bill Banaszak was one of four on defense. "Little Notre Dame," a moniker coined by CC basketball coach and football aide Jack Young, who would die from complications due to the flu during the second week of the season, lacked too much game experience at too many positions to rationalize the early accolades.

Catholic Central 25
Muskegon 19
Friday, September 15 at Houseman Field

Sowle's argument didn't hold much water after his "green" team handled Muskegon, led by future Michigan State College and NFL star quarterback Earl Morrall, 25-19, in the Cougars' 15th victory in a row spanning three seasons. In an oddly prophetic *Grand Rapids Herald* story written by Charles L. Clapp, Catholic's "old black magic" was gone, but its speed, finesse and precision were too much for Muskegon to counter despite the wizardry of coach Harry Potter.

The Cougars, in their sharp blue-and-gold uniforms, got three touchdowns out of little Jack Doran in his varsity debut and one out of Naimo. Doran sprinted to a 9-yard touchdown in the first quarter but Morrall's 26-yard touchdown pass gave Muskegon a 7-6 lead. Catholic stormed right back, covering 67 yards in 11 plays, to take a 12-7 lead on Doran's pinball 7-yard TD run. Then, with about two minutes remaining in the first half, Doran did most of the damage on a 54-yard scoring drive that ended on his 3-yard score for a 19-7 lead. A 50-yard pass from quarterback Larry Schmitt to halfback LaVern Wolf set up Naimo's 13-yard touchdown that gave CC a commanding 25-7 lead. Morrall sneaked in a touchdown in the fourth quarter, but Catholic Central commemorated the end of the CC-Muskegon series with a second consecutive victory.

Catholic Central 33
Muskegon Heights 6
Friday, September 22 at South Field

Catholic Central's tenuous grasp on the No. 1 spot among the state's Class A teams after the first weekend of the season became a little surer following a 33-6 drubbing of Muskegon Heights. It was Sowle's 50th victory as the CC head coach against just seven defeats and two ties.

The Cougars stumbled out of the gate, but Hal Russell's interception late in the first quarter set up his 54-yard touchdown run for the first of five unanswered scores. Later in the first quarter, Ron Makowski made the score 13-0 when he returned an interception 70 yards for a TD. Midway through the second quarter, Doran, the elfin halfback with a shock of red hair and freckled face, cruised 15 yards around end for a 19-0 lead and a 20-yard pass from Schmitt to Naimo made it 26-0 just before halftime. The final CC TD was set up in the third quarter by a short Heights punt to its own 30 and came on Wolf's plunge from inside the 1-yard line.

Catholic Central 20
Toledo Scott Catholic 20
Friday, September 29 at Toledo

Catholic Central traveled to Northwestern Ohio with the expectations of coming home with an easy victory over Toledo Scott Catholic, a team it crushed 42-13 a year earlier. The Cougars, however, were fortunate to escape with a 20-20 tie.

After falling behind 7-0 in the first quarter, Catholic took to the air and scored on Schmitt's 19-yard pass to Jack

Archives, Grand Rapids Public Library

Catholic Central Cheer Squad

Dumas. Toledo Scott fumbled the ensuing kickoff and Wolf recovered at the 38. Schmitt converted the turnover on the final play of the first half when he threw a 16-yard touchdown pass to end Dick Vorenkamp.

On the first play of the fourth quarter, Schmitt and Doran combined for an 80-yard pass play to the Toledo Scott 5-yard line, and Naimo tossed an option pass to Vorenkamp for a 20-7 lead. The Cougar defense couldn't hold Toledo Scott out of the end zone as its lead shrunk to seven points, and then, with less than a minute to go, it surrendered a 25-yard touchdown run and failed to block the extra point. The deadlock snapped Catholic's 16-game win streak and dropped it to No. 2, behind Flint Northwestern, in the state Class A poll.

Union 19
Catholic Central 14
Monday, October 9 at Houseman Field

The matchup between Union and Catholic Central didn't figure to be much of a contest after the Red Hawks lost to Muskegon Heights, which fell to CC by 27 points, 27-13. But the Cougars looked vulnerable in their 20-20 tie on the road against Toledo Scott Catholic as Union roared to a 31-0 mauling of Creston. Nevertheless, Catholic Central was favored to win by three touchdowns.

After the game pitting the previous two Class A state champs was moved from Friday to Monday night because of soggy conditions at Houseman Field, the showdown for early supremacy in the City League went to the Red

Hawks, who improved to 2-0 with a stunning 19-14 come-from-behind victory. What was considered among the greatest upsets in City League history ended CC's streak of games without a loss at 17.

Wolf's fumble, the first of three costly CC turnovers, as he headed toward the end zone cost the Cougars a touchdown in the first quarter, and Union worked its single-wing offense with dizzying perfection to take a 7-0 lead. Wolf made up for his mistake with a 42-yard touchdown run to tie the score in the second quarter. Then Schmitt put CC ahead with a 41-yard bomb to Wolf for a 14-7 lead that stood until the fourth quarter.

A 69-yard run by Naimo put Catholic Central in business at the Red Hawk 20, but the Cougars couldn't cash in and Union closed the gap to one point on an 84-yard touchdown drive in the fourth quarter. Union put the game out of reach with under three minutes to play when quarterback Reggie Wiktorowski unleashed a 67-yard TD pass to Billy LeBaron.

"They were better than we were," Sowle said.

Catholic Central 19
South 6
Saturday, October 14 at South Field

The one-two combination of Wolf and Naimo ran for second-quarter touchdowns to get the Cougars headed toward their first City League victory of the season. Wolf darted through the South defense for a 7-yard touchdown that capped a 66-yard drive and Naimo powered in from 4 yards out with 10 seconds left to give CC a 13-0 halftime lead en route to a 19-6 victory.

GR Herald Photo

Tony D'Amico hauls in a touchdown pass against Central.

The Trojans capitalized on a third-quarter Cougar fumble to get on the scoreboard, but Wolf added an insurance marker in the fourth quarter. The victory was enough to return CC to No. 10 in the Class A state poll.

Catholic Central 47
Central 6
Friday, October 20 at Houseman Field

By 1950, the term "Cinderella team" was already considered a worn-out cliché when it was applied to a Central High squad that started the season with a 5-0 record. Catholic Central brought the Hilltoppers' hackneyed rags-to-riches tale to an abrupt end with a 47-6 victory.

"Pistol" Pete Naimo posted CC to a 7-0 lead with a 15-yard sweep, which was the 14th play of a 73-yard drive in the first quarter. Wolf made it 14-0 when he galloped 20 yards for a touchdown with five minutes left in the first half, and Schmitt connected on a 40-yard touchdown pass to backup end Tony D'Amico with two seconds left for a 21-0 halftime lead.

Schmitt pushed the lead to 27-0 in the third quarter on his 1-foot sneak, and tackle Jerry Schoen's fumble recovery at the Central 5 set up Doran's touchdown run on the next play. After the Hilltoppers finally scored in the fourth quarter, Schmitt hit D'Amico with a 3-yard TD toss, and D'Amico completed the scoring with a 34-yard interception runback with 25 seconds to go.

Catholic Central 33
Creston 6
Saturday, October 28 at Houseman Field

Trailing Union, which had tied Ottawa Hills 40-40, by only a half-game, Catholic Central remained in the City League title hunt with an impressive 33-6 victory over Creston. Striking dramatically from long range, the Cougars had done all their scoring before the Polar Bears got on the board in the final quarter.

Wolf led off the touchdown parade with a 69-yard run in the first quarter and tacked on a 76-yarder a few minutes later. Doran scooted 59 yards to give CC a 21-0 lead in the second quarter and Jerry Kozminski, who replaced the injured Schmitt for a game, threw a 29-yard touchdown pass to speedy Roman Zobro for a 27-0 halftime lead. Kozminski put the finishing touches on the win when he returned an interception 100 yards in the third quarter.

Catholic Central 27
Ottawa Hills 7
Friday, November 3 at Houseman Field

"Frankly, I'm scared to death," Sowle said about Catholic Central's City League finale against Ottawa Hills, which played Union to a standstill a couple of weeks earlier.

Naimo took the fright out of the night when he covered all the ground for CC's first touchdown in a smashing 27-7 victory. After retuning the opening kickoff to the 38, the "human fire hydrant" chugged the final 62 on the first play from scrimmage for a 7-0 lead. After a fumble recovery at its own 21-yard line and a 57-yard gain by Wolf, halfback Ted Olewinski slithered in from the 1 and CC led 14-0. The Cougars got the ball back on a punt one more time before halftime, and the two-play possession consisted of a 26-yard sweep by Naimo and a 27-yard tackle-breaking run by Wolf.

Sowle substituted liberally in the third quarter, and after two touchdown runs were nullified by penalties, Zobro broke free for a 31-yard run to set up his 8-yard score for a 27-0 lead. Catholic Central outgained the Indians, 315-149, and earned a share of the City League title by virtue of Central's victory over Union.

Catholic Central 27
LaPorte (Ind.) High School 18
Friday, November 10 at Houseman Field

In Catholic Central's two-game series with LaPorte (Ind.) High School, Naimo was just two points shy of dominating the Slicers all by himself. As an encore to his four-touchdown, 24-point performance in the Cougars' 40-28 victory in '49, Naimo closed out his career with three touchdowns and three extra points for 21 points in the 27-18 win in a snowstorm on home turf.

The Slicers took a 6-0 lead early in the second quarter, but Naimo finished CC's ensuing drive off with a 28-yard touchdown run and the first half ended in a deadlock. Russell's interception return to the Cougar 27 was followed by Naimo's 73-yard touchdown dash, and runs of 23 and 21 yards led to Wolf's 21-yard TD for a 20-6 lead. After Naimo's final trip to the end zone, LaPorte tacked on two late scores. Catholic piled up an amazing 428 rushing yards.

"Pistol Pete" led the first-team All-City squad which included fellow Cougars Bill Banaszak, a center and linebacker, and guard Paul Sheldon.

1950 Schedule/Results
Head Coach – Ted Sowle

Date	Opponent	Result		Location
Sep. 15	Muskegon	Won	25-19	Houseman Field
Sep. 22	Muskegon Heights	Won	33-6	South Field
Sep. 29	Toledo Scott	Tie	20-20	Toledo, OH
Oct. 9	Union	Lost	14-19	Houseman Field
Oct. 14	South	Won	19-6	South Field
Oct. 20	Central	Won	47-6	Houseman Field
Oct. 28	Creston	Won	33-6	Houseman Field
Nov. 3	Ottawa Hills	Won	27-7	Houseman Field
Nov. 10	LaPorte, IN	Won	27-18	Houseman Field

	Record	Pts. Scored	Pts. Allowed
Overall	7-1-1	245	107
City League	4-1	140	44

-1951-

Catholic Central continued to build momentum in the new decade and was installed as the preseason favorite to win the state championship and the City League title. Head coach Ted Sowle, of course, pooh-poohed the notion with a time-honored list of coaching conditions in the local papers.

"If we don't have injuries we'll have a very fine team before the season is over," said Sowle. "Our championship prospects depend on how fast the team shapes up. They're wrong about rating us for any title at this stage of the game."

Sowle had some noteworthy holes to fill. All-State linebacker Bill Banaszak and All-City touchdown maven "Pistol" Pete Naimo were gone. However, the offensive line returned five starters, including All-City guard Paul Sheldon, tackles Jerry Schoen and Leo Debri and Rocky Nawrocki at center. And a promising fullback named Ted "All the Way" Olewinski appeared to be capable of picking up where Naimo left off, but new starting quarterback Jack Dumas was untested.

Catholic Central 14
Muskegon Heights 6
Saturday, September 15 at Phillips Field

The Cougars didn't exactly refute Sowle's reservations with a 14-6 season opening victory at Muskegon Heights. Either that, or the Tigers showed they would be a tough team before the season was over, as well.
Catholic Central's expected offensive firepower was conspicuous by its absence and the Heights took an early

GR Herald Photo
Cougar Back Roman Zobro

6-0 lead on a 16-yard drive after the Cougars first possession stalled and Dumas, who set up to punt on fourth down, couldn't handle a poor snap from center. Catholic Central countered immediately and Dumas' 27-yard pass to end Gordon Schmuker set up Olewinski's first of many touchdowns, this one from 10 yards out, for the season. Olewinski also kicked the extra point and the Cougars led 7-6 at halftime. Catholic Central put the game out of reach with a 92-yard possession that concluded on halfback Roman Zobro's 5-yard touchdown run and then dominated the rest of the game on defense.

Catholic Central 44
Ottawa Hills 7
Saturday, September 22 at Houseman Field

Even though the emergence of his defense was a pleasant surprise, Sowle bristled at Catholic's No. 1 ranking in the first state poll of the season. "Don't believe it," he reportedly told the Cougars at a Tuesday practice. "We're not that good, not yet at least." The voters were so impressed with CC after its season-opener, they ranked the team it defeated, Muskegon Heights, No. 10 by virtue of losing to the Cougars by only one touchdown.

Sowle would have hard time convincing Ottawa Hills the Cougars weren't worthy of the top spot after an easy 44-7 City League-opening victory. Oh, CC looked the part while losing two of three fumbles in the first quarter and coughing the ball up four times in all. But that Cougar defense was a sight to behold while Dumas led the offense to seven touchdowns, including one through the air with one of his soft, wobbly passes that were said to be easy to catch.

Catholic Central 26
Saginaw Arthur Hill 20
Friday, September 28 at Saginaw Memorial Stadium

Whatever doubts Sowle had about Catholic's top ranking were dissolved by the Cougars' magnificent come-from-behind road victory over No. 3 Saginaw Arthur Hill before more than 10,000 fans in new Memorial Stadium.

After spotting the powerful Lumber Jacks a 14-0 second-quarter advantage, CC roared to life behind the tough running of Olewinski and Zobro, and rugged defense. After breaking loose for a 64-yard gain, Zobro cut the deficit in half just before intermission with a 3-yard rushing TD. In the third quarter, Dumas, playing safety on defense, intercepted a pass and returned it 34 yards to the Saginaw Arthur Hill 16, and three plays later Zobro scored on a 2-yard run, but the conversion failed and CC trailed 14-13.

Later in the quarter, Jerry Cook blocked a Lumberjack punt and CC recovered at the 28. It took the Cougars just three plays to cover the distance and Zobro's 4-yard TD provided a 19-14 lead. Bill Bergin's interception set up what proved to be CC's game-winning touchdown. After Zobro's 20-yard rush put the ball at the Hill 1-yard line, fleet-footed Cougar halfback Bob Fox did the rest. Saginaw Arthur Hill scored again, but with only 40 seconds remaining in one of the biggest wins in Catholic Central history.

The Cougars were so impressive they retained the No. 1 spot by garnering 157 of 160 votes. Hill, meantime, dropped only to fifth.

Catholic Central 32
Holland 12
Saturday, October 6 at Holland Riverview Park

For the third time in four games, Catholic Central had to come-from-behind to protect its bid for the state championship. The Cougars actually scored first for a change, but then had to overcome a 12-6 halftime deficit before crushing Holland High, 32-12.

Catholic made the best of the rain-soaked conditions when Fox capped a 60-yard drive with a 2-yard touchdown run in the final seconds of the first quarter. However, as the weather worsened, so did the Cougars' grip on the ball and a pair of fumbles led to two Dutchmen scores.

Holland returned the favor with three fumbles that led to CC touchdowns in the third quarter. Dumas' 2-yard sneak completed a 42-yard drive, Jack Doran scored from 11 yards out less than a minute later and Olewinski carried for the final two touchdowns on runs of 4 and 19 yards.

GR Herald Photo

Ted "All the Way" Olewinski

Catholic Central 33
Union 7
Friday, October 12 at Houseman Field

The biggest obstacle standing between Catholic Central and a shot at its second state title in three seasons was Union. The Red Hawks won the crown four years earlier, were ranked as high as fourth before losing to Muskegon Heights, 26-6, and were the Cougars' next opponent in what was dubbed the City League's biggest rivalry.

The 2-0 Red Hawks went into the game knowing they would take control of the city race with a win, but that CC would be out for revenge. A year earlier, CC's 19-13 loss to Union cost it the city title.

Olewinski wore that red-and-white obstacle down to a nub by scoring all of Catholic's points in a 33-7 pounding before an overflow crowd of more than 11,000 at Houseman Field. The first of Olewinski's five touchdowns came on a 66-yard blast after a series of well-executed play-fakes by Dumas, early in the first quarter. Five minutes later, Schoen recovered a Union fumble and Olewinski accounted for 32 of the 54 yards on the ensuing possession, including 2 for the score.

Christened "140 pounds of Demon" by a *Grand Rapids Herald* headline writer, Olewinski, the shortest player on the field, gashed Union for 16 yards and his third touchdown, and also kicked the first of his three extra points. The Red Hawks momentarily interrupted the Olewinski show with Jack VerDuin's 7-yard rushing touchdown, which cut the CC advantage to 19-7, but Olewinski ended their comeback hopes by taking a pitchout from the Union 1 into the end zone.

GR Herald Photo

Ted Olewinski on his way to a 35-yard touchdown run against South wears a mask to protect a broken jaw suffered in the Union game a week earlier.

It didn't look to be all Olewinski all the time when Doran struck for what appeared to be a 41-yard TD, but the officials nullified the play with a holding penalty that set up Olewinski's 10-yard score for one of the greatest individual performances in City League history. Olewinski did most of his damage on a simple off-tackle play Sowle said "calls for split-second timing."

Catholic Central 35
South 6
Friday, October 19 at South Field

Catholic Central took a 2-0 lead on Dave Dorgan's blocked punt and never looked back en route to a 35-6 rout of South High. Olewinski scored the first of his 15 points on a 2-yard touchdown run a short time later to give the Cougars an 8-0 first-quarter lead, and Sowle began substituting liberally in the second period.

Doran made it 15-0 on an 18-yard halfback option pass to end Dick Vorenkamp on the fourth play of the second quarter and backup quarterback Bob Murphy increased the lead to 21 points with a 15-yard TD pass to end Don Cook, the son of former Union High all-time great Frank Cook. The play was set up by Melvin Pospiech's recovery of a fumbled punt. Zobro bumped the score up to 28-0 with a 25-yard run, and after the Trojans tagged a touchdown on the CC reserves, Olewinski put the finishing touch on the win with an off-tackle burst good for a 35-yard TD in the final quarter.

Catholic's sixth straight win, and 11th in a row over two seasons, kept it atop the state Class A poll, but Muskegon continued to breathe down its neck for the mythical state championship.

Catholic Central 31
Central 13
Saturday, October 27 at Houseman Field

Catholic Central wrapped up a share of its sixth City League championship, and fourth under Sowle, with a decisive, but penalty-marred, 31-13 victory over the Central High Rams, formerly known as the Hilltoppers, and their sensational halfback Terry Barr. The Cougars struck early and often, with a pair of touchdowns in each of the first two quarters.

Vorenkamp opened the touchdown floodgates when he recovered Olewinski's fumble in the end zone after a 5-yard gain, but Doran stole the show with his best game in a CC uniform. Doran also scored from 5 yards out a few minutes later, and Zobro's 3-yarder early in the second quarter upped the score to 19-0. Then, with 30 seconds remaining in the first half, Doran slammed through the middle of the line for a 10-yard TD and Catholic led, 25-0, at halftime. Doran's 9-yard touchdown midway through the third quarter ended CC's scoring spree, and the officials, who were booed lustily by the fans, were a factor in holding the score down.

While Doran ran for 129 yards on 16 carries, the Cougars gave 115 yards back on penalties. The Rams, who got two touchdowns on a 1-yard run and a 15-yard reception by Barr, lost 40 yards on penalties.

Despite the lopsided score, Catholic continued to lose ground to Muskegon in the state poll, which was becoming the center of a bitter controversy.

Catholic Central 46
Creston 13
Friday, November 2 at Houseman Field

After leading Creston just 7-6 at halftime, Catholic Central broke open a 46-13 victory over Creston to wrap up the undisputed City League crown. Despite striking for 39 second-half points, the Cougars apparently didn't score enough style points to satisfy newspaper poll voters around the state.

Catholic Central racked up all 469 yards of total offense on the ground, and Zobro had the lion's share with 225 on 21 carries in one of the greatest performances in City League history. Olewinski's 35-yard touchdown run and extra point held up for the first two quarters against Creston's spread-formation offense patterned after Texas Christian's, and then Catholic Central's punishing ground game pounded the Polar Bears into submission.

Zobro finished a 68-yard drive with a 24-yard touchdown early in the third quarter and Doran added a 3-yarder before the second half was seven minutes old. Doran scored again in the third quarter, and after the Polar Bears added one more marker, Catholic scored three touchdowns in the fourth quarter, one by Doran and two by Olewinski, to beef up its resume for the pollsters. The effort went for naught because for the first time all season, CC dropped out of the No. 1 spot in favor of Earl Morrall-led Muskegon High, which drilled Kalamazoo Central 33-0.

Catholic Central 51
Detroit Catholic Central 0
Saturday, November 10 at Houseman Field

Sensing Catholic Central's season-long grip on the No. 1 spot in the Class A poll being weakened by the subjectivity of voters around the state, Coach Ted Sowle resorted to a little politicking in the press going into the season finale against Detroit Catholic Central.

"We have scouted Detroit Catholic Central three times and each time it has looked very powerful," Sowle said. "The club is expertly coached, deep at most positions and has two tackles and two halfbacks who would be standouts in any corner of Michigan. I will be surprised if more than two touchdowns are scored and with that in mind, we are stressing defense this week."

GR Herald Photo
Cougars celebrate their City Championship after blasting Creston 46-13.

After practicing in 14 inches of snow all week long, the Cougars ran like they were on roller skates on the fast Houseman

Field surface meticulously cleared by maintenance workers. Catholic Central, which knew Muskegon clobbered Muskegon Heights 26-6 earlier in the day, did everything it could to demonstrate its dominance with a 51-0 victory. And local media reports prematurely designated CC as the No. 1 team in Class A after Fox and Zobro scored three touchdowns apiece and Olewinski and Schmuker tallied one each against the Shamrocks.

However, Sowle was far from being a happy camper. At a Knights of Columbus dinner honoring the Cougars' accomplishments, Sowle said the rating system used to judge teams was "cancerous and vicious" and forced top teams to play out of character. He also lamented the fact that he was booed for the first time in his career after inserting substitutes into the game against Detroit Catholic instead of letting the regulars stay in for another score.

"I'm not blaming anyone in particular," Sowle said. "We are entering an era of overemphasis in that winning state championships are (sic) creating dangerous pressure. I simply feel the situation is all wrong. We won the city title, but this major accomplishment became insignificant alongside the desire to win the state crown. The first string, gunning for state honors, begged me to keep them in against Catholic of Detroit in order to win a decisive victory and enhance the state championship possibilities.

"When we piled up that big score Saturday night, we were battling the polls and not Detroit. The only reason Muskegon has an unbeaten record this season is because they refused to play us."

Muskegon coach Harry Potter supported Sowle by saying the players on his undefeated team have been "accused of pouring it on. It has been like holding frisky horses in check. The boys themselves feel the poll rivalry keenly and want to go all out."

And yet, despite boasting the state's top touchdown scorer in Olewinski, a 9-0 record against arguably tougher competition than Potter's Big Reds who had a close call in a 7-0 win over Benton Harbor, an endorsement from Detroit CC coach Bob Wines calling the Cougars hands-down the best team in the state, and winning for the 32nd time in 34 games, Catholic Central finished second to Muskegon in the final Associated Press poll by two first-place votes, 160-158. The Cougars were named the No. 1 team by the United Press International wire service poll of coaches, sportswriters and game officials.

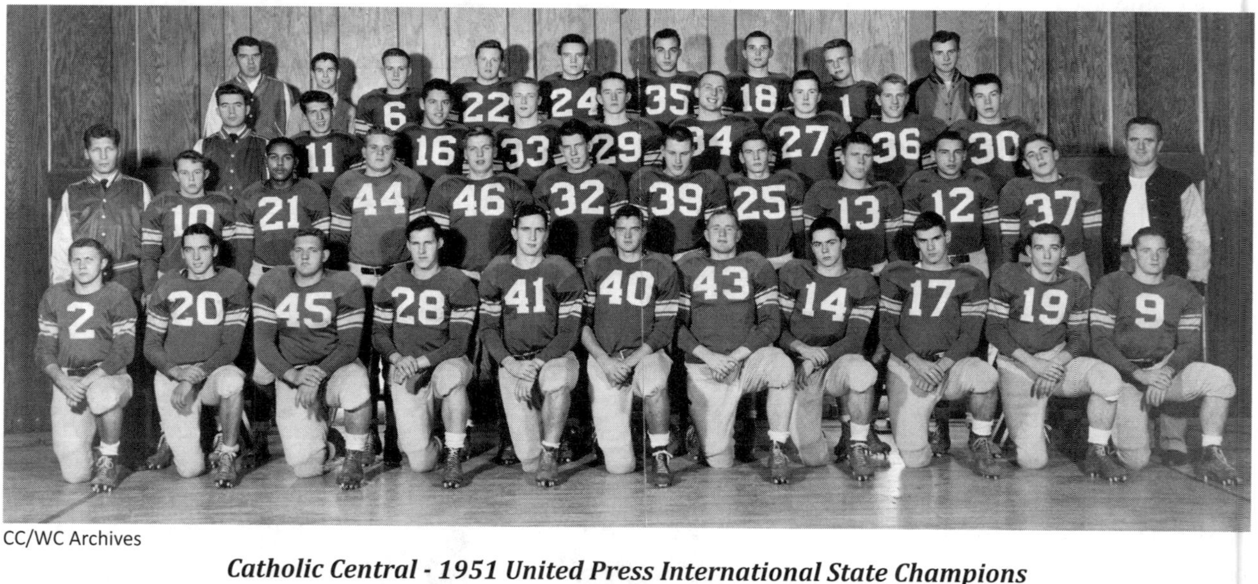

CC/WC Archives

Catholic Central - 1951 United Press International State Champions

First Row (l-r) - Olewinski, Bergin, Nawrocki, Debri, Schoen, Dumas, Vorenkamp, Schmuker, Sheldon, Zobro, Doran
Second Row - Coach Godleski, McGough, Hayes, D. Cook, Rose, Robinson, J. Cook, Heynen, Stanitzek, Chero, Jacobitz, Coach Sowle
Third Row - Coach McEvoy, Endres, Kowalczyk, Pospiech, J. Sowle, Jendrasiak, Janik, Surman, Palaszek
Fourth Row - Coach Geary, Fitzgerald, Huff, Murphy, McGavin, Biondo, Murphy, Fox, Coach Lennon

In a way, Sowle foretold the results when early in the season he said CC wasn't that good, even if it was a tongue-in-cheek declaration designed to keep his players hungry. Nevertheless, he didn't need a bunch of newspaper sports editors, most of whom never saw the Cougars play, validate what he already knew about his team, which boasted 10 seniors in 11 starting positions. "This is the finest team I've ever coached," he said.

Catholic Central placed a City League record seven players on the first-team All-City squad: Olewinski, Dumas, Nawrocki, Sheldon, Debri, Schoen and guard Frank Stanitzek. Zobro and Schmuker were named to the second team.

1951 Schedule/Results

Head Coach – Ted Sowle

Date	Opponent	Result		Location
Sep. 15	Muskegon Heights	Won	14-6	Phillips Field
Sep. 22	Ottawa Hills	Won	44-7	Houseman Field
Sep. 28	Saginaw Arthur Hill	Won	26-20	Saginaw
Oct. 6	Holland	Won	32-12	Holland
Oct. 12	Union	Won	33-7	Houseman Field
Oct. 19	South	Won	35-6	South Field
Oct. 27	Central	Won	31-13	Houseman Field
Nov. 2	Creston	Won	46-13	Houseman Field
Nov. 10	Detroit Catholic Central	Won	51-0	Houseman Field

	Record	Pts. Scored	Pts. Allowed
Overall	9-0	312	84
City League	5-0	189	46

-1952-

The defense of Catholic Central's split state championship would be put in the hands of an attrition-addled team that returned just one starter, All-State guard Frank Stanitzek. The good news was that all of the Cougars' City League counterparts also suffered major losses due to graduation. It's not that CC lacked talent. Many of the backups played big roles on the undefeated team that settled for the highly respected United Press International coaches' poll state title after Muskegon came from behind to capture the No. 1 spot from the more popular Associated Press balloting of sportswriters from around Michigan.

Coach Ted Sowle, who sported a five-year record of 38-4-2, sensed an air of complacency from the team which was envied around the state for its organization, top-of-the-line equipment and fan interest. He planned to clear the situation up with competition.

"Don't be surprised to see a lot of new faces if we don't find a remedy soon," he told *The Grand Rapids Press* during the run-up to the season opener against Muskegon Heights. "(The Cougars) just don't have it."

Sowle saw Central, with Terry Barr and Clarence "Bobo" Bouknight returning, as the team to beat in the city.

GR Herald Photo
All-State Guard Frank Stanitzek

Muskegon Heights 13
Catholic Central 0
Saturday, September 20 at Houseman Field

Sowles' worst fears were realized in a 13-0 season-opening shutout at the hands of the Tigers. Catholic, which saw its 14-game win streak snapped, crossed midfield just twice and one of those forays was the result of a pass-interference call that put the ball at the Heights 26-yard line. The Cougars also committed six fumbles, including one that led to a Tiger TD. The only consolation came from knowing that Union, Central and Creston also lost their openers. The bad news was that CC's next opponent, Ottawa Hills, which just made the jump from Class B to Class A, won a 37-26 shootout against East Grand Rapids.

Catholic Central 52
Ottawa Hills 0
Friday, September 26 at Houseman Field

Whatever malaise affected Catholic Central was cured by a 52-0 drubbing of Ottawa Hills. The margin of victory was the biggest in a City League game since eventual state champ Union clubbed Creston, 62-0, in 1948. Repeating as state champ was all but out of the question, but CC put the rest of the conference on notice, with Red Hawks coach Milo Sukup and Central mentor Chuck Irwin watching from the Houseman Field press box, that they had the weapons and the will to defend their City League crown.

"Any hope local coaches may have had about Catholic's shortcomings in 1952 must have been written off the books in the 52-0 runaway," wrote legendary *Grand Rapids Press* sportswriter Clank Stoppels.

The Cougars scored on eight of 11 possessions. The CC defense forced fumbles on each of the Indians' first two plays from scrimmage and the offense promptly converted the turnovers into 5-yard touchdown runs by halfbacks Bob Fox and Frank Brocato, respectively. The third score, another 5-yarder by Fox, came after Catholic Central end Don Cook blocked a punt. Stanitzek personally recovered four Ottawa fumbles, and his scoop early in the second quarter led to quarterback Bobby Murphy's 10-yard sneak for a 26-0 lead. Following another Stanitzek fumble recovery, Murphy threw six straight passes and completed five, including one in the end zone to Tom Larkin for a 32-0 halftime advantage.

The Cougars proved they didn't need Indian generosity to score in the second half, and drove 64 yards for a TD. The final play covered 10 yards on a pass from Murphy to Mel Pospiech. Fox then romped 41 yards for a score and Murphy closed out the point spree with a 1-yard jump pass to end Don Cook.

Catholic Central 19
Saginaw Arthur Hill 7
Friday, October 3 at South Field

With Murphy leading the way, Catholic Central continued to flex its considerable muscle against powerhouse Saginaw Arthur Hill, which was undefeated and unscored-upon when it showed up at South Field looking like a maize and blue prep version of the University of Michigan. The Cougars dominated the Lumberjacks in a 19-7 victory that put them back in the running for a state title.

Murphy scooted 56 yards, after being sprung by Joe Biondo's savage block on the safety, to give Catholic a 7-0 lead midway through the first quarter. The Cougars pounced on an Arthur Hill fumble on the ensuing kickoff, and Murphy finished off the 36-yard drive with a 2-yard sneak into the end zone.

The Lumberjacks cut the CC lead to 13-7 late in the second, but backup running back Dick Szarowicz's 19-yard run set up a 1-yard TD plunge by Jimmy Huff early in the third period and the Cougars coasted the rest of the way.

GR Press Photo

Bob Fox scores the first touchdown against Ottawa Hills.

Catholic Central 34
Holland 26
Saturday, October 11 at South Field

In what was considered a statement-making non-league upset, Catholic Central downed highly touted Holland High School 34-26. In a sense, the Cougars avenged their costly season-opening loss to Muskegon Heights because the Dutchmen had subsequently defeated the Tigers to earn a Top-10 ranking.

Catholic Central broke out on top in the second quarter, 7-0, on Murphy's 13-yard touchdown pass to Pospiech. Murphy set up the score with a 27-yard pass to Pospiech and a 12-yarder to Larkin. Holland countered almost immediately with a 49-yard touchdown pass, but missed the extra point.

The Cougars wasted no time while rebuilding their cushion, and Szarowicz scored 14-6 with a 7-yard blast. Then, just before halftime, Dick Heynen, Fox and Szarowicz battered the Dutchmen defense until Fox plowed over the goal line for a 21-6 bulge. In the third quarter, Murphy carried out a magnificent series of play fakes before tucking the ball into the gut of Huff, who rambled 22 barely noticed yards for a score. Holland scored twice against CC's reserves in the third quarter, but Murphy put the game out of reach with an 8-yard keeper.

Catholic Central 13
Union 7
Saturday, October 18 at Houseman Field

Union had triple-threat sensation Billy LeBaron but Catholic Central had a three-headed monster. Bob Fox, Dick Heynen and Jim Huff were too much for the Red Hawks to handle in the Cougars' pivotal 13-7 victory over their ancient Westside rival. The trio led CC to a whopping 329-115 advantage in rushing yards and a 16-6 bulge in first downs.

On a possession that started late in the first quarter, Fox and Heynen did most of the legwork during an eight-play, 60-yard drive that ended on Heynen's 3-yard touchdown run one minute into the second quarter. After getting the ball back at their own 36 midway through the second quarter, Huff, Fox and Szarowicz pounded the ball to the Union 13 from where Fox swept into the end zone with a minute remaining in the half.

Union converted a fourth-and-1 at the CC 21 and LeBaron zipped up the sideline past the Cougar defenders for a 20-yard score, but Catholic held on for the victory that set up a first-place showdown against undefeated South High.

Catholic Central 27
South 0
Saturday, October 25 at Houseman Field

South entered its game against fifth-ranked Catholic Central with arguably its best team in a decade, riding a seven-game win streak that started at the end of the previous season, ranked in the Top 10 and in position to win the City League championship. And then the Cougars took it all away with a resounding 27-0 victory that put them back in the state title race conversation.

Catholic Central crossed the Trojans up with a ball-hawking pass defense and by attacking through the air with better success than on the ground. The Cougars intercepted South's first four passes. Murphy came up with the first pickoff of Trojan quarterback Ed Jackson late in the first quarter, and on the first play of the second quarter, Huff raced 24 yards for the only score CC would need.

But, there was more. Later in the first half, Chuck Kreuger intercepted another Jackson pass and returned it to the South 43. Five plays later, Fox busted loose off tackle for an 8-yard touchdown with 25 seconds remaining. In the third quarter, Huff crashed through the middle of theTrojan defense for a 26-yard TD that capped a 61-yard possession, and the second-string offense moved the ball 63 yards in the fourth quarter, with backup Marty Schnur going in from the 12. South's only first down came in the opening moments of the third quarter, and the victory pushed CC all the way up to No. 2 in the state, right behind Ann Arbor Pioneer.

GR Press Photo

Jim Huff crosses the goal line during the South game.

Catholic Central 20
Central 6
Friday, October 31 at Houseman Field

Everybody in Grand Rapids knew Central was going to put up a fight against Catholic Central. And after the Rams took a 6-0 lead early in the second quarter on a 40-yard pass from future Michigan and Detroit Lions star Terry Barr to Bobo Bouknight, who eluded two tacklers at the CC 20 and then got away from three more thanks to a devastating downfield block by guard Loren DeGroot, anything seemed possible. And then, when Catholic failed to cash in from the Central 7-yard line when Fox fumbled with time running out in the first half, Rams fans were saying, "Why not us? Why not tonight?"

But, coach Chuck Irwin used just 13 players against the waves of talented Cougars, and Catholic Central earned a share of its second City League title in a row with a 20-6 victory. After Catholic avoided going down by two touchdowns when Stanitzek stopped Bouknight for no gain on fourth-and-inches at the CC 4-yard line, the Cougars went 96 yards on eight plays, including a 38-yard run to the Central 3 by Fox, to tie the score. Huff powered across the goal line for CC's first score.

With just over two minutes remaining in the third quarter, Catholic capitalized on a 6-yard Bouknight punt when Fox ran for a 5-yard touchdown, and Kreuger's interception at midfield allowed Fox to clinch the victory in the fourth quarter.

GR Press Photo
Frank Stanitzek pulls down Central's Terry Barr .

Catholic Central 41
Creston 7
Saturday, November 8 at Houseman Field

Catholic Central wrapped up its second undisputed City Championship with an anti-climactic 41-7 drubbing of outmanned Creston. Once the Cougars took a 14-0 first-quarter lead on Larry Endres' 8-yard gallop and Miles Murphy's 44-yard TD scamper, Sowle went mostly with backups and odd combinations the rest of the way. All-State tackle Frank Stanitzek even tried his hand as a ball-carrier out of the backfield.

Fox got into the act with a 46-yard gain that led to Heynen's 4-yard touchdown for a 21-0 lead in the third quarter, and later, with CC facing a fourth-and-9, Fox ran for a 44-yard touchdown. Szarowicz dashed around end for a 20-yard score in the fourth quarter and Jerry Karas plunged in from the 1 for the Cougars' final tally.

Catholic Central 35
Detroit Catholic Central 7
Friday, November 14 at Detroit McCabe Field

The Cougars did everything they could to boost their state-title resume with a 35-7 road victory over well-respected Detroit Catholic Central, but it wasn't enough to unseat undefeated Ann Arbor Pioneer from the No. 1 spot.

The Shamrocks were by far the best team CC faced and Sowle said, "It was the best game our boys have played this season. Maybe we didn't win any state titles this year because of our opening defeat by Muskegon Heights, but I dare say that by the way the boys clicked tonight, we'd give any high school team in the country a mighty tough evening of it if any playoffs were concerned."

With 19 seniors playing their final game in the blue and white, CC won with total team collaboration that created a 362-58 disparity in total offensive yards. Sowle let outgoing players have one last moment in the spotlight while playing numerous second- and third-stringers in preparation for the '53 season.

Endres scored the first CC TD on a 37-yard run and he made it 14-0 in the third quarter with a 15-yard TD. Terry Rose blocked a Detroit CC punt at the 32 and Cook scooped up the ball and returned it to the 9 to set up Catholic's third touchdown, which came on an 8-yard pass from Murphy to Pospiech. Endres made it 28-0 when he broke loose for a 28-yard rush to the 1-foot line to set up his third TD of the game. The heirs apparent to the Catholic Central dynasty completed the scoring on a 9-yard pass from Dick Erhardt to Gerry Nye.

Nine Cougars were selected to the official first- and second All-City Teams as selected for *The Grand Rapids Press* by the seven City League head coaches. Stanitzek, the only unanimous selection, Pospiech, Cook, Heynen, Fox and center Jim Sowle were named to the first unit and Rose, Biondo and Murphy were on the No. 2 squad.

GR Press Photo

City League Coaches Pick the All-City Team

(l-r) - Gil Powers (Creston), Ted Sowle (Catholic), Lendy Davis (GR Press), Wendell Emery (Asst. Director of Athletics), Milo Sukup (Union), Don Schriemer (South), Charles Irwin (Central) and Charles Davidson (Ottawa)

1952 Schedule/Results

Head Coach – Ted Sowle

Date	Opponent	Result		Location
Sep. 20	Muskegon Heights	Lost	0-13	Houseman Field
Sep. 26	Ottawa Hills	Won	52-0	Houseman Field
Oct. 3	Saginaw Arthur Hill	Won	19-7	South Field
Oct. 11	Holland	Won	34-26	South Field
Oct. 18	Union	Won	13-7	Houseman Field
Oct. 25	South	Won	27-0	Houseman Field
Oct. 31	Central	Won	20-6	Houseman Field
Nov. 8	Creston	Won	41-7	Houseman Field
Nov. 14	Detroit Catholic Central	Won	35-7	McCabe Field

	Record	Pts. Scored	Pts. Allowed
Overall	8-1	241	73
City League	5-0	153	20

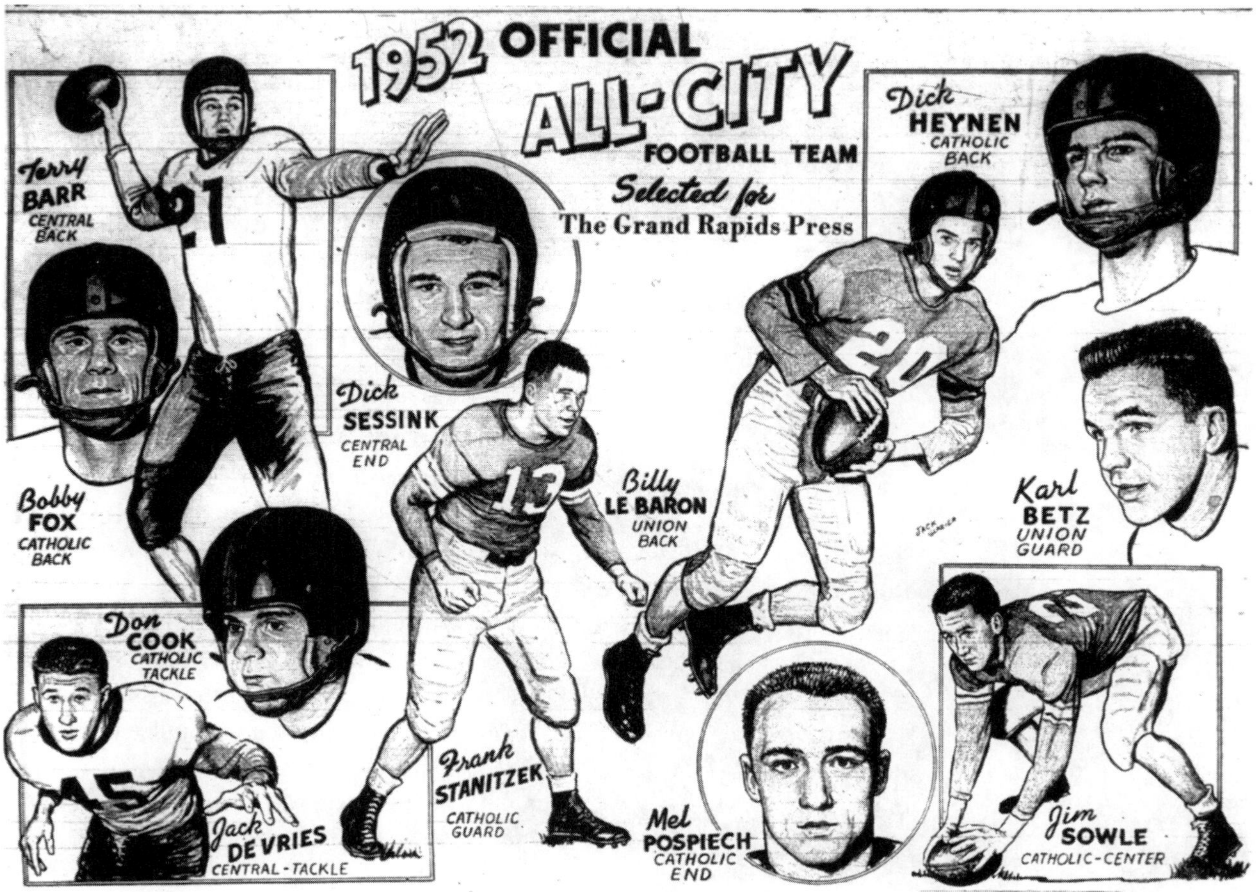

-1953-

The departure of 19 seniors, including every key starter, presented Coach Ted Sowle with yet another rebuilding project. However, the 1953 season would be an indicator of whether the program was to the point where it just needed to be reloaded with groomed talent waiting in the wings. Even with a new quarterback in place, lefty Dick Erhardt, CC was picked to win its third consecutive City League championship. Light and fast, the '53 Cougars were significantly different than their predecessor, which overpowered opponents with a big offensive line and a punishing ground game.

Flint Northern 19
Catholic Central 0
Friday, September 18 at Flint Atwood Stadium

"I don't know when we've been, well, so low, especially in respect to that manpower, as we are this year," Sowle said. "It's probably the lightest team Catholic has fielded in seven years, but the boys are plenty fast, tough and scrappy." And, the Cougars went into their first preseason intrasquad scrimmage with 10 seniors on offense.

Sowle's inexperienced charges ran headlong into a brick wall of reality in their season opener against Flint Northern, a team *The Grand Rapids Press* reported could stand up to many college squads. Despite being battered, bruised and bowed while being held to minus-3 passing yards in the 19-0 shellacking, the Cougars outgained the Vikings 175-153.

GR Press Photo

Quarterback Dick Erhardt

"We fumbled the ball seven times and most of those resulted in Flint recoveries," Sowle said of CC's sixth loss in seven seasons. "But more important, we bobbled the ball 14 times in our backfield. That means 14 plays went screwy. You cannot afford that type of sloppy play against a good club. We were beaten by a better club, no mistake about that, but we have a lot of work to do and are not sure we'll be in good shape by this weekend."

Catholic Central 27
Creston 0
Friday, September 25 at Houseman Field

The Cougars continued their error-prone ways in the City League opener against Creston, which was without the services of injured star fullback Johnny DeBlaay. But, Erhardt, the CC starting quarterback, was also hurt and on the sideline, so no one could say the 27-0 thumping of the Polar Bears wasn't a credible win, especially since Catholic lost five of its seven fumbles.

The Cougars dominated the first half and piled up 125 yards of total offense to minus-6 for Creston in the first quarter alone. The teams exchanged fumbles on the first three possessions of the game, but fullback Marty Schnur held on long enough during a 64-yard run to score Catholic's first six points of the season. Another CC fumble recovery on the final play of the first quarter led to Jerry Karas' 12-yard TD run off right tackle on the first play of the second.

Following the ensuing kickoff and three more fumbles, Jim Parente, who was filling in at quarterback for Erhardt, threw a 29-yard pass to Dick Szarowicz who did the rest with his legs on a 79-yard scoring play. Although the Polar Bears performed better in the second half than Catholic Central, the Cougars scored its final touchdown in the fourth quarter when Bruce Yarrington rushed up the middle to block Dave Fleming's punt and Tom Grego fell on the ball in the end zone. Creston fumbled five times and lost four.

Catholic Central 39
Ottawa Hills 12
Saturday, October 3 at Houseman Field

The theme of Catholic Central's season continued to be mistakes as it overcame 175 yards of penalty yardage and two of four lost fumbles to crush Ottawa Hills 39-12. The Indians won a moral victory by holding the Cougars scoreless in the first quarter, but CC exploded for 19 points in the second and the only question remaining was how big the winning margin would be.

Karas pushed Catholic's first scoring drive forward with a 19-yard gain in what was left of the opening stanza and then swept around right end for a 28-yard TD. Szarowicz outdid Karas with a 60-yard touchdown a few minutes later and Erhardt threw a 7-yard scoring strike to end Gerry Nye for a 19-0 halftime lead. In the third quarter, Schnur bested both Szarowicz and Karas with a 65-yarder and after recovering a fumble, Szarowicz scored on a 12-yard run through a huge hole for a 32-0 advantage. After Ottawa scored against CC's reserves, Denny Cook swept 11 yards for the Cougars' final touchdown in Sowle's 40th win as their head coach.

Catholic Central 54
Holland 7
Friday, October 9 at South Field

Scoring on each of its five first-half possessions against an injury-riddled and shell-shocked Holland High School team, Catholic Central showed how daunting it could be when it played mistake-free football. The game ended with a humane score of 54-7 only because Sowle played his second- and third-teamers the entire second half.

On the third play of CC's game-opening drive, Szarowicz sprinted home for an 81-yard touchdown and two minutes later, Karas cracked the Dutchmen line for a 7-yard score. Holland momentarily made it a game with a 70-yard drive that ended on Bob VanDyke's 3-yard plunge to cut the deficit to 14-7, but it was all Catholic Central the rest of the way.

The Cougars' third touchdown of the first half came on Erhardt's 34-yard pass to Grego early in the second quarter. Schnur scored the fourth on a 5-yard rush. After taking the handoff on a simple dive play behind center, Karas broke for the sideline and rambled 42 yards for the TD that gave CC a 33-7 halftime lead. Catholic's subs were just as effective against the Dutchmen in the second half. Frank Huizenga added a 5-yard touchdown, and Chuck Tomajezyk's interception set up the final score, also by Huizenga. The Cougar defense held Holland to 6-for-28 passing for 80 yards.

GR Press Photo

Lineman Stan Moleski

Saginaw Arthur Hill 20
Catholic Central 13
Friday, October 16 at Saginaw Memorial Stadium

If the competition between Catholic

Central and Saginaw Arthur Hill were an eyeball test, the Cougars won going away. Unfortunately, the Cougars suffered lapses during Lumberjack touchdown runs of 92 and 91 yards by twin brothers Bill and Bob Plater, and what was otherwise a dominating performance went for naught in a 20-13 road defeat.

After falling behind 6-0 in the first quarter on Bill Plater's long-gainer, the Cougars got the ball back in the second on Cook's fumble recovery at his own 47. Schnur and Szarowicz took turns pounding the ball to the Arthur Hill 3. Erhardt sneaked in from there and Catholic took a 7-6 lead. The Lumberjacks regained the lead late in the second quarter on a 12-yard touchdown run, and Bob Plater completed the twin-killing after starting out from his own 9-yard line in the third quarter. Jim Parente intercepted a Saginaw pass in the fourth quarter and Karas did some long-distance scoring of his own with a 52-yard scamper, but time ran out on the CC comeback bid.

Catholic Central 19
Union 14
Friday, October 23 at Houseman Field

Denny Cook's 3-yard touchdown plunge with 75 seconds remaining and Schnur's 10-yarder a minute or so later allowed Catholic Central to pull out a 19-14 last-second victory over Union. The Red Hawks controlled play early and took a 7-0 lead on a possession that gobbled up 10 minutes of the first quarter. Quarterback Ray Heidenga completed the 67-yard drive with a 1-yard sneak, and when Union converted Jack VanDuinen's recovery of Karas' fumble on CC's ensuing possession into a 7-yard TD run by halfback Dick Green, the Hawks had the Cougars on the ropes.

Catholic made up some of the ground late in the second quarter with Schnur's 10-yard TD run off tackle to complete a 60-yard drive. However, Union protected its 14-7 advantage until late in the fourth period when Catholic got the ball back at the 50-yard line with four minutes remaining.

It wasn't going to be easy for the Cougars, who promptly moved back to their own 35 thanks to a clipping penalty, but Szarowicz got it all back, and then some, with a 25-yard run that paved the way for Cook's TD. Catholic then executed a perfect onside kick, which the Cougars recovered at the Union 44.

Erhardt moved CC into scoring position with a 21-yard pass to Tom Larkin with 50 seconds remaining, and then preserved the clock with sweeps by Scnhur and Ralph Hauenstein that ended up out of bounds. Erhardt then crossed the Hawks up by faking a handoff for one more sweep before giving the ball to Schnur whose inside run didn't stop until he crossed the goal line untouched.

GR Press Photo

CC's Dick Szarowicz brought down after a 25-yard gain.

Catholic Central 31
South 19
Friday, October 30 at Houseman Field

The never-say-die attitude Catholic Central demonstrated in its dramatic last-gasp victory over Union paid dividends a week later during its successful bid for a third straight City League title. The Cougars fell behind South twice and came back both times for a 31-19 triumph.

The Trojans scored first early in the opening quarter on Jack Dornan's 1-yard run. However, Szarowicz returned the ensuing kickoff 42 yards into South territory and five plays later Catholic gained a 6-6 tie on running back Ken Duchene's 2-yard dive across the goal line. In the second quarter, Trojan quarterback Ed Jackson orchestrated a 56-yard drive that took advantage of Catholic's porous pass defense until he plowed in from the 4-yard line for a 13-6 lead. The Cougars countered quickly when Erhardt caught the South defensive backs cheating up to stop the run and threw a 30-yard touchdown pass to Grego, but the conversion run was stopped short and CC trailed 13-12 at halftime.

The Cougars regained the lead, 19-13, in the third quarter when backup quarterback Jim Parente threw a 37-yard touchdown pass to Grego, who got behind Trojan defensive back Richard Mayfield at the 5. Midway through the third quarter, Chuck Pease recovered Jackson's fumble at the CC 38 and after 12- and 20-yard runs by Larry Endres and Duchene, Endres evaded five South defenders throughout the course of a 30-yard scoring jaunt and in the fourth quarter put the game out of reach with a brilliant 71-yard broken-field excursion to paydirt.

Catholic Central 0
Central 0
Saturday, November 7 at Houseman Field

It wasn't the most glamorous way to clinch a third undisputed City League title in a row, but Catholic Central's 0-0 tie with Central did the trick. The Rams, who needed a win to earn a share of the top spot, dropped to second place.

Both defenses repeatedly rose to the occasion in a game ranked among the best played in the area all season despite the lack of points. The statistics were nearly as close as the score. The Cougars had four scoring chances as did Central, and while the Rams had a 16-15 edge in first downs, CC finished with a 324-315 edge in total offense.

Central advanced to the Catholic Central 18-yard line in the first period, but the Cougars thwarted the threat by forcing Bobo Bouknight into fumbling the ball away. Catholic Central drove to the Central 3-yard line on two occasions, only to be derailed by the hard-tackling Rams who forced two fumbles. In the second half, Erhardt ran to the Ram 10, but almost immediately after taking the handoff on the next play was separated from the ball by a jolting tackle and Central recovered at the 18. The Cougars had one more golden opportunity with 4 ½ minutes remaining when Hauenstein valuted to the Central 38. However, at the end of a 10-yard gain by Hauenstein on the next play, Ram tackle Richard Simmons stripped the ball out of Hauenstein's hands. Bouknight efficiently passed Central down the field all the way to the CC 9, but on the last play of the game, he inexplicably handed off to Buzzy Brown, who the Cougars gang-tackled 5 yards shy of the goal line as time expired.

Sowle, when reminded of the way he poor-mouthed his team during preseason drills, said Catholic simply did a good job of taking advantage of the opportunities that came its way.

"We had the breaks," he said. "I might add, we made a few of those breaks. We had a bunch of youngsters who were upholding the prestige of the school. They knew they were defending champions and that meant an added burden on their shoulders. I've had more alert teams. I've had better all-around clubs. But I've never had a squad of kids as eager-beaver and ready to capitalize on the other guy's mistakes as these youngsters."

Catholic Central 31
Muskegon Catholic Central 7
Friday, November 13 at Houseman Field

GR Press Photo

All-City Back Larry Endres

Catholic Central wrapped up another successful season with a pretty bow that came in the form of a 31-7 victory over Muskegon Catholic Central. The 6-2-1 Cougars piled up five touchdowns against the Crusaders, who completed the first football season in school history.

Bruce Yarrington brought Muskegon's opening drive to an end by recovering a fumble at its 30-yard line and a 20-yard pass from Erhardt to Nye and Schnur's 9-yard carry to inside the 1 set up a very short TD run by Endres. On CC's next possession, Haunenstein found plenty of room to operate out of the spread formation and his 18-yard gain set up an 8-yard touchdown pass from Erhardt to Nye, and the outcome was determined.

Hauenstein added a 32-yard TD run before halftime and Endres carried the ball in from the 5 in the third quarter. Muskegon's Dick Seymour shocked the CC defenders with an 84-yard scoring run in the final period, but the Cougars came right back to cap a 64-yard TD drive, and the season, with Erhardt's 3-yard quarterback sneak.

Sowle's blue-collar, overachieving appraisal of his team was reflected in the All-City squad. Endres was the only Cougar named to the first team and guard Stan Moleski was the school's only representative on the second team. It was the first time in several years that the city champ didn't dominate the All-City team, but the Cougars didn't care. They had the only hardware that mattered in their trophy case.

CC/WC Archives

1953 City League Champions

Row One (l-r) - T. Richard, T. Larkin, J. Jacobitz, J. Nye, C. Pease, D. Golczynski, L. Endres, L. Bilski, D. Erhardt
Row Two - S. Moleski, R. Hauenstein, M. Schnur, D. Emaus, D. Lucas, D. Szarowicz, M. Anderson, T. Grego, B. Yarrington, J. Karas
Row Three - D. Cook, D. Tietema, F. Huizenga, P. Willacker, F. Marger, J. Parenta, C. Tomajczyk, J. Milan, P. Paskiewicz, R. Gaudet
Row Four - T. Sowle, J. Godleski, D. Lennon, J. Sommers, M. Allen, K. Duchene, D. Wittkowski, K. Hanraham, F. Dobrygowski, M. Erhardt, J. Wilkes, F. Geary

1953 Schedule/Results
Head Coach – Ted Sowle

Date	Opponent	Result		Location
Sep. 18	Flint Northern	Lost	0-19	Atwood Stadium
Sep. 25	Creston	Won	27-0	Houseman Field
Oct. 3	Ottawa Hills	Won	39-12	Houseman Field
Oct. 9	Holland	Won	54-7	South Field
Oct. 16	Saginaw Arthur Hill	Lost	13-20	Saginaw
Oct. 23	Union	Won	19-14	Houseman Field
Oct. 30	South	Won	31-19	Houseman Field
Nov. 7	Central	Tie	0-0	Houseman Field
Nov. 13	Muskegon Catholic Central	Won	31-7	Houseman Field

	Record	Pts. Scored	Pts. Allowed
Overall	6-2-1	214	98
City League	4-0-1	116	45

-1954-

Less than a year after winning its unprecedented third consecutive City League title, Catholic Central was picked by rival coaches to win a fourth in a row. Coach Ted Sowle wasn't complaining about having that 500-pound gorilla placed on the Cougars' back, but he was lamenting the fact he was putting his most inexperienced team in years, maybe ever, through its paces during preseason camp. Catholic would be bigger, Sowle acknowledged, but also slower. It must have had a high football IQ, however, because future Cougar coach Jerry Sieracki was slated for duty at tackle and Larry Barcheski, who would go on to become the head coach at Central, was making his varsity debut at end.

Flint Northern 26
Catholic Central 20
Saturday, September 18 at Houseman Field

Believers in omens thought the season couldn't have started better for the Cougars, who lost a seesaw battle against powerful Flint Northern 26-20 with 2 ½ minutes remaining. Yes, the defeat put an early crimp in CC's state championship aspirations, if there were any for such a young squad, but it lost its previous two openers as well and still ended up as city champs.

Northern opened the biggest game on the statewide schedule with a methodical 78-yard touchdown drive that ended on quarterback Tony Burton's 7-yard off-tackle keeper into the end zone. The Cougars finally canceled out that score late in the second quarter when linebacker Terry Morton blocked a punt, Larry Eggelston covered the loose ball at the Viking 4-yard line and new CC starting quarterback Jim Parente flipped a 2-yard touchdown pass to end Pete Sowle, the son of the Cougars' head man.

Burton single-handedly regained the lead on Northern's first play of the second half when he blasted through the line for a 95-yard touchdown, but the conversion failed. Undaunted, the Catholic Central offense started to operate with its trademark efficiency during a 54-yard drive. Halfback Dave Huizenga tied the score with a 3-yard touchdown run and Isidore Dobrygowski kicked the extra point for a 14-13 advantage.

G. R. Press Photo

CC's Dave Huizenga eludes a Flint Northern tackler for a five-yard gain.

The Vikings marched 88 yards to regain the lead early in the momentous fourth quarter, but the Cougars put together a 70-yard possession and drew even on Huizenga's 8-yard burst off tackle. The decisive play occurred as CC was advancing to midfield for the game-winning score. As Parente dropped back to pass, he dropped the ball when he collided with Northern defensive end Dave Copeland, who picked up the loose ball in stride and galloped 46 yards for the backbreaker. In addition to the fumble, Parente had two of his three passes intercepted. But, take away Burton's long run and Copeland's fluky TD, and it was clear to see that CC stacked up well against the state's elite teams.

Catholic Central 27
Creston 0
Saturday, September 25 at Houseman Field

Two touchdowns by the latest running back to emerge in Catholic Central's vaunted rushing attack spurred CC to its 14th straight win over Creston, 27-0. Walt Stein, a leg-pumping, 5-foot-8, 149-pound dynamo scored two touchdowns in the first stage of the Cougars' title defense. Pete Sowle's recovery of a Polar Bear fumble 35 yards from the goal line led to Stein's 5-yard TD run five plays later. Catholic traveled 75 yards for another Stein 5-yarder that put CC in front 13-0 early in the second quarter and that's how the first half ended.

The Cougars continued to churn up yardage in the second half. Fullback Denny Cook made the score 20-0 early in the third quarter and a 12-yard touchdown pass from Parente to Barcheski accounted for the final TD a few minutes later. Catholic gained 327 of its 339 yards on the ground and held Creston to a total of 97 yards.

Catholic Central 41
Ottawa Hills 14
Friday, October 1 at Houseman Field

Catholic Central looked scary-good when all it did was run the ball. Now, interject some passing into the offensive attack, as the Cougars did in a 41-14 obliteration of Ottawa Hills, and they were all but unstoppable. The defense set the tone early for a 10th straight win over the Indians on the game's first play when defensive tackle Kevin Hanrahan recovered a fumble at the Ottawa 10-yard line. Two plays later, Cook slogged his way through the muddy terrain for a 3-yard touchdown.

Early in the second quarter, Stein charged forward for a 16-yard TD and Cook scored his second touchdown a few minutes later on a 65-yard pass-and-run from Parente for a 20-0 halftime lead. On the second play of the third quarter Huizinga turned a quick-hitter into the middle of the line into a 53-yard score and early in the fourth quarter backup quarterback Joe Schmitz lofted an 18-yard TD pass to Barcheski. Reserve fullback Dave Feutz did his "Crazy Legs Hirsch" imitation on a rollicking 49-yard touchdown run to close out the Indians. Catholic rushed for 300 yards and added another 130 through the air.

Catholic Central 39
Holland 7
Friday, October 8 at Holland

Cook scored early and often in Catholic Central's 39-7 dismantling of Holland High School. His first of three touchdowns came from 15 yards out at the end of an amazing seven-play, 57-yard possession that took all of 60 seconds. Cook limited the number of handoffs on a drive later in the first quarter by breaking into the open for a 53-yard touchdown run.

The Dutchmen cut into CC's lead in the second quarter and trailed 13-7 at halftime. Then, after Ron Van Dyke ticked off 50 yards to the Catholic 15-yard line, it looked like an upset was brewing. However, the CC defense stopped Holland for zero yards on its next four plays and took over on downs and 11 plays later Stein put the game out of reach with an 18-yard scoring sweep around end. Stein ripped off a 56-yard touchdown run in the fourth quarter and Cook made the Dutchmen pay for fumbling with a 32-yard run up the sideline. Cook had what would have been his fourth touchdown, on a 44-yard interception return, called back because of a penalty, but reserve running back Tom Hanna eventually went over from the two. Dobrygowski, who was becoming known as a place-kicking sensation, converted three extra points to bring his total to 13 for the season.

Saginaw Arthur Hill 19
Catholic Central 13
Friday, October 15 at South Field

A nine-point swing on an unusual sequence of events proved costly in Catholic Central's 19-13 loss to Saginaw Arthur Hill. Trailing 13-6 late in the first half, coach Ted Sowle sent his kicking specialist, Isidore "The Cougar Toe" Dobrygowski in to try a 20-yard field goal from the hashmark. Hurried by a furious Lumberjack rush, Dobrygowski got off a low kick that traveled just 10 yards and was fielded by defensive halfback Floyd Wright, who returned it 90-yards for the decisive touchdown.

G. R. Press Photo

Catholic Central's 1954 Offensive Unit

Backfield (l-r) - Frank Huizenga, Ken Duchene, Jim Parente, Denny Cook

Lineman - Pete Sowle, Stan Rubleski, Ed Wybranowski, John Wilks, Dave Tietema, Chuck Tomajczyk, Fred Marger

The Cougars were their own worst enemy. They fumbled on the second play of the game, and then, two plays after putting up a goal-line stand, fumbled again at their own 10-yard line to set up Saginaw's first touchdown. Huizinga quickly evened the score with a 58-yard TD, but the Lumberjacks regained the lead early in the second quarter. Huizinga cut into the Saginaw lead with a 3-yard touchdown run early in the second half, but CC couldn't mount an effective attack the rest of the way.

G. R. Herald Photo

Union's Dick Droski (12) slices through the Catholic defense.

Union 20
Catholic Central 6
Friday, October 22 at Houseman Field

Union scored on its first possession, and for the first time in four City League seasons, heavily favored Catholic Central didn't have an answer. The Red Hawks' staggering 20-6 upset of the three-time defending champs put them in command of the conference race with a 3-0 record. Meantime, 2-1 CC suffered its first loss in 20 conference games dating back to a defeat, also dealt by eventual champion Union, in 1950.

Halfback John Johnson took it to the Cougars before more than 9,000 fans at Houseman Field. Johnson's 12-yard leaping touchdown gave the Red Hawks an early 7-0 lead which held up until the second half, which started with a Union kickoff. However, Catholic had difficulty getting to the ball and and Bill Veerecken covered it for the Red Hawks at the CC 22-yard line. Two plays later, Johnson rambled in from the 10 for a tenuous 13-0 lead.

The Cougar offense finally sprung to life following the ensuing kickoff and cut into the deficit when Stein capped a 75-yard possession with a 24-yard TD burst. However, as Catholic appeared to be mounting a game-winning drive in the fourth quarter, Union's Jerry Hendrickson recovered a Cougar fumble at his own 25, and Johnson did the rest with a 75-yard dagger into the heart of CC's championship machine.

Catholic Central 21
South 14
Saturday, October 30 at South Field

Catholic Central converted two South fumbles into touchdowns in the first quarter, and then broke a tie in the fourth quarter to sew up second place in the City League with a 21-14 victory. Two-way tackle Fred Boylen's recovery of a Trojan giveaway at the CC 33-yard line led to Huizenga's 1-yard TD. Later in the quarter, Fred Marger latched onto another South fumble at the Trojan 38 and Walt Stein put the Cougars ahead 14-0 with a 27-yard sprint.

Leroy Davis threw a 29-yard touchdown pass to Jerome Benton late in the first half, and Gill Lyon stung Catholic with a 58-yard touchdown in the third quarter to tie the score. But Stein completed a 62-yard drive with a 16-yarder that sealed the win with 3:30 remaining.

Catholic Central 12
Central 0
Friday, November 5 at Houseman Field

Catholic Central quickly adjusted to a surprising change in Central's offense and intercepted four of the 14 passes thrown by quarterback Ernie Brazil to stay alive in the City League race with a 12-0 victory. After beating the Cougars, league-leading Union settled for a tie with Ottawa Hills, meaning CC could still end up alone in first place if the Red Hawks were upset by South in their season finale.

Central opened the game in an unbalanced single-wing formation instead of its typical split-T, and picked up good yardage. But the Cougars stopped the Rams in their tracks the rest of the way. Defensive back Terry Morton had Catholic's first pickoff and returned it to the Central 16-yard line. Huizinga needed just one play to give Catholic Central a 6-0 lead which stood until Cook plowed in from the 1 with less than a minute remaining in the game. All 219 of CC's yards came on the ground and the Cougars limited the Rams to 136 yards.

G. R. Press Photo

CC's Denny Cook runs over a Central player.

Catholic Central 47
Muskegon Catholic 19
Saturday, November 13 at Muskegon CC Stadium

In an uncharacteristic departure from the norm, Catholic Central came out passing in its season finale against Muskegon Catholic, and ran away with a 47-19 victory. Parente, who was named All-City quarterback before the game, completed 5 of 10 passes for 117 yards and also ran for a touchdown. Huisinga and Cook scored two touchdowns apiece and Hanna and Tom Przybysz had one each as the Cougars built a 41-0 lead before Sowle sent in the subs.

Union, which defeated South to win the City League title, placed four on the All-City team. Parente was joined by teammates Dave Tietema, a guard, and center John Wilks on the first team.

1954 Schedule/Results
Head Coach – Ted Sowle

Date	Opponent	Result		Location
Sep. 18	Flint Northern	Lost	20-26	Houseman Field
Sep. 25	Creston	Won	27-0	Houseman Field
Oct. 1	Ottawa Hills	Won	41-14	Houseman Field
Oct. 8	Holland	Won	39-7	Holland
Oct. 15	Saginaw Arthur Hill	Lost	13-19	South Field
Oct. 22	Union	Lost	6-20	Houseman Field
Oct. 30	South	Won	21-14	South Field
Nov. 5	Central	Won	12-0	Houseman Field
Nov. 13	Muskegon Catholic Central	Won	47-19	Muskegon CC Stadium

	Record	Pts. Scored	Pts. Allowed
Overall	6-3	226	119
City League	4-1	107	48

-1955-

Catholic Central 13
Flint Northern 13
Friday, September 16 at Atwood Stadium

What was it about Catholic Central and the inability to win season-openers? Despite all of his success as a head coach after the first weekend of competition, Ted Sowle's first-game record since 1952 dropped to 0-3-1 thanks to a 13-13 tie with Flint Northern. Two of those losses also were against the Vikings.

Despite playing in front of a hostile Atwood Stadium crowd in excess of 5,000, Catholic gave every indication that it was going to shake the first-game blues. The Cougars showed no fear early in the first quarter when they

G. R. Herald Photo

Catholic Central's 1955 Backfield
(l-r) - Tom Hanna, Denny Cook, Hermie Miller and Walt Stein

methodically marched 77 yards to take a 7-0 lead on Walt Stein's 2-yard dive. However, in addition to facing a perennial tough Northern team, something bigger, what *The Grand Rapids Herald* called "a jinx," seemed to stand in CC's path to victory. The Cougars drove all the way to the Viking 4-yard line on their next possession but turned the ball over on downs. They made it to the 27 in the second period, but the offense stalled again.

With little to show, relatively speaking, for its first-half domination, Catholic paid for keeping Northern in the game. The Vikings, who should have been trailing by three touchdowns, successfully completed a 51-yard drive in the third quarter to take a 7-6 lead. Catholic quickly reasserted itself by covering 63 yards in just six plays, the last of which was Stein's 16-yard flash into the end zone, and held a 13-7 lead early in the final period. But the defense couldn't keep Northern from crossing the goal line and the offense appeared to be running into an invisible brick wall the rest of the way.

CC/WC Archives

All-City Back Walt Stein

Catholic Central 36
Central 12
Saturday, September 24 at Houseman Field

Catholic Central's fears of Central being a darkhorse turned out to be unfounded. The Cougars launched their assault on an eighth City League championship in 14 seasons on the first play of their second possession when pile-driving fullback Denny Cook charged through the Ram defensive line and didn't stop running until he had a 73-yard TD in the bag.

Not to be outdone, Central quarterback Ernie Brazil lulled the Cougars to sleep with a delayed fake handoff, and then raced 70 yards to cut CC's lead to 7-6. The fireworks continued in the second quarter when CC quarterback Hermie Miller Jr.'s first pass ended up in the hands of hulking 200-pound right end Fred Sauer and he sprinted away from the Rams for a 67-yard TD.

The Cougars added to their 14-7 halftime lead with a 71-yard drive that ended on Miller's 1-yard sneak, and Miller made it 27-6 when he completed a 28-yard pass to Sauer to set up an long scoring toss to Cook. Jim Augustyn blew the game open in the fourth quarter with a 23-yard field goal and reserve running back Jerry Couturier added another long-distance score with a 72-yard jaunt. The game remained entertaining until the end and with a minute left, Brazil threw a 40-yard touchdown pass to fullback Gordy VanPutten to put the final score at 36-12.

Catholic Central 32
Creston 6
Friday, September 30 at Houseman Field

The victory machine took awhile to get rolling, but thanks to a fumble recovery and an interception that thwarted a pair of Creston threats in the second quarter, Catholic Central just bided its time. Then, once the ever-evolving offense of coach Ted Sowle started to click with its double-wing and twin-flanker sets, the all-too predictable outcome came to fruition. The Cougars scored four touchdowns in the second half to whip the Polar Bears, 32-6.

CC/WC Archives

All-City Tackle Jerry Sieracki

The rout appeared to be on from the initial drive, which took all of three plays. Cook, who moved through Creston defenders like a bowling ball through bowling pins, banged his way for a 40-yard gain on the first play from scrimmage, Miller passed 12 yards to Sauer and halfback Tom Hanna crashed into the end zone from the 1-yard line. The Polar Bear defense rose to the occasion, however, and CC led only 7-0 at halftime.

Creston couldn't hang with Catholic's balanced attack in the second half. After the Cougars recovered a fumble early in the third quarter, Miller threw his first of two long touchdown passes to Sauer which served as bookends to Stein's 65-yard quick-hitter. Catholic Central's lead grew to 32-0 in the fourth quarter on backup halfback Russ Smith's 6-yard marker. Miller completed 3 of 6 passes to increase his proficiency in two league games to 6-for-10.

Catholic Central 32
Ottawa Hills 13
Saturday, October 8 at Houseman Field

Five, as in touchdowns, was a charm for Catholic Central in a third consecutive game. Meanwhile, the Cougars' long-distance scoring express continued to roll in a 32-13 runaway against Ottawa Hills. Cook was the first to break out of the starting gate with a 43-yard touchdown trot that put CC ahead 7-0 with the game just four minutes old.

Sparked by 5-for-5 passing by ace quarterback Mike Coddington in their first scoring drive, the Indians cut the lead to 7-6 on a 3-yard run by Tom Cargill. However, Hanna erased that score with a 50-yard TD blitz to give the Cougars a 14-7 halftime lead, and then upped the advantage to 21-7 with a 60-yard scoring dash in the third quarter. The defense got into the act when linebacker Ken Duchesne picked off Coddington's pitchout and returned it 35 yards for a touchdown. Then, after defensive halfback Dave Feutz intercepted a Coddington pass and returned it 70 yards to the Ottawa 10-yard line, halfback Dave Navigato ran it in from there for a 32-6 lead.

Catholic Central 29
Saginaw Arthur Hill 7
Friday, October 14 at Saginaw Memorial Stadium

Revenge is a dish best served cold, and Catholic Central took no mercy on Eastern nemesis Saginaw Arthur Hill on its own turf. Cook got the 29-7 blood-letting started with a 90-yard return of the opening kickoff for a 7-0 lead. Arthur Hill battled back to tie the score in the first quarter, but the stalemate was only temporary.

Augustyn's second field goal of the season, from 21 yards, increased the CC lead to 10-7 in the second quarter and Stein converted Dan Grego's interception and 21-yard return to the Arthur Hill 19 into a 5-yard TD run for a 17-7 halftime lead.

The ball-hawking Grego recovered a fumble at the Lumberjack 20 in the third quarter to set up Cook's second score, which required him to run just 1 yard this time around. Cook was far from finished, however, and his 39-yard run set up his 14-yard TD in the fourth quarter. The victory snapped the Cougars' two-game losing streak to Arthur Hill and gave them a 3-2 series lead. The win was doubly satisfying given the fact the Lumberjacks had previously defeated Flint Northern, which tied CC 13-13 in the opener. Catholic held a 267-216 advantage in total offense.

Catholic Central 26
Detroit Catholic Central 7
Friday, October 21 at South Field

As he had throughout the season, Cook set the stage with a long run and Catholic Central never lost the momentum in a 26-7 victory over Detroit Catholic Central. Cook staggered the Shamrocks with a 21-yard gain up the middle on the first play of the game, but the Cougars momentarily lost momentum when the drive ended on a fumble at the Detroit 21-yard line. Catholic Central got the ball right back when Detroit fumbled after a 1-yard gain and Stein set up his first of three touchdowns with a 21-yard surge to the 1.

Stein's next scoring excursion covered 33 yards to complete an 83-yard drive and he put the Cougars ahead 20-0 in the third quarter by angling through a crease for a 7-yard TD. After Detroit scored, Couturier was on his way to a long touchdown but tripped on his own shoelaces after a 57-yard gain. Stein's first attempt at his third touchdown came in the fourth quarter when he followed a wall of blockers for 41 yards to the end zone, but the play was nullified by a holding penalty. He moved into a tie with Cook for the city scoring lead a few minutes later.

Catholic Central 48
Union 7
Friday, October 28 at Houseman Field

What went around came around for defending city champion Union High, which endured a 48-7 thrashing by Catholic Central just over a year after spoiling the Cougars' title defense with a stunning 20-6 upset. Unbeaten Catholic went way over its 33-point-per-game scoring average in City League play and Cook highlighted the seven-touchdown barrage with a 95-yard dash on the first play of the second half. The Cougars (6-0-1, 5-0 City League) assured themselves of a share of the championship, which they could win outright with a victory against South, 3-0 in league play.

Catholic Central pounded out 350 rushing yards and Navigato, a 5-foot-5, 132-pound gnat of a player, scored twice in place of the injured Stein. Couturier posted CC to a 7-0 lead in the first quarter, the only period in which the Cougars didn't score two touchdowns, with a 3-yard sweep. After Boylen blocked a punt, Navigato navigated his way to a 34-yard TD in the second quarter, which Miller followed with a touchdown pass to Fuetz.

CC/WC Archives

All-City Guard Roger Plachecki

Cook opened the second half with the City League's longest play of the year and Barcheski returned a fumble 24 yards for a defensive score. Navigato knew the way to a 33-yard touchdown in the fourth quarter and Hanna, who was kept out of the first three quarters with a minor injury, scored on an 8-yard run with the third-string offense.

Catholic Central 32
South 0
Friday, November 4 at South Field

It was billed as "The game of the year." It pitted South High's City League-leading defense against Catholic Central's offensive juggernaut, which had outscored its opponents 215-65.

It was, in a word, anticlimactic.

The Cougars feasted on turnovers before 8,300 fans in sub-freezing weather to turn back the Trojans 32-0 for their fourth city championship in five seasons and eighth in 14. Afterward Sowle called it one of the greatest teams he ever coached. Catholic scored all of its points in the first half and South didn't even cross into CC territory until late in the game.

As it turned out, Cook scored all the points Catholic Central would need when he gashed the Trojans for an 18-yard touchdown run that completed a 72-yard drive on the fifth play of the game. Crego intercepted South quarterback Delvin Bishop's pass and returned it 10 yards to the Trojan 45 to set up CC's second TD of the first quarter. Navigato took the ball into the end zone from 5 yards out a few plays later, and the Cougars scored their third TD of the period seconds later when Crego recovered a Trojan fumble and returned it 15 yards.

The first of linebacker Ed Wybranowski's two interceptions came on the first play of the second quarter and led to a 35-yard touchdown pass from Miller to Sauer. Midway through the second quarter, defensive back Jim Wysocki scooped up another South fumble and returned it to the 41 and a minute later Couturier swept around the left flank and into the end zone for the final score of the game. Wybranowski snuffed out the Trojans' only scoring threat of the game by picking off a Bishop pass at the CC 2-yard line with under five minutes remaining.

Catholic Central 20
Muskegon Catholic Central 7
Saturday, November 12 at Houseman Field

Fullback Denny Cook scored one of Catholic Central's three first-half touchdowns to hold off teammate Walt Stein for the City League scoring title. Stein also had a TD, but trailed Cook by 12 points going into the game. Navigato had the other six-pointer.

Stein cut into Cook's lead with a 1-yard touchdown that finished off a 56-yard drive featuring Navigato's 18-yard run in the first quarter. Navigato didn't play favorites, however, and contributed a pair of 12-yard gains during a 59-yard drive that ended on Cook's 1-yard TD on the first play of the second quarter. Navigato took matters into his own hands when on the third scoring drive Miller lost the handle on the ball while attempting a pitchout. Navigato completed the 10-yard scoring play by fielding the ball on one hop, leaping over a Crusader defender and keeping his balance long enough to cross the goal line.

Not surprisingly, the Cougars dominated the All-City balloting just as they did their opponents while amassing an 8-0-1 record. Cook, Stein and Sauer, offensive tackles Boylen and Sieracki and the guard tandem of Wybranowski and Roger Plachecki were named to the first team. The four linemen were the squad's only unanimous choices. South, with two, and Ottawa, with one, were the only other teams to place players among the starting All-City 11.

CC/WC Archives

1955 City League Champions

Row One (l-r) - R. Piachecki, R. Grinnewald, F. Boylen, L. Eggleston. F. Sauer, L. Barcheski, J. Sieracki, D. Cook, E. Wybranowski, W. Stein, K. Duchene

Row Two - E. Idziak, J. Wysocki, D. Feutz, D. Grego, H. Miller, J. Schmidt, J. Augustyn, R. Boonstra, T. Ryan, J. Couterier, R. Wybranowski, T. Hanna, F. Geary, J. Sommer

Row Three - R. Smith, P. Tietema, T. Fox, T. Kaywood, G. Andrie, S. Sichterman, G. Barto, E. Rutowski, J. Kailunas, T. Bieberlie, N. Smith, W. Navigato, D. Lennon

Row Four - T. Sowle, M. Hickey, R. Ciucci, G. Zainea, M. Elliot, W. O'Brien, J. Bowen, S. Zurek, R. Brocato, T. Walsh, S. Wisinski, J. Cook, T. Flickenger, J. Rauch, R. Satkowski, J. Godleski

1955 Schedule/Results

Head Coach – Ted Sowle

Date	Opponent	Result		Location
Sep. 16	Flint Northern	Tie	13-13	Atwood Stadium
Sep. 24	Central	Won	36-12	Houseman Field
Sep. 30	Creston	Won	32-6	Houseman Field
Oct. 8	Ottawa Hills	Won	32-13	Houseman Field
Oct. 14	Saginaw Arthur Hill	Won	29-7	Saginaw
Oct. 21	Detroit Catholic Central	Won	26-7	South Field
Oct. 28	Union	Won	48-7	Houseman Field
Nov. 4	South	Won	32-0	South Field
Nov. 12	Muskegon Catholic Central	Won	20-7	Houseman Field

	Record	Pts. Scored	Pts. Allowed
Overall	8-0-1	268	72
City League	5-0-0	180	38

-1956-

Ted Sowle played the "we're inexperienced" card again, to which the rest of the City League rolled its collective eyes and said, "seriously Coach?" It was the same lament uttered in 1955 before Catholic Central won its fourth conference championship in five seasons and eighth in 14 campaigns. Truth be told, Sowle did lose most of his top players such at Denny Cook, Walt Stein and Jerry Sieracki. However, even the most casual observers would have a hard time missing the return of Hermie Miller Jr. at quarterback, Fred Boylen at left tackle, Dan Grego at end and Bill Navigato and Jerry Couturier to the backfield.

Flint Northern 21
Catholic Central 19
Friday, September 14 at Houseman Field

Maybe inexperience was to blame, after all, when the Cougars failed to beat Flint Northern in a fourth consecutive season opener. Catholic fell to 0-3-1 in those games after losing a hard-luck 21-19 decision at Houseman Field.

In a game of big breaks, the last ones favored the visitors especially when Navigato was separated from the ball by a hard tackle after a 44-yard gain to the Viking 3-yard line, and Northern recovered in the end zone. What likely would have been the Cougars' game-winning touchdown turned into a game-losing touchback. Catholic's first touchdown resulted from Grego's recovery of a Northern fumble on the first play of the game. Navigato charged in for a 6-yard touchdown to give the Cougars a 7-0 lead before the game was a minute old.

The Vikings countered at the end of the opening period in similar fashion when Phil Gaines intercepted a Miller pass. On the next play, state track champ John Sharp, who ran the quarter-mile in a record-breaking 50 seconds the previous spring, sprung loose for a 59-yard TD. Catholic didn't need any luck while completing an 83-yard drive on Couturier's 7-yard touchdown late in the second quarter to take a 13-7 halftime advantage. But a Navigato fumble gave Northern the ball for its go-ahead touchdown, 14-13. Ned Smith regained a five-point lead for CC with a soaring leap of 3 yards into the end zone late in the third quarter. However, a 15-yard holding penalty called on Boylen during a Viking punt gave Northern the new life it needed for Sharp's 35-yard game-winning TD, and set the stage for Navigato's fatal fumble.

Catholic dominated statistically. The Cougars picked up all 263 of their yards on the ground to Northern's 138 yards of total offense. CC had 16 first downs to just two, including one on Boylen's fateful hold, by the Vikings. The bottom line was, however, that with inexperience like that, Catholic could win a lot of games.

Catholic Central 33
Central 13
Friday, September 21 at Houseman Field

Rainy conditions dictated the style of play in Catholic Central's City League opener against Central, and the Cougars couldn't have been happier. All but four of their snaps started off a running play, typically for Navigato or Couturier, and the result was a scrappy 33-13 triumph before 5,000 soggy souls. It was Catholic's 10th consecutive victory over the Rams.

When Miller did throw, he was the picture of perfection. He went 4-for-4 including two touchdown passes to Navigato. The first publicized contribution of George Andrie, who would go on to fame at Marquette University and fortune as a five-time Pro-Bowler with the Dallas Cowboys, took place in the first quarter when he recovered a fumbled punt at the 17. Moments later Couturier scored from the 2-yard line and Catholic never trailed. A fumble recovery by Gene Idziak later in the first quarter set up a 43-yard TD pass from Miller to Navigato. In the second quarter, Miller bamboozled the entire Ram defense with a deft play fake to Couturier and eventually tucked the ball into the stomach of Navigato, who streaked up the sideline for a 62-yard TD. Navigato set up his third score with a 21-yard reception and reached the end zone on a 14-yard toss from Miller.

Central scored on an 80-yard drive that was aided by a 15-yard CC penalty and cut its deficit to 26-7, but Jack Bowen recovered another Ram fumble in the fourth quarter and Couturier put the game away with a 25-yard streak around left end. The Cougars lost 125 yards on penalties and Couturier had a 62-yard TD wiped out in the third quarter because of a 5-yard infraction.

Catholic Central 40
Creston 20
Saturday, September 29 at Houseman Field

It's often said that luck is the residue of design, so maybe Fred Boylen was being prepared for this opportunity every minute he was coached by Ted Sowle and Catholic Central assistant Joe Godleski. On the second play of CC's game against Creston, Miller threw a jump pass that ricocheted off a Polar Bear defender and into Boylen's arms. Sixty-five yards later, the Cougars had a first down at the Creston 15, and after an exchange of fumbles, Miller threw a 17-yard touchdown pass to Grego for a 7-0 lead.

Catholic Central never trailed in an opportunistic 40-20 victory. The Cougars' next possession covered 61 yards and the 11th play was a 1-yard plunge into the end zone by fullback Jim Wysocki for a 13-0 lead. The Polar Bears tied the score with two second-quarter touchdowns, including one with 37 seconds remaining, but Catholic went ahead for good when Navigato turned a simple pass in the flat into a 53-yard touchdown reception as time ran out.

Couturier added a 34-yard touchdown run and Miller scored on a 1-yard sneak in the third quarter, and on the first play of the fourth quarter Ed Ruthkowski intercepted a Creston pitchout and ran it in for CC's final TD. Andrie was treated for a broken arm at St. Mary's Hospital after the game.

CC/WC Archives
All-State Tackle Fred Boylen

Catholic Central 26
Ottawa Hills 0
Friday, October 5 at Houseman Field

The halfback combo of Couturier and Navigato and lead blocking of tackle Fred Boylen rammed into the City League's best defense until it caused a dam burst that resulted in Catholic Central's 26-0 victory over Ottawa Hills. The high-powered CC offense reached Indian territory only once in the first half, but that was enough to create a crack. The Cougars used 13 plays to cover 94 yards and Couturier wedged into the end zone from 10 yards away to provide a 7-0 halftime advantage.

It was the play of the CC defense, however, and blocking of the Cougar offensive line that gave Sowle the confidence to go for it on fourth-and-3 at his own 15 midway through the third quarter. Catholic picked up the first down and on the next play, Navigato broke Ottawa's heart with a 67-yard touchdown run. Shortly after the fourth quarter got underway, Jerry Barto stripped the ball out of the Indian quarterback's hand and recovered it 10 yards from the end zone. Navigato's burst from there gave CC a 19-0 lead and Couturier added a 70-yard lightning strike.

Ottawa's defense was being ballyhooed all week prior to the game, but it was the Cougar stoppers who rose to the occasion on five Indian forays into scoring position. Catholic Central ended up with a 461-316 advantage in total offense.

CC/WC Archives

All-City End Dan Grego

Catholic Central 31
Saginaw Arthur Hill 20
Friday, October 12 at South Field

Catholic Central threw its hat in the state championship ring with an impressive 31-20 victory over Saginaw Arthur Hill. The win snapped the Lumberjacks' six-game win streak, which began in 1955, and evened CC's season record against Saginaw Valley Conference teams at 1-1.

The Cougars were so dominant, they ran up 348 yards of rushing offense to Arthur Hill's 97, and would have had even more if they weren't assessed 165 penalty yards. Catholic's penchant for scoring from anywhere on the field continued when Couturier, who ended the scoring against Ottawa a week earlier with 70-yard TD, started it against the Lumberjacks with a 73-yard romp. Arthur Hill answered with a 64-yard scoring drive, but Navigato's 4-yard touchdown gave CC a 12-7 lead in the second quarter.

Capable backup halfback Ned Smith's 11-yard TD put the Cougars ahead 19-7 before halftime, and with the Lumberjacks picking up just 33 rushing yards in the final three quarters, Couturier's second touchdown was all CC needed to salt the game away. The Lumberjacks completed 8 of 20 passes for 103 yards, and CC was 1 of 4 for 4 yards, but who needed to throw with ground-gainers like Navigato and Couturier?

Catholic Central 7
Detroit Catholic Central 0
Friday, October 19 at Detroit McCabe Field

It was ironic that a bruising defensive battle would be decided by the City League's top offensive scoring threat. Catholic Central and Detroit Catholic Central played to a stalemate for all but a brief instance early in the third quarter when the Cougars capitalized on a break for the game's only score.

Although Catholic reached the Shamrock 10-yard line in the first quarter, it couldn't punch the ball into the end zone. Then, on the first play of the second half, Detroit fumbled at its own 23-yard line and a committee of Cougar defenders covered the ball. Six plays later, Couturier upped his league-leading point total to 60 with a 4-yard TD that provided the difference in the 7-0 win. In a desperate bid to tie the score, Detroit made its deepest penetration into Cougar territory in the third quarter. However, the CC defense was up to the task and took over on downs at its own 18-yard line after stopping the Shamrocks for no gain on three straight plays. Catholic Central reached the Detroit 10-yard line again in the final quarter but the drive stalled out, not that it mattered.

CC/WC Archives

All-City Back Jerry Couturier

Catholic Central 40
Union 7
Saturday, October 27 at Houseman Field

The 45th renewal of the storied rivalry between No. 2-ranked Catholic Central and Union barely lived up to its milestone as the Cougars quickly moved on with an overwhelming 40-7 shellacking. The Red Hawks still held a commanding series advantage, 24-16-5, but CC won the last two meetings by a combined score of 88-14.

CC/WC Archives

All-State Guard George Zainea

The win, before a sellout crowd of 9,100, provided Catholic with no less than a share of its fifth City League crown in six seasons. Couturier put the Cougars ahead in typical fashion with a 6-yard run that completed an all-rush, 10-play, 52-yard drive. But then, CC deviated from past form. First Miller threw a 13-yard touchdown pass to Grego at the end of a 12-play, 73-yard possession. Then, after Union scored its only touchdown on Ken Folkertsma's 43-yard run, and Jim Wysocki got the ball back for CC on an interception with time running out in the first half, Miller threw a 16-yard scoring strike to end Paul Tietema, who collected the ball in the end zone.

After the Cougars returned the second-half kickoff to the Red Hawk 47, a two-play scoring driving, with runs of 10 and 37 yards by Navigato, made the score 26-7. Navigato hit for runs of 20 and 27 yards to set up his second TD, from 1 yard out, and Smith also scored on a 1-yard dive. Aside from its scoring drive, Union made it across midfield on only one other occasion and CC outgained the Red Hawks, 309-161.

Catholic Central 34
South 7
Saturday, November 3 at Houseman Field

It took just 10 minutes and 12 plays for the Cougars to capture their second straight outright City League championship, their fifth in six seasons, their sixth in eight and their ninth in 15. Catholic scored three touchdowns in that span against South at the beginning of the first quarter and then coasted to a 34-7 victory. The Cougars were the living example of a juggernaut while collecting 347 yards, for a 12.2-yards-per-play average, in the first half. CC finished with a 447-yard rushing total for the game.

After Wysocki returned the opening kickoff to the CC 38-yard line, Smith, who started in place of the injured Navigato, ripped through the Trojan defense for 28 yards and on the next play, Ron Wybranowski went around right end for 34-yard score. Catholic's next drive started at its own 34, and after Couturier advanced the ball 31 yards, Smith scored two plays later on a 28-yard rush. A South punt sent the Cougars back to their own 18, but they needed just seven plays to go the distance and take a 20-0 lead on Couturier's 30-yard TD run. Couturier delighted the Homecoming crowd with 130 rushing yards and two TDs.

Catholic Central 25
Muskegon Catholic Central 21
Saturday, November 10 at Muskegon CC Stadium

As talk of dropping the powerful Catholic Central football program from the City League gained steam, the Cougars seemed to lose some in their season finale at Muskegon Catholic Central. The city champs had to battle from behind three times and then hold on for a spine-tingling 25-21 win against a Crusader team that finished with a 5-3-1 record.

CC/WC Archives

All-City Guard Gene Idziak

Couturier put the Cougars ahead 6-0 with a 3-yard touchdown run in the first quarter, but Muskegon mounted a six-play, 90-yard drive to take its first lead, 7-6. The Cougars led 12-7 at halftime on the strength of Couturier's second score, but Muskegon marched 77 yards in the third quarter for a 14-12 advantage. Wybranowski returned the ensuing kickoff 56 yards to the Muskegon 24, and the Cougars regained the lead, 19-14, a few minutes later on Navigato's 4-yard dive. There was no quit in the Crusaders, however, and they took advantage of a Cougar fumble to move back out on top, 21-19.

The Cougars avoided what would have been an embarrassing loss by driving 80 yards in 18 plays in the final four minutes of the game. Wysocki had the honor of finishing off the Crusaders and the season with a 1-yard plunge.

Couturier, Boylen, Grego, Idziak and guard George Zainea represented the Cougars on the first-team All-City squad and Navigato, Miller, Tietema and tackle Tom Ryan earned second-team regocnition.

1956 Schedule/Results

Head Coach – Ted Sowle

Date	Opponent	Result		Location
Sep. 14	Flint Northern	Lost	19-21	Houseman Field
Sep. 21	Central	Won	33-13	Houseman Field
Sep. 29	Creston	Won	40-20	Houseman Field
Oct. 5	Ottawa Hills	Won	26-0	Houseman Field
Oct. 12	Saginaw Arthur Hill	Won	31-20	South Field
Oct. 19	Detroit Catholic Central	Won	7-0	McCabe Field
Oct. 27	Union	Won	40-7	Houseman Field
Nov. 3	South	Won	34-7	Houseman Field
Nov. 10	Muskegon Catholic Central	Won	25-21	Muskegon CC Stadium

	Record	Pts. Scored	Pts. Allowed
Overall	8-1	255	109
City League	5-0	173	47

-1957-

It had become a rite of early September in the City League: Catholic Central coach Ted Sowle's publicly despairs about lacking experience, and the Cougars picked to win the conference title.

Poor Sowle groaned that "only one outstanding veteran," end Jerry Barto, returned from the 1956 squad that successfully defended its '55 title. Nevermind that CC returned a bevy of outstanding non-vets, which was plain for rival coaches to see. It is fair to say Catholic would open the season with all new starters on offense and that the defense, with a handful of regulars, would have to carry the team until the offense was up to speed. However, the cupboard wasn't entirely bare. In addition to Barto, end George Andrie and guard Jack Bowen were among the talented reserves who contributed significantly to an 8-1 record and No. 2 ranking.

"As I see, we'll have to work much harder this year before the opening game," Sowle said.

Saginaw Arthur Hill 10
Catholic Central 0
Saturday, September 21 at Saginaw Memorial Stadium

Either the Cougars let up at some point during preseason drills or they ran out of time, because for the fifth straight season they failed to win their opener against a team from the Saginaw Valley Conference. Except this time, it wasn't Flint Northern that spoiled CC's debut, it was Saginaw Arthur Hill protecting its home turf with a 10-0 victory.

It wasn't as if the Cougars were overmatched. They weren't even particularly mistake-prone despite being in the first stage of the season and playing in rainy and muddy conditions that favored the defenses. However, Catholic's inexplicable streak of bad luck in openers against the Valley continued. Midway in the third period, the CC defense had just stopped Arthur Hill's most effective drive by forcing and recovering a fumble at the Cougar 7-yard line. However, Catholic Central promptly fumbled the ball back to the Lumberjacks, who recovered at the 4, and they converted CC's only turnover of the game into the game-winning touchdown. Garron Weiker added a 31-yard field goal for insurance in the fourth period.

The Cougars played well. They didn't allow a first down in the first half and outgained Arthur Hill, 307-221. But, after they got their best opportunity to score when halfback Tim Baragar broke loose for a 42-yard gain and the offense made it to the Lumberjack 23 in the fourth quarter, they couldn't finish the job.

Catholic Central 12
South 0
Friday, September 27 at South Field

True to the form that resulted in so many City League championships in previous seasons, Catholic Central shook off a season-opening disappointment to win its first conference game. The Cougars made it over a major hurdle standing in the way of a third straight title with a 12-0 victory over South High.

The running-back corps of Baragar, Bob Misner, Bill Shuple and Ron Ciucci combined for 281 rushing yards, while the Trojans could scratch out just 79 yards on the ground against the stout CC defense. The wind left South's sails in the opening moments when the Catholic Central defense repelled its scoring opportunity 8 yards from the end zone.

The Cougars were in command the rest of the way and got their first scoring opportunity when Andrie recovered a fumble at the South 38-yard line in the second quarter. On first down, Baragar ran for 28 yards. On the second play of the drive he took the ball inside the 1, and he banged in from there on the third play for a 6-0 lead. A combination of penalties and another CC defensive stand caused the Trojans to give the ball back on downs inside the Cougar 15-yard line in the third quarter and Catholic put the game out of reach with a 10-play drive that covered 73 yards. Misner rushed for 43 yards, including the final 4 for the TD, during the possession. The score was somewhat misleading because two Cougar drives ended on fumbles, and they turned the ball over after failing to covert three fourth-down plays in South territory.

G. R. Herald Photo

Brothers Stan (left) and Ron Zurek

CC/WC Archives

Bob Misner runs to daylight.

Catholic Central 25
Central 6
Friday, October 11 at Houseman Field

A week after its game against Flint Northern was canceled by City League officials due to a flu epidemic affecting Grand Rapids schools, Catholic Central rode on Misner's shoulders to a 25-6 victory over Central. Misner contributed mightily to CC's rushing total of 286 yards and provided a 7-0 first-quarter lead on a 4-yard burst into the end zone. The score came at the end of a 70-yard drive.

Shuple made it 13-0 with a 5-yard touchdown in the second quarter. Rams' ball-carrier Don Faasen punched across the goal line from 2 yards out before halftime, but the CC defense pitched a shutout in the final two quarters. A high snap from center caused Faasen to abort his punt attempt and four plays after he was tackled at the Central 38, Misner scored his second 4-yard TD. The Cougars drove to within the Ram 10-yard line in the fourth quarter, and after an exchange of fumbles, backup quarterback Tom Ryan's fourth-down pass to Don Blain resulted in an 8-yard score.

Catholic Central 18
Creston 6
Friday, October 18 at Houseman Field

Running back by committee was working well for Catholic Central. A week after Misner led the Cougars to a victory over Central, Shuple was the difference in an 18-6 victory over Creston. Shuple broke a 6-6 tie with less than five minutes remaining with a spectacular 75-yard touchdown run that left the 6,500 spectators at Houseman Field gasping.

A Polar Bear punt set the Cougars back to their own 25-yard line. On the first play, Shuple blasted off right tackle, broke into the clear at midfield and was 20 yards ahead of the closest Creston pursuer when he crossed the goal line. Trailing by a score of just 12-6, the Polar Bears still had enough time to stage a comeback, but CC defensive back Mike Krzykwa intercepted a pass thrown by quarterback Fred Challa and returned it to midfield. A few plays later, Krzykwa converted the turnover into an 8-yard touchdown with 10 seconds remaining.

Catholic took a 6-0 lead in the first quarter on a 2-yard touchdown pass from quarterback Mart Elliott to Andrie, but Challa tied the score in the second quarter with a 17-yard touchdown pass to fullback Dave Annis. Shuple, who ran for 46 yards on the first play of the game, finished with 132 of Catholic's amazing 349 rushing yards. Bob Borlet added 109 yards on 13 carries and Misner, a 166-pound junior, had 98 yards on 14 attempts. Led by linemen Barto, Andrie, Jim Wysocki, Chuck Collins, Stan Zurek and Tom Tenfelde, the suffocating Cougar defense limited Creston to 4 rushing yards in the first half and 15 in the second half and dropped Challa for 28 yards in losses while attempting to pass.

Catholic Central 13
Ottawa Hills 13
Friday, October 25 at South Field

Catholic Central's bid to defend its back-to-back City League championships sustained a devastating blow in the form of a 13-13 tie with Ottawa Hills. It marked the first time CC failed to defeat the Indians in 13 years. The Cougars couldn't hold a pair of first-half leads and then couldn't find the end zone in the second half.

Catholic's game-opening possession covered 66 yards, including 32 on Misner's draw play, after Shuple powered across the goal line from 2 yards out, but Barto's missed extra point proved costly. Ottawa needed just four plays to answer, with quarterback Steve Graves and right end Dave Smith combining for a 56-yard pitch-and-catch touchdown to tie the score.

The Cougars regained the lead in the second quarter on Krzykwa's 4-yard tackle-breaking TD effort and extra-point run, but Ottawa canceled out that score with a 39-yard halfback option pass from Frank Breen to Smith.

Catholic Central 28
Detroit Catholic Central 13
Friday, November 1 at Houseman Field

With the Cougars' backs against the wall in the second half, it was a lineman, senior Jerry Barto, who led them to a 28-13 victory over Detroit Catholic Central. Trailing 7-0 at the start of the second half, GRCC ran repeatedly around right end where Barto was clearing a path with savage blocks during a 68-yard scoring drive. On the final play of the possession, Ciucci followed a Barto block for a 14-yard game-tying score.

Less than three minutes later, Barto blocked a Shamrock punt and the Cougars took over at the 10-yard line from where Misner crashed in for the go-ahead touchdown. On the second play of Detroit's ensuing drive, Barto hit the ball-carrier so hard he fumbled the ball and Stan Zurek recovered at the 25. Misner carried four times and finally scored from the 1-foot line. Early in the fourth quarter, Ryan put the Cougars ahead 28-7 with a 17-yard TD pass to Andrie.

Union 22
Catholic Central 7
Saturday, November 9 at Houseman Field

Catholic Central found itself in familiar territory, a championship game against Union, but as the defensive stalwart instead of an offensive juggernaut as in previous seasons. Both teams sported 4-1-1 records, but the Red Hawks were a perfect 3-0 against City League competition while CC was 2-0-1.

G. R. Herald Photo
Running Back Bill Shuple trys to evade a trio of Union defenders.

In this case, however, the axiom that defense wins championship applied to Union, which clinched its fifth city title of the modern era with a 22-7 victory over the Cougars on snow-covered Houseman Field.

The Red Hawks charged out to a 16-0 first-quarter lead on 4- and 43-yard touchdown runs by speedy 5-foot-4 halfback Kenny Folkerstma and a safety that resulted when Catholic Central fumbled in the end zone and Shupe covered the ball. Union then subdued the Cougar offense until the final period.

Midway through the final quarter, Ciucci cut Union's lead to 16-7 with a 6-yard touchdown through the snow. The Cougars quickly added what appeared to be another touchdown to draw to within three points, but it was nullified by a penalty and Red Hawks back Bill Stacy sealed the victory with an 8-yard TD run.

Catholic Central 20
Muskegon Catholic Central 19
Friday, November 15 at Houseman Field

Catholic Central used a ball-control offense to defeat Muskegon Catholic Central for a fifth time in as many meetings, 20-19. Touchdown runs of 1 and 6 yards by Baragar allowed the Cougars to forge 7-7 and 13-13 ties in the first half and they took the lead for the first time, 20-13, on Ciucci's 1-yard dive early in the fourth quarter. Muskegon's Harry Allore countered with a 50-yard touchdown dash, but the Cougars secured the victory by stopping Jerry Wolski short of the goal line as he attempted to run for the extra point.

Andrie and Cougar guard Mike Ward were the only members of CC's 5-2-1 team to earn first-team All-City accolades. Zurek, Bowen and Collins were named to the second team.

George Andrie
Catholic Central
1958

Following his graduation from Catholic Central, George Andrie enrolled at Marquette University. Andrie led Marquette in receiving in 1959 and 1960 and was a standout on the defensive line.

Andrie was drafted in the sixth round of the 1962 NFL Draft by the Cowboys as a defensive end, despite not playing his senior season because the sport was dropped at Marquette.

As a rookie, Andrie won the starting job at right defensive end and also made the NFL All-Rookie team.

In 1964, after playing on the left side of the defense, he was switched back to his original position at right defensive end, where he stayed throughout the remainder of his career.

He played most of his career next to hall of fame defensive tackle Bob Lilly. Together they helped to form the Cowboys' original "Doomsday Defense", that dominated the NFL for the next several years.

A starter at defensive end for the Cowboys for 11 seasons (1962-72) Andrie was named to the Pro Bowl five straight times (1965–69), All-Pro once and three times second team All-Pro during his career. He was also named the Pro Bowl MVP in 1970.

1957 Schedule/Results

Head Coach – Ted Sowle

Date	Opponent	Result		Location
Sep. 21	Saginaw Arthur Hill	Lost	0-10	Saginaw
Sep. 27	South	Won	12-0	South Field
Oct. 11	Central	Won	25-6	Houseman Field
Oct. 18	Creston	Won	18-6	Houseman Field
Oct. 25	Ottawa Hills	Tie	13-13	South Field
Nov. 1	Detroit Catholic Central	Won	28-13	Houseman Field
Nov. 9	Union	Lost	6-22	Houseman Field
Nov. 15	Muskegon Catholic Central	Won	20-19	Houseman Field

	Record	Pts. Scored	Pts. Allowed
Overall	5-2-1	122	89
City League	3-1-1	74	47

-1958-

With 200-pound Chuck Collins and 190-pound Mike Ward returning to reprise their All-City selections at the guard spots, coach Chuck Sowle had to temper his poor-mouthing about how inexperienced Catholic Central was going into the season. Rival coaches certainly weren't buying it anyway when they picked the Cougars to finish first again after a one-season hiatus from the top spot. Furthermore, Ward and Collins would be blocking for three proven ball-carriers, fullback Bill Shuple and halfbacks Bob Misner and Tim Baragar along with quarterback Jim Ryan.

Catholic Central 26
Saginaw Arthur Hill 6
Saturday, September 20 at Houseman Field

All that "experience" paid off as CC broke a six-year streak of winless season openers by crushing Saginaw Aurthur Hill, 26-6. The Cougars improved to 1-4-1 in those games, all against representatives of the Saginaw Valley Conference.

G. R. Herald Photo
Tim Baragar (10) breaks off a 72-yard run against Arthur Hill only to be nullified by a penalty.

Catholic Central 32
South 13
Saturday, September 27 at South Field

Catholic Central opened its bid for a 10th City League title in 17 seasons with 20 unanswered points before going on to beat South, 32-13. The Cougar point avalanche didn't start until the second quarter when a 53-yard, 10-play drive reached its climax on Misner's 2-yard touchdown run. Later in the period, Baragar completed a 50-yard possession by bouncing off the line at the 9 and into the end zone.

Catholic notched its third TD of the second quarter when Tom Nystrom threw a 33-yard option pass to Ryan, who was standing all by himself at the 10 and trotted into the end zone as two Trojan defenders closing in on him crashed into each other. The teams combined for four touchdowns in the fourth quarter with scoring runs of 3 and 33 yards by Shuple and Nystrom, respectively, canceling out South's pair.

Flint Northern 19
Catholic Central 7
Saturday, October 4 at Houseman Field

Flint Northern's place on Catholic Central's schedule changed but the result stayed pretty much the same for the Cougars, who lost 19-7. Since CC defeated the Vikings in 1932, it lost four and tied one in the frustrating series, mostly in season-openers.

Catholic actually led 7-0 on Shuple's 34-yard touchdown run with 8:21 remaining in the first quarter. However, after picking up 91 yards in the opening stanza alone, the Cougars were able to gain just 104 in the remaining three periods. After Northern cut its deficit to 7-6 a few minutes later, CC drove all the way to the Viking 10-yard line. However, the Northern defense put up a stand, and after taking over on downs, the Vikings traveled 90 yards in 10 plays to effect a 12-point swing from which the Cougars could not recover.

Catholic Central 31
Central 7
Saturday, October 11 at Houseman Field

Four fumbles caused Catholic Central to go into the locker room with a 7-7 halftime tie against Central. Four touchdowns in the second half lifted the Cougars to a 31-7 victory that kept their title dreams in clear focus. Ryan's 27-yard touchdown pass to Jim Wysocki put CC ahead 7-0 in the first quarter and it seemed as if the win would come easy. But then, turnover fever set in.

G. R. Herald Photo
CC sophomore Bob Quist picks up yardage against Creston.

Central tied the score with 41 seconds remaining in the first half on a 1-yard smash by city scoring leader Doug Eggleston. After getting a talking-to from Sowle during intermission, the Cougars came alive to run for 240 of their 370 rushing yards in the second half.

Misner, who rushed for 114 yards on 15 carries, broke the tie with a 2-yard plunge early in the third quarter. Sophomore fullback Bob Quist and junior halfback

Pat Dennis, subbing for the injured Shuple and Baragar, scored CC's next two TDs. Quist squirmed through the middle of the line for a 3-yarder that gave Catholic a 19-7 lead and Dennis opened the fourth quarter with a 75-yard shot up the sideline. Misner ran for 52 yards on CC's final scoring drive and picked up his second TD of the game from the 1-yard mark. Dennis led the Cougars with 149 yards on nine carries and Quist had 65 on nine. Ward, CC's star guard, also missed the game because of an arm injury.

G. R. Herald Photo

CC Running Backs

(l-r) Tim Baragar, Bill Shuple, Tom Ryan and Bob Misner

Catholic Central 28
Creston 6
Friday, October 17 at Houseman Field

One mistake cost Catholic Central an 87-yard interception return for a Creston touchdown, but an otherwise flawless performance netted an easy 28-6 victory to set a championship showdown against Ottawa Hills.

Quist continued his stellar fill-in duty by racing 29 yards for a TD on the 10th play of the game. Dennis, another super-sub, doubled the first-quarter advantage to 14-0 with a 30-yard rush. Creston defensive back Jim Grutter interrupted the point flow when he picked off a short pass that Ryan threw into coverage, but Misner countered with a plunge from inside the 1 to give CC a 21-6 halftime lead.

Dennis added a 2-yard TD in the third quarter to close out the Polar Bears, who suffered their 19th straight loss to CC. Creston had the ball for just 10 plays in the first half, including two in the second quarter, and both of its first downs came after halftime. All 392 of Catholic's yards came via the rush while the Polar Bears totaled 60 through the air and on the ground.

Catholic Central 27
Ottawa Hills 6
Saturday, October 25 at Houseman Field

Unbeaten, untied and unscored-upon in three City League games, Ottawa Hills had to get past Catholic Central to win its first conference championship since 1938. It was not to be for the Indians, who had no answer for the Cougars' punishing ground attack. The 27-6 victory gave CC a share of its 10th title in 17 seasons.

Although attendance was generally, and problematically from a budgetary standpoint, down for city schools, more than 10,000 watched the Cougars out-rush Ottawa 257-115. Jim Wysocki, an end on CC's defense, set up the first score of the game in the second quarter when he intercepted a Raleigh Smith pass and ran it back 6 yards to the Ottawa 14-yard line. On fourth-and-goal at the 2, Baragar caved in the Indian defense for a 6-0 lead. The CC defense forced an Indian punt on the ensuing possession, and after an 18-yard pass from Ryan to Wysocki moved the ball to the Ottawa 45, Quist carried the ball on four identical running plays over right tackle to the 7. On the

G. R. Herald Photo

Catholic Central's 1958 Defense
Down (l-r) - Ron Zurek, Karl Stanitzek, George Jackoboice, Chuck Collins, Mike Ward
Standing - Jim Wysocki, Bob Quist, Ed Wysocki, Volkers Thiry, Pat Dennis, Bill Shuple

final play of the drive, Ryan faked the same play to Quist and handed off to Baragar, who scored standing up.

The Indians temporarily made it a game with a 24-yard touchdown pass from Smith to Larry Stanley on the final play of the first half to cut CC's lead to 13-7, but a defensive struggle ensued the rest of the way. Catholic Central recovered an Indian fumble at their 45-yard line and Quist eventually scored on the third play of the fourth quarter on a pitchout from the 4 for a 20-7 lead. Misner's 14-yard TD a few minutes later wrapped up the Cougars' championship effort.

The following week, Ottawa team physician, Dr. Howard P. Porter Jr., retracted his charges made in a letter to the Grand Rapids Board of Education that injuries sustained by the Indians during the game were caused intentionally by Cougar fists. Porter's charges resulted in a full review, involving board, school and game officials, held in the Catholic Central gymnasium.

After interviewing Ottawa players and watching a tape of the game Monday night, Porter, in an open letter published by *The Grand Rapids Herald*, wrote: "… I find no evidence to support the allegations or implication of foul play previously presented in my letter to the Grand Rapids Board of Education. … This was simply a hard-fought game between two top city teams in which there were more than the average number of serious injuries. I wish in this way to make a public apology to the Catholic Central coach and squad members."

During the meeting, Porter said his accusations were borne of the exaggerated comments made by players "during the heat of battle by excited youngsters." Ottawa coach Rip Collins denied in the aftermath that any of his players were injured as a result of foul conduct, and said he had no knowledge of Porter's letter to the Board. "It was a good, hard, clean football game," Collins said. "I thought so at the time of the game (and) I think so now after reviewing the films with Ted and after looking at our own films. We saw nothing in them that we could call dirty football or unsportsmanlike conduct."

Said Sowle, "We have never played dirty football and never will. In 25 years of coaching, I have never had as fine a group of boys as this team."

Catholic Central 38
Detroit Catholic Central 6
Friday, October 31 at Detroit McCabe Field

After Central upset Ottawa, 19-0, to give Catholic Central the outright City League crown, the Cougars ended their series against Detroit Catholic Central with an emphatic 38-6 drubbing. Shuple led the way for CC with touchdown runs of 1, 62 and 48 yards and finished with 148 yards on just 11 rushes for a 14.4-yards-per-attempt average.

The Cougars took a 7-0 lead in the first quarter on a 6-yard pass from Ryan to Tom Zegunis, and Quist set up Shuple's first TD with a 23-yard run. After Shuple's time in the end zone finally came to an end, Misner scored from the 6 in the final quarter and Nystrom finished things up on offense with a 1-yard plunge that followed a 55-yard pass from Ryan to Bob Everin.

Catholic Central 29
Union 6
Friday, November 7 at Houseman Field

With the City League title race already completed, traditional rivals Catholic Central and Union lined up with nothing but pride on the line. Powered by two Shuple touchdowns, the Cougars dispatched the 1957 city champs with a clean 29-6 victory.

In between Shuple's 4- and 32-yard touchdowns in the first and second quarters, Misner inserted a 3-yard score for a 20-0 CC lead at halftime. Ryan's touchdown made the score 27-0 in the third quarter and the Cougar defense added a safety in the fourth period when they swarmed Red Hawk running back Dick Jarmosco in his own end zone.

CC/WC Archives

1958 City League Champions

Row One (l-r) - Tom Barager, Bill Shuple, Mike Ward, Dan Blain, George Jackobioce, Bob Dill, Chuck Collins, Jim Wysocki, Wolker Thiry, Bob Misner, Ed Wysocki

Row Two - Mitch Zainea, Bernie Tolfel, Leo Golembiewski, Karl Stanizek, Tom Zegunis, Ed Zyniewicz, Paul Sydloski, Bob Erhardt, Bob Everin, Ron Zurek, Dick Kalinowski, Jim Ryan

Row Three - Ted Sowle, Laverne Wolf, Pat Dennis, Bob Quist, Chuck Karas, Ed Powell, Dave Seamon, Mike Stalec, Bill Boylen, Mike Akey, Terry Huyge, Jerry Krenslewski, Joe Godleski

Row Four - Gene Jaglowski, Don Lennon, Jim Galvin, Mike Koskuc, Jerry Bieberle, Dave Delaney, Jim Gardiner, Tom Nystrom, Jim Schultz, Jules Sommers

CC/WC Archives

Coaches Ted Sowle (left) and Joe Godleski reflect on another City Championship.

Catholic Central 27
Muskegon Catholic Central 6
Saturday, November 15 at
Muskegon CC Stadium

Once an anticlimactic finish between an established state power and a fledgling program, Catholic Central's season finale against Muskegon Catholic Central took on added significance in 1958. Both teams were highly ranked in Class A and the contest was billed as "the game of the year" in Western Michigan. The 8-0 Crusaders had never defeated the Cougars in five previous meetings since their program began, but Grand Rapids CC won the previous two games in come-from-behind fashion by a total of five points.

The Cougars settled two scores with its 27-6 domination of the Crusaders: they also beat the team that beat the Flint Northern team (27-21) that beat them (19-7 on Oct. 4). A crowd of more than 8,500 watched underclassmen score all four Grand Rapids CC touchdowns.

Shuple set up the first of his three touchdowns with a 42-yard rush on the game's first play, and his 4-yard run on fourth-and-goal put the Cougars ahead 7-0. Grand Rapids CC blew a chance to two take a 14-0 lead when it failed to convert Ward's blocked punt. Dick Pasco accounted for Muskegon's touchdown on a 17-yard run off an option pitch from his younger brother Tom, who was being tackled.

The Cougars regained the lead in the waning moments of the first half when they traveled 65 yards in three plays, with Misner picking up 31 and Quist covering the final 30 for the score and a 13-6 hafltime lead. The game turned in Grand Rapids CC's favor in the third quarter when Quist's fumble recovery at his own 38-yard line snuffed out what had been a promising Crusader drive. The Cougars scored on their first two series of the fourth quarter when Shuple cashed in from the 4-yard line and again from the 3 after being set up by Misner's 51-yard gain.

Shuple, Ward, Collins, center George Jackoboice and end Don Blain represented the Cougars on the first-team All-City squad and Misner and Jim Wysocki were second-team selections.

1958 Schedule/Results

Head Coach – Ted Sowle

Date	Opponent	Result		Location
Sep. 20	Saginaw Arthur Hill	Won	26-6	Houseman Field
Sep. 27	South	Won	32-13	South Field
Oct. 4	Flint Northern	Lost	7-19	Houseman Field
Oct. 11	Central	Won	31-7	Houseman Field
Oct. 17	Creston	Won	28-6	Houseman Field
Oct. 25	Ottawa Hills	Won	27-6	South Field
Oct. 31	Detroit Catholic Central	Won	38-6	McCabe Field
Nov. 7	Union	Won	29-6	Houseman Field
Nov. 15	Muskegon Catholic Central	Won	27-6	Muskegon CC Stadium

	Record	Pts. Scored	Pts. Allowed
Overall	8-1	245	75
City League	5-0	147	38

-1959-

The methodology to the sometimes maddening approach Ted Sowle used while coaching Catholic Central should have been evident after all those years. Renowned for poor-mouthing his team in preseason preview stories that ran in the newspapers during early fall drills, especially after his fellow City League coaches picked the Cougars to win the championship, Sowle's pattern was well-worn. Then, more often than not, Catholic would go on to win a title and finish the season with a high ranking. However, Sowle outdid himself heading into the 1959 season.

"It's not only the worst squad I've had here, but what really worries me is the lack of football spirit and enthusiasm for the sport," Sowle said. "In fact, there's only one boy I could praise right now, and he's one of our big tackles, Ron Zurek. The others? They haven't shown much of anything. The troubles are compounded by a general lack of experienced manpower. I knew we would make mistakes and that we would have to go along with youngsters pretty green in some spots, but I didn't think we would run into this general lack of effort."

It was a familiar song-and-dance routine, and yet different. It could only mean one thing. Sowle knew this CC team was good, with a chance to be really good, if not special.

G. R. Herald Photo
Running Back Pat Dennis

Catholic Central 31
Saginaw Arthur Hill 2
Saturday, September 19 at Saginaw Memorial Field

The Cougars immediately validated such suspicions with a 31-2 season-opening smack-down of perennial powerhouse Saginaw Arthur Hill, in

G. R. Herald Photo
Cougar Quarterback Paul Sydloski

Saginaw! The lightest and fastest Catholic Central team in at least 10 years completely bewildering the big, lumbering Lumberjacks to such a degree that many of Sowle's starters took the fourth quarter off. The Cougars were poised to pounce from the opening whistle and after tackle Dick Rossi plucked an Arthur Hill fumble out of midair on the second play of the game, halfback Tom Nystrom went the distance from 28 yards out on the third.

Five minutes later, fullback Bob Quist, who drew Sowle's ire in preseason camp, intercepted a pass at his own 44, and a few plays later bowled over two defenders on his way to an 8-yard TD for a 12-0 lead. On the final play of the first quarter, quarterback Paul Sydloski, the ace of the CC baseball team's pitching staff, threw a perfect strike to end Bob Everin for a 60-yard pickup to the Lumberjack 4-yard line. Two plays later, Quist's 2-yard touchdown increased CC's lead to 19-0.

Nystrom's 2-yard TD capped an 82-yard drive before halftime, and the Cougars had 159 rushing yards at intermission. Catholic's final touchdown came on an 8-yard rush by halfback Pat Dennis in the third quarter. Arthur Hill finally got on the board midway through the third quarter when it tackled backup CC quarterback Jim Gardiner in the end zone for a safety.

Catholic Central 25
Union 20
Friday, September 25 at Houseman Field

Sowle remained coy after Catholic's stunning win at Saginaw Arthur Hill, especially with the league opener against archrival Union on the horizon. "How good are we?" Sowle said to a reporter. "Well, frankly I don't know. I wonder if we're as good as the score indicates or if Saginaw Arthur Hill just isn't as strong as we think it is."

The Cougars looked every bit as dominant against the Red Hawks while building a 19-0 first-half lead, but then needed a good bit of luck to escape Houseman Field with a 25-20 victory. If not for a miscommunication that put Union in the wrong single-wing formation at the CC 3-yard line with 52 seconds remaining, Catholic might have dropped out of the ranks of the unbeaten after only two games. But when the perfect pass-back from center sailed between the Red Hawks' fullback and halfback untouched, the Cougars knew they just dodged a major bullet.

The ball bounced CC's way early in the second quarter when Dennis fell on a mishandled punt at the Union 10-yard line. Three plays later, Quist, the rugged halfback, barged into the end zone for a 7-0 lead. Slightly more than five minutes later, Quist twisted and turned for a 26-yard TD that completed a 53-yard drive. The rout appeared to be on when Catholic's Dave Cyronoski recovered a Red Hawk fumble at their 30 and Nystrom swept into the end zone from 9 yards.

Union, however, didn't get the message that it was time to fold its tent and scored on its next three possessions, including a 13-yard TD reception by Tony Symko, who made a leaping circus catch over Everin in the end zone just before halftime. With the momentum shifted to the Westsiders, Union opened the second half with a 53-yard scoring drive that cut CC's lead to six points on Ken Betz's 4-yard run. Then, after Catholic dropped a punt and Symko covered the ball at the Cougar 15, Tom Ver Hoeks reached down to make a shoestring catch of Dennis Goble's low pass for a 6-yard touchdown and a 20-19 lead.

Three minutes later, Catholic Central shifted into power mode with Quist and Nystrom pounding the Red Hawks during a 68-yard drive that ended on Bob Taylor's 3-yard smash. Catholic actually had the game in hand until a

15-yard penalty and a fumble, recovered at its 7-yard line by Union's Charles Warning, set up the fateful call of play No. 31, which the Red Hawk halfback mistook for No. 21.

G. R. Herald Photo

Catholic Central's 1959 Backfield

(l-r) - Paul Sydloski, Bob Taylor, Bob Quist, Tom Nystrom

Catholic Central 21
South 0
Friday, October 2 at South Field

Sowle came out of the near-miss against Union an unhappy man and so determined to avoid a repeat, completely shook up the entire left side of his defensive front. "We were lucky," Sowle said. "It's bound to run out on us unless we stop this daydreaming and concentrate on football. Outside of halfback Bob Quist, who played his best game for Catholic, our running and blocking still needs more zing and punch."

Given Sowle's fire-and-brimstone rant earlier in the week, it was hard to determine what was more amazing: that the No. 3-ranked Cougars came out flat against South, or that they were able to win 21-0 while putting on a completely uninspired performance.

Catholic had a commanding lead before breaking a sweat. On the game's first play from scrimmage, Trojan halfback Jack Jones fumbled. The Cougars recovered at the South 8-yard line and after a 4-yard loss on first down, Sydloski pitched to Taylor who skated in for a 12-yard touchdown. Catholic's second touchdown also came gift-wrapped after Tom Zegunis blocked a punt, Chuck Wierzbicki covered it at the 10 and two plays later Quist scored from the 3. In the third quarter, CC wasted Taylor's 93-yard run when Quist fumbled the ball away on the next play, but Sydloski got the points in the fourth quarter with a 24-yard TD toss to Cyranoski. Unlike Union, South didn't have the offensive weaponry to stage a comeback.

Catholic Central 33
South Bend St. Joseph's 18
Saturday, October 10 at South Field

Perhaps Catholic Central was just one of those teams that played up, or down, to its opponent. The third-ranked Cougars wouldn't have had a chance to beat South Bend (Ind.) St. Joseph's if they played the way they did a week earlier against South. However, with an effort equal to the one that resulted in a 29-point win over Saginaw Arthur Hill, CC handed St. Joe's its first loss in six games.

Quist was once again tenacious as a bulldog and bit off big chunks of yardage on 67- and 53-yard scoring runs in the second half. Catholic took a 7-0 lead on a 23-yard touchdown pass from Sydloski to Everin, but South Bend quickly scored to cut CC's lead to 7-6. The Cougars marched 92 yards in five plays, including a 40-yard pass from Sydloski to Nystrom who barreled into the end zone from 3 yards out with 25 seconds remaining in the first half.

In the third quarter, a 60-yard punt return by St. Joe's cut CC's lead to 14-12, but then Quist took over. On the first play of Catholic's ensuing drive, Quist broke off his first long run to increase the advantage to eight points. Then, after CC defensive tackle Karl Stanitzek recovered a fumble at the South Bend 16, Sydloski's second TD toss of the game also ended up in Everin's hands and was good for 6 points. St. Joe's scored one more time to keep things close in the fourth quarter until Quist delivered the knockout punch.

Catholic Central 21
Central 0
Friday, October 16 at Houseman Field

The victory over South Bend St. Joseph's elevated Catholic Central to the No. 2 spot in the state Class A poll, but Central, 1-3 overall but 1-0 in the City League, was looking to make a name for itself at the Cougars' expense. Those aspirations were summarily quashed when three turnovers and two penalties that wiped out a pair of long touchdown runs couldn't prevent CC from throttling the Rams, 21-0.

The Cougars did a better job of stopping themselves than Central did. They started their first drive at their own 48-yard line, but it ended on a fumble inside the Ram 5. Then Quist had a 78-yard touchdown called back. Then Taylor suffered the same fate after reaching the end zone on a 34-yard run.

Catholic finally got it right with 3:29 remaining in the first half when Quist, who had a 31-yard run during the 82-yard drive, powered in for a 1-yard TD. Dennis took a pitchout for a 1-yard score in the third quarter and Nystrom evaded tacklers en route to a 15-yarder in the fourth. The Cougars outgained the Rams, who netted just 8 rushing yards in the second half, 330-117, in total offense.

Catholic Central 26
Creston 13
Saturday, October 24 at Houseman Field

Second-ranked Catholic Central closed the gap between it and No. 1 Bay City Central to four points going into its game against Creston. How much of a bump the Cougars would get from a city-championship-clinching 26-13 victory over the Polar Bears remained to be seen.

After a scoreless first quarter, CC built up a 13-0 halftime lead on a 21-yard play that started with a pass from Sydloski to Cyranoski, who lateraled to Nystrom at the 5, and Quist's 2-yard plunge with 1:30 remaining. The Polar Bears cut into the lead with a third-quarter touchdown, but Taylor's off-tackle sprint with 33 seconds remaining in the period put the Cougars ahead, 20-6. Quist added a 12-yard score in the fourth quarter and Creston got its second marker against the CC reserves.

Catholic Central 33
Ottawa Hills 13
Friday, October 30 at Houseman Field

Bay City Central increased its first-place lead over No. 2-ranked Catholic Central to six points after beating No. 6 Midland, 13-0. The Cougars made up a little ground, one point to be exact, with a 33-13 trouncing of once-beaten Ottawa Hills to win the City League title outright, but it was evident they would need help in the form of an upset of Bay City Central to win the state crown.

Ottawa's Raleigh Smith startled Catholic by returning the opening kickoff 68 yards, and if not for a touchdown-saving tackle by Dick Kolenda at the CC 17-yard line, the Cougars would have found themselves in an early hole. As it was, the Catholic Central defense took the ball on downs after three running plays netted the Indians just 2 yards and a fourth-down pass fell incomplete. The Cougars started their first drive from their 15 and ended it in the end zone on Quist's 4-yard run. Ottawa countered in the second quarter on quarterback Ted Texer's 2-yard sneak which he set up with a 33-yard pass to future Detroit Tigers outfielder Mickey Stanley.

But Nystrom returned the ensuing kickoff 79 yards for a touchdown to trigger a surge of 26 unanswered Cougar points. The CC offense had nothing to do with the next two touchdowns, either. Zegunis blocked an Indian punt and returned it 32 yards for one score and rover Larry Baragar ran an interception back 39 yards to give Catholic a 27-9 halftime bulge. Taylor put the finishing touches on Catholic's 11th City League title in 19 seasons with a 70-yard touchdown romp in the third quarter.

Despite the impressive win, the Cougars trailed Bay City Central by seven points in the following week's Class A poll.

Catholic Central 38
Muskegon Heights 6
Friday, November 6 at Muskegon Phillips Field

Catholic Central got the help it needed when Pontiac Central upset No. 1 Bay City Central, and then took care of business with a 38-6 thumping of Muskegon Heights in freezing weather. The victory propelled the Cougars to the top spot in the Associated Press Class A poll and set up a faceoff for the state title with No. 2-ranked Muskegon Catholic Central in the season finale.

With Quist kept under wraps to shield him from the prying eyes of Muskegon CC scouts, Taylor scored three touchdowns against the Tigers while Sydloski completed all four of his passes including two that resulted in 24- and 27-yard touchdown receptions by Everin. Gardiner, the reserve quarterback, also threw a 45-yard touchdown pass to backup end Ed Powell.

Catholic Central 6
Muskegon Catholic Central 0
Saturday, November 14 at Houseman Field

The "worst team" Ted Sowle had ever seen during preseason drills in early September turned out to be the best Michigan had to offer in 1959.

Top-ranked Catholic Central delivered Sowle's fourth Class A state championship with a dramatic 6-0 victory over No. 2 Muskegon Catholic Central in front of close to 10,000 spectators at Houseman Field. The rush-oriented Cougars seemed perfectly suited for the sloppy field conditions created by a snowfall earlier in the week, but they crossed up the Crusaders with well-timed passes.

Sowle tipped his hand on the game's first series after the Cougars advanced the ball from their own 45 to the Muskegon CC 12-yard line. Instead of running for it on fourth-and-2 as everyone in the stadium expected, Sydloski tossed a flat pass to Nystrom who ran to the 4 for a first-and-goal. After three running plays lost 2 yards, Sydloski's fourth-down pass to Nystrom fell incomplete and the Crusaders took over on downs.

G. R. Herald Photo

Cougar's Dave Cyranoski goes up for a pass in the endzone but fails to come down in bounds during the Catholic Central Muskegon Catholic game.

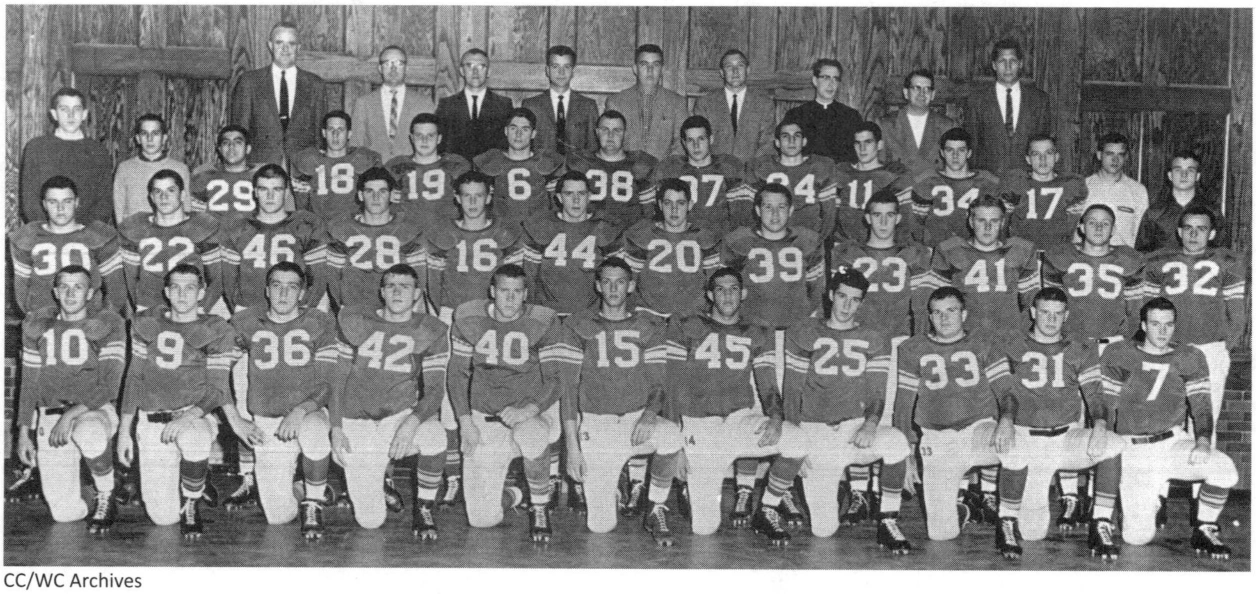

CC/WC Archives

1959 City League and State Champions

Row One (l-r) - T. Nystrom, P. Dennis, R. Kolenda, R. Zurek, K. Stanitzek, P. Sydloski, T. Zegunis, R. Everin, B. Boylen, J. Bieberle, J. Gavlin

Row Two - R. Rossi, R. Quist, L. Barager, D. Cyranoski, M. Stalec, D. Seamon, E. Powell, G. Wierzbicki, M. Akey, J. Kahnoski, R. Taylor, C, Karas

Row Three - M. Burns, P. Cavera, S. Zainea, J. Gardiner, T. Berry, T. Burns, D. Troeger, D. Trap, D. Dill, D. Dill, T. McCormick, G. Smith, D. Kozminski, L. Prangley

Row Four - T. Sowle, J. Sommer, J. Krenselewski, D. Lennon, J. Schultz, L. Wolf, Fr. J. Murphy, A. Marsiglia, J. Godleski

Grand Rapids CC wasn't discouraged by its failure to score and stuck to the game plan on a possession that started at its own 15-yard line. A running play moved the ball just 2 yards and Sydloski dropped back on second-and-8. As he scanned the field, he saw Cryanoski break into the clear at the 40, and the left-hander put the ball on the money. Cyranoski ran for 9 more yards after the catch to complete the 32-yard pass play.

The Cougars picked up 16 more yards on three running plays, and then, their most effective weapon all year, 5-foot-10, 180-pound fullback Bob Quist, took the handoff on CC's most reliable play, cut inside of his right tackle, spun out of the grasp of two Crusader defenders at the 20 and sprinted untouched the rest of the way for a championship-clinching 35-yard touchdown.

"Not only did he break away for the only score, but he did a vital job on defense for us," Sowle said of Quist, a player he challenged to play up to his potential in preseason camp. "Muskegon's long-gainer, the play that killed several teams this year, is a pitchout from the quarterback to left halfback Rolando Jones. All week we gave Quist special work on evading blockers and stopping this thrust. They tried it five times and never reached the line of scrimmage."

As for his preseason assessment, well, Sowle didn't take anything back.

The Cougars "wouldn't have gone far if these kids hadn't progressed so rapidly," he said. "We knew we had a good, solid team only four weeks ago when we really jelled in beating South Bend St. Joseph. Why, Union should have beaten us except for the weird happenings of the last couple minutes."

The All-City team featured five Cougars: Sydloski, Zurek, Kolenda, Stanitzek and, of course, Quist, the only junior on the squad.

An Invocation given by Msgr. William J. Murphy, Principal of Catholic Central High School, Grand Rapids, Michigan, on the occasion of the Annual Football Banquet honoring the school's State Championship Football Team of 1959.

Almighty God, our good and gracious Father, we find ourselves gathered here tonight on a festive and joyous occasion. We gather in a traditional American fashion to do a traditional American thing - to give some small honor to a group of American boys and to those men who have directed their activities in football. This is not, dear Lord, an occasion on which we should be puffed up with hollow pride in our own marvelous achievements, for all good things must begin in Thee and in Thee be happily ended. Through Your goodness You have blessed the brains and the brawn of these young men, you have for the most part kept them from serious injury, and you have allowed them the fulfillment of a boyhood football dream. We pray that the sacrifice and effort required of them in the achievement of their goal will stand them in good stead in the years stretching out before them. Perhaps heaven is not too concerned with football, but You and all in heaven are concerned with men -- men of principle and honesty and integrity, men who can and will make sacrifices to accomplish good things, and we pray that because of football these young men will do far greater and nobler things in the years that lie ahead. You have told us that life is a constant warfare and through Your great Apostle Peter that the "devil is a roaring lion seeking whom he may devour". Give these young men the grace to meet this common adversary of us all with the right block or the right tackle at the right moment. May we also remind You, Lord, that football terminology is almost as old as the Church, for we read in the life of one of Your great athlete martyrs, St. Lawrence, that he died on the gridiron. Therefore, we ask Your gracious indulgence with all the football words that shall be spoken here this evening. And now as we go about the first part of these festivities we call to mind the words of the great St. Paul "whether you eat or drink or whatever else you do, do it all for the honor and glory of God". We are sure You know the appetites of athletes, and therefore we are about to give you much honor and much glory. And so we humbly ask that You will bless us and these Thy gifts which we are about to receive from Thy bounty through the Knights of Columbus and Christ, Our Lord, Amen.

CC/WC Archives

1959 Schedule/Results
Head Coach – Ted Sowle

Date	Opponent	Result		Location
Sep. 19	Saginaw Arthur Hill	Won	31-2	Saginaw
Sep. 25	Union	Won	25-20	Houseman Field
Oct. 2	South	Won	21-0	South Field
Oct. 10	South Bend St. Joseph's	Won	35-18	South Field
Oct. 16	Central	Won	21-0	Houseman Field
Oct. 24	Creston	Won	26-13	Houseman Field
Oct. 30	Ottawa Hills	Won	33-13	Houseman Field
Nov. 6	Muskegon Heights	Won	38-6	Phillips Field
Nov. 14	Muskegon Catholic Central	Won	6-0	Houseman Field

	Record	Pts. Scored	Pts. Allowed
Overall	9-0	234	72
City League	5-0	126	46

-1960-

How's this for an encore? Catholic Central coach Ted Sowle didn't bemoan the fact that his team was uninspired and inexperienced heading into the new decade. He may have thought it, but he didn't bemoan it. With the state's best backfield tandem, fullback Bob Quist and halfback Bob Taylor, returning from CC's 9-0 Class A state championship team, such talk would be pointless. In addition to retaining much of their speed, the Cougars were bigger by close to 10 pounds per man. No one was going to feel sorry for them. Even Sowle had to know his poor-mouthing ran its course once the "worst squad I've had here" won it all. So, he took a different tack. Compared to the Catholic Central's team at this point a year ago, the 1960 edition is "considerably better," Sowle allowed, but knew all too well that titles aren't won on Sept. 13.

G.R.Press Photo

An Arthur Hill Defender deflects a pass intended for Mike Neuman.

Catholic Central 41
Saginaw Arthur Hill 12
Friday, September 16 at Houseman Field

The Cougars picked up right where they left off with a 41-12 mashing of Saginaw Arthur Hill in the season opener. The performance was so complete, so dominant, many wanted to give CC the state title right then and there and cancel the rest of the season. Four of Catholic's six touchdowns went for 30 yards or more. Taylor stole the show from his all-state running mate with 175 yards and touchdown runs of 45 and 61 yards on 11 carries, but Quist averaged 9.4 yards on seven attempts and scored from 9 and 21 yards out. Two newcomers to the running back rotation, Terry Burns and John Lovell, added 31- and 32-yard TDs, respectively. New CC starting quarterback Jim Gardiner had an easy night. All he had to do is hand the ball off as CC amassed 391 rushing yards and no one noticed, or cared, that all five Cougar passes fell incomplete.

CC/WC Archives
All-State Center Dave Seamon

Catholic Central 40
Union 6
Saturday, September 24 at Houseman Field

The Cougars took a big step toward becoming the balanced team they needed to be to defend their state and city championships with a 40-6 romp over undermanned Union. Although Quist & Co. continued to run wild, Gardiner provided the fireworks with his arm.

Quist accounted for 108 of CC's 352 rushing yards and three touchdowns and Taylor covered 62 yards of real estate. However, Gardiner completed 3 of 4 passes for 128 yards and two touchdowns. The game was flip-side of Catholic's opener against Saginaw Arthur Hill when the running backs turned the game into a track meet. After Quist spotted the Cougars to a 7-0 lead with a rather ordinary 5-yard run, Gardiner made it 13-0 in the second quarter with a sensational 83-yard scoring pass to end Dave Cryanoski, another standout on the '59 team. The ball traveled 23 yards through the air and Cryanoski did the rest with his long legs while hugging the left sideline.

Gardiner set up Quist's final TD, just another ho-hum 10-yarder, with a 20-yard pass to end Mike Akey and hit Burns for a 22-yard score in the final quarter. If there was a weakness, it was in the pass-defense department which was burned with a 30-yard touchdown pass from Jack Van Duinen to Tom Symko late in the third quarter.

South 20
Catholic Central 14
Saturday, October 1 at Houseman Field

Then, disaster struck.

Catholic Central's 16-game win streak came to an end on a numbing 20-14 loss to a South High team that managed just two first downs. The good fortune that favored the Cougars a year earlier in a close call against Union turned against them this time. Just as a miscommunicated formation cost the Red Hawks a shot at the go-ahead touchdown that would have prevented CC from going on to win the state title, botched execution in the backfield did major damage to the mistake-plagued Cougars' efforts to defend it.

CC/WC Archives
All-American Back Bob Quist

Leading 14-13 late in the fourth quarter but backed up to its own goal line by a Larry Portice punt, Catholic Central fumbled the ball in the end zone and a host of Trojans fell on the ball for the game-winning touchdown. The Cougars had a chance to pull out a win in the final three minutes and drove the ball all the way to the South 20-yard line. But the game was lost for good when two passes fell incomplete and the Trojans took over on downs.

The game was a struggle for CC from the start. Although Quist and Taylor drove the ball 50 yards on the game's first possession, the penalty-riddled possession ended with a punt, which South fielded at its 11. Another Catholic penalty moved the ball to the 15, but rushing lineman Larry Baragar deflected a pass to John Jackoboice, and the giant tackle lumbered

G.R.Press Photo
CC's Terry Burns is pulled down by a South defender.

33 yards with an interception return for a touchdown. In the second quarter, a series of runs, including Taylor's 24-yarder, set the ball at the Trojan 10 and Taylor covered the remaining distance with two tries for a 14-0 halftime lead.

But, things turned south for Catholic in the third quarter when shifty Trojan halfback Ira Ward took the handoff, went off left tackle and sprinted out of the grasp of a CC defender for an 88-yard touchdown. A loss of composure resulted in the ejection of Quist and South center Doug Deliefde for unsportsmanlike conduct after the play, and the Cougars were in trouble. Later in the third quarter, South downed a Portice punt at the Cougar 2-yard line. The Trojans recovered Taylor's first-down fumble at the 4, and two plays later Portice dove in to cut CC's lead to 14-13 and set the stage for Catholic's most disappointing ending in years. The Cougars were penalized nine times for 75 yards.

Catholic Central 39
South Bend (Ind.) St. Joseph's 7
Thursday, October 6 at South Bend

Whatever pain, frustration and disappointment Catholic Central harbored from its error-prone loss to South was left on a field in northwest Indiana after it destroyed South Bend St. Joseph's 39-7. Quist, who was disqualified from the previous game, returned with a vengeance and scored on runs of 57, 25 and 6 yards. Taylor bounced back from his devastating fumble against South with his best game of the season. He scored on TD runs of a 22 and 50 yards and a long touchdown on a hook-and-ladder pass thrown by Gardiner.

The Cougars vented their angst with power football and out-rushed St. Joe's 358-102. Gardiner added 92 yards on just two pass completions. With two minutes remaining in the first half, Gardiner dropped back from his own 45-yard line and threw a pass to Cyranoski, who ran a button-hook pattern to the South Bend 35. After making the catch, Cyranoski flipped the ball to Taylor who completed the 55-yard play for a 26-0 halftime lead. Eight busloads of Cougar fans attended the game.

Catholic Central 46
Central 13
Saturday, October 15 at Houseman Field

Quist continued to take quantum leaps for Catholic Central in a 46-13 Homecoming rout of Central. The bruising fullback averaged nearly 14 yards per carry and scored four touchdowns on runs of 51, 2, 20 and 11 yards.

"He's not only the best running back I've coached here, but he's also one of the best blockers," Sowle said of Quist, who riddled the Rams for 180 yards on 13 carries. "It's a team operation but individuals like Quist are sure handy to have around."

Quist was totally committed to the team concept.

"I like blocking maybe even more than carrying the ball," Quist told *The Grand Rapids Press*. "In our offense, it's my job usually to knock down the first man I meet, the end rushing in or the linebacker in close. When you get in a good block and the play goes for a lot of yardage, there's something about it that gives you a thrill."

The Cougars took a 7-0 lead on the first play of the game when Taylor threw a halfback option pass to Cyranoski for a 62-yard touchdown. Baragar and fellow defensive lineman Dave Seamon combined to block two Central punts to set up a pair touchdowns.

G.R.Press Photo
First-Team All-Staters Bob Quist (left) and Dave Seamon

Catholic Central 34
Creston 0
Friday, October 21 at Houseman Field

After Quist scored 24 points in the first 24 minutes, Catholic Central stayed in contention to defend its city championship with a 34-0 wipeout of Creston. The victory set up a title game against Ottawa Hills, which remained undefeated in City League play. Even though the Polar Bears stacked 10 defenders at the line of scrimmage just to stop Quist, he rushed for 193 yards on 23 carries and added a 25th point by rushing for an extra point before retiring for the night midway through the third quarter.

Quist's first TD came on a 2-yard run and he made it 14-0 with a 4-yard scamper. His third score was a work of art as he slanted off left tackle, spun out of the grasp of one Polar Bear and dragged another across the goal line for an 18-yard tally. Finally, as CC was faced with a fourth down at the Creston 45-yard line with under a minute remaining in the first half, Quist took the handoff from Gardiner, cut back across the grain and went the distance to put the Cougars ahead, 27-0. Quist then carried five times for 37 yards on a 56-yard drive that ended on Burns' 3-yard bolt into the end zone. The Cougars held a 321-85 advantage in total offense.

Catholic Central 46
Ottawa Hills 7
Saturday, October 29 at South Field

It was Catholic Central's power vs. Ottawa Hills' speed in the City League championship showdown at South Field.

"Let's be realistic about the matter," Indians coach Rip Collins said the Wednesday before the game. "Our defense isn't going to contain Catholic's running power. We must match Catholic score-for-score and that's got to be accomplished by our overall speed and wide-open passing." Collins went on to guess that Ottawa would need to score three or four touchdowns just to have a chance at upsetting the slightly favored Cougars.

Collins' estimate was woefully short as was the Indians' point production. The Cougars' rock crushed Ottawa's scissors to claimed a share of their 12th City League championship in 20 seasons with a 46-7 demolition. Taylor shook off a leg injury to complement Quist in the running department. The duo combined for five touchdowns and led CC to a remarkable 401-yard rushing performance against an Indian defense stacked to stop the run. Quist's three scores gave him an even 20 touchdowns on the season and quarterback Dave Kosminski threw a 25-yard touchdown pass to Tom Kathan and a 35-yarder to halfback John Lovell. The victory evoked as many emotions among the Cougar faithful, who stormed the field and tore down the goalposts barely after Lovell crossed the goal line, as winning the state title did a year earlier.

The Cougars finished in a first-place tie with South.

Catholic Central 27
Muskegon Heights 0
Friday, November 4 at South Field

The Catholic Central defense helped the Cougar offense overcome four fumbles by holding Muskegon Heights to just 39 yards of total offense in a mud-spattered 27-0 victory. After a scoreless first period, Sowle let some of his future stars go to work, and halfback Dave Roach put CC ahead 6-0.

However, the old mainstays weren't to be denied, and later in the second quarter, Quist played off the block of sophomore end Mike Neuman for a 74-yard touchdown. The loose field conditions didn't hinder Quist, who ended up with 192 rushing yards. Taylor also got into the act with 89 yards and rushing TDs of 10 and 12 yards.

Catholic Central 14
Muskegon Catholic Central 0
Saturday, November 12 at Muskegon CC Stadium

A rematch of the 1959 state championship game had a familiar ending. Catholic Central upped its series record against Muskegon Catholic Central to 7-0 with a 14-0 season-ending victory. Roach was the hero of the game for the Cougars.

His interception of a Dick Brothers pass led to Taylor's 21-yard touchdown for a 7-0 lead with 3:02 remaining in the first quarter. Both teams were hampered by penalties in the scoreless second and third periods, but Roach

sealed the victory for Grand Rapids CC when he picked off another Brothers pass and raced 45 yards for a touchdown with 1:40 remaining in the game. Quist, used primarily by Sowle as a decoy, had a relatively quiet game, and Taylor had two other touchdowns nullified by illegal motion penalties.

Quist was the only City League player to repeat All-City honors and he was joined on the first team by six other Cougars including: Taylor, Cyranoski, Baragar, center Dave Seamon, guard Sam Zainea and tackle Mike Cwik.

1960 Schedule/Results
Head Coach – Ted Sowle

Date	Opponent	Result		Location
Sep. 16	Saginaw Arthur Hill	Won	41-12	Houseman Field
Sep. 24	Union	Won	40-6	Houseman Field
Oct. 1	South	Lost	14-20	Houseman Field
Oct. 6	South Bend St. Joseph's	Won	39-7	South Bend
Oct. 15	Central	Won	46-13	Houseman Field
Oct. 21	Creston	Won	34-0	Houseman Field
Oct. 29	Ottawa Hills	Won	46-7	South Field
Nov. 4	Muskegon Heights	Won	27-0	South Field
Nov. 12	Muskegon Catholic Central	Won	14-0	Muskegon CC Stadium

	Record	Pts. Scored	Pts. Allowed
Overall	8-1	301	65
City League	5-0	180	46

-1961-

Muskegon Catholic Central 12
Catholic Central 0
Saturday, September 16 at Muskegon CC Stadium

The day Muskegon Catholic Central coach Ed Farhat dreamed of finally arrived. The Crusaders, who had never won a game in its series with Grand Rapids Catholic Central, achieved a measure of revenge for eight straight losses, including one in the 1959 state championship game, with 12-0 season-opening victory over the Cougars.

G.R.Press Photo

The Right Side of the Cougar Line
(l-r) - Mike Neuman, Mike Cwik, Saul Balys

Picked to battle it out with Central for the City League title, a red flag shot up for coach Ted Sowle when Grand Rapids CC couldn't run the ball against the nine-man Muskegon defensive line designed to neutralize the Cougars' vaunted rushing attack. Senior fullback

Bill Wolski scored both of the Crusaders' touchdowns on runs of 1 and 76 yards. The Cougars' only serious scoring opportunity came at the end of the fourth quarter when they made it to the 4-yard line, but on fourth-and-goal, Dennis Patterson's pass to end Mike Neuman went incomplete. Grand Rapids CC rushed for just 145 yards, its lowest total in years.

"We were not ready to go against a good team," Sowle said. "Muskegon Catholic was primed and eager for this one. We have plenty of work ahead and I promise a number of new boys will be given the opportunity to show their talent."

G.R.Press Photo

CC's Dave Roach tries to elude a Flint Northern defender.

Catholic Central 7
Flint Northern 6
Friday, September 22 at Houseman Field

The revenge theme continued into Catholic's second game, but this time it was the Cougars who were enjoying it after a 7-6 victory over long-time nemesis Flint Northern. It was Sowle's first win over the Vikings in six tries. A revamped lineup afforded CC with a slight improvement over the opening-game debacle. The Cougars upped their rushing total to 185 yards. Senior halfback John Lovell led the attack with 96 yards and the game-winning touchdown on 23 carries and fullback Dave Roach had 59 on 17.

After Northern got new life when CC was called for offside on a punt, it took a 6-0 lead in the second quarter. The Cougars roared right back from their own 35-yard line with a 16-play drive to score the desive TD. The key play came on fourth-and-5 at the Viking 29 when quarterback Dave Kosminski's only pass of the game was caught by Roach for a 6-yard pickup. Lovell picked up 22 yards on back-to-back carries, and then plunged in from the 1-yard line with 1:30 remaining in the first half. Roach's block on a wide sweep then sprung Lovell for the all-important extra point. Northern's bid at a comeback ended at the CC 24 as time expired. The win was costly for Catholic, however, because standout guard Chuck Merdzinski sustained a knee injury and would be out for up to a month.

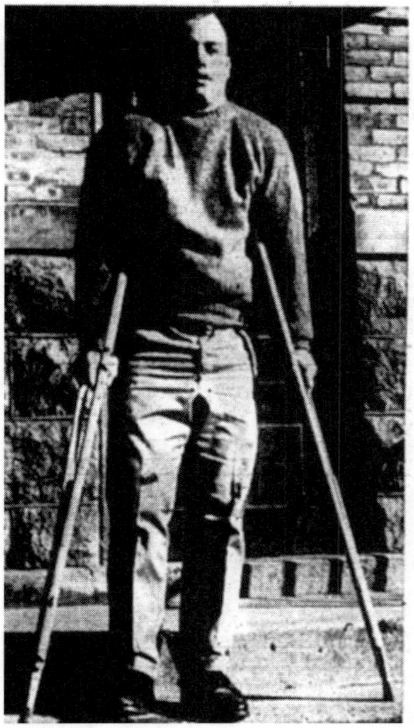

G.R.Press Photo

Injuried Linebacker Chuck Merdzinski.

Union 18
Catholic Central 13
Friday, September 29 at Houseman Field

Next, it was Union's turn for a payback. The Red Hawks, who suffered a demoralizing defeat that kept Catholic Central's 1959 state title hopes alive and were beaten down last season by a 40-6 count, gave the Cougars a dose of their own medicine with an 18-13 victory.

Operating out of the single-wing formation, which backfired disastrously on Union two years earlier, halfback Mike VanDuinen stole the win from CC with a 10-yard touchdown pass to halfback Dave Lawrence with 14 seconds remaining in the game. This time, the formation sucked the Cougar secondary up to the line to stop the run and VanDuinen lofted the ball over the Cougars' heads.

Lawrence fouled up CC's strategy on the game-opening drive as well. The Cougars stacked the line with 10 defenders and only one safety, and once Lawrence made it into the secondary, he was off to the races for a 48-yard touchdown and a 6-0 lead. A 3-yard Red Hawk punt gave Catholic the ball just 28 yards from the end zone and Lovell capped the short, two-play drive with a 5-yard sweep for a 7-6 lead.

VanDuinen quickly regained the lead, 12-6, with a 67-yard lightning bolt, but CC went ahead in the fourth quarter after a bizarre sequence of events. After the Cougars advanced the ball from its own 32 to Union's 31, Kosminski fire a pass to Patterson who caught the ball at the 5 but fumbled it out of the end zone for a touchback. Lawrence fumbled the ball back to CC after getting clobbered by a host of Cougars on the next play, and Roger Schlosser recovered at the 28. Halfback Erwin Ratajczak picked up 3 yards and a Red Hawk penalty put the ball at the 13. Lovell's 4-yard run around the right end gave Catholic a 13-12 lead with 3:33 remaining, but the Cougars couldn't protect it after giving up a 30-yard run to VanDuinen on Union's fateful winning drive.

Catholic Central 40
South 18
Friday, October 6 at South Field

Catholic Central settled a score with South High, whose victory over the Cougars in 1960 caused the two teams to share the City League championship, with a reassuring 40-18 victory. With 248 rushing yards, including 201 in the first half, it looked like the CC of old.

Lovell, who accounted for all of Catholic's points up to this point in the season, got his 26th when he singed the Trojans with a 55-yard blast on the first play of the game. But it was Roach who did most of the damage by scoring three subsequent touchdowns of 3, 31 and18 yards. After South converted Edmund Karas' fumble at the Catholic 5-yard line, Roach increased the lead to 19-6 with his first two tallies. His first TD was set up by a 14-yard pass from Kosminiski to Lovell on fourth down.

The turning point of the game came in the second quarter after South scored on halfback Willie Smith's 2-yard run to pull to within seven points. On fourth-and-1 from its own 45, South set the gamble in motion, but the Cougars stuffed Smith for no gain. Roach put the game out reach with his next score and backup sophomore halfback Dick Brougham's 4-yard dive with four seconds remaining gave CC a 33-12 halftime lead. Brougham added a 6-yarder in the second half.

Bay City Central 25
Catholic Central 0
Friday, October 13 at South Field

It was two years in coming, but Bay City Central finally got a chance to make a statement with regard to Catholic Central. The Wolves were the No. 1 team in Class A during the 1959 season until they yielded the top spot to CC following a loss to Pontiac Central. The Cougars went on to win the state championship but no one ever knew if Bay City was the better team.

The sixth-ranked Wolves left no doubt with a 25-0 blanking of Catholic Central in '61. The Cougars suffered a third defeat in the same season for the first time since 1954 partly because the ground attack netted just 87 yards, partly because they fumbled six times and lost two, and partly because they threw two interceptions.

Catholic Central 12
Central 6
Friday, October 20 at Houseman Field

Trials and tribulations aside, Catholic Central remained in the thick of the City League race with a last-minute 12-6 victory over Central, which was picked along with the Cougars to contend for the championship. Catholic improved to 2-1, a game behind undefeated Union.

After asserting itself early, CC battled the Rams to a standstill for just under four quarters. The Cougars started their first possession of the game when Roach intercepted a Fred Barr pass and returned it 22 yards to Central's 36-yard line. On CC's first play from scrimmage, Lovell broke to the outside and tiptoed his way down the sideline for a 6-0 lead. The Rams dodged a bullet after Catholic blocked a punt and took over on their 2-yard line. However, Central backed the Cougars up with 26 yards in losses and got the ball back on downs. Two plays later, Ram fullback Jim Otterbridge tied the score on a 66-yard burst up the gut with 25 seconds remaining in the first quarter.

The teams traded body blows via the running game, but no one could score a knockout until Central got the ball back at its own 26 with under two minutes remaining. Jim Nixon got outside the Cougar defense and was headed for daylight until he fumbled when he was hit by a pair of CC defenders. Ratajczak, who was having his best game as a Cougar, recovered the ball at the 41 and on the first-down play looped around end for a 6-yard gain. Sophomore quarterback Bert Fortuna then connected on a 25-yard pass to Neuman, who was hauled down at the 10. Lovell swept around right end on the next play and reached the ball out to the flag for the game-winner with 54 seconds to play.

Catholic Central 33
Creston 13
Thursday, October 26 at Houseman Field

A triumvirate of blockers made it possible for Catholic Central halfback John Lovell to gash Creston for big yardage, and consequently keep the Cougars on Union's heels in the City League race. Lovell used the interference provided by tackle Mike Cwik and end Mike Neuman on the right side, along with that of backfield-mate Dave Roach, to perfection while leading CC to a 33-13 victory. Lovell carried the ball 15 times for 135 yards and three touchdowns against the Polar Bears. Roach had a productive night as well with 47 yards on seven attempts.

The Cougars struck for all of their points in the first 26 minutes. Ratajczak scored CC's second TD with 2:01 left in the first quarter on a 5-yard rush and backup halfback Bob Fredericks pushed through for a 1-yard score with 3:53 to go in the first half. Merdzinski, the burly middle linebacker, shined on defense especially in the second quarter when he threw Creston blockers aside like ragdolls before dropping Polar Bear quarterback Tom Annis for a 15-yard loss and fullback Bill Kellogg 5 yards behind the line on successive plays to set up a fourth-and-35. Creston finished the first half with minus-33 rushing yards and ended up being outgained 301-95 by the Cougars.

Catholic Central 13
Ottawa Hills 0
Friday, November 20 at Houseman Field

Union's upset loss to Central opened the door for Catholic Central to defend its city crown with a victory over Ottawa Hills. And the Cougars still had a chance at the outright title if the Red Hawks were to lose to Creston.

Based on how the season had developed to this point, CC was happy to end up with half a championship after it beat the Indians 13-0 and Union toppled the Polar Bears, 20-18. Catholic's path to victory was paved by

Merdzinski, the hard-hitting, 190-pound middle linebacker.

Ottawa had reached midfield and was driving in the second quarter when Merdzinski drilled halfback Bob Carpenter as he tried to sweep around right end. Merdzinski's beastly hit separated Carpenter from the ball, which flew right into the hands of CC defensive back Dave Roach at the Indian 44-yard line. It took 13 plays by Roach, Lovell and Ratajczak to cover the distance and Lovell went in from the 3 for a 6-0 lead with 1:26 to play in the first half. Catholic got an insurance marker in the third quarter when Roach's block allowed Dale Miedzielec to break into the open for a 37-yard TD.

When the Cougars returned to school on Monday, they had their 12th city championship since 1947 and 14th in school history.

Catholic Central 27
Muskegon Catholic Central 7
Friday, November 10 at South Field

The "revenge" storyline carried through right to the very end of Catholic Central's season. The Cougars avenged their season-opening loss the Muskegon Catholic Central with an easy 27-7 win in the campaign-ending rematch.

Merdzinski blocked a punt to set up the Cougars' first score, which came on a 4-yard run up the middle by Roach. Grand Rapids CC had the game all but won with four minutes remaining in the first quarter when Ratajczak completed a 52-yard drive with a 5-yard sweep into the end zone behind a caravan of blockers. Fredericks increased the lead to 20-0 in the second quarter when he converted a fourth-and-2 situation into a 39-yard touchdown. Ratajczak pushed CC out to a 27-0 lead with a 1-yard plunge which he followed up by scoring the extra point.

After losing three of their first five games, Grand Rapids CC finished the season with four straight wins for a 6-3 record and a share of the league title.

Merdzinski led a contingent of three Cougars on the All-City team, which also included Cwik and Neuman.

1961 Schedule/Results
Head Coach – Ted Sowle

Date	Opponent	Result		Location
Sep. 16	Muskegon Catholic Central	Lost	0-12	Muskegon CC Stadium
Sep. 22	Flint Northern	Won	7-6	Houseman Field
Sep. 29	Union	Lost	13-18	Houseman Field
Oct. 6	South	Won	40-18	South Field
Oct. 13	Bay City Central	Lost	0-25	South Field
Oct. 20	Central	Won	12-6	Houseman Field
Oct. 26	Creston	Won	33-13	Houseman Field
Nov. 3	Ottawa Hills	Won	13-0	Houseman Field
Nov. 10	Muskegon Catholic Central	Won	27-0	South Field

	Record	Pts. Scored	Pts. Allowed
Overall	6-3	145	98
City League	4-1	111	55

-1962-

A lackluster preseason scrimmage against East Grand Rapids High School left Catholic Central coach Ted Sowle down in the dumps. And this time, his appraisal seemed to be less about motivating talent-laden players and more about the reality of the situation.

"It was a disappointing performance on offense for us," Sowle said. "Our blocking was mediocre. The zing wasn't there. Our backfield was too slow." The Cougars looked tough on defense, however, and Sowle hoped they could carry the freight until the offense, with its heavy but short line, caught up.

Catholic Central 27
Muskegon Catholic Central 7
Saturday, September 15 at Houseman Field

Neither unit was a concern in the 27-7 season-opening victory against Muskegon Catholic Central. The Cougars scored four unanswered touchdowns in the first three quarters, including a pair in the second quarter, to cruise to an easy decision. The Cougars took a 6-0 lead in stunning fashion on the first play of their second possession when Bob Franzak took advantage of a devastating block by Dick Brougham on the linebacker and exploded for a 53-yard touchdown. Unfazed by a penalty that nullified quarterback Bert Fortuna's 37-yard keeper for a touchdown in the second quarter, Grand Rapids CC persevered until Fortuna tossed a 5-yard touchdown pass to Paul Korte. Fortuna's second and final pass of the game resulted in a 47-yard TD connection with Dan Reagan with 32 seconds showing in the first half. Franzak's long punt return, which would have ended in the end zone had he not tripped after running 54 yards, set up Reagan's 13-yard touchdown midway through the third quarter.

Sowle was still grumpy three days after the game.

"I am surprised we rolled up 27 points," he said. "Our linemen were missing their blocking assignments and the backs were missing their holes. We were slow all the way around. If we expect to win Saturday (against Flint Northern), we'll have to sharpen up."

Catholic Central 19
Flint Northern 0
Friday, September 21 at Flint Atwood Stadium

Flint Northern came out of its 40-7 season-opening victory against Midland in the state championship conversation, and a victory over perennial power Catholic Central away from establishing itself as the team to beat.

The Cougars put an end to that talk with an unequivocal 19-0 thumping of the Vikings on their home turf, while inserting themselves into the statewide race. Middle linebacker Dick Merdzinski almost single-handedly dominated the Northern offense and Reagan was impressive on offense. All-City end Mike Neuman blocked a punt to set up Catholic's first touchdown, which came on Reagan's 8-yard scamper through a huge hole with 11:15 remaining in first half. Merdzinski unintentionally mishit the ball on the ensuing kickoff and the Cougars covered the loose ball at the Northern 41-yard line. The Cougars drove the ball to the 4 with a series of rushes into the line, and Reagan powered in from there.

Jerry Wilks, CC's 210-pound defensive tackle, recovered Lane Ellis' fumble at the Viking 38, and fullback Ed Karas dotted the "I" in win with a 2-yard plunge.

Catholic Central 13
Union 0
Saturday, September 29 at Houseman Field

G.R.Press Photo
Catholic's Ted Pasikowski (21) tries to sweep the end as Union's Ed Nylander moves up to make a tackle.

The Catholic Central defense pitched its second consecutive shutout and the offense scored just enough in a 13-0 victory over Union to put the undefeated and No. 2-ranked Cougars in the driver's seat for city and state championships.

Although the Red Hawks penetrated the CC 20-yard line on two occasions and even reached the 5 the second time around, they couldn't get past the Cougar defenders. Catholic scored on its first series, Karas banged in from the 5 to complete a 78-yard, 9-play drive, and then put the game in the hands of its defense. The Cougars even punted three times from inside the Red Hawk 45-yard line.

Considering the way Catholic Central was playing on defense, it all but put the game out of reach in the third quarter after getting the ball back on punt on its own 26. The Cougars pounded the Red Hawk defense relentlessly until on the 11th play of the drive, Brougham took the handoff from his fullback position and rocketed through the center of the Union defense for a 17-yard score with 5:06 remaining in the period.

South 13
Catholic Central 0
Saturday, October 6 at Houseman Field

An ill wind blew up Sheldon Avenue and across the entrance to Catholic Central High School. The Cougars were just voted No. 1 in Class A, but Merdzinski, the barrel-chested heart and soul of the sensational CC defense, was sidelined by a tender ankle.

A angry storm ensued and after everything calmed down, the Cougars came off Houseman Field with a monumental 13-0 upset loss to South. It was the second time in three years the Trojans played the role of spoiler in Catholic's championship scenario.

Ossie Holt, South's 140-pound halfback, scored the first touchdown on an 8-yard pass reception with 41 seconds remaining in the first half after tackle Juan Garcia recovered a Cougar fumble at their 29-yard line. With Catholic Central being held to under 100 rushing yards, 99 to be exact, for the first time anyone could remember, Holt delivered the coup de grace with an 81-yard TD dagger with 1:29 left in the game.

Bay City Central 31
Catholic Central 13
Friday, October 12 at Bay City

What was left of No. 3-ranked Catholic Central's world following the loss to South came crashing down with a 31-13 road defeat against Bay City Central. It was a slow painful process as the Cougars came out of the first quarter with a 7-6 lead provided by Reagan's 65-yard scoring sprint on a daring fourth-and-1 call.

Catholic only trailed 12-7 at the start of the second half and played the Wolves to a scoreless stalemate in the third quarter. But, the Wolves erupted for three fourth-quarter touchdowns, and just like that, the Cougars were beaten into submission. Fortuna's 51-yard touchdown pass to Reagan made the final score look only a little bit more respectable.

Catholic Central 34
Central 6
Thursday, October 18 at Houseman Field

Catholic Central averted what would have been a catastrophic loss to winless Central by breaking from tradition and attacking through the air. Fortuna completed 6 of 10 passes for 112 yards and two touchdowns. He also set up two of CC's running TDs with his arm.

Fortuna's 12-yard pass to Korte on fourth-and-10 set up Reagan's 1-yard score that put the Cougars ahead 6-0 with 6:34 remaining in the first half. The Cougars completed a 52-yard scoring drive just before intermission on a 9-yard pass from Fortuna to Korte. Central cut into CC's lead when flanker Ed Ripmaster fell on teammate Bob Jourdan's fumble in the end zone, but the Cougars responded with three fourth-quarter touchdowns.

Reagan scored from the 3 on the first play of the final period, Fortuna set up a 1-yard TD run by fullback Tom Reens with a 19-yard pass to Korte and a 21-yarder to Paul Schaab, and after Korte returned an interception to the Ram 28, Fortuna connected with him for the final touchdown.

Catholic Central 24
Creston 0
Saturday, October 27 at Houseman Field

Sporting a new-look hurry-up offense, Catholic Central defeated Creston for the 22nd straight time, 24-0, to move into a first-place tie with Union. With Bob Franczak back in the starting lineup and leading the way, the Cougars rushed for 288 yards.

Franczak completed CC's 63-yard game-opening drive with a 15-yard TD burst. And when quarterback Tom Annis fumbled the Polar Bears' first snap, Wilkes jumped on it for CC at the 34. A couple of plays later, immediately after taking the snap, Fortuna zipped a long pitchout to Schaab, who scored on an 18-yard run.

Neuman's recovery of another Annis fumble early in the third quarter led to Catholic's third touchdown. After taking an unusually deep drop, Fortuna passed to Reagan down the middle for a 56-yard TD. In the final quarter, Neuman grabbed another Creston fumble and Fortuna relied on his legs, instead of his arm, for a 20-yard TD.

Ottawa Hills 20
Catholic Central 13
Saturday, November 3 at Houseman Field

It figured that Catholic Central's vulnerable 1962 team would be the one that would pay the price for years of misery inflicted on Ottawa Hills High School. The Indians healed a number of wounds with a 20-13 victory over the team that was ranked No. 1 earlier in the season. It was their first win over Catholic since 1944 and it knocked the Cougars out of the city championship scenario for the first time in five seasons. Catholic's loss gave Union the undisputed City League title.

It appeared to be business as usual when Tom Reens returned a second-quarter punt to the Ottawa 20-yard line and scored four plays later on a 2-yard dive for a 7-0 lead. But after Ottawa's Dick Watcher recovered a fumbled CC punt at the Cougar 35, Pete Salamone completed the 12-play possession with a 1-yard TD plunge.

In the third quarter, Indians guard Gordon Mendels recovered another Catholic fumble just 6 yards from the goal line, and Salamone gave Ottawa its first lead, 13-7, with a 3-yard run. The Cougars turned the tables on Ottawa late in the fourth quarter after tackle John Ficeli recovered a fumble and Brougham eventually tied the score with a 1-yard bash. But Salamone sunk the Cougars with a 78-yard touchdown pass to end Jim Guedry, and Catholic dropped into a second-place tie with the Indians in the final standings.

Still boiling over on the following Monday, Sowle turned the team over to the underclassmen he'd been counting on in 1963 heading into the finale at Muskegon Catholic Central.

"I'm not taking anything away from Ottawa," Sowle said. "(Coach) Rip Collins had his team fired up. Ottawa out-charged and out-hustled us all the way, but our seniors were not putting out. I'm disappointed in the lack of improvement and enthusiasm of the players. The blocking was horrible and the tackling wasn't much better."

Catholic Central 46
Muskegon Catholic Central 6
Saturday, November 10 at Muskegon CC Stadium

The Cougars ended the season with a 46-6 win in the rematch with Muskegon Catholic, but it was a bittersweet victory all the way around. The Cougars completed a disappointing campaign against a Crusader team that lost all nine of its games, beginning with the opener against Grand Rapids CC.

Fortuna threw for two of Catholic's four touchdown passes, the Cougars ran for two more and Merdzinski returned an interception 45 yards for a score that resulted in a 6-0 lead. Fortuna's 14-yard touchdown pass to Neuman gave Grand Rapids CC a 13-0 halftime lead, and Fortuna hit Schaab for a 53-yard score in the third quarter.

Cougar reserves completed the rout with William Schumaker running for a 35-yard TD and Dick Brennan barging in from the 2. Reserve quarterback Tom Popiel threw touchdown passes of 23 and 32 yards to Steve Sowle, son of the CC head coach.

Merdzinksi, who bore a striking resemblance to former Illinois and Chicago Bear linebacker Dick Butkus, and played like him, too, garnered All-City honors along with Neuman, who was on the receiving end of most of CC's passes.

1962 Schedule/Results

Head Coach – Ted Sowle

Date	Opponent	Result		Location
Sep. 15	Muskegon Catholic Central	Won	27-7	Houseman Field
Sep. 21	Flint Northern	Won	19-0	Atwood Stadium
Sep. 29	Union	Won	13-0	Houseman Field
Oct. 6	South	Lost	0-13	Houseman Field
Oct. 12	Bay City Central	Lost	13-31	Bay City
Oct. 18	Central	Won	34-6	Houseman Field
Oct. 27	Creston	Won	24-0	Houseman Field
Nov. 3	Ottawa Hills	Lost	13-20	Houseman Field
Nov. 10	Muskegon Catholic Central	Won	46-6	Muskegon CC Stadium

	Record	Pts. Scored	Pts. Allowed
Overall	6-3	145	98
City League	3-2	111	55

-1963-

Catholic Central coach Ted Sowle was nothing, if not a product of his times. When it suited the Cougars to grind teams into submission, he featured a punishing ground game that relegated the forward pass to novelty status. But by 1963, Sowle embraced change and introduced the Cougars to a wide-open passing attack that featured flankers in motion and split ends.

"We have changed our basic approach on offense this season," Sowle told *The Grand Rapids Press* reporter Joe VanderHoff. "We have geared our practices to a wide-open style, and we plan to use this system when needed. We will line up in our usual T-formation but will lean more to flankers and split ends to loosen the opponent's defense. This gives us more options and striking power."

Catholic shared preseason City League favorite honors with Creston, which hadn't enjoyed contender status for more than 20 years.

Catholic Central 20
Muskegon Catholic Central 6
Saturday, September 14 at Muskegon CC Stadium

Sowle liked his team going into the season, and the Cougars unveiled a portion of their new attack during a 20-6 season-opening victory against Muskegon Catholic Central. Quarterback Bert Fortuna completed 4 of 7 passes for 52 yards and the running attack churned out 236 yards. The Cougars started with a short field after tackling the punter, who had to field a low snap, for a loss. Halfback Dick Brougham scored the first TD of the season on a 9-yard run on fourth-and-goal. Dan Reagan, the other starting halfback, put the Cougars ahead 13-0 with a 3-yard rush that capped a systematic 58-yard possession just before halftime.

The Crusaders stayed close with a 1-yard TD in the third quarter, but the Grand Rapids CC defense held them at bay the rest of the way and after a Cougar punt return to the 36, fullback Dave Walski finished things off with runs of 26 yards and 10 to reach the end zone for the final score with 12 seconds remaining.

Flint Northern 27
Catholic Central 20
Friday, September 20 at South Field

Twice Catholic Central built two-touchdown leads on Flint Northern, and twice the Cougars couldn't hold them before falling 27-20. And in the end, when they could have pulled out the win, they couldn't and instead fell victim to a 93-yard quarterback sneak that padded the Vikings' margin of victory.

Catholic got the first break of the game when the opening kickoff bounced off a Northern player and Mart Heyboer recovered the loose ball for the Cougars at the Viking 45. A 15-yard penalty called on Northern and 20-yard gain by Reagan set up Walski's 2-yard tumble over the goal line. Reagan upped CC's lead to 14-0 later in the first quarter with a 62-yard sprint to paydirt.

Track sprinter Willie Buck closed the gap for Northern with a 78-yard dash on the first play after the ensuing kickoff, but the Cougars regained their two-TD advantage in the second period with an 83-yard drive, shortened by two 15-yard Viking penalties, that culminated in Walski's 5-yard grinder into the end zone.

Northern's Leroy Scott, a powerful 187-pound fullback, cut into CC's 20-6 lead with a 66-yard rumble with 8:45 remaining in the first half. Then, after the Cougars squandered a scoring opportunity by turning the ball over on downs at the Viking 20, Scott burrowed through the CC defense for the final yard of an 80-yard possession and Northern led 21-20 at halftime. After a scoreless third quarter, Catholic drove all the way to the Viking 7 in the fourth, but couldn't cash in. The Cougars got another chance later in the period, but Northern executed another successful goal-line stand when end Steve Sowle was stopped at the 1-yard line after catching a fourth-down pass from Fortuna. Two plays later, Viking quarterback Dan Stamos would have been content to run out the final 20 seconds with a quarterback sneak, but when no Cougar bothered to tackle him, he kept going all the way for a 97-yard score.

Catholic Central 34
Muskegon Heights 7
Friday, September 27 at Houseman Field

New-fangled football may be fine for some teams, but Catholic Central stayed true to its rushing heritage under Sowle with a 34-7 mauling of Muskegon Heights. The Cougars' rushing attack plowed up 368 yards, with Brougham contributing 160 of them on just nine carries. The 172-pound halfback was one of five CC players to score a touchdown with the help of offensive linemen Dick Krulis, Mart Heyboer, Dan Rogalski, Jim Campione and Dennis Pospiech, who overpowered the Tigers.

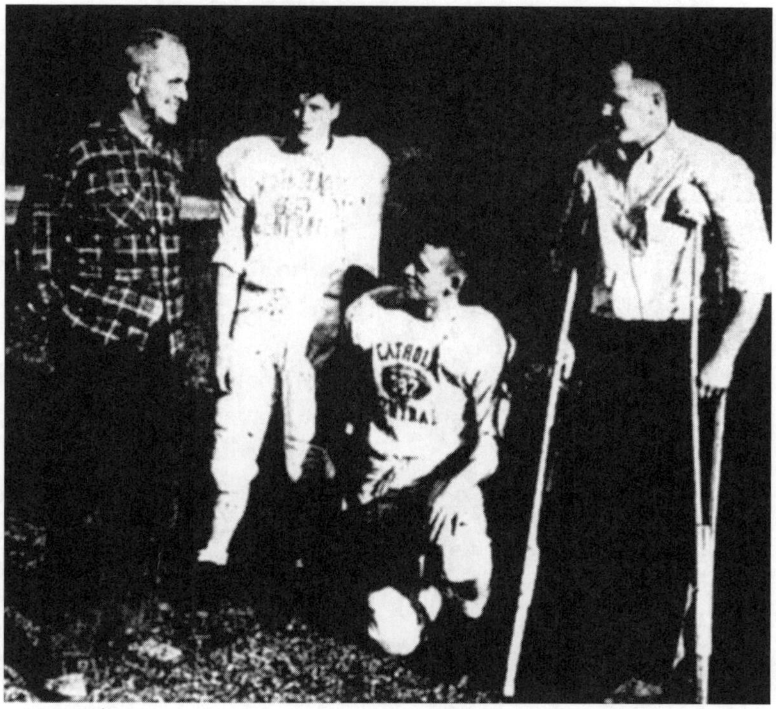

G.R.Press Photo

Coach Ted Sowle talks to injured Paul Korte (right) while Gerald Idziak and Steve Larkin look on.

Reagan scored first on a 4-yard power sweep and Brougham followed with a 5-yard dive four minutes later. Walski went in from 12 yards out after halftime and was joined in third-period scoring by

G.R.Press Photo

CC's 5'5" 149-pound halfback Dave Walski (14) finds daylight and the goal line in the game against Union.

Tom Zerfas with a 2-yarder touchdown and 5-foot-5, 128-pound Jim Kuzma added some excitement with a 35-yard jaunt. Brougham set up two touchdowns with runs of 37 and 44 yards.

Catholic Central 27
Union 7
Friday, October 4 at Houseman Field

The time finally came for the diversified offensive attack Sowle talked about unleashing at the proper time, to be unleashed. Catholic Central mixed up the run with the pass to upend defending city champ Union, 27-7.

Walski, the elusive 5-foot-5, 149-pound scatback, set the tone for the Cougars with 136 yards and three touchdowns on 17 carries. Fortuna complemented his efforts on the ground by completing 4 of 6 passes for 110 yards and one touchdown. He also set up a pair of running scores with pinpoint passes.

After returning a short opening kickoff to its own 40-yard line, Catholic marched 60 yards with a series of power runs, and Walski's 13-yard smash presented the Red Hawks with a 6-0 deficit. The Cougars' next possession looked decidedly different. Fortuna's first pass covered 23 yards to Steve Sowle, who was tackled at the Union 48. His second was caught by Reagan for a 35-yard pickup that set up Walski's 2-yard drive for a 13-0 lead. The Red Hawks rallied for a 63-yard scoring drive, which ended on Ed Major's 6-yard touchdown run in the third quarter.

G.R.Press Photo

Quarterback Bert Fortuna

But when Fortuna completed another 60-yard drive with a 35-yard laser pass to Sowle for a 20-7 lead and Union failed to counter, the game was virtually over. Walski's 36-yard gain and a 15-yard Fortuna-to-Sowle completion set up Walski's final 1-yard plunge.

South 25
Catholic Central 21
Friday, October 11 at South Field

South looked eminently beatable after losing to upstart West Catholic, a future member of the city high school football league, but Sowle wasn't buying it. "South isn't as weak as the 25-12 loss to West Catholic indicates," he warned. "South has the capability of doing it again."

And yet, despite all the determination in the world to avenge losses to South that cost Catholic Central state titles in 1960 and 1962, the Cougars couldn't prevent it from happening again. The Trojans put a major crimp in Catholic's city championship aspirations with a 25-21 defeat.

The turning point came in the first quarter when the Trojans shrugged off what appeared to be a crucial fumble. The Cougars scored first on an 11-yard touchdown pass from Fortuna to end Bob Gregorski. South looked to counter and drove all the way to the CC 4, but handed the ball over to

Catholic, which advanced the ball just 9 yards. Faced with fourth-and-inches at the Cougar 13 early in the second quarter, Sowle lost a risky bet when Walski was stopped cold for no gain. Quick-stepping halfback Ernie Green dashed into the end zone to cut CC's lead to 7-6, but while the extra point failed, South had the momentum.

Steve Watchman's recovery of a Catholic fumble at the Cougar 23 set up quarterback Ed Matthew's 5-yard TD pass to King for a 12-7 lead with 10 seconds left in the first half. South increased its lead 19-7 in the third quarter when fullback Steve Giammona broke tackle after tackle en route to a 68-yard touchdown and King put the game out of reach with a 58-yard TD early in the fourth period. The Cougars gamely fought back for two late touchdowns on a 6-yard pass from Fortuna to Steve Sowle and 12-yarder from Fortuna to Schumaker. And, Fortuna had Catholic on the move with a minute to go, but he was hit before he could get off another pass, lost the ball and South's Teddy Tett recovered the fumble to seal CC's fate once again.

Catholic Central 44
Saginaw Arthur Hill 6
Saturday, October 19 at Houseman Field

Catholic Central's balanced attack produced more favorable results in a 44-6 drubbing of Saginaw Arthur Hill. Buoyed by Fortuna's accurate passing, the Cougars quickly jumped out to a 19-0 lead. First, Fortuna's 20-yard pass to Steve Sowle set up Zerfas' 1-yard plunge. Then, six plays after CC recovered a Lumberjack fumble at their 20 after the ensuing kickoff, Zerfas scored again. Dennis Patterson scored the Cougars' third touchdown on a 23-yard pass from Fortuna with 3:55 still remaining in the first quarter.

The Fortuna-Patterson combination produced a 15-yard touchdown with time running out in the second quarter and CC led 25-0 at the start of the third quarter. The Cougars recovered a blocked punt in the end zone for their fifth TD and Patterson's 75-yard interception return put CC ahead 37-0. Hungry reserve running backs Tim Carmody, Joe Murphy and Kuzma went for the kill by racking up big gains in the third quarter, and Murphy's 4-yard TD resulted in a 44-0 bulge.

Catholic Central 32
Central 13
Friday, October 25 at Houseman Field

Catholic Central remained in contention for the league title with a 32-13 whipping of Central, which hadn't defeated the Cougars since 1947. Walski and Brougham led a ground attack that pounded out 303 yards at the expense of the light Ram defenders. Walski started the onslaught with a 23-yard touchdown and Zerfas ended it with a 1-yard marker.

G.R.Press Photo

CC's Larry LaMange (5) sweeps the end for a 19-yard touchdown run aided by a Tom Zerfas (11) block.

The victory was overshadowed four days later when Ted Sowle announced he was stepping down at the Catholic Central head coach after 19 years due to poor health. The 52-year-old mentor had been ailing with severe bronchial asthma and informed principal Fr. James P. Yager that after a brief stay at the University of

Michigan Hospital, he was leaving for Arizona almost immediately.

"Ted needs the benefit of a warm, dry climate and plenty of rest," his personal physician told *The Grand Rapids Press*.

While Catholic Central was preparing as if the move would be permanent, Sowle said, "I hope to be back in the harness next fall. Coaching is my life and I sure would hate to give it up now.'

Joe Godleski, Sowle's long-time chief assistant, was placed in charge of the team for the remainder of the season.

Catholic Central 39
Creston 27
Friday, November 1 at Houseman Field

For the first time in 19 years, Catholic Central's Cougars took to the football field of battle without Ted Sowle leading them from the sideline. It was a rough debut for Godleski, who took over for his long-time boss. But after trailing Creston, 20-19, at halftime, CC rallied for a 39-27 victory.

Brougham got the seesaw battle started by completing Catholic's game-opening 70-yard drive with a 7-yard touchdown for a 6-0 lead. Creston, at times operating out of a shotgun formation, responded with a 70-yard possession of their own which ended on halfback Mike Dunham's 3-yard TD off a trap play for a 7-6 lead. A 15-yard Polar Bear punt gave CC good field position in the second quarter, and Fortuna's 22-yard pass to Steve Sowle set up Brougham's 23-yard score.

Creston put up two touchdowns in the next three minutes but Fortuna made it a one-point game with an 18-yard scoring toss to Steve Sowle with 11 seconds left in the first half. The Cougars got a huge break at the start of the second half when their kickoff was allowed to hit the ground at the 31-yard line and Herm Bilski beat the Polar Bears to it. Though CC was set back 15 yards by a holding penalty, Zerfas zoomed over the final 15 yards for a 26-20 lead four plays lalter and the Cougars wouldn't trail the rest of the way. Zerfas added a 19-yard scoring strike and Larry LaMange converted Murphy's fumble recovery into a 10-yard deal-closer. Brougham finished with 180 yards on 18 carries.

G.R.Press Photo

Steve Sowle hauls in the extra point conversion to clinch a 13-13 tie with Ottawa Hills.

Catholic Central 13
Ottawa Hills 13
Friday, October 8 at Houseman Field

The storied Ted Sowle era ended at Catholic Central with a 13-13 tie against Ottawa Hills.

The deadlock propelled 4-1 South to the City League championship and left the 3-1-1 Cougars wondering what happened during a season that began with so much promise. It was the second time in as many seasons that the Indians spoiled Catholics championship aspirations. Ottawa defeated CC, 20-13, to hand the outright title to Union in 1962.

The 2-6-1 Indians lined up with four linebackers behind four- and five-man defensive fronts to stop Catholic's potent rushing attack throughout the evening, and the Cougars ended up with just 187 yards on the ground. Ottawa converted a Zerfas fumble into a 6-0 first-quarter lead with the help of a CC pass-interference penalty but the Cougars battled back to force a tie. The Indians' second TD drive also got a boost by an interference infraction, and they led 13-6 at halftime.

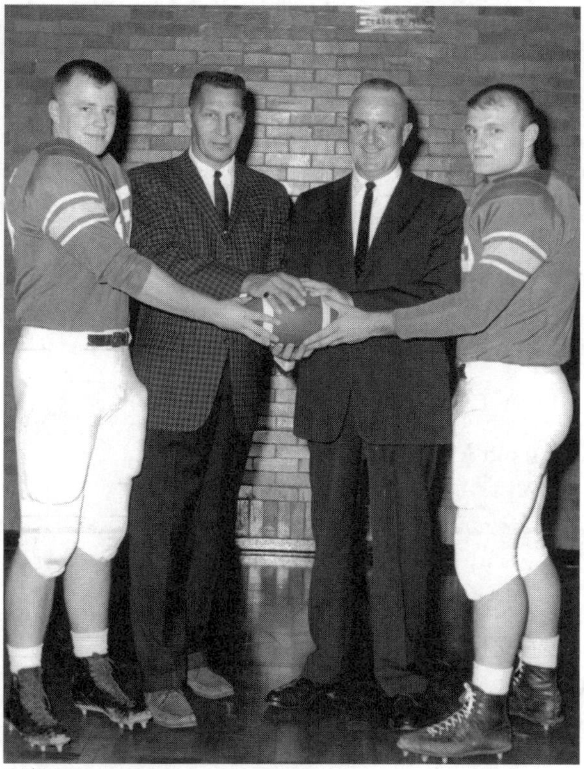

CC/WC Archives

(l-r) - Paul Korte, Coach Joe Godleski, Coach Ted Sowle and Denny Pospiech

Catholic's game-tying touchdown started with LaMange's recovery of a Jack Kinsman fumble at the CC 28. Fortuna kept the drive alive when he ran for a first down out of punt formation while facing a fourth-and-6 situation. Fortuna had to jump to field a high snap from center, and after sidestepping two rushers, ran around end for 7 yards to the Ottawa 47. The Cougars were backed up to their own 40 with another 15-yard penalty, but Fortuna converted on a third-and-18 with a 24-yard pass to Carmody. Catholic used running plays to get to the 5-yard line, and on the first play of the fourth quarter, Steve Sowle snagged a low Fortuna pass from his shoetops for the equalizer. Ottawa and CC each had scoring opportunities end with interceptions down the stretch.

Sowle's last Catholic Central team sent five to the All-City squad including: Steve Sowle, Fortuna, Campione, Krulis and Pospiech.

1963 Schedule/Results
Head Coach – Ted Sowle

Date	Opponent	Result		Location
Sep. 14	Muskegon Catholic Central	Won	20-6	Muskegon CC Stadium
Sep. 20	Flint Northern	Lost	20-27	South Field
Sep. 27	Muskegon Heights	Won	34-7	Houseman Field
Oct. 4	Union	Won	27-7	Houseman Field
Oct. 11	South	Lost	21-25	South Field
Oct. 19	Saginaw Arthur Hill	Won	44-6	Houseman Field
Oct. 25	Central	Won	32-13	Houseman Field
Nov. 1	Creston	Won	39-27	Houseman Field
Nov. 8	Ottawa Hills	Tie	13-13	Houseman Field

	Record	Pts. Scored	Pts. Allowed
Overall	6-2-1	250	131
City League	3-1-1	132	85

EPILOGUE

Known and admired for its tenacious and hard-nosed approach to football since its inception, even while being trounced 81-0 by Hope College in 1913, Catholic Central moved into another dimension when Ted Sowle came onto the scene in 1943. The Cougars immediately responded to the Sowle touch with a mythical state championship in his first season as head coach. And although Sowle had a one-year hiatus when Ed Killoran returned from WWII in '46, Catholic Central never really missed a beat.

There was talk of drumming the Cougars out of the City League in football because they were just too dominant, and when Sowle retired to Arizona before the end of the 1963 season because of health issues, he had 11 City championships, four Class A titles and a few near-misses along the way to his credit.

Just as Notre Dame was the pre-eminent college program during Sowle's time at Catholic Central, so were the Cougars in Michigan high school football.

Faith, Honor, Integrity, and Tradition - Volume II will continue the story of the Catholic Central football program, starting with Coach Hollarn and the post-Sowle era and continuing through the 2012 season. Look for *Volume II* in the fall of 2013.

Catholic Central Alumni (1910-1963) Who Played Collegiate Football

A

Andrie, George - 1958
Marquette University
Dallas Cowboys

Andrie, Stan - 1951
Marquette University

B

Banaszak, Bill - 1951
Central Michigan University

Baragar, Larry - 1960
Arizona State University

Bartnick, Lucien - 1937
Central Michigan University

Barto, Jerry - 1958
Marquette University
Drake University

Bockheim, Jerry - 1944
Central Michigan University

Boruta, Roman - 1946
Wayne State University

Boylen, Fred - 1957
Michigan State University

Brogger, Jim - 1941
University of Notre Dame

C

Cary, John - 1915
University of Michigan

Couturier, Jerry - 1957
Western Michigan University

Cummings, Ted - 1927
University of Dayton

Cyronoski, Dave - 1961
Northwestern University

D

Dumas, Jack - 1952
University of Notre Dame

F

Fitzgerald, Robert - 1948
Central Michigan University

G

Galant, Ed - 1936
Central Michigan University

Godleski, Joe - 1935
University of Notre Dame
Central Michigan University

Gorski, Ed - 1942
University of Detroit

Grego, Danny - 1957
University of Wyoming

H

Jack Hart - 1939
Grand Rapids Junior College
University of Detroit

Hartnacke, Frank - 1934
Michigan State University

Heynen, Dick - 1953
University of Michigan

J

Jaglowski, Gene - 1949
Washington State University

Jarosch, Robert - 1932
Eastern Michigan University

Jebb, Jim - 1949
Michigan State University

K

Kaman, Roman - 1938
Michigan State University

Kampfschulte, Elmer - 1927
Marquette University

Koelzer, Jim - 1950
Purdue University

L

Lennon, Don - 1942
University of Detroit
Western Michigan University

M

McGovern, Jerry - 1946
Michigan State University

Milito, Jack - 1942
University of Detroit
Purdue University

Montroy, Jack - 1925
University of Notre Dame

Mysliewiec, Dick - 1945
University of Portland
Central Michigan University

N

Neuman, Mike - 1963
U.S. Military Academy

Norman, Louis - 1924
University of Notre Dame

O

O'Donnell, Hugh - 1911

University of Notre Dame

Olewinski, Ted - 51
Marquette University

P

Pins, Richard - 1948
Western Michigan University

Pobojewski, Dan - 1947
Michigan State University
Purdue University

Q

Quist, Bob - 1961
University of Michigan
University of Connecticut

R

Rataczak, Erwin - 1962
Central Michigan University

Roach, Tom - 1928
University of Michigan
University of Notre Dame

Romani, Romulus - 1935
Albion College

Ruth, Audrey - 1940
University of Detroit

S

Schnur, Martin "Cowboy" - 1928
University of Dayton
Schultz, Jim - 1946
Central Michigan University

Seamon, Dave - 1961
University of Michigan

Shada, John - 1934
University of Detroit

Shuple, Bill - 1958
University of Iowa

Grand Rapids Junior College
Central Michigan University

Sieracki, Jerry - 1956
Central Michigan University

Snow, Roman - 1938
University of Detroit

Soboleski, Joe - 1943
University of Michigan

Spielmaker, Terry - 1949
Michigan State University

Stanitzek, Frank - 1953
University of Notre Dame

Sydlowski, Paul - 1960
University of Michigan

V

VandenBerg, Bob - 1944
Marquette University

W

Wisneski, Leo - 1934
Central Michigan University

Wilks, Jerry - 1962
University of Nebraska

Wolf, LaVerne - 1951
Central Michigan University

Z

Zakem, John - 1940
University of Detroit

Zegunis, Tom - 1960
Western Michigan University

Zwers, Joe - 1933
University of Notre Dame

Season Coaching Records

Year	Wins	Loses	Ties	Coach
1912	1	1	0	Tierney
1913	3	5	0	Phil Holloway
1914	3	2	1	Phil Holloway
1915	0	5	0	Phil Holloway
1916	2	4	0	Phil Holloway
1917	2	5	0	Phil Holloway
1918	0	1	0	John Cary
1918	0	1	0	Holland
1918	0	1	0	Ray Murray
1919	0	5	0	Heine Lightner
1920	0	4	1	Will Cary
1921	7	2	0	George Fitzpatrick
1922	7	3	2	George Fitzpatrick
1923	10	1	0	George Fitzpatrick
1924	5	4	1	George Fitzpatrick
1925	5	5	0	George Fitzpatrick
1926	8	4	0	George Fitzpatrick
1927	6	1	2	George Haller
1928	0	2	0	George Haller
1928	3	4	0	Louis Norman
1929	3	5	1	George Haller
1930	2	7	0	Tony McCraken
1931	6	3	0	Tony McCraken
1932	6	1	1	Tony McCraken
1933	5	2	1	Tony McCraken
1934	1	4	2	Edward Killoran
1935	4	3	1	Edward Killoran
1936	4	3	1	Edward Killoran
1937	7	2	0	Edward Killoran
1938	4	4	1	Edward Killoran
1939	4	3	1	Edward Killoran
1940	2	5	1	Edward Killoran
1941	3	2	2	Edward Killoran
1942	6	0	2	Edward Killoran
1943	7	0	0	Ted Sowle
1944	2	4	1	Ted Sowle
1945	5	3	0	Ted Sowle
1946	2	7	0	Edward Killoran
1947	6	2	1	Ted Sowle
1948	7	1	0	Ted Sowle
1949	9	0	0	Ted Sowle
1950	7	1	1	Ted Sowle
1951	9	0	0	Ted Sowle
1952	8	1	0	Ted Sowle
1953	6	2	1	Ted Sowle
1954	6	3	0	Ted Sowle
1955	8	0	1	Ted Sowle
1956	8	1	0	Ted Sowle
1957	5	2	1	Ted Sowle
1958	8	1	0	Ted Sowle
1959	9	0	0	Ted Sowle
1960	8	1	0	Ted Sowle
1961	6	3	0	Ted Sowle
1962	6	3	0	Ted Sowle
1963	6	2	1	Ted Sowle

Career Coaching Records

Coach	Wins	Loses	Ties	Winning %
Tierney	1	1	0	.500
Phil Holloway	10	21	1	.323
John Cary	0	1	0	.000
Holland	0	1	0	.000
Ray Murray	0	4	0	.000
Heine Lightner	0	5	0	.000
Will Cary	0	4	1	.000
G. Fitapatrick	42	19	3	.689
George Haller	9	8	3	.529
Louis Norman	3	4	0	.429
T. McCraken	19	13	2	.594
Ed Killoran	37	33	12	.529
Ted Sowle	136	30	7	.819

Index

A

B

C

D

O

P

Q

R

S